W9-AOE-700

Peacemakers

WINNERS OF THE NOBEL PEACE PRIZE

Peacemakers

WINNERS OF THE NOBEL PEACE PRIZE

ANN T. KEENE

OXFORD UNIVERSITY PRESS
NEW YORK · OXFORD

BR BR
YA
JZ5540
.K44
1998

This book is for Trevor Huddleston,
a lifelong peacemaker.

Oxford University Press
Oxford   New York
Athens Auckland Bangkok Bogotá Bombay
Buenos Aires Calcutta Cape Town Dar es Salaam Delhi
Florence Hong Kong Istanbul Karachi
Kuala Lumpur Madras Madrid Melbourne
Mexico City Nairobi Paris Singapore
Taipei Tokyo Toronto Warsaw
and associated companies in
Berlin   Ibadan

Copyright © 1998 by Ann T. Keene

Published by Oxford University Press, Inc.,
198 Madison Avenue, New York, New York 10016

Oxford is a registered trademark of Oxford University Press

All rights reserved. No part of this publication may be reproduced, stored in a retrieval system,
or transmitted, in any form or by any means, electronic, mechanical, photocopying, recording,
or otherwise, without the prior permission of Oxford University Press.

Library of Congress Cataloging-in-Publication Data
Keene, Ann. T.
Peacemakers : winners of the Nobel Peace Prize / Ann T. Keene.
p. cm.
Includes bibliographical references and index.
ISBN 0-19-510316-5 (library; acid-free paper)
1. Pacifists—Biography—Juvenile literature. 2. Peace—Awards—History—Juvenile literature.
3. Nobel Prizes—History—Juvenile literature.
[1. Pacifists. 2. Nobel Prizes—Biography.]
I. Title
JZ5540.K44   1998
327.1'72'0922—dc21   98-13522
                                            CIP
                                            AC

1 3 5 7 9 8 6 4 2

Printed in the United States of America
on acid-free paper

On the cover: (Clockwise from top left) Albert Schweitzer, Desmond
Tutu, Jane Addams, and Theodore Roosevelt
Frontispiece: The front and back of the Nobel Peace Prize medal

Design: Sandy Kaufman
Layout: Loraine Machlin
Picture research: Lisa Kirchner,
Andrea Lynch

Contents

Note: The Nobel Peace Prize was not awarded for the following years: 1914, 1915, 1916, 1918, 1923, 1924, 1928, 1932, 1939, 1940, 1941, 1942, 1943, 1948, 1955, 1956, 1966, 1967, and 1972.

Preface

THE STORY OF PEACEMAKERS

The English word "peacemaker" has been used since the 15th century to describe someone who creates peace by ending conflict between individuals, groups, or nations. But the word occurred much earlier in other languages. Many of us are probably most familiar with its use in the Bible—specifically in the New Testament, which was originally written in Greek. In the Gospel of St. Matthew, chapter 5, verse 9, the apostle quotes one of the Beatitudes of Christ, which is usually translated in English as "Blessed are the peacemakers, for they shall be called the sons of God."

Other religions besides Christianity have praised peacemakers and condemned human conflict. Yet despite this desire for peace, warfare has been part of the human condition as long as people have walked the earth—some 2 million years. Moreover, despite religious teachings to the contrary—and the efforts of generations of peacemakers throughout history—warfare was considered a noble activity in most of the world until the mid-19th century.

The actions of a single man challenged the widespread belief that war was both glamorous and necessary. His name was Henri Dunant, and in 1863 his opposition to war led him to create the Red Cross—the same organization that most of us are familiar with today for its many services to people throughout the world. Dunant was one of the founders of the modern peace movement, and most of the organizations working today for world peace owe their origins to him and to his followers. It is therefore appropriate that in 1901 Dunant became the first winner of the first award established to honor men and women who have devoted their lives to peace: the Nobel Peace Prize, established by the Swedish industrialist Alfred Nobel.

In the following pages, you will learn about Alfred Nobel and why he created a special annual prize for peacemakers. You will also read the moving stories of more than 100 winners—both individuals and organizations—of the Nobel Peace Prize. As you learn about their achievements, you will be introduced as well to major events in world history, from the 1850s to the 1990s. And you will meet other peacemakers who deserved, but did not win, the Nobel Peace Prize.

As you read this book, you will learn that peacemakers come in several categories. Many of them were brilliant, highly educated people who made major contributions in their chosen careers long before their efforts on behalf of world peace: men and women like U.S. President Theodore Roosevelt (1906); Norwegian explorer and scientist Fridtjof Nansen (1922); French medical missionary and musician Albert Schweitzer (1952); U.S. scientist Linus Pauling (1962), who also won a Nobel Prize for Chemistry; and Swedish sociologist Alva Myrdal (1982).

However, some of the most extraordinary peacemakers seemed destined for lives as ordinary individuals—until they discovered an opportunity to act on behalf of peace and chose to do so. They were like Dunant, a not-very-successful Swiss businessman; U.S. social worker Jane Addams (1931), crippled from birth and unable to pursue a career in medicine; two office workers, Mairead Corrigan and Betty Williams (1976), in Northern Ireland, caught in the midst of a civil war; and Mother Teresa (1979), a high school teacher in India for nearly two decades before she began working directly with the poor.

You will discover, too, that some of the winners were not always on the side of peace. At first they supported warfare, either by fighting themselves or by encouraging others to do so. But during the course of their lives, they changed direction, moving toward peace and away from war, and that change made a profound difference in the world.

—Ann T. Keene

Introduction

ALFRED NOBEL AND THE NOBEL PEACE PRIZE

The 19th-century Swedish inventor and industrialist Alfred Nobel hated war, and he often wished that he could use his creative genius to invent an antiwar "substance or machine." He could not, of course, and so he did the next best thing: in his will, he directed his heirs to create an annual prize worth a great deal of money for the person or persons who had done "the most or the best work for fraternity among nations, for the abolition or reduction of standing armies, and for the holding and promotion of peace congresses."

In 1901, five years after Nobel's death, the first Nobel Peace Prize was awarded. Today, nearly a century later, some 100 men, women, and organizations have won the award for their activities on behalf of world peace. In its early years, the prize—awarded in Swedish kronor—was the equivalent of several thousand dollars. In the late-1990s, it is worth around $1 million—a consequence of investments that have made the Nobel estate increasingly valuable. The Nobel Peace Prize has a much greater value than the money that accompanies it, however: it is recognized as the most prestigious award in the world that a peacemaker can receive.

The bulk of Alfred Nobel's fortune came from the manufacture of explosives. The most important of these was dynamite, which he invented. In the century since Nobel's death, many false stories have been circulated about him. The most common is that he created the Nobel Peace Prize because he had a guilty conscience about making money from the manufacture of weapons. In fact, although some of Nobel's explosives were used to make ammunition, he made little or no money from that application of his inventions. The Nobel fortune came from peacetime uses of dynamite throughout the world to blast roads, tunnels, canals, railways, and oil wells.

If Alfred Nobel had been able to choose a career for himself, it might not have been science or invention or business. Instead, he might have become a professional writer. Nobel was born in 1833 in Stockholm, the capital of Sweden. He was the fourth of eight children, of whom only four lived beyond childhood. His father was an architect, builder, and inventor who became financially successful during Alfred's childhood by manufacturing simple explosives and small machines.

As a child, Alfred Nobel was sickly. He was closer to his mother, who encouraged his interest in literature and the arts, than he was to his father, who was often absent on business. When he was nine, the family moved to St. Petersburg, Russia, where his father had established his business. His parents hired private tutors for him, and when they discovered that he had an aptitude for chemistry, his future career in the family business seemed assured.

Alfred Nobel also pursued the study of literature and languages, and he became fluent in Russian, German, French, and English as well as his native Swedish. He read the works of many leading writers in all these languages, and he began writing himself at a young age. In the course of his life he composed many stories, poems, plays, and novels for his own pleasure.

Nobel went abroad for the first time in 1850, when he was 17. During the next three years, he visited several European countries as well as the United States, and he studied chemistry for a while in Paris. He returned to St. Petersburg in 1853 to join his father's business, which was now producing small arms for the Crimean War (1853–56). After the war ended three years later, the business began to fail, and the Nobels returned to Stockholm.

In a laboratory that his father established on the family estate, Alfred Nobel began tinkering with various explosive devices and obtained several patents from the Swedish government. He and his three brothers helped their father to rebuild the family explosives business in Stockholm, and Alfred began experimenting with the most powerful explosive material then known: a compound called nitroglycerin.

Nitroglycerin posed a major problem to those who tried to use it, however: no one had yet discovered how to control its detonation, the means by which it was transformed from a harmless-looking liquid into a powerful explosive, and many lives had been lost as a consequence.

In 1863, following a series of experiments in the family laboratory, Alfred Nobel invented a safer and more practical detonating process that used gunpowder to ignite nitroglycerin. This creation paved the way for his future success, but it also caused a tragedy: during experiments to perfect it, the laboratory blew up. Eight people were killed, including one of Alfred Nobel's brothers. In response to the catastrophe, Nobel's father suffered a stroke and remained bedridden for the rest of his life.

Nobel was determined to succeed in order to improve the family's financial situation. He persuaded the Swedish government to use his new "blasting oil," as he called it, to construct a series of railway tunnels, and he talked a local merchant into giving him a loan to build a factory for its manufacture. His success in Sweden led him to market his blasting oil in other European countries and in the United States, where it was used to blast tunnels through the Sierra Nevadas for the new Central Pacific Railroad.

Nobel built another factory in the German city of Hamburg and moved there in 1865. A year later he set up an additional blasting oil factory in the United States. Nobel was pleased by the success of his product, but he was troubled by the fact that it was still not totally safe to use. Accidents still occurred from time to time, and workers were killed or injured. He continued to experiment and the result was dynamite, which he patented in 1867.

Dynamite was made by mixing liquid nitroglycerin with solid but absorbent material that was formed into sticks. The sticks, which were safe to handle, were placed in holes drilled into rock. Their explosive power was released only from a burning fuse. Workers could ignite the fuse and then take cover before the flame reached the dynamite and caused an explosion.

Nobel's new invention was revolutionary, and it was quickly adopted for major construction projects around the world, including the construction of railway tunnels through the Swiss Alps.

Alfred Nobel

BORN
October 21, 1833
Stockholm, Sweden

DIED
December 10, 1896
San Remo, Italy

EDUCATION
Privately tutored

OCCUPATION
Chemist; inventor; industrialist

MAJOR ACCOMPLISHMENTS
Patented several inventions related to explosives, including a simple detonator for nitroglycerin; invented the blasting powder known as dynamite; left provisions in his will for the creation of international prizes in the fields of peace, chemistry, physics, physiology or medicine, and literature

"I should like to invent a substance or machine with such terrible power of mass destruction that war would thereby be impossible forever."

— Alfred Nobel

One of its major applications in the late 19th century was its use to blast oil wells in Baku, an oil-rich region in central Russia.

Nobel established factories throughout Europe to manufacture dynamite. For the rest of his life he spent nearly all his time managing his business affairs. Many people tried to steal his various patents, and Nobel had to go to court to reclaim his rights. For relaxation he visited spas (health centers) in Germany and Austria. At one of them, in 1876, he met a young flower seller named Sophie Hess, who became his nearly lifelong companion.

Despite his heavy work schedule, Nobel found time for cultural pursuits. In Paris, where he moved in 1873, he became acquainted with men and women who were prominent in the arts and public affairs, and he often hosted them at large dinner parties. Nobel preferred his own company, however. He continued to conduct chemical experiments in a home laboratory, and he enjoyed literature—reading works by other authors and creating his own. Despite his great wealth, Nobel lived simply. He did not smoke or drink alcoholic beverages, and he did not play cards or other games.

Nobel was aware of the growing European peace movement that had begun in the 1860s, and he entertained men and women in his home who supported that movement. One of them was a writer named Bertha von Suttner, who with her husband became a friend of Nobel's in Paris in the mid-1880s. With Suttner's encouragement, Nobel donated large amounts of money to various peace organizations. Suttner herself had decided to devote her life to the cause of peace, and she published a number of books on that cause.

It is Bertha Suttner who deserves part of the credit for the creation of the Nobel Peace Prize. After she returned to her home in Vienna in the late 1880s, she continued to correspond with Nobel. In her letters she encouraged him to donate at least some of his substantial fortune to the cause of international peace. By 1893 Nobel had agreed, and he wrote to Suttner to tell her so.

Two years earlier, Nobel had moved from Paris to a home in sunny San Remo, on the Italian Riviera. He was now ill with heart disease, but he continued his chemical experiments whenever his health permitted. Homesick for his native land, Nobel established a second home and laboratory in Varmland, Sweden, in 1894 and spent the last two summers of his life there.

In the fall of 1896, back at his home in San Remo, Nobel began to write his will. In it he made provisions not only for a peace prize but also for annual awards to outstanding individuals in four other fields: literature, chemistry, physics, and physiology or medicine. In the early hours of December 10, 1896, not long after completing his will, Alfred Nobel died in bed of a cerebral hemorrhage. He was 63 years old.

To carry out Alfred Nobel's wishes, the Nobel Foundation was established in 1900 for the purpose of administering all the Nobel Prizes. In his will Nobel specified that winners could be chosen from any country in the world. He also specified that the selection of winners in each field would be carried out by different institutions. The prizes in literature were to be supervised by the Swedish Academy; in chemistry and physics, by the Royal Academy of Sciences in Stockholm; and in physiology or medicine, by the Karolinska Institute, a prominent medical research center in Stockholm.

Responsibility for choosing the winner of the Nobel Peace Prize was given by Nobel in his will to the Norwegian parliament, called the Storting. Norway and Sweden had been united since 1814, although Norway had been trying to separate from Sweden for some time. Norway finally achieved independence in 1905, but the Norwegian Nobel Committee—five members of parliament elected by the Storting—continues to administer the Peace Prize.

The first Nobel Prizes were awarded on December 10, 1901, the fifth anniversary of the death of Alfred Nobel. The Peace Prize is awarded in Oslo, the Norwegian capital, and the other prizes are presented in Stockholm. In 1968 a sixth Nobel Prize, in the field of economics, was created by a grant of the Bank of Sweden to the Nobel Foundation. This prize is also administered by the Royal Academy of Sciences and is presented in Stockholm; it was awarded for the first time in 1969.

In accordance with rules established by the Nobel Foundation, no more than three individuals can receive any Nobel Prize jointly in any given year. Although multiple winners are fairly common in the scientific fields, most of the annual Peace Prize awards have been given to single individuals or organizations.

Nobel Prize winners in every field are chosen with great care. For each prize, the supervising institution invites more than 1,000 experts in the field from countries throughout the world to nominate candidates. Those experts always include previous Nobel Prize winners. The invitations are sent out in the fall prior to the year of the award. To choose the Nobel Peace Prize winner, the Norwegian Nobel Committee requests nominations from philosophers, historians, and legal and political scholars, as well as individuals who are prominent in the international peace movement.

Nominations in all fields must be received by their supervising institutions no later than February 1 of the award year. The various Nobel committees then begin the work of choosing the winners, and by early fall they have completed their task. Sometimes a committee may decide not to award a prize for that year. Since 1901 the Norwegian Nobel Committee has chosen not to name a Peace Prize winner 19 times—in 1914, 1915, 1916, 1918, 1923, 1924, 1928, 1932, 1939, 1940, 1941, 1942, 1943, 1948, 1955, 1956, 1966, 1967, and 1972.

The names of the year's Nobel Prize winners are announced in October, more than a year after the selection process began. The winners, called laureates, and their families are invited to the December 10 award ceremonies. The ceremonies in both Oslo and Stockholm are gala affairs, and all the participants dress formally for the occasion.

The Stockholm ceremony is held in the city's Concert Hall, and the awards are presented by the king of Sweden. The Peace Prize ceremony takes place in the Assembly Hall of the University of Oslo, in the presence of the king of Norway and the royal family. The chairman of the Norwegian Nobel Committee presents the award, and the prizewinner usually gives a lecture. And even as the Nobel Prizes are being awarded in Oslo and Stockholm, the search is already under way for the next year's winners.

Henri Dunant
Frédéric Passy

1901

I n June 1859, a young Swiss businessman traveled to Solferino, Italy, hoping to see Emperor Napoleon III of France. The emperor was in Italy to command his troops, and those of his Italian allies, against an invasion by the Austrians. The Swiss businessman, whose name was Henri Dunant, had bought land in the French colony of Algeria, in North Africa. He intended to raise livestock and grain there, and to do so he needed permission to pipe water from government-owned property. Algerian officials were not helpful to him, so Dunant decided to make a personal appeal to the French emperor.

But instead of seeing the emperor, Dunant arrived in time to witness one of the bloodiest battles of the 19th century: on June 24, 1859, the Battle of Solferino, whose hand-to-hand slaughter Dunant would later describe in vivid terms, claimed 40,000 lives. Putting aside his mission,

Henri Dunant pursued a career as a businessman while helping the poor and less fortunate. His concern for the welfare of others, especially in time of war, led him to found the Red Cross.

Dunant joined rescue efforts to evacuate the wounded to the nearby town of Castiglione. Over the next few days he worked heroically to save lives, directing volunteers, gathering food, finding doctors, and securing medical supplies.

The Battle of Solferino changed Henri Dunant's life. He could never get over the horrors and brutality that he had seen there. He was so overwhelmed by the experience that he wrote a book about it, *Un Souvenir de Solferino* (A Memory of Solferino). Virtually overnight, *Un Souvenir de Solferino* made Henri Dunant known throughout the Western world.

Dunant's interest in helping others had begun years earlier, in his childhood. He was born Jean Henri Dunant in Geneva, Switzerland, in 1828 to a family that was well educated, wealthy, and devoted to works of charity. His father, a member of the Geneva town council, was the official in charge of the city's orphanages. One of Henri Dunant's grandfathers was the director of a leading hospital in Geneva, and an uncle was a prominent physicist. A strong Protestant religious faith underlay the family's belief in working hard for the benefit of the community.

As a youth, Henri Dunant did charitable work among the city's poor and sick. As a university student, he found time while studying economics to be a volunteer chaplain at a local prison. He also became active in the Young Man's Christian Association (YMCA). After meeting the American abolitionist and writer Harriet Beecher Stowe in 1853, Dunant became a lifelong opponent of slavery.

In 1854, Dunant became a representative of one of Geneva's largest banks, with responsibility for the bank's affairs in North Africa and Sicily. He settled in Algeria, where he continued to perform charitable acts while working for the bank. Among his accomplishments was the forming of a YMCA branch in Algeria; he also published a book of essays about North Africa that included a section on slavery.

Dunant left the bank in the spring of 1859 to become a private investor, and in June he made his fateful trip to Solferino. After doing all that he could for the wounded there, Dunant went on to organize relief efforts at battle sites in Brescia and Milan. He amassed local support for the survivors and arranged for charitable organizations in Geneva to send medical supplies.

Back in Algeria, Dunant was obsessed by what he had witnessed on the battlefields of Italy. War, he had always assumed, was probably inevitable between nations. Seeing its consequences firsthand distressed him deeply. As a person who had always sought to serve others, he now asked himself what he could do to relieve suffering in future wars.

As a way of trying to sort out his feelings about what he had seen, Dunant wrote *Un Souvenir de Solferino*. The book not only described what Dunant had seen on the battlefield and the relief efforts that followed; it also called for the creation of a cooperative war relief organization among nations. The book was published in 1862 to instant acclaim. In the following months, many prominent public figures throughout Europe wrote Dunant to express support for his plan.

The first concrete step toward the creation of Dunant's proposed organization was taken early in 1863, when the Public Welfare Society of Geneva decided to take up his cause. The society, a private humanitarian organization to which many of Geneva's leading citizens belonged, appointed a committee of five, including Dunant, to plan its strategy. Dunant, who was now dividing his time between Algeria and Geneva, led the committee in organizing widespread public support for an international conference. He traveled throughout Europe on behalf of his cause, giving lectures and meeting with

During the bloody Battle of Solferino in 1859, Dunant organized efforts to aid the wounded. His book about the battle, *Un Souvenir de Solferino* (*A Memory of Solferino*), published in 1862, awakened the public to the horrible suffering caused by warfare and became an international bestseller.

government officials. He also sought and received the support of many well-known figures, including the English writer Charles Dickens and the French writer Victor Hugo, as well as the founder of modern nursing, the Englishwoman Florence Nightingale.

On October 26, 1863, 39 delegates representing 16 countries assembled in Geneva to found an international war relief organization that they named the International Committee of the Red Cross. They adopted as their symbol a red cross on a white background (a reversal of the colors on the Swiss flag) and drafted a treaty that guaranteed neutral status to relief workers on the battlefield. That treaty, known as the Geneva Convention, or agreement, was signed in Paris in 1864 by representatives of 12 nations.

While Dunant worked to establish the Red Cross, he had little time for his business interests in Algeria. By 1867 he had lost most of his money as well as funds that had been entrusted to him

for investment by others, and he had to declare bankruptcy. Dunant fell into disgrace, and was accused falsely of fraud. Virtually overnight he became a social outcast. Yet he continued his efforts on behalf of the cause he had chosen as his life's work—war relief.

At the height of his financial distress, Dunant still managed to attend the general meeting of the Red Cross in 1867 in Paris. At that meeting, he made what was then a radical proposal: that prisoners of war be granted the same status as the wounded. What had seemed to upset Dunant the most about his experiences in Italy was the treatment of captured enemy soldiers. According to the customs of war, prisoners were not supposed to receive medical attention or be dealt with humanely; they were treated roughly and were often even killed by their captors. Indeed, Dunant had intervened several times in Castiglione to rescue badly wounded Austrian soldiers from brutal treatment by the Italians.

Fair treatment of prisoners of war now became the focus of Dunant's humanitarian crusade. Though living in poverty, he worked hard to enlist others in support of his view. In 1871, during the Franco-Prussian War, he founded the Provident Society, later renamed the World Alliance for Order and Civilization, for the purpose of protecting war prisoners and declaring them neutral. The society established branches in several European countries and the United States.

Dunant worked for the World Alliance full time for three years and was able to persuade Czar Alexander II of Russia to organize an international conference in Brussels in 1874 that drew up an agreement on the rules of war and the treatment of prisoners. That year Dunant assumed a prominent role in opposing the slave trade, which still flourished in parts of Africa and the Middle East. He also continued his strong support of Zionism, a movement among European Jews to return to their homeland in Palestine. A decade earlier, while establishing the Red Cross, Dunant had also founded the International Society for the Revival of the Orient for the purpose of establishing a Jewish colony in Palestine.

Despite all that he had achieved, Dunant became dismayed by his personal situation. His family had virtually disowned him, and old friends shunned him. In the mid-1870s he began keeping more and more to himself. He traveled to England to try to raise funds for the World Alliance but soon became discouraged and retreated to live alone in a small village in the south of England. Sometime during the 1880s he went to Paris to work briefly for Frédéric Passy, who had founded the French Society for Friends of Peace. Eventually he returned to Switzerland and became a beggar, wandering from village to village.

No one knows exactly why Henri Dunant adopted such a life in middle age, but he probably felt that he had little choice. There was also a spiritual aspect to his poverty: although he had abandoned the conventional piety of his youth years earlier, he still considered himself a religious man. Simple living was for him a religious vocation. Significantly, he was always well groomed and took pains to make sure that his worn clothing was still presentable. He even used ink to blacken his suit, and he rubbed chalk on his shirt to whiten it.

Dunant eventually made his way to the village of Heiden, and in 1892, at the age of 64, he entered a small lodging house for the elderly there, run by a local charitable organization. It became his home for the rest of his life. Meanwhile, during the years that Dunant had been withdrawing from the world, the organization that he had been instrumental in founding was flourishing. Red Cross units were being established throughout the world; in 1881 Clara Barton had founded the first U.S. chapter.

Henri Dunant was "rediscovered" in 1895 by a Swiss journalist, Wilhelm Sondregger, who tracked him down and interviewed him. A sympathetic article written by Sondregger was published in newspapers throughout Europe, and Dunant suddenly became the focus of international attention, as he had three decades earlier when he wrote *Un Souvenir de Solferino*. Many people sent him money, including the Dowager Empress of Russia, who gave him a small pension. Peace activist Bertha von Suttner came to visit him in Heiden, encouraged him to write again, and saw that his articles were published.

During the following years Suttner herself wrote frequently about Dunant and his achievements. Suttner's championing of Dunant was largely responsible for the great honor he was accorded in 1901, when he was named the co-recipient, with Frédéric Passy, of the

Henri Dunant

BORN
May 8, 1828
Geneva, Switzerland

DIED
October 30, 1910
Heiden, Switzerland

EDUCATION
Studied economics at the University of Geneva (late 1840s)

OCCUPATION
Businessman

MAJOR ACCOMPLISHMENTS
Wrote *Un Souvenir de Solferino* (1862); founded the International Committee of the Red Cross (1863); helped write the first Geneva Convention (1864)

Frédéric Passy, who shared the first Nobel Peace Prize with Henri Dunant, devoted much of his life to improving economic and political cooperation among nations. He believed that such cooperation would lead eventually to world peace.

first Nobel Peace Prize for his work on behalf of peaceful cooperation between nations. Old and bedridden, Dunant was unable to travel to Stockholm to receive the prize, and he never spent the money he was awarded. He lived another nine years at the simple lodging house and died there quietly in 1910. In his will, Henri Dunant left most of his prize money to charities in Norway and Sweden. The rest of the money went to the lodging house for the endowment of a free bed for the poor.

Dunant, who had never married and was long estranged from his family in Geneva, was buried in the Heiden churchyard. Carved on his tombstone is the figure of a man offering water to a dying soldier.

Frédéric Passy, who shared the first Nobel Peace Prize with Henri Dunant, was a native of France. He was born in Paris in 1822 to a wealthy couple; his father, as well as relatives on both sides of the family, held important positions in the French government. He was privately tutored and then attended prestigious secondary schools in Paris, where he studied philosophy, law, and economics. He later earned a law degree at the University of Paris. Through his education and through discussions with family members, Passy became a supporter of liberty, free trade, peace, and internationalism.

Passy began his professional career in 1844 as an accountant for the French State Council. However, when he received a substantial inheritance three years later, he resigned from the post to become an independent scholar. He became interested in the new European peace movement in 1856, as the Crimean War (1853–56) was drawing to a close. The war—in which Great Britain, Turkey, and France fought against Russia—resulted in enormous casualties, which disturbed Passy very much. About the time that the war was ending, an enormous flood

in the Loire Valley of France killed many people and did extensive damage. The public response to the flood was overwhelming, as French men and women protested the destruction it caused.

Passy was amazed by a great contrast: people were upset by the damage caused by natural disasters but were indifferent to the horrors of war—despite the fact that warfare could be avoided, whereas natural disasters could not. Passy decided to do all that he could to end war, which he believed was not only immoral but also had huge economic costs. He reasoned that if only people understood this, they would come together and demand an end to all conflict. They would then further their interests by drawing up international peace agreements and working for the establishment of unrestricted trade among nations throughout the world.

Passy began a one-man campaign to spread his views. In 1857 he published a collection of essays, *Mélanges Économiques* (later published in English as *Problems in Economics*), and gave many lectures during the next decade. In 1867 he and several of his colleagues wrote a letter to the Paris newspaper *Le Temps* calling for an end to recent tensions between the French and Prussian governments. They also urged the creation of a peace society in France. Many people responded enthusiastically to this letter, and as a result the International League for Peace and Freedom was established in Paris later that year, with Passy as its director. In this capacity, Passy contributed a column on pacifism to *Le Temps* and sponsored the Library of Peace, a series of publications on pacifism.

Despite the efforts of Passy's organization, the Franco-Prussian War broke out in 1870 and the French army was defeated. During the occupation of Paris by Prussian troops, the International League was forced to end its activities. When peace was finally restored in 1871, Passy created a new pacifist organization, the French Society of the Friends of Peace.

Passy had long refused any government appointments because accepting them meant he had to take an oath of allegiance to the French monarch, and this was something that his conscience would not allow him to do. He was therefore pleased when a republican form of government replaced the monarchy in 1871, and to show his support of the new regime he taught in the Paris school system during the 1870s.

In 1881 Passy decided to seek office and was elected to the Chamber of Deputies, the lower house of the French parliament. During his two terms of service, he supported legislation for free trade, the improvement of working conditions for French laborers, and calls for international arbitration (the peaceful settlement of disputes through mediation rather than warfare). He also spoke out against the French acquisition of colonies in Africa and Southeast Asia and their exploitation of native peoples.

In the late 1880s Passy learned of British peace leader William Cremer's attempts in Parliament to get his nation and the United States to sign an arbitration agreement to resolve future disputes. Passy introduced similar legislation in the French parliament calling for arbitration of any future disputes between his own country and the United States. In 1888 Passy and Cremer organized a conference in Paris of representatives from the French and British parliaments to discuss the passage of an arbitration treaty between their governments and the United States. They met again a year later in Pairs, together with representatives of eight other European nations and the United States. There they founded the Interparliamentary Union for the purpose of promoting the cause of interna-

tional arbitration. Passy served as its first president and continued in that role for more than a decade. During that time he worked tirelessly for peace, lecturing throughout Europe and publishing articles on the subject.

Passy's dedication to world peace earned him a share of the First Nobel Peace Prize in 1901. For the remaining 11 years of his life, Passy was considered the undisputed leader of the European peace movement. One of his major contributions to the cause of peace occurred in 1906, when he persuaded Russia and Japan to end the Russo-Japanese War by submitting to arbitration by U.S. President Theodore Roosevelt.

In private life, Passy was married and the father of 12 children. He was offered many other awards besides the Nobel Peace Prize, including membership in the French Legion of Honor, but he declined them all. He died at home in June 1912 at the age of 90 and was buried at Père-Lachaise Cemetery in Paris.

FURTHER READING

Gray, Charlotte. *Henry Dunant*. Milwaukee: Gareth Stevens, 1988.

Dunant, Henri. *A Memory of Solferino*. 1862. Reprint. Washington, D.C.: American National Red Cross, 1939.

Gumpert, Martin. *Dunant: The Story of the Red Cross*. Oxford: Oxford University Press, 1938.

Hart, Ellen. *Man Born to Live: The Life and Work of Henry Dunant, Founder of the Red Cross*. London: Victor Gollancz, Ltd., 1953.

Puech, Jules L. "Frédéric Passy." In *The Interparliamentary Union from 1889 to 1939*. Geneva: Interparliamentary Union, 1939.

Rich, Josephine. *Jean Henri Dunant: Founder of the International Red Cross*. New York: Julian Messner, 1956.

Frédéric Passy

BORN
May 20, 1822

DIED
June 12, 1912
Neuilly-sur-Seine, France

EDUCATION
Studied law at the University of Paris

OCCUPATION
Economist

MAJOR ACCOMPLISHMENTS
Founder, International League for Peace and Freedom (1867) and the French Society of the Friends of Peace (1871); cofounder, Interparliamentary Union (1889)

Élie Ducommun

Albert Gobat

1902

Growing up in Geneva, Switzerland, Élie Ducommun was told not to expect too much from life. As the youngest of three sons of Jules Ducommun, a clockmaker from Neuchâtel, Elie knew that he would not be offered any special advantages by his family, for they had little money. Although he was a brilliant student, a university education was out of the question.

After completing secondary school at the age of 17, Ducommun was hired as a tutor to the children of a wealthy family in Saxony, a region of Germany. There he mastered German, and three years later he returned to Geneva to teach languages in a public secondary school.

Bright and ambitious, and with a strong interest in politics, Ducommun turned to freelance journalism as a sideline. In 1855 he became editor of the *Revue de Genève* (*Geneva Review*), a political journal. This led Ducommun to prominence in local politics, and two years later he was named vice-chancellor of the canton of Geneva; in 1862 he became chancellor.

Ducommun left his post as chancellor in 1865 to return to journalism. He became editor of a political newspaper, *Progrès* (*Progress*), in Delémont, a watchmaking town in the Jura Mountains of northwestern Switzerland. Here he grew interested in the new Western European peace movement and reported on its development. Several pacifist organizations were forming at this time, including the International League of Peace and Freedom, founded in Paris in 1867. The following year, Ducommun became coeditor of that organization's newspaper, *Les États-Unis d'Europe* (*The United States of Europe*).

Ducommun believed that peace was essential to a democratic society. As a longtime supporter of liberal—not radical—politics, he also believed that a necessary ingredient of a peaceful society was a workforce that received fair wages and had decent living conditions. As a political journalist, Ducommun often participated in discussions of several workingmen's groups. He became aware of the need for a credit organization that would lend money to Swiss workers and also help them save. In 1869, responding to that need, Ducommun founded the Swiss Popular Bank with an initial membership of 93. By 1907, the bank had more than 40,000 members; today it continues to be one of the leading banking societies in Switzerland.

Following a year of service in the Swiss army, Ducommun joined with a journalistic colleague, Auguste Schneegans, to found the newspaper *L'Helvetia* (*Switzerland*) in 1871, but the paper folded a year later. Through political connections, Ducommun was appointed in 1873 as secretary-general of the proposed Jura-Bern (later Jura-Simplon) Railroad and moved to Biel, a community near Bern, to oversee its construction. During the next 14 years, while the railroad was being built, Ducommun continued to be active in the peace movement. Always civic-minded, he also served on the Grand Councils of Geneva and Bern. When the line was completed in 1887, Ducommun moved to Bern, where he continued as an administrator of the railroad.

In 1891 Ducommun traveled to Rome as a Swiss delegate to the third international conference of the Interparliamentary Union, the European peace organization founded in 1889 by Frédéric Passy and William Cremer. While attending that meeting, Ducommun founded the International Peace Bureau as a clearinghouse for information on the numerous peace societies in Europe. Ducommun served without pay as director of the bureau, headquartered in Bern, while continuing his job with the railroad.

Over the next decade Ducommun worked tirelessly on behalf of the Peace Bureau, corresponding with member organizations, organizing annual conferences, preparing publications, and assembling a library of books and other printed material on peace and disarmament. These efforts—combined with decades of public service on behalf of his fellows—earned Ducommun a share of the Nobel Peace Prize in 1902.

Never a wealthy man, Ducommun nonetheless gave his prize money to the peace movement. In tribute, the International Peace Bureau presented him with money donated by all of the bureau's chapters. Ducommun was able to resign from the railroad in 1903, and he devoted the remaining years of his life to the bureau and other activities for peace.

In his private life, Ducommun enjoyed literature and the theater and

Élie Ducommun founded the International Peace Bureau in 1891 and served as its head until his death 15 years later. Under his direction, the bureau became the largest peace information center in the world, and in 1910 it received its own Nobel Peace Prize.

also found time to write poetry; *Derniers sourires* (*Last Smiles*), a volume of his verse, was published in 1886. In addition, he founded two cultural societies for the French-speaking population of Switzerland. Ducommun was married to a cousin but had no children. He died in 1906 at the age of 73.

In contrast to Élie Ducommun, his fellow laureate Albert Gobat probably never doubted that he was destined to play an important role in the life of his country and perhaps even the world. Born in 1843, Charles Albert Gobat was the only son of an educated family. His father was a Protestant minister in Tramelan, a town in northwestern Switzerland, near the French border.

Gobat seems to have always had enormous self-assurance. After completing secondary school he studied philosophy, history, and literature at the universities of Basel and Bern, in Switzerland, then went on to Heidelberg University in Germany, where he

PEACEMAKERS

Élie Ducommun

BORN
February 19, 1833
Geneva, Switzerland

DIED
December 7, 1906
Bern, Switzerland

EDUCATION
Attended elementary and secondary schools in Bern

OCCUPATION
Journalist; public official

MAJOR ACCOMPLISHMENTS
Founder, Swiss Popular Bank (1869); founder and director, International Peace Bureau (1891–1906)

Albert Gobat was awarded the Nobel Peace Prize for his efforts to promote arbitration instead of warfare as a means of settling disputes among nations. Gobat succeeded his cowinner, Élie Ducommun, as head of the International Peace Bureau after Ducommun's death.

earned a doctorate in law in 1867, graduating with the highest honors. This was followed by a year of post-graduate study in economics and international law in Paris.

Gobat returned to Switzerland in 1868 and settled briefly in Bern. There he joined the university faculty as a lecturer in law, a position he held until 1912. In the late 1860s Gobat moved to the town of Delémont and established a large law practice. Here he became acquainted with Élie Ducommun, who was then working as a journalist in Delémont. Like Ducommun, Gobat also became involved in politics and held seats on local as well as national governing bodies. In the late 1880s he was elected president of the canton of Bern and in 1890 became a member of the National Council, a position he held until his death 24 years later.

The combination of Gobat's impressive educational background, professional success, and commanding presence—he was powerfully built and had a forceful debating style—led to his appointment in 1882 as superintendent of Bern's Department of Public Education. In this position, which he held until 1906, Gobat was responsible for putting through major reforms in the curriculum, or course of study, in the public schools. He expanded instruction in modern languages and the natural sciences, forced the state to pay for fine arts education, and created a program of vocational education. In his role as education superintendent, Gobat was also able to establish an adult education program at the University of Bern, and he was active in raising funds for the expansion of the university.

Gobat's interest in the spreading European peace movement seems to have grown out of his academic training in international law and politics. He continued to teach those subjects at the University of Bern, and as a public figure he sought out active members of various peace organizations to learn their views.

In 1889 Gobat attended the founding conference of the Interparliamentary Union, held in Paris. He was especially drawn to one of the goals advocated by the organization: the international adoption of arbitration agreements between nations. By adopting such agreements, nations would agree to seek peaceful mediation of any disputes that arose between them. They would bring their disputes to the Permanent Court of Arbitration at The Hague in the Netherlands and abide by that court's decision.

Not surprisingly, the forceful Gobat soon emerged as a leading voice within the Interparliamentary Union, and in 1891 he headed the Swiss delegation to the union's third international conference, in Rome. The following year he organized the union's fourth international conference, held in Bern, and at that conference he was chosen as director of the Interparliamentary Bureau, the administrative organization that coordinated activities of the union's member countries. From 1893 to 1897 Gobat also edited *La Conférence Interparlementaire*, the union's monthly newsletter.

As director of the Interparliamentary Bureau, Gobat focused his attention on international arbitration. Through speeches, the newsletter, and other writings, he urged nations to adopt arbitration as a centerpiece of their foreign

Albert Gobat

policy. Putting his beliefs into practice at home, he was the sponsor of a bill passed by the Swiss legislature in 1902 that applied arbitration to commercial treaties. Under the new law's provisions, any trade agreements signed henceforth by the Swiss government had to include a clause requiring all parties to the agreement to submit to the Permanent Court of Arbitration any disputes that might arise between them.

For his efforts on behalf of international arbitration, as well as his effective leadership of the Interparliamentary Bureau, Gobat was named cowinner of the 1902 Nobel Prize for Peace, along with Élie Ducommun. Winning the award did not mean that Gobat was ready to retire, however. He continued his vigorous work on behalf of the bureau, as well as his teaching. In 1904 he visited the United States as the leader of the Swiss delegation to an Interparliamentary Union conference in St. Louis. Following the conference, he delivered a petition to President Theodore Roosevelt in Washington, D.C., urging Roosevelt to encourage international participation in the Second Hague Peace Conference, which took place in 1907.

Upon Élie Ducommun's death in 1906, Albert Gobat succeeded him as director of the International Peace Bureau while continuing to serve as director of the Interparliamentary Bureau. Now Gobat was directing the affairs of the two largest organizations in the world working for peace, and he held both posts simultaneously for three years. He resigned as director of the Interparliamentary Bureau only after its headquarters moved to Brussels, Belgium, in 1909.

Gobat, who never married, wrote several books. His scholarly study, *La République de Berne et la France pendant les guerres de religion* (*The Republic of Bern and France During the Religious Wars*), was published in 1891. Gobat's *Le Cauchemar de l'Europe* (*The Nightmare of Europe*, 1911), which warned against the growing European arms race, was widely read. He was also the author of a popular history of Switzerland (*Histoire de la Suisse*, 1900).

To the end of his life, Gobat was active on behalf of peace. He presided for the last time over an international conference of the Interparliamentary Union in 1912, in Geneva. In 1913 he arranged a conference on arms reduction between members of the French and German parliaments, but to his disappointment little was accomplished. Gobat died of a stroke on March 16, 1914, while addressing a meeting of the International Peace Bureau in Bern. Five months later, the conflict he had worked so hard to avert—World War I—began.

FURTHER READING

Abrams, Irwin. "Albert Gobat." In *The Nobel Peace Prize and the Laureates*. Boston: G. K. Hall, 1988.

"Ducommun, Élie." In *Biographical Dictionary of Modern Peace Leaders*. Edited by Harold Josephson. Westport, Conn.: Greenwood Press, 1985.

Ducommun, Élie. "The Permanent International Bureau of Peace." *The Independent*, March 19, 1903, pp. 660–61.

Simon, Werner. "The International Peace Bureau, 1892–1917." In *Peace Movements and Political Cultures*. Edited by Charles Chatfield and Peter van den Dungen. Knoxville: University of Tennessee Press, 1988.

BORN
May 21, 1843
Tramelan, Switzerland

DIED
March 16, 1914
Bern, Switzerland

EDUCATION
Attended universities of Basel and Bern; doctorate in law, Heidelberg University (1867); postgraduate work in economics and international law, University of Paris and College de France

OCCUPATION
Attorney; professor; public official

MAJOR ACCOMPLISHMENTS
Director, Interparliamentary Bureau (1892–1914); director, International Peace Bureau (1906–9); author of several works on history and current affairs, including *Le Cauchemar de l'Europe* (1911), one of the first books to warn against the arms race

William R. Cremer

1903

ike Élie Ducommun, William R. Cramer became involved in pacifism through his interest in the needs of workingmen. Cremer did not, however, develop that interest as an outsider. He was a workingman himself; from his childhood onward Cremer knew the rough life and poverty of the laboring classes.

William Randal Cremer was born in 1828 to an often unemployed coach painter and his wife in the southern English town of Fareham, several miles from Portsmouth. The father deserted the family, which included two older sisters, soon after his son's birth, and Mrs. Cremer, who had some education, eked out a living by giving lessons in reading and writing to children of other poor families. Young William was probably taught at home by his mother. He was able to attend a local church-sponsored grammar school for only a brief period, and as a youth he began working in a local shipyard. At the age of 24 he moved to London and became apprenticed to an uncle who was a carpenter.

William Cremer worked hard at his job and soon became active in the growing trade union movement. This

English trade union leader William Cremer helped bring the working classes into the peace movement. He devoted much of his life to the cause of international arbitration.

was an organized effort by workingmen who banded together to seek better pay and working conditions from their employers. Whenever he had the time, Cremer also took classes at a workingmen's institute in London. Such institutes had been organized by church groups and private charities in the mid-19th century to offer educational opportunities to workers in non-professional occupations; like William Cremer, such workers usually had little or no formal education.

An important event in Cremer's life occurred in 1856, when he was 28 years old. That year Cremer attended a lecture by a representative of the London Peace Society at the workingmen's institute. The speaker urged his audience to make the achievement of world peace their goal. Nations, the speaker said, had to renounce war as a means of settling their differences; they had to agree instead to resolve disputes by negotiating with one another. At this lecture, Cremer was introduced for the first time to the ideal of world peace through international arbitration.

Cremer did not begin working for world peace immediately, however. He believed that his talents and responsibilities lay with the trade union movement, and during the next two decades he became a leading figure in that movement among the building trades industry. His prominence as a labor leader was a consequence not only of his intelligence but of his remarkable skill as a public speaker. In 1860 Cremer cofounded the Amalgamated Society of Carpenters and Joiners, which became a leading building trades labor union. Four years later he helped to found the International Workingmen's Association, the IWA, and became secretary of the British division.

Not surprisingly, given his commitment to decent working conditions, Cremer was a strong foe of slavery. Although Great Britain had abolished slavery earlier in the century, the British supported the South during the American Civil War (1861–65) because British textile mills depended on imports of cotton grown there. In protest against his government's position, Cremer organized working-class support for the North in the form of rallies, speeches, and pamphlets, and he welcomed the Union victory over the Confederates in the spring of 1865.

Cremer traveled abroad for the first time in 1866, when he attended the annual IWA conference, held in Geneva, Switzerland. Along with other members of the British delegation, he argued that reforms should be achieved gradually and through peaceful efforts. Their stance put the British delegates at odds with a strong radical faction, led by the German Karl Marx, a founder of Communism who advocated violent revolution by workers to gain their rights.

Conflict between nations was never far from the surface during the 19th century. When another war erupted in Europe, this time between the French and the Germans in 1870, Cremer's attention was drawn wholeheartedly to the need for international peace. Joining with several trade union associates, he founded the Workingmen's Peace Association (WPA) to oppose the entry of Great Britain into the war. Cremer's effort was successful: that conflict—known as the Franco-Prussian War—ended a year later without British involvement.

Now fully committed to the cause of peace, Cremer continued his work for the WPA, serving as the organization's secretary for the remainder of his life. Cremer recognized that the growing European peace movement was largely composed of members of the upper and middle classes, and he believed strongly that the working class needed to be involved, too. Through his efforts, the WPA, as the voice of the common man, became a major

William R. Cremer

BORN
March 13, 1828
Fareham, Hampshire, England

DIED
July 22, 1908
London, England

EDUCATION
Briefly attended a local grammar school

OCCUPATION
Carpenter; labor leader

MAJOR ACCOMPLISHMENTS
Cofounder, Amalgamated Society of Carpenters and Joiners; cofounder, International Workingmen's Association; cofounder and secretary, Workingmen's Peace Association, later called the International Arbitration League (1870–1908); cofounder and British secretary, Interparliamentary Union (1889–1908); Member of Parliament; knighted by King Edward VII (1907)

force in the quest for international peace.

Increasingly, Cremer had come to believe that commitment to international arbitration—the subject of that speech he had heard as a young man in London years earlier—was the only way to achieve peace among nations. In recognition of that goal, the WPA changed its name to the International Arbitration League in 1875. Cremer and his organization focused their energies on trying to keep the British out of conflict with other nations during the final decades of the 19th century. Their efforts were not always successful: despite their opposition, Great Britain became involved in wars in Russia, Turkey, and South Africa.

But Cremer never gave up his quest. He achieved a new platform to spread his views in 1885, when he was elected to a seat in the House of Commons as a representative of the London working-class district of Haggerston. Such an event was fairly new in England: only since 1867, with the passage of the Reform Act, had British urban workingmen been allowed to vote and to stand for public office.

Cremer's increasing prominence led to a meeting in 1887 with American industrialist Andrew Carnegie while Carnegie was vacationing in England. Carnegie, who had been born in Scotland, was also a leading philanthropist—a major donor to charitable causes—and he was a longtime peace advocate. At Carnegie's suggestion, Cremer drafted a treaty calling for Great Britain and the United States

to agree to resolve any future differences by arbitration, and he circulated it among fellow members of the House of Commons; more than 200 of them signed the draft treaty. Carnegie also arranged for Cremer to visit the United States, where he received support from President Grover Cleveland for the proposed treaty at a meeting in October 1887.

The following year, Cremer traveled to Paris and, with Frédéric Passy, organized a meeting of French and British legislators to discuss an arbitration treaty among the three nations. A year later, in June 1889, a second arbitration conference, initiated by Cremer and others, was held in Paris. At this conference the Interparliamentary Union was formed, and Cremer was elected secretary for Great Britain. During the following decade, the Interparliamentary Union, which included representatives from many nations in Western Europe, met annually to consider various peace proposals, including arbitration agreements. A draft plan by the union laid the groundwork for the establishment of the Permanent Court of Arbitration at The Hague in 1899.

For his efforts on behalf of international peace through arbitration, William Cremer was awarded the 1903 Nobel Peace Prize. And there would be a further honor for William Cremer, the highest that his country can bestow: in 1907 he was knighted by King Edward VII. As a spokesman for labor, Cremer had refused earlier offers of a knighthood, but now he accepted the award—on behalf of the working class

that he had been a part of and fought for all his life.

Cremer remained active on behalf of peace to the end of his life. When he died in 1908—from pneumonia, at the age of 80—he still held the offices to which he had been elected years earlier: secretary of the International Arbitration League and British secretary of the Interparliamentary Union. Married twice, he had outlived both wives and had no children.

William Cremer had at least one survivor, however, a "child" born six years after his death: In 1914, on the eve of World War I, a permanent arbitration treaty was signed by the United States and Great Britain, ensuring that future relations between the two nations would be grounded in peace. That treaty was a direct outcome of the effort Cremer had begun in the House of Commons nearly three decades earlier. It is the basis for the peaceful relations between the two nations that continue to this day.

FURTHER READING

"Cremer, William Randal." In *Dictionary of National Biography, 1901–1911*. Twentieth Century Supplement. London: Oxford University Press, 1912.

Evans, Howard. *Sir Randal Cremer: His Life and Work*. 1909. Reprint, New York: Garland, 1973.

Institute of International Law

1904

The Institute of International Law, awarded the 1904 Nobel Prize, was formally founded at a conference in Ghent, Belgium, in September 1873. There, 11 experts in international law representing Argentina, Belgium, Germany, Italy, the Netherlands, Russia, Scotland, and the United States met to establish a permanent institution devoted to advancing the principles of international law and the peaceful solution of international disputes.

Although modern international law dates from the early 17th century, there had never before been a single institution devoted exclusively to its formal study, codification (arrangement in a systematic form), and advancement. The idea for such an institute apparently originated with Francis Lieber, a law professor who taught at Columbia University in New York City in the mid-19th century. Lieber had initially proposed the establishment of a congress to settle international disputes in 1861.

A decade later, in 1871, a French legal scholar, Gustave Rolin-Jacquemyns, along with fellow scholars John Westlake of England and Tobias Asser of the Netherlands, founded the first scholarly journal of international law, *Revue de Droit International et de Legislation Comparée* (*Review of International Law and Comparative Legislation*). After learning of the journal, Lieber wrote to its editor, Rolin-Jacquemyns, and repeated his proposal. The Frenchman responded by organizing the 1873 conference that led to the founding of the Institute of International Law.

From the outset, the institute was a private organization of legal experts. Although the establishment and maintenance of peace among nations was an ideal underlying the founding of the institute, its members were realists who knew that the immediate abolition of warfare was an impossible dream. What they hoped for, instead, was the steady improvement of international relations through widespread acceptance of and adherence to the principles of international law, which in its own right was continuing to expand through the adoption of various agreements and treaties between nations.

In its early years the institute concentrated on trying to find common ground in the different judicial systems of various countries. One of its first accomplishments was the successful sponsorship of a series of extradition treaties among major Western nations; under such treaties, criminals who escaped to other countries were returned to their country of origin. The institute also undertook comparative legal studies that paved the way for the eventual establish-

Institute of International Law

FOUNDERS

Eleven international law scholars representing Argentina, Belgium, Germany, Italy, the Netherlands, Russia, Scotland, and the United States

FOUNDING

September 11, 1873
Ghent, Belgium

HEADQUARTERS

Geneva, Switzerland

PURPOSE

To advance the principles of international law, and to promote peace, justice, and humanity in international relations

MAJOR ACCOMPLISHMENTS

Organized the creation of major international treaties, including the Suez Canal Convention (1888) and the Declaration of the International Rights of Man (1929)

Francis Lieber, a law professor at Columbia University in New York City in the mid-19th century, was the first person to suggest the creation of an international organization to settle disputes among nations.

ment of international tribunals, or courts of justice, to resolve international disputes.

In an attempt to reduce the harmful effects of war, the institute published *A Handbook of Rules and Observances of War* (1879); many of its principles were later adopted at the First and Second Hague Conferences (1899 and 1907). In an effort both to reduce the likelihood of war and to further limit its consequences, the institute drew up a list of international arbitration procedures and went on record as supporting a neutral status for all areas vital to international communication. At least two treaties resulted: In 1884 representatives of 27 countries signed an agreement in Paris that placed all underwater cables under international protection. Four years later, nine countries signed the Suez Canal Convention in Constantinople, which

declared that the waterway would always remain free and open.

For these and other efforts to establish law and justice as the basis for lasting international peace, the Institute of International Law was named the recipient of the fourth Nobel Peace Prize in 1904. In the decades that followed, the institute continued its work of formulating important principles of international law. Among its milestones was the adoption in 1929 of the Declaration of the International Rights of Man, an important statement on the rights of emigrants and refugees. In the 20th century, several organizations—the League of Nations, the United Nations, and the International Court of Justice—were created to apply and enforce international law; in many ways their existence was a consequence of the pioneering accomplishments of the institute.

More than a century after its founding, the institute is still in operation as a scholarly society for the study and improvement of international law. Headquartered in Geneva, Switzerland, it limits its membership to 132 legal scholars from around the world; new members are recommended and elected by the entire body. The institute is funded by membership fees and private grants.

The Institute of International Law continues to follow new developments in international law as social and technological changes create new issues for study. In recent years it has devoted its attention and resources to such modern problems as airline hijacking, environmental pollution, and weapons of mass destruction.

FURTHER READING

Abrams, Irwin. "The Emergence of the International Law Societies." *Review of Politics* 19 (1957), 361–80.

Bertha von Suttner

1905

I n 1876, when Bertha von Suttner first met Alfred Nobel, neither of them could have predicted that three decades later she would be awarded a world-famous prize bearing his name—and one that she had urged him to create. This young woman, who was then Bertha Kinsky, had traveled to Paris to see Nobel, hoping to become his housekeeper and personal secretary. Just after their meeting, however, Nobel was called back to Sweden on business, and she had to return to her home in Vienna. She and the wealthy industrialist would not encounter each other again for 10 years.

When she first met Nobel, Bertha Kinsky desperately needed a job. She was 33 years old, unmarried, and had been unable to establish a singing career. Her family, once wealthy, was now virtually penniless. Bertha Kinsky had found work as a governess—only to fall in love with the eldest son in the family. The family had disapproved of their

Austrian writer Bertha von Suttner was a leading supporter of the peace movement in the late 19th century. She persuaded her friend Alfred Nobel to establish the Nobel Peace Prize.

relationship, however, and Bertha looked elsewhere for employment. Through friends she had learned of the job with Nobel, and now that, too, had fallen through.

On the surface, Bertha Sophia Felicita Kinsky seemed until recently to have led an idyllic existence, but in reality her life had always been far from easy. Born in Prague in 1843 to the widow of an Austrian field marshal—her father had died a few months before his daughter's birth—Bertha grew up in hotels, palaces, and the homes of her mother's friends in cities throughout Europe, including Paris, Venice, and Baden-Baden, the German spa. Mme. Kinsky, who was independently wealthy, spent most of her time at parties or in gambling casinos, and Bertha was looked after by a series of caretakers and governesses. There was one advantage to such a life: through her frequent travels, Bertha soon became fluent in English, French, and Italian in addition to her native German.

As a young single woman, Bertha Kinsky continued to live with her mother, studied music privately, and appeared on the concert stage from time to time. As she grew older, her hopes of finding a suitable husband—women who did not enter a convent were expected to marry—began to fade. So did the family's wealth: by the time Bertha Kinsky was 30, her mother had spent nearly all their money. Bertha had to go to work to help support them, and she found employment in Vienna, the capital of the Austro-Hungarian (formerly Habsburg) Empire, as governess to the four young daughters of the Suttner family.

Bertha Kinsky's romance with Baron Arthur von Suttner proved stronger than his parents' opposition. When she returned to Vienna from her interview with Alfred Nobel in 1876, Arthur defied his family's wishes and married her secretly. The couple, with very little money, left Austria-Hungary to live in eastern Russia, in the Caucasus Mountains, where Bertha had friends. During the following decade, the Suttners earned a living teaching music and languages. Through her husband's influence, Bertha von Suttner became interested in European politics, and the couple, who never had children, educated themselves in that field.

The Suttners, both of whom had been raised in the conservative upper class of the Habsburg Empire, became political liberals committed to peaceful social change and opposed to war. In the late 1870s, as the Russian-Turkish War raged about them, Arthur von Suttner began sending articles on the conflict to periodicals in Vienna. Bertha von Suttner decided to take up writing, too, publishing essays, short stories, and a nonfiction book called *Inventarium einer Seeler* (*Inventory of a Soul*, 1883), a plea for social progress and world peace. The couple also collaborated on four novels in the late-19th-century literary style known as naturalism, with plots that focused on social issues.

The Suttners returned to Vienna in 1885 well established as writers. Back in Vienna, while her husband continued his work as a journalist, Bertha von Suttner turned again to fiction to express her growing commitment to peaceful social progress: between 1885 and 1894, she published five novels with political and social themes.

In the mid-1880s the Suttners lived for a time in Paris, and there Bertha von Suttner once again met Alfred Nobel. Nobel became a close friend of the couple and introduced them to many leading literary and political figures. In Paris Bertha von Suttner heard more about the growing European peace movement and learned for the first time of the founding in London of the International Arbitration and Peace Association; this organization had been formed to work for the creation of an international court to resolve disputes between nations. Later, in her memoirs, she recalled the strong impact of this news upon her; it seemed to strengthen her belief in the possibility of world peace.

Returning to Vienna, Bertha von Suttner felt that she could best serve the cause of peace through her writing. That feeling was confirmed by the enthusiastic public response to her novel *Die Waffen nieder* (later published in English as *Lay Down Your Arms*), which appeared for the first time in 1889. In its pages, Suttner recounted the grim effects of warfare on a young woman during the European wars of the 1860s. With its vivid descriptions of battle, the book was viewed as a strong indictment of war, and it was widely praised not only by literary critics and the reading public but also by leading pacifists, including the Russian novelist Leo Tolstoy. Parts of the book were serialized in newspapers, and eventually it was translated into 12 languages.

The fame of *Die Waffen nieder* made Bertha von Suttner a leader of the European peace movement virtually overnight. She became a participant in various peace groups, and in 1891 she traveled to Rome to attend the third international conference of the Interparliamentary Union. Later that year she founded the Austrian Peace Society, the first such organization in that country. She was also a cofounder, with Élie Ducommun and Charles

Albert Gobat, of the International Peace Bureau, headquartered in Bern, Switzerland, and served for 20 years as the group's vice president. During the 1890s, she edited the peace journal *Die Waffen nieder,* named after her famous novel and founded by Alfred Fried, a journalist who was the author of more than 70 books and pamphlets and numerous articles on the peace movement.

Bertha von Suttner's friendship with Alfred Nobel, which had begun in Paris, continued through an extensive correspondence. In her letters to him, she wrote often of her hopes for international peace, and she is credited with persuading Nobel to share that goal. In the early 1890s she began urging him to donate his substantial fortune to the cause of peace. By 1893, he had agreed. In a letter to Bertha von Suttner written that year, he told her that he had decided to "set aside a portion of my estate for a prize . . . to be awarded to the individual who has advanced furthest in the direction of a peaceful Europe." Thus the Nobel Peace Prize was born.

During the 1890s and on into the 20th century, Bertha von Suttner worked vigorously on behalf of peace. She traveled throughout Europe, attending numerous peace conferences—usually as the only female delegate—and giving lectures. She also wrote articles and for a while edited a pacifist journal. In 1904–5, Bertha von Suttner made lecture tours of Germany and the United States, where she met with President Theodore Roosevelt.

In 1905, Bertha von Suttner received the Nobel Peace Prize—an award that many thought she should have been granted several years earlier. By this time, she and Frédéric Passy had become without question the most important leaders of the European peace movement. Unfortunately, her husband did not live to see her receive this honor; Arthur von Suttner had died in 1902.

Winning the Nobel Peace Prize further increased Bertha von Suttner's popularity as a lecturer, and her writings were also in demand. She continued to contribute articles on peace to various European periodicals; some of them were published in translation in England and the United States. In her last years, Suttner warned in both her lectures and her writings against increasing militarism throughout the world, including China. She also expressed concern about the military use of a new invention—the airplane.

Suttner's last novel, *Der Menschheit Hochgedanken* (English title: *When Thoughts Will Soar*), was published in 1911; it had both peace and women's rights as its themes. She made a second lecture tour of the United States in 1912, and in 1913 she addressed the International Peace Congress held at The Hague.

In the last year of her life, Bertha von Suttner was accorded another honor: she was named honorary president of the International Peace Bureau. Ill for several months with cancer, she died in Vienna in June 1914, less than two weeks after her 71st birthday.

FURTHER READING

Lengyel, Emil. *And All Her Paths Were Peace: The Life of Bertha von Suttner.* Nashville: Thomas Nelson, 1975.

Suttner, Bertha von. *Lay Down Your Arms.* 1889. Reprint, New York: Garland, 1972.

———. *Memoirs of Bertha von Suttner: Records of an Eventful Life.* 2 vols. 1909. Reprint, New York: Garland, 1972.

Bertha von Suttner

BORN
June 9, 1843
Prague, Bohemia (then part of the Habsburg Empire)

DIED
June 21, 1914
Vienna, Austria

EDUCATION
Privately tutored

OCCUPATION
Writer

MAJOR ACCOMPLISHMENTS
Founder, Austrian Peace Society; cofounder and vice president, International Peace Bureau; author of numerous essays, short stories, and books, including the best-selling antiwar novel *Die Waffen nieder* (1889); editor of the European peace periodical *Die Waffen nieder,* named after her novel

Theodore Roosevelt

1906

Theodore Roosevelt—historian, author, outdoorsman, explorer, soldier, politician, and U.S. President—became a peacemaker when he ended the Russo-Japanese War.

Theodore Roosevelt never intended to enter politics, or to be an American historian. Nor did he grow up dreaming of becoming President of the United States. From childhood until he had nearly finished college, Theodore Roosevelt wanted more than anything else to be a naturalist, a person who studies nature.

Born in 1858 to a wealthy New York businessman and his wife, young Theodore was fascinated by wildlife. That interest was created by family camping trips and later by extended trips abroad, including a year that the four Roosevelt children spent with their parents on a houseboat on the Nile River in Egypt. Theodore collected birds' nests and animal skulls, and learned to stuff small animals. His natural history collection was displayed on a floor of the Roosevelt mansion in New York City, and he also contributed specimens to the American Museum of Natural History, which his father helped found in 1869.

Roosevelt entered Harvard University in the fall of 1876 as a science major. He was an excellent student, making nearly all A's in his courses. However, the university offered no training to someone who wanted to do fieldwork in natural history, and Roosevelt knew he did not want to spend his life in a laboratory. By the time he graduated with honors in 1880, he had turned his attention to American history.

Roosevelt was independently wealthy—his father had died in 1878, leaving him a large fortune—and he took his time trying to decide what career to pursue. He studied law briefly at Columbia University, then began writing about history. His first book, *The Naval War of 1812*, was published in 1882. Over the next three decades, Roosevelt would write 14 more nonfiction books, including additional works on American history, politics, and outdoor life.

Roosevelt first dabbled in politics in the early 1880s, when he served three terms as a Republican member of the New York State legislature. Following the sudden death of his first wife in 1884, he temporarily abandoned political life and moved to a ranch he owned in the Dakota Territory. There Roosevelt pursued a vigorous life as a sportsman while continuing to write.

In 1889, about the time Roosevelt began publishing the first volume of his best-known work, *The Winning of the West* (4 vols., 1889–96), he was appointed U.S. Civil Service Commissioner by Republican President Benjamin Harrison, whom Roosevelt had supported in the 1888 Presidential election. He held this post for six years, during which he lived in Washington, D.C., with his second wife and growing family. (Roosevelt eventually had six children.)

Roosevelt's competence as an administrator led him to his next appointment, this time back in New York as the city's police commissioner. For two years he performed this job with vigor, effectively opposing both corrupt politicians and underworld gangs. In 1897 he returned to Washington, D.C., as Assistant Secretary of the Navy under Republican President William McKinley. In this post he distinguished himself by promoting military preparedness in the face of an impending war between Spain and the United States.

When the Spanish-American War did in fact begin a year later, Roosevelt resigned abruptly to take an active role in the conflict in Cuba. He fought bravely in several important battles, but he became famous in one that was of little military importance: he led a volunteer cavalry regiment known as the Rough Riders, took San Juan Hill—and came home a national hero. That fall, on the basis of his newfound popularity, Theodore Roosevelt was elected governor of New York State.

Again Roosevelt demonstrated leadership as he used his position to make state government an instrument of reform. During his two years in office, the state legislature enacted legislation that taxed corporations for public services, improved housing for the poor, and established a civil service system for state employees.

While the public seemed happy with Roosevelt and his accomplishments as governor, more conservative members of his own party were alarmed by his independence and reforming zeal. Working behind the scenes, they supported his nomination as William McKinley's running mate in 1900, believing that as Vice President he would have little power. The McKinley-Roosevelt ticket was elected overwhelmingly that fall, but the conservatives' scheme to rein in Roosevelt's political power backfired: In September 1901, six months after taking office for a second term, William McKinley was assassinated. Forty-two-year-old Theodore Roosevelt immediately became President of the United States, the youngest man ever to hold the office. Three years later, he was elected to a full term.

Roosevelt was one of the most reform-minded Presidents in history. He believed that the federal government should act as defender of the common good, at home as well as abroad. Roosevelt's domestic policy championed individual economic freedom and successfully opposed industrial monopolies. He oversaw the passage of the first federal laws regulating the manufacture and sale of food and drugs. Not surprisingly, many of his major accomplishments were in the field of conservation, a consequence of his early interest in natural history and his later activities as a sportsman. He proposed and vigorously supported legislation that preserved land and other natural resources, and he protected animals through the creation of national parks and wildlife refuges.

In foreign affairs, Roosevelt was equally energetic and self-assured. He believed that the nation should ensure peace by having a powerful defense force, in particular a strong navy. He also believed that the United States should seize opportunities to maintain its position as the leading nation in the western hemisphere. To that end, he supported a revolution in 1903 by the residents of Panama, a region in Central America that was then part of Colombia, against the Colombian government. U.S. support led to the creation of the independent nation of Panama and the creation of the Panama Canal Zone; U.S.-sponsored construction of the Panama Canal began in 1904.

A central tenet of Roosevelt's foreign policy was his restatement of the Monroe Doctrine. In 1823 President James Monroe had issued his famous

Theodore Roosevelt

BORN
October 27, 1858
New York, New York

DIED
January 6, 1919
Oyster Bay, New York

EDUCATION
Tutored privately; A.B., Harvard College (1880)

OCCUPATION
Politician; statesman; historian

MAJOR ACCOMPLISHMENTS
President of the United States (1901–9); Vice President of the United States (1901); Assistant Secretary of the Navy (1897–98); governor, New York State (1898–1900); drew up the Treaty of Portsmouth (1905), which ended the Russo-Japanese War; president, American Historical Association; author of 15 books, most of them about American history; awarded numerous honorary degrees; first American to win a Nobel Prize

Roosevelt (center) with Russian and Japanese delegates to the Portsmouth Conference, held in Portsmouth, New Hampshire, in 1905. Roosevelt's skill as a mediator helped the two sides come to an agreement and end the armed conflict between their nations by signing the Treaty of Portsmouth.

1890s, Russian foreign policy had focused on extending the government's influence in the Far East. Japan, increasingly alarmed, finally declared war on Russia in February 1904. As the Russo-Japanese War dragged on, Roosevelt viewed the situation as potentially dangerous for the United States. He did not want either side to achieve victory, for this would upset the balance of power among Asian nations and might threaten American interests in the Pacific.

Proposing himself as a mediator between the two warring countries, Roosevelt called their representatives to a meeting in Portsmouth, New Hampshire, in August 1905. As a result of his mediation, Russia and Japan reached an agreement that ended the war. Called the Treaty of Portsmouth, it was signed on September 5, 1905. A year later, Roosevelt was named the winner of the Nobel Peace Prize for his role in ending the conflict. He was the first American to win a Nobel Prize in any field.

While Roosevelt's selection for this award was applauded by many, it was also widely criticized: longtime European peace advocates believed that the prize should have been awarded to a pacifist, and not to a man who emphasized military preparedness. Roosevelt's supporters argued that his mediation had saved thousands of lives that might have been lost if the war had continued, but this argument did not silence the critics.

Such criticism, however, misrepresented or ignored several important facts about Roosevelt. Although he was not a pacifist, he also did not believe in warfare as a means of resolving disagreements; he believed that if all

proclamation warning European powers not to interfere in the affairs of the western hemisphere. To this warning Roosevelt added a corollary: if other western hemisphere nations had political or economic crises that might make them vulnerable to outside interference, the U.S. government would step in to protect them even before Europe acted.

It was not only the western hemisphere that Roosevelt kept an eye on, however. He also watched European and Asian affairs closely. During the nations maintained a strong military force, any single nation would be reluctant to attack another. Furthermore, Roosevelt had often acted as a peacemaker in other troublesome situations, both domestic and foreign. In 1902, for example, he had used the federal government as an arbitrator to settle a major coal strike peacefully at a time when labor unrest often led to violence and death. And he was on record as a declared supporter of international peace efforts: in 1904 he had called for the formation of the Second Hague Conference, held three years later to discuss arms limitation. Finally, because of his many successful efforts to improve human welfare, it could be argued that Roosevelt had spent his entire professional life working for the establishment of a peaceful society.

Roosevelt continued to be a prominent public figure after his second term as President ended in 1909. Following a year of travel in Europe and Africa, he became a cofounder of the Progressive party, a group of reform-minded Republicans who wished to separate themselves from the conservative wing of the Republican party. In 1912, Roosevelt again ran for President, this time as the Progressive party candidate. During the campaign, he narrowly escaped an assassination attempt in Milwaukee: a bullet shot at him by a fanatic was deflected by his glasses case and a folded copy of his speech in his breast pocket. Following his defeat by the Democratic party candidate, Woodrow Wilson, Roosevelt took a break from politics and turned his attention to other interests. He wrote more books, including his autobiography, and served as president of the American Historical Association, an organization of histori-

ans. Still an active outdoorsman, he led an expedition in 1914 to the South American wilderness to explore the La Plata River, and later that year published a book about his adventures.

The eruption of war in Europe in August 1914—the conflict that would later be known as World War I—drew Roosevelt back into politics. He became a strong public critic of President Woodrow Wilson, believing that Wilson was too cautious and hesitant as a leader both at home and abroad. When the United States finally entered the war nearly three years later, Roosevelt supported the move, for he believed that victory by the enemy forces—Germany and its allies—would endanger democracy throughout the world.

Eager to serve his country and to support a cause he strongly believed in, Roosevelt tried to enlist as a soldier, although he was nearly 60 years old—and was angry when the army turned him down because of his age. All four of Roosevelt's sons served in World War I, and one of them was killed in action. In 1917, Roosevelt, through an act of the U.S. Congress, donated his long-saved Nobel Peace Prize money to war relief agencies, including the Red Cross.

As early as 1910, Roosevelt had proposed the formation of an international organization, which he called a "League of Peace," that would work to maintain and even enforce peaceful relations among nations. However, following the armistice that ended World War I in November 1918, he did not support the League of Nations, the peacekeeping organization that Woodrow Wilson had proposed. Roosevelt believed that the President was naive and unrealistic about world poli-

tics, and that the League agreed to by Wilson and the leaders of the victorious European nations might even draw the United States into another war.

During his South American trip in 1914, Roosevelt had contracted several severe tropical infections, and he never fully recovered. Although his health declined steadily in the years that followed, he still tried to lead a vigorous life. He died in his sleep in January 1919, at the age of 60. That fall, 13 years after Roosevelt received the Nobel Peace Prize, his longtime political opponent Woodrow Wilson was named the 1919 winner for his own efforts on behalf of peace.

FURTHER READING

Fritz, Jean. *Bully for You, Teddy Roosevelt!* New York: Scholastic, 1992.

Hagedorn, Hermann. *The Roosevelt Family of Sagamore Hill*. New York: Macmillan, 1954.

McCullough, David. *Mornings on Horseback*. New York: Simon & Schuster, 1981.

Miller, Nathan. *Theodore Roosevelt: A Life*. New York: Morrow, 1992.

Morris, Edmund. *The Rise of Theodore Roosevelt*. New York: Coward, McCann, 1979.

"Roosevelt, Theodore." In *Dictionary of American Biography*, vol. 8, part 2. New York: Scribners, 1935.

Roosevelt, Theodore *An Autobiography*. 1913. Abridged ed. New York: Scribners, 1958.

Ernesto Moneta
Louis Renault

1907

From the time of his birth in Milan in 1833, it was assumed that Ernesto Moneta would grow up to become a soldier. Warfare was a common occurrence in 19th-century Italy, and nearly every able-bodied man served in a military unit of some sort. Much of the fighting that occurred was in revolt against outside rule: Italy was not yet a single nation but a collection of individual kingdoms and city-states, many of which were under foreign control. Milan, for example, had belonged to Austria, except at short intervals, since 1713.

Ernesto was the third of 11 children born to a family that was aristocratic but had little money. He was educated in the local schools of Milan until the age of 15, when he, his father, and several of his brothers joined in the fight against Austrian forces during an uprising in 1848. The revolt was not successful, and Italians who had fought and survived had to flee the city, in fear of being punished by the Austrians. Moneta escaped to the independent kingdom of Piedmont, northwest of Milan.

Ernesto Moneta fought with the Italian patriot Garibaldi for the unification of Italy. Later, as a journalist, he became a leader in the movement for world peace.

During his years in Piedmont, where he was joined by other family members, Moneta resumed his education, this time at a military academy in the town of Ivrea. He also became a member of a secret society that was working to overthrow Austrian rule in Milan. In 1859, he went to war again when conflict broke out between Piedmont and Austria. That year he and his brothers joined troops led by Giuseppe Garibaldi, a prominent leader in the fight for Italian unification. Moneta became a member of Garibaldi's general staff and served him for seven years.

During the 1860s, a united Italy began to emerge as some principalities joined to form a single kingdom under King Victor Emmanuel II of Sardinia. However, there were still setbacks and defeats for Italian nationalists in several regions that remained under foreign control; final unification would not be accomplished until 1870. Throughout the struggle, Moneta remained committed to the nationalist cause, but he became increasingly discouraged by disorganization within the army. Finally, in 1866, at the age of 33, he resigned from the military.

Returning to Milan, Moneta decided to pursue his support of a united Italy through a career as a journalist. He began by contributing drama reviews to a local newspaper, *Il secolo*, while he looked for other opportunities. In 1867, Moneta's fortunes changed suddenly when several of his friends became owners of *Il secolo*. Moneta was named editor-in-chief, and during the next few years he transformed the small daily into Italy's leading newspaper. Leading issues of the day were discussed and debated in its pages. Through *Il secolo* Moneta supported unification efforts; at the same time he urged the new nation to drop old hatreds and to pursue peaceful relations with other countries. He also pressed the government to reduce the

size of the army and convert it to a civil peacekeeping force, or home guard.

Moneta's support of Italian unification and the peaceful role he wished the new nation to play in international affairs drew him into the European peace movement. During the 1870s, the editorial policy of *Il secolo* reflected that growing involvement. Step by step, Moneta himself became a peace activist. In 1878, he organized and hosted a peace conference in Milan. Nine years later he helped found an Italian peace society, the Lombard Union for International Peace and Arbitration, and supported it with his own money. In 1890, Moneta began publishing an almanac called *L'amico della pace* (*Friend of Peace*), which described various activities of the peace movement. A year later, he became the Italian representative to the International Peace Bureau, newly founded by Élie Ducommun.

After 28 years as editor-in-chief of *Il secolo*, Moneta retired in 1896. He continued to contribute essays and reviews to the newspaper, and in 1898 he founded *La vita internazionale*, a periodical that published articles by Moneta and others on issues in the peace movement. *La vita internazionale* had considerable influence in Italian politics and is credited with many contributions to the cause of peace, including a series of articles that paved the way for the signing of an arbitration treaty between Italy and France in 1903.

For his many years of work on behalf of peace, in particular his contributions to Italo-French relations, Ernesto Moneta was named cowinner, with Louis Renault, of the 1907 Nobel Peace Prize. However, because he continued to support a nation's right to fight, if necessary, to achieve self-government, Moneta's selection was criticized by many pacifists.

Moneta remained active in journalism and politics until the end of his

Ernesto Moneta

BORN
September 20, 1833
Milan, Italy

DIED
February 10, 1918
Milan, Italy

EDUCATION
Attended secondary schools and a military academy

OCCUPATION
Journalist

MAJOR ACCOMPLISHMENTS
Editor-in-chief, *Il secolo*; founder, Lombard Union for International Peace and Arbitration; founder and publisher, *L'amico della pace* and *La vita internazionale*; Italian representative, International Peace Bureau; author of *Le guerre, le insurrezioni, e la pace nel secolo XIX* (4 vols., 1903–10), a major history of 19th-century Europe

Louis Renault, a French legal scholar, began his career as an expert in criminal law. He later became an authority on international law and served as a member of the Hague Tribunal.

1914, he also supported Italy's entry into the conflict against the aggressors, Germany and Austria.

Moneta was married and had two sons; his wife died in 1899. In the winter of 1918, Moneta fell ill with pneumonia. He died in Milan on February 10 at the age of 84.

The man who shared the 1907 Nobel Peace Prize with Ernesto Moneta and who worked much of his life on behalf of peaceful relations between France and Italy was, appropriately, a Frenchman, Louis Renault. Beyond that, however, neither the lives of these two men nor their contributions to peace were connected. Unlike Moneta, Renault was a legal scholar who used his intelligence and considerable knowledge to further the development of international law. From birth, he was raised by his family to be an intellectual, never a soldier.

Louis Renault (pronounced *ruh-NO*) was born in Autun, an historic town in east-central France first settled by the ancient Romans. His father was a wealthy bookseller who closely directed the boy's education. Louis excelled in all his subjects at the local schools, then continued his studies at the University of Dijon, where he received a bachelor's degree in literature in 1861. He then enrolled at the University of Paris, and during the next seven years earned three degrees with honors, including a doctorate in law.

Renault became a law professor at the University of Dijon in 1868. He developed a specialty in criminal law, which he taught at the University of Paris after joining its faculty in 1873. A year later, he was appointed to a professorship there in the relatively new field of international law. Although Renault was reluctant to develop a new specialty, he agreed to the appointment. During the next few years he soon became widely known as an authority on the

life, despite the gradual loss of his sight because of glaucoma. He also wrote a four-volume history of the 19th century, *Le guerre, le insurrezioni, e la pace nel secolo XIX* (*Wars, Insurrections, and Peace in the Nineteenth Century,* 1903–10). He continued to be a strong supporter of both international peace efforts and Italian nationalism, and saw no contradiction between these activities. When Italy annexed Libya in 1911, Moneta supported his country's action as necessary for its security. Following the outbreak of World War I in subject through his lectures and the publication of his textbook, *Introduction à l'Étude du droit international* (*Introduction to the Study of International Law*, 1879). Renault was named the highest-ranking professor of international law at the university in 1879 and remained on the faculty for the rest of his life.

Renault's reputation as a legal scholar grew considerably during the next decade, following his appointment as director of the French diplomatic archives in 1880. By 1890 he was acknowledged as the nation's leading authority on international law. That year he was appointed legal consultant to the French Foreign Office. In this capacity he traveled as France's representative to international conferences throughout the world that met to consider a variety of topics, including revision of the 1864 Geneva Convention.

In 1899, Renault, along with Léon Bourgeois, represented France at the First Hague Conference. At this conference, held in The Hague, Netherlands, representatives of leading nations met to consider arms limitation and other issues relating to peace. There Renault concentrated on issues surrounding naval warfare. He was also appointed to the Permanent Court of Arbitration, also known as the Hague Tribunal, founded at the conference to help resolve international disputes. During his 14 years of service on the Hague Tribunal, Renault heard and helped settle many controversial cases involving countries throughout the world, including Japan, Morocco, and India.

At the Second Hague Conference, held in 1907, Renault served on a committee that specified the rights of neutral nations during sea warfare. He also made proposals to extend the application of the Geneva Convention from land to sea battles. At the conclusion of the conference, Renault was one of the authors of the official proceedings, which were later published.

Louis Renault shared the 1907 Nobel Peace Prize in recognition of his contributions to both Hague conferences, and for his scholarly work in the field of international law. In his acceptance address, Renault declared his belief in international peace as a goal of nations but reminded his audience that war, unfortunately, was still a possibility. Because of this, he urged that further progress be made in adopting measures to protect civilian populations, as well as the sick and wounded, in times of conflict.

Renault received other awards for his years of public service, including membership in the French Legion of Honor, honorary degrees from many universities, and decorations by 19 foreign nations. In 1903, the French government granted him the joint honorary title of minister plenipotentiary and envoy extraordinary. Renault was elected president of the Academy of International Law in 1914.

Renault was married and had five children. He remained active professionally until the end of his life. He died suddenly at his villa outside Paris in February 1918, a few months before his 75th birthday and a few days after giving what would be his last lecture. Two days after Renault's death, his Nobel cowinner, Ernesto Moneta, died in Milan.

FURTHER READING

Cooper, S. E., ed. *Internationalism in Nineteenth-Century Europe*. New York: Garland, 1976.

Rhodes, Anthony. *Louis Renault: A Biography*. New York: Harcourt, Brace & World, 1970.

Louis Renault

BORN
May 21, 1843
Autun, France

DIED
February 8, 1918
Barbizon, France

EDUCATION
Baccalaureate, University of Dijon (1861); Docteur en Droit, University of Paris (1868)

OCCUPATION
Attorney; legal scholar

MAJOR ACCOMPLISHMENTS
Highest-ranking professor of international law, University of Paris; director, French diplomatic archives; French delegate, First and Second Hague Conferences (1899, 1907); member, Hague Tribunal; president, Academy of International Law

Klas Arnoldson
Fredrik Bajer

1908

I n 1860, at the age of 16, Klas Arnoldson was not sure what he wanted to do to earn a living, but he was fairly certain that he would not be a musician like his father. Klas did not have to decide yet, however, and he enjoyed his classes at the school he attended in Göteborg, Sweden, the city where he had been born and spent his youth; he thought he might like to attend the local university after graduation.

Then tragedy struck. His father died suddenly, and young Klas had to leave school to help support his mother. He took the best job he could find, as a railway clerk, and for the next 21 years he worked for Swedish railroads. Only in 1881, at the age of 37, was Klas Arnoldson able to afford to leave that job and work full time at his chosen career—journalism.

The decision to become a journalist was not made hastily. During his years working for the railroad, Arnoldson had educated himself by reading widely in history, philosophy, and religion. Influenced by liberal political and religious

As a journalist and politician, Klas Arnoldson was a leader in the movement to establish Sweden's neutrality. He also championed Norway's peaceful efforts to separate from Sweden.

ideas, he came to believe strongly in individual freedom as the basis for a peaceful society. The European conflicts that raged during this period, including the Franco-Prussian War (1870–71), troubled him deeply. He was also disturbed by the increasing manufacture and stockpiling of weapons by major European powers. In the 1870s, he began writing essays that expressed his beliefs, and they were published in several Swedish newspapers and magazines. By 1881, he was prepared to devote himself full time not only to journalism but to advancing the cause of peace.

Settling in Stockholm as a freelance journalist, Arnoldson increased his output of articles on contemporary political and social issues, in particular the quest for international peace. He quickly became well known to the Swedish public, and in 1882 his prominence earned him election to the lower chamber of parliament, where he served for five years.

In parliament, Arnoldson supported legislation for universal male suffrage (voting rights) and religious tolerance, and became a major voice for peace and for arms limitation. He convinced his colleagues that Sweden, a relatively small country, should not try to arm itself on the scale of the major European powers; instead, he argued, Sweden's best form of defense was a proclamation of neutrality. Under his leadership, parliament passed a resolution in 1883 calling on the government to declare Sweden a neutral country. Sweden finally adopted that position 21 years later, on the eve of World War I. Today, Sweden continues to be a neutral nation.

Arnoldson continued to pursue his career as a journalist while serving in parliament, and he also became active in peace organizations, including the Swedish Peace and Arbitration Union, which he helped found in 1883. During the 1880s and 1890s he edited as well

as wrote for several political periodicals, and he made popular speaking tours of Sweden and Norway on behalf of the peace movement. Arnoldson was a strong supporter of international arbitration as a means of preventing war, and a plea for the adoption of arbitration became the focus of many of his speeches. Convinced by his arguments, the Norwegian parliament in 1890 endorsed arbitration as a national policy—the first parliamentary body in the world to do so.

In the mid-1890s, Arnoldson became sympathetic to the Norwegian independence movement. Norway had been ruled by the Swedish king for 80 years and was now demanding its freedom. Many Swedes opposed Norwegian independence, but Arnoldson worked long and hard on its behalf. As a consequence of his efforts, the Swedish government granted Norway its independence in 1905.

Arnoldson was awarded the 1908 Nobel Peace Prize for his many years of dedication to the cause of peace; he shared the honor with the Danish pacifist Fredrik Bajer. In his address at the presentation ceremony, Arnoldson said that pacifism had to replace war so that humanity could progress to a more civilized stage in its development. As a step toward ending war—a step that was discussed at both the First and Second Hague Conferences—he urged nations to limit their military expenditures. Arnoldson proposed the abolition of national armies and the creation in their place of an international police force to keep order. He further proposed an international referendum—a popular vote—in which citizens throughout the world could declare their support for such action.

Arnoldson donated his share of the prize money to several peace organizations. He remained active as a peace advocate to the end of his life, speaking and writing on behalf of the referendum that he had proposed.

Klas Arnoldson

BORN
October 27, 1844
Göteborg, Sweden

DIED
February 20, 1916
Stockholm, Sweden

EDUCATION
Attended local public schools

OCCUPATION
Railroad worker; journalist

MAJOR ACCOMPLISHMENTS
Member, Swedish parliament; cofounder, Swedish Peace and Arbitration Union; author of numerous articles and several books about peace, including *Pax Mundi* (1892)

Experiencing the horrors of war turned Fredrik Bajer, a Danish military officer and strong supporter of his nation's army, into a leader of the European peace movement.

Arnoldson died of a heart attack in Stockholm in February 1916, at the age of 71. Married twice, he was survived by his second wife; he had no children.

Fredrik Bajer (pronounced BY-er), the Danish writer and politician who shared the 1908 Nobel Peace Prize with Klas Arnoldson, was fascinated by warfare as a child. His boyhood hero was Napoleon Bonaparte, the French emperor who had tried to conquer all of Europe only decades before Fredrik's birth in Vester Egede, Denmark, in 1837.

Fredrik Bajer's father was a clergyman who hoped that his son would follow in his footsteps. To that end, the boy was enrolled in Denmark's most distinguished boarding school to prepare him for eventual attendance at a university. Fredrik did not like the course of study, however, and begged his father to send him to military school. At the age of 17 he enrolled in the National Cadet Academy in Copenhagen and graduated two years later with a commission as a cavalry lieutenant.

Bajer served from 1856 to 1864 in the Danish army. During those years he also received further training at a military college. As he matured, he developed an interest in social issues, particularly education, and began to read widely for the first time about nonmilitary subjects. When Prussia went to war with Denmark in 1864 to claim the duchies of Schleswig and Holstein as Prussian territory, Bajer participated in actual combat for the first time. He served with distinction, but the experience changed his attitude toward warfare: He had once believed it was glamorous. Now he thought that war was horrible.

Bajer's new interest in pacifism coincided with the downsizing of the Danish army in 1865. As a consequence, Bajer was decommissioned and had to find other work. He turned briefly to teaching in a secondary school; he also wrote newspaper articles on contemporary social issues. He read all that he could find about peace and pacifism, including writings by the Frenchman Frédéric Passy. Passy's ideas inspired Bajer to try to form a Danish peace society, but his fellow Danes scoffed at his proposal, for they were still angry over their loss to Prussia in the recent war.

Gradually Bajer came to believe that peace could be achieved only through the replacement of monarchies—governments by kings and queens who inherited their titles—with a republican, or elected, form of government. In 1870, he founded the Association of Scandinavian Free States, an organization that worked to transform the monarchies of Sweden, Norway, and Denmark into a federation of republican governments. Such a federation, he thought, would serve as a model for the eventual establishment of a worldwide union of all nations.

Bajer became active in the Liberal party, one of several political parties in Denmark, and in 1872 he was elected on the Liberal ticket to the lower house of the Danish parliament. For 13 years Bajer served in parliament, where he became a major supporter of legislation to reduce military spending and to promote peace. He also strongly supported women's rights, a cause that he shared with his wife, Mathilde Schluter, whom he had married in 1867. In 1871, the Bajers had founded the Danish Women's Association to work for political equality for women. When female suffrage—the right of women to vote—was finally achieved in Denmark more than 40 years later, the Bajers' association was given much of the credit.

In 1882, Bajer founded another organization, the Association for the Neutralization of Denmark, for the purpose of maintaining Danish neutrality in the event of future conflicts. Later renamed the Danish Peace Society, this organization became the primary outlet for Bajer's peace activities.

On behalf of the Peace Society, Fredrik Bajer traveled to Paris in 1889 as the only Danish representative to the international peace conference at which Frédéric Passy and William Cremer established the Interparliamentary Union. The union was formed to promote world peace by bringing together members of parliaments in different countries for mutual discussion. Despite initial opposition in the Danish parliament, Bajer persuaded a number of his fellow legislators to participate in the union. In 1893, Bajer himself was elected the Scandinavian representative to the Interparliamentary Union's governing council.

Bajer is credited with proposing the formation of an information clearinghouse for the European peace movement during his attendance at the annual Interparliamentary Union conference held in London in 1890. His proposal led to the founding a year later of the International Peace Bureau by Élie Ducommun. Bajer was elected chairman of the bureau's governing board and held this position for six years.

During the following decade, Bajer made speeches and wrote articles sup-porting the adoption of arbitration treaties by Denmark, the establishment of a Scandinavian Interparliamentary Union, and the proclamation of Danish neutrality. He eventually achieved victories in all three areas. Denmark signed arbitration treaties with Portugal, Italy, and the Netherlands in the early 1900s, and in 1908 the Scandinavian Interparliamentary Union became a reality. Later that year, Fredrik Bajer, the onetime soldier, shared the Nobel Peace Prize with Klas Arnoldson for his many contributions to the cause of peace.

Although Bajer suffered from a crippling illness in his later years, he remained active in the peace movement after winning the Nobel Peace Prize. He was dismayed at the outbreak of World War I in 1914 but was pleased to see one of his goals achieved when Denmark proclaimed its neutrality soon afterward.

Bajer died at his home in Copenhagen in January 1922, several months before his 85th birthday. His wife and longtime collaborator, who was his only survivor, continued his work for many years despite her own advanced age.

FURTHER READING

Abrams, Irwin. "Fredrik Bajer." In *The Nobel Peace Prize and the Laureates*. Boston: G. K. Hall, 1988.

"Arnoldson, Klas Pontus." In *Biographical Dictionary of Modern Peace Leaders*. Edited by Harold Josephson. Westport, Conn.: Greenwood Press, 1985.

The Interparliamentary Union from 1889 to 1939. Geneva: Interparliamentary Union, 1939.

Fredrik Bajer

BORN
April 21, 1837
Vester Egede, Denmark

DIED
January 22, 1922
Copenhagen, Denmark

EDUCATION
Graduated from the National Cadet Academy, Copenhagen (1856)

OCCUPATION
Soldier; writer; politician

MAJOR ACCOMPLISHMENTS
Member, Danish parliament; founder, Association of Scandinavian Free States; cofounder, Danish Women's Association; founder, Danish Peace Society; chairman, International Peace Bureau; founder, Scandinavian Interparliamentary Union; author of numerous articles and several books on modern history and social issues

Auguste Beernaert

Paul d'Estournelles de Constant

1909

In retirement, Belgian politician and government official Auguste Beernaert devoted the remainder of his life to the cause of peace, especially international arbitration and arms limitation.

uture peace leader Auguste Beernaert (pronounced *bare-NARR*) grew up comfortably with his sister and their parents in the town of Namur, Belgium. His father, who worked for the tax division of the Belgian government, had been transferred from Oostende to Namur shortly after Auguste's birth in 1829. The Beernaert family became well known and respected in Namur, and the two children were raised to be hardworking and responsible citizens. Auguste's mother assumed responsibility for his education, hiring private tutors to supplement her own teaching as she prepared him for the university. As a child, he also developed his talent as an artist and became an accomplished painter.

Auguste Beernaert enrolled at the University of Louvain in 1846 and excelled in his classes; five years later he received a law degree. After graduating, Beernaert accepted an appointment from the Belgian government to study legal education in French and German universities. In 1853, he submitted an extensive report on his findings to the government and was widely praised for his work.

Beernaert then began practicing law in Brussels. He interned under a well-known business attorney who became a major influence on Beernaert's career. Beernaert decided to specialize in fiscal law, a branch of law relating to financial matters, especially taxation. He soon became one of the city's leading tax attorneys, and during the next two decades maintained a thriving practice. In 1870, he married the daughter of a Swiss diplomat; the couple had no children. In his private life, Beernaert continued to paint and served as chairman or board member of several arts organizations.

In 1873 Beernaert was appointed to the Belgian cabinet as minister of public works by the prime minister, Jules Malou. That job was usually held by someone trained as an engineer, and there was criticism of the appointment, but Beernaert accepted the post. According to law, however, he had to be a member of parliament before he could hold a cabinet-level position. The following year, Beernaert succeeded in winning election from the district of Thielt. He remained in parliament until his death nearly 40 years later.

Despite lacking an engineering degree, Beernaert proved to be an excellent minister of public works. During the next four years, he improved the country's railways, roads, and canals, built new port facilities at Antwerp and Ostende, and through new construction and renovation made Brussels, Belgium's capital, a more attractive city. Beernaert also worked to end child labor in Belgian coal mines.

Beernaert lost his cabinet post in 1878 when Malou's party was defeated in national elections, but he continued to be an active member of parliament. When Jules Malou became prime min-

ister again six years later, Beernaert was appointed head of the department of agriculture, industry, and public works, a job with even greater responsibility than his earlier cabinet post. After four months, the king, Leopold II, asked Malou to resign, and Beernaert submitted his resignation, too. The king then appointed Beernaert to the dual positions of prime minister and minister of finance.

Beernaert distinguished himself during his 10 years of service. His accomplishments included the passage of labor reform laws as well as legislation that extended voting rights. In support of King Leopold II, he gained parliamentary approval for Leopold's rule of the Belgian Congo, a colony in Africa. Beernaert resigned from his dual post as prime minister and finance minister in 1894, following his failure to pass a law that would have guaranteed fairer representation in parliament.

Although he continued to serve in parliament, Beernaert now had the time to devote to a new interest, developed in old age: the cause of international peace. In 1896, at the age of 69, he became an active member of the Interparliamentary Union, which had been founded seven years earlier by William Cremer and Frédéric Passy.

Beernaert focused on one of the union's primary objectives, the adoption of arbitration by European nations as a means of solving conflicts between them. As Belgium's chief representative to the Interparliamentary Union, he presided over its conferences in 1897, 1905, and 1910 in Brussels. In 1899, he was elected president of the union's newly created governing body, the Interparliamentary Council, and held that position until his death.

Beernaert became a strong advocate of arms limitation as more and more countries increased their production of weapons. At the First Hague Conference, held in 1899, he served as chairman of the first commission on

Auguste Beernaert

BORN
July 26, 1829
Oostende, Belgium

DIED
October 6, 1912
Lucerne, Switzerland

EDUCATION
Doctor of Jurisprudence, University of Louvain (1849)

OCCUPATION
Attorney; statesman

MAJOR ACCOMPLISHMENTS
Member, Belgian parliament (1874–1912); prime minister and finance minister of Belgium (1884–94); president, Interparliamentary Council (1899–1912); chairman, first commission on arms limitation, First Hague Conference (1899); member, Hague Tribunal (1899–1912)

Paul d'Estournelles de Constant turned from diplomacy to law in an effort to end warfare. As a longtime member of the French parliament, he supported arms reduction and peaceful cooperation among European nations.

arms limitation. His support of disarmament was opposed by King Leopold II, who believed that Belgium had to have an increasingly strong defense force to protect its neutral status. Beernaert refused to change his position, however.

When the Permanent Court of Arbitration, also known as the Hague Tribunal, was established by delegates to the First Hague Conference, Beernaert was appointed as a member. In this capacity, he helped to resolve several international disputes and to standardize codes of international maritime law (law that governs a nation's rights on the world's oceans).

At the age of 80, Auguste Beernaert shared the 1909 Nobel Peace Prize with the Frenchman Paul d'Estournelles de Constant for his continuing work on behalf of arbitration and arms limitation. Never intending to retire, Beernaert next turned his attention to the new field of military aviation and became its outspoken opponent. At the Interparliamentary Union conference held in Geneva in the fall of 1912, he persuaded reluctant delegates to pass a resolution calling for the banning of air warfare.

Beernaert served as the Belgian delegate to the second commission on arms limitation, which met during the 1912 Geneva conference. Here he argued for the adoption of proposals guaranteeing humane treatment for war prisoners. In early October, while the commission was still meeting, Beernaert became ill and decided to return home for treatment. En route to Belgium by train, his condition worsened and he interrupted his journey to enter a hospital in Lucerne, Switzerland. He died there several days later from pneumonia. Beernaert's body was taken back to Brussels for a state funeral.

Paul d'Estournelles de Constant was a man as gifted and energetic as Auguste Beernaert, with whom he shared the 1909 Nobel Peace Prize. Unlike Beernaert, however, d'Estournelles became committed to pacifism at a relatively young age.

D'Estournelles was born into wealth in 1852 in a château in the Loire Valley of western France. His aristocratic family had many prominent members, including Paul's great-uncle, the noted author Benjamin Constant. Paul's father was a baron, and Paul inherited the title upon his father's death.

From childhood on, Paul d'Estournelles seemed to do everything well, from painting to fencing to sailing a yacht. Because of his brilliance and charm, and the asset of being a member of the French aristocracy, d'Estournelles's family prepared him for a career in diplomacy, a field then reserved only for men from society's upper class. After earning a law degree in Paris in 1874, d'Estournelles studied Eastern languages and traveled through Asia. Upon his return to France, he joined the French foreign service.

From 1876 to 1882, d'Estournelles served as a diplomat in a series of posts that included Montenegro, Turkey, the Netherlands, England, and Tunisia. He then returned to Paris to become assistant director of the Near Eastern Bureau within the Ministry of Foreign Affairs. During the 1880s, he wrote a political study, *La Politique française en Tunisie* (*French Politics in Tunisia*, 1891), which was widely acclaimed and earned him an award from the Académie Française.

D'Estournelles became chargé d'affaires at the French embassy in London in 1890. It was during his years of service there that he began to reconsider his choice of a career. As he tried to resolve disputes that arose between France and England, d'Estournelles became convinced that diplomacy alone could not maintain peace among nations. Only through the rule of law, he believed, could warfare be abolished. D'Estournelles therefore decided to leave the foreign service, enter politics, and become a legislator.

In 1895, d'Estournelles was elected to the lower house of parliament, the Chamber of Deputies, from the district of Sarthe—the same district that his great-uncle Benjamin Constant had represented in the chamber several decades earlier. After nine years of service, d'Estournelles was elected in 1904 as Sarthe's representative to the upper house, the senate, as a Radical-Socialist. He held that seat until his death 20 years later.

As a member of parliament, d'Estournelles became a brilliant advocate of pacifism. In 1899, he and fellow legislator Léon Bourgeois represented France at the First Hague Conference. There they supported resolutions calling for weapons restriction, laws governing warfare, and the establishment of the Hague Tribunal. For d'Estournelles, the First Hague Conference was an exhilarating experience, and the establishment of the tribunal—for the purpose of settling international disputes through arbitration—convinced him that world peace would ultimately be achieved. He believed that this goal could be reached through a massive education effort: if people learned about the benefits of arbitration, he reasoned, they would then put pressure on their governments to outlaw war. D'Estournelles decided to undertake that effort himself, and to devote the rest of his life to it.

During the next few years, d'Estournelles traveled throughout Europe giving lectures on the accomplishments of the First Hague Conference. He also visited the United States frequently, bringing with him his American wife and their son. D'Estournelles had strong respect and admiration for the United States, whose support he believed was crucial to the achievement of world peace. He became a respected authority on American politics and later published a book-length study of the country.

Because of his fluency in English—and his diplomatic skills—d'Estournelles felt completely at ease in his meeting with American political leaders, including President Theodore Roosevelt. In 1902, d'Estournelles persuaded Roosevelt to bring a U.S. dispute with Mexico to the Hague Tribunal, where a settlement was reached—in large part through the efforts of tribunal member Auguste Beernaert.

In the early 1900s, d'Estournelles became active in the Interparliamentary Union and attended its annual conferences with other members of the French parliament who were committed to achieving peace. In 1904 he organized exchange visits of members of the French and British parliaments who supported arbitration. These exchanges paved the way for an important agreement between France and Great Britain the same year, the Franco-British Entente Cordiale. D'Estournelles sponsored similar exchanges between the French and the Scandinavian parliaments. One of d'Estournelles's major achievements was the creation of the Association for International Conciliation in 1905 and the founding of its journal, *International Conciliation*.

At the Second Hague Conference, held in 1907, d'Estournelles once more represented France and again campaigned for the adoption of interna-

Paul d'Estournelles de Constant

BORN
November 22, 1852
La Flèche, France

DIED
May 15, 1924
Paris, France

EDUCATION
Law license, École de droit, Paris (1874); studied at the École des langues Orientales, Paris (1874–75)

OCCUPATION
Diplomat; statesman

MAJOR ACCOMPLISHMENTS
French chargé d'affaires, London (1890–93); member, French parliament (1895–1924); founder, Association for International Conciliation (1905) and its journal; member, Hague Tribunal (1907–14); author of numerous articles and books on politics and history

tional arbitration. That same year he was appointed to a seat on the Hague Tribunal. D'Estournelles's tireless work on behalf of peace earned him a share of the Nobel Peace Prize two years later. The citation accompanying the award gave him credit for the signing of several French arbitration treaties, and it praised his efforts to persuade other nations to adopt similar treaties.

During his visits to the United States, d'Estournelles had met Andrew Carnegie, the industrialist and philanthropist who had used his fortune for the betterment of humanity.

In 1910, Carnegie founded a leading peace organization, the Carnegie Endowment for International Peace, whose director was the educator Nicholas Murray Butler. D'Estournelles had established a friendship with Butler, and their relationship paved the way for d'Estournelles's appointment as head of the Carnegie Endowment's European branch. The Carnegie Endowment subsequently took over the publication of *International Conciliation*.

The historical bitterness that existed between France and Germany had long been of concern to d'Estournelles, and in the years prior to the outbreak of World War I, he tried to improve their relationship. Hatred of Germany was very strong among the French, particularly since France's defeat by the Germans in the Franco-Prussian War (1870–71). In 1903, d'Estournelles had traveled to Munich to found a Franco-German society for mutual understanding. Six years later, he returned to Germany, this time to Berlin, where he delivered a speech to the legislature calling for the two countries to put aside their differences as a step toward world peace.

Despite the efforts of d'Estournelles and others, Germany and France again went to war with each other in 1914.

During the four years that World War I raged in Europe, d'Estournelles turned his attention to helping his countrymen through the conflict. He made extensive studies of submarine warfare and advised the government on methods of countering German sub attacks. To help care for the thousands of casualties, he turned the family château in the Loire Valley into a hospital. At the end of the war, he joined with Léon Bourgeois in drawing up a proposal for the formation of the League of Nations, and submitted the proposal to the prime minister, Georges Clemenceau.

In the remaining years of his life, d'Estournelles encouraged and organized more parliamentary exchange visits. For relaxation, he turned to writing, making translations of ancient Greek literature, and publishing a history of classical Greece as well as a play. His last public act occurred in 1921, when he attended the Interparliamentary Union conference in Stockholm. There he made an impassioned plea for fairness toward the German delegation, who were being treated with hostility. The plea was a failure, and he returned to his home in Paris sad and dejected. D'Estournelles died there in May 1924, at the age of 71.

FURTHER READING

Abrams, Irwin. "Paul d'Estournelles de Constant." In *The Nobel Peace Prize and the Laureates*. Boston: G.K. Hall, 1988.

"Beernaert, Auguste." In *Biographical Dictionary of Modern Peace Leaders*. Edited by Harold Josephson. Westport, Conn.: Greenwood Press, 1985.

Davis, Hayne, ed. *Among the World's Peacemakers*. 1907. Reprint, New York: Garland, 1972.

International Peace Bureau

1910

T he suggestion for an International Peace Bureau was first made by the Danish writer and peace activist Fredrik Bajer. Bajer offered the proposal in 1890, while he was in London attending the second international conference of the Interparliamentary Union, which had been founded a year earlier. During the preceding decade, peace societies had sprung up all over the world, and Bajer thought that an organization was needed to gather and share information about them.

At the Interparliamentary Union's next annual conference, held in 1891 in Rome, Bajer's idea took root. A Swiss representative, Élie Ducommun, was named by an organizing committee to create the International Peace Bureau—IPB—to be headquartered in Bern, Switzerland. The IPB became the central office of the International Union of Peace Societies—IUPS—and began work in December 1891. Its statement of purpose promised "to coordinate the activities of the peace societies and promote the concept of peaceful settlement of international disputes." The IPB was financed by contributions from IUPS members. Ducommun became the first director of the IPB and held that post for 15 years.

Ducommun worked tirelessly—and without pay—on behalf of the International Peace Bureau. He organized annual international peace conferences, prepared and circulated publications describing the activities of IUPS member organizations, and assembled a library of books and other printed materials on peace and disarmament. After Ducommun's death in 1906, his fellow Swiss Charles Albert Gobat served as director of the IPB for three years.

In 1910, nearly two decades after its founding, the International Peace Bureau was awarded the Nobel Peace Prize. The citation from the Nobel Committee that accompanied the award noted that Alfred Nobel had intended his money to "support, accelerate, and promote the peace movement," and it expressed the hope and expectation that the IPB would use the prize money with those goals in mind.

When World War I broke out in 1914, the IUPS ceased to function, but the International Peace Bureau remained open in Bern. When the war ended in 1918, the IPB became active in coordinating the work of various relief and humanitarian organizations. The IPB played an active role in the formation of the League of Nations in 1919, and henceforth worked closely with this new international organization. In 1925, the IPB moved its offices to Geneva, Switzerland, the site of the League's headquarters.

The League of Nations all but collapsed with the outbreak of World War II in 1939, and the International Peace

International Peace Bureau

FOUNDERS

Proposed by Fredrik Bajer of Denmark; founded by Élie Ducommun of Switzerland

FOUNDING

1891
Rome, Italy

HEADQUARTERS

Geneva, Switzerland

PURPOSE

To coordinate the activities of peace societies and to promote the concept of peaceful settlement of international disputes

MAJOR ACCOMPLISHMENTS

Sponsored major conferences on peace and peace-related topics and published their proceedings principal backer of the League of Nations; today works closely with the United Nations on peace issues, such as disarmament and weapons testing

Bureau became inactive. During the war years, its assets were placed under the supervision of the Swiss government. After the war, representatives of former member organizations met in Geneva to reactivate the IPB. At that time they formed the International Liaison Committee of Organizations for Peace—ILCOP. In 1961, ILCOP was formally recognized by the Swiss government as the legal successor to the International Peace Bureau, and it received IPB's monetary assets. IPB's archives, including its extensive library, were transferred to the United Nations library in Geneva. One year later, in 1962, ILCOP renamed itself the International Peace Bureau.

More than a century after its founding, the International Peace Bureau continues to function as an organization dedicated to furthering the cause of peace. It serves as a clearinghouse for information about peace organizations, organizes international conferences on specific peace-related issues, and works closely with the United Nations on various activities. It has an official status within the UN as permanent consultant to the United Nations Economic and Social Council.

One of the major postwar concerns of the International Peace Bureau has been disarmament. In 1974, the IPB sponsored a nongovernmental conference on weapons reduction at Bradford University, in England. Proposals made at the Bradford Conference paved the way for the UN's First Special Session on Disarmament in 1978. IPB-organized symposia on compulsory military service and human rights have also led to United Nations conferences on these issues, and the International Peace Bureau has played a prominent

role in international efforts to ban nuclear testing.

Membership in the International Peace Bureau is open to any organization working for peace and international cooperation; representatives of member organizations determine policy and elect IPB officials. Nonvoting membership is open to individuals who support the organization's aims. In addition to conference reports, books, and pamphlets, the IPB publishes a bimonthly journal, *Geneva Monitor,* which is circulated throughout the world.

Officially, the International Peace Bureau was awarded only one Nobel Peace Prize, in 1910. But many other winners of the prize have been closely associated with the IPB, including Klas Arnoldson, Tobias Asser, Fredrik Bajer, Élie Ducommun, William Cremer, Henri Dunant, Alfred Fried, Charles Albert Gobat, Henri La Fontaine, Seán MacBride, Ernesto Moneta, Alva Myrdal, Philip Noel-Baker, Frédéric Passy, Linus Pauling, and Bertha von Suttner. This list includes not only the IPB's "founding fathers" but also men—and one woman—who were able to use the resources of the IPB in their own efforts to promote the cause of peace.

FURTHER READING

Ducommun, Élie. "The Permanent International Bureau of Peace." *The Independent,* March 19, 1903, pp. 660–61.

Simon, Werner. "The International Peace Bureau, 1892–1917." In *Peace Movements and Political Cultures.* Edited by Charles Chatfield and Peter van den Dungen. Knoxville: University of Tennessee Press, 1988.

The International Peace Bureau: History, Aims, Activities. Geneva: International Peace Bureau, 1969.

Tobias Asser
Alfred Fried

1911

Dutch legal scholar Tobias Asser helped found the Institute of International Law in 1873 and devoted the remainder of his life to promoting the cause of internationalism.

A
t the age of 73, and less than two years before his death, Dutch statesman and jurist Tobias Asser was named cowinner of the 1911 Nobel Peace Prize for his work on behalf of international arbitration. Asser had undeniably spent most of his lifetime in the cause of peace, but he made two of his most significant contributions nearly 40 years earlier, when he was a young attorney. At the age of 31, he had cofounded the first scholarly journal on international law. Four years later, he cofounded the Institute of International Law, the first organization dedicated to peaceful resolutions of disputes among nations.

Tobias Asser seemed destined from the day of his birth, in 1838, to enter the legal profession. His father, grandfather, and an uncle were lawyers and prominent members of the Jewish community in their home city of Amsterdam. Tobias briefly considered becoming a businessman when he won an essay competition on economic theory while in his teens. However, he entered Amsterdam's law school, the Athenaeum, after completing secondary school, and received a doctorate in the field in 1860.

Asser had his first encounter with international law after graduation, when he served on a commission to negotiate the end of shipping fees on Europe's Rhine River. Afterwards, he practiced law privately for a year, then accepted an appointment in 1862 as professor of international and commercial (business) law at the Athenaeum. Despite his relative youth—he was only 24 when he joined the faculty—Asser soon became well established as a scholar in the growing field of international law through the publication of many articles and books. Throughout his career, Asser urged that nations develop peaceful relations with one another through adherence to law. In particular, in his writings and later as a negotiator, he encouraged national legislatures to pass laws in their own countries that conformed to the principles of international law.

In 1869, Asser, together with fellow legal scholars Gustave Rolin-Jacquemyns of Belgium and John Westlake of England, founded the *Revue de Droit International et de Legislation Comparée* (*Review of International Law and Comparative Legislation*). The *Revue*, the first scholarly journal on the subject of international law, became the leading publication in the field, and Asser contributed many articles. The success of the journal led Asser to join with Rolin-Jacquemyns and others in founding the Institute of International Law in Ghent, Belgium, in 1873.

Beginning in the mid-1870s, Asser served as a legal adviser to the Dutch government. He became a sought-after

Tobias Asser

BORN

April 29, 1838
Amsterdam, Netherlands

DIED

July 29, 1913
The Hague, Netherlands

EDUCATION

L.L.D., Amsterdam Athenaeum
(1860)

OCCUPATION

Jurist; statesman

**MAJOR
ACCOMPLISHMENTS**

Cofounder, *Revue de Droit International et de Legislation Comparée;* cofounder and later honorary president, Institute of International Law; cofounder and member, Hague Tribunal

The "Peace Palace" at The Hague in the Netherlands, site of the Hague Tribunal.

negotiator in his country's dealings with other nations, not only because of his legal knowledge and skills but also because he was fluent in several languages, including English. Virtually every treaty signed by the Dutch between 1875 and 1913 was negotiated by Asser. Among the most important of these was the Suez Canal Convention of 1888, which guaranteed the neutrality of this major waterway in time of war. Asser's contribution to the signing of the Suez Canal Convention was twofold: not only was he a major negotiator on behalf of the Dutch government, but the Institute of International Law, which he had cofounded, is given credit for drawing up the convention and securing its adoption by representatives from countries around the world.

Asser retired from the law faculty at the Athenaeum (which is now part of the University of Amsterdam) in 1893, when he was appointed to the Dutch Council of State, the administrative governing body of the Netherlands. As a member of the council, he helped organize and presided over four major international law conferences that were held at The Hague, Netherlands, in the 1890s and early 1900s. He also served as the chief delegate from the Netherlands to the First and Second Hague Conferences, in 1899 and 1907, respectively.

At both Hague Conferences, Asser was a strong supporter of compulsory arbitration, calling for international treaties that would require feuding nations to settle their differences by negotiation instead of going to war. At the First Hague Conference, Asser helped create the Permanent Court of Arbitration, also known as the Hague Tribunal, the first world court. He was appointed a judge of the Hague Tribunal in 1900, and during the following decade he helped resolve a number of international disputes, including one between the United States and Russia over fishing rights in the Bering Strait.

Asser's career reached its peak in 1904 with his appointment as Dutch minister of state. This was the highest-ranking government position then open to a commoner in the Netherlands, and he served in this post for the rest of his life. Asser received many honors, including honorary degrees from major European and British universities. Several of his books became standard texts in the fields of international and commercial law.

Asser was married and had four children. He left behind his famous library, which included major works on international law. After his death, the library was donated to the Peace Palace at The Hague, where it is known as the Asser Collection.

Alfred Fried, cowinner of the 1911 Nobel Peace Prize, had only a high school education. He was born in Vienna in 1864 to Jewish parents; the occupation of his father is unknown, but one of his uncles was the publisher of a leading periodical in the city. Why Fried left school at the age of 15 is unclear; perhaps there were financial problems, or perhaps he was just impatient to begin earning his own living. Whatever the reason, Fried became a bookseller in Vienna—and prospered. He moved to Berlin and in 1887 founded his own publishing company. Two years later he married for the first time.

During the next two decades, he married a second and a third time, but there is no record of his having any children.

As a publisher of books and magazines, and to further educate himself, Fried read widely and taught himself several other languages in addition to his native German. Around 1890 he discovered the works of the Viennese pacifist Bertha von Suttner, whose antiwar novel *Die Waffen nieder* had become a bestseller in 1889. Suttner's writings changed Fried's life, and he decided that he would devote himself to the cause of world peace. Perhaps Fried thought that he was destined for such a role: his name, after all, was the German word for "peace."

In 1891, Fried founded a peace journal with the same name as Suttner's famous novel, *Die Waffen nieder* (literally, "No More Arms") and persuaded Suttner to be the editor. A year later, inspired by Suttner's creation of the Austrian Peace Society, Fried created the German Peace Society in Berlin. In 1894, Fried replaced *Die Waffen nieder* with a new peace journal, *Die Friedenswaret* (*The Peace Watch*), which he edited himself. *Die Friedenswarte* became a well-known and well-respected periodical, and the leading publication of the worldwide peace movement.

During most of the 1890s, as nations increased their manufacture of weapons, Fried published books and articles calling for arms limitation and the adoption of international laws to prevent war. After attending the First Hague Conference in 1899, he became convinced that peace activists could not just support these positions and expect them to be adopted. The public needed to be educated about the meaning of war before it could be made to understand why disarmament and international arbitration had to be the basis for lasting peace. Fried believed that war was a *symptom* of an even

Alfred Fried

BORN

November 11, 1864
Vienna, Austria

DIED

May 6, 1921
Vienna, Austria

EDUCATION

Attended local secondary school

OCCUPATION

Publisher; journalist

MAJOR ACCOMPLISHMENTS

Founded peace journals *Die Waffen nieder*, *Die Friedenswarte*, and *Annuaire de la Vie Internationale*; author of more than 70 books and pamphlets and numerous articles on the peace movement, including *Handbuch der Friedensbewegung* (1911); cofounder, Society for International Understanding

Alfred Fried was introduced to pacifism through the writings of Bertha von Suttner and became a leader of the German peace movement.

greater problem, international anarchy. (Anarchy is the absence of government, usually resulting in disorganization and violence.) Peace could thus be achieved only through internationalism—that is, by all nations placing themselves under world law.

Fried tried to redirect the attentions of the German Peace Society to his new commitment but was unable to do so. Finally, in 1903, he withdrew from the society and moved back to Vienna, where he continued his publishing efforts on behalf of internationalism. In 1905, he founded the *Annuaire de la Vie Internationale* (*Annual of International Life*), a yearbook chronicling the achievements of various peace societies throughout the world.

In the following years, he wrote several books in support of internationalism, the most important of which was the *Handbuch der Friedensbewegung* (*Handbook of the Peace Movement*). Published in 1911, the *Handbuch* included a history of the peace movement and its major conferences as well as biographies of leading pacifists; it also contained a directory of leading peace societies.

Fried was named cowinner of the 1911 Nobel Peace Prize for his commitment to pacifism and his work on behalf of internationalism. The citation accompanying the award noted that Fried was self-educated, and it praised him for his persistence in mastering scholarly writings on international law and politics.

During the next three years, Fried continued his work in Vienna as a publisher and writer, and as an editor of peace publications. He was active in several peace organizations, including the Society for International Under-

standing, which he helped to establish. When World War I broke out in 1914, Fried openly criticized Austria for its role in the conflict. The government responded by accusing him of high treason, and he had to flee the country to escape prosecution. He settled in Switzerland and worked for four years on behalf of humane treatment for prisoners of war.

Fried remained in Switzerland after the 1918 armistice and later published a memoir of his experiences during the war called *Mein Kriegstagebuch* (*My War Journal*). He supported the League of Nations when it was founded in 1919 and voiced his hopes that the organization would keep the peace by inspiring adherence to the rule of law. He opposed the use of the League as an international police force.

But no one seemed to care any more about Fried's views. Ironically, Austria's defeat, which Fried had supported, led to the loss of most of his assets, and he returned to Vienna in 1920 a poor and forgotten man. He spent the last year of his life suffering from illness and extreme poverty, and died of a lung infection in May 1921.

FURTHER READING

Abrams, Irwin. "The Emergence of the International Law Societies." *Review of Politics* 19 (1957), 361–80.

———. "Tobias Asser." In *The Nobel Peace Prize and the Laureates*. Boston: G. K. Hall, 1988.

"Fried, Alfred Hermann." In *Biographical Dictionary of Modern Peace Leaders*. Edited by Harold Josephson. Westport, Conn.: Greenwood Press, 1985.

Elihu Root

1912

As U.S. Secretary of State, Elihu Root was a firm supporter of international arbitration. He believed that world peace would come only when people were no longer willing to tolerate war.

G rowing up in the small college town of Clinton, New York, in the mid-19th century, young Elihu Root seemed likely to distinguish himself someday as a mathematician. The boy was brilliant in all his school subjects, but the family's interests focused on math and science. His father was a widely respected mathematics professor at Hamilton College, a short walk from the family home, and when Elihu entered Hamilton at the age of 15, a career like his father's seemed likely.

More than 50 years later, Elihu Root received a Nobel Prize, which is generally considered the most prestigious award in the world. In old age, Root had clearly fulfilled his early promise. But he did not win the Nobel Prize for Mathematics. Root was awarded the 1912 Nobel Peace Prize—in recognition of his service as one of America's, and the world's, most distinguished statesmen.

The third oldest of four brothers, Elihu Root was born in 1845 in Clinton. The family was warm and close-knit, and Oren and Nancy Root encouraged a love of both learning and nature in their sons, as well as a strong sense of civic responsibility. After Elihu graduated from Hamilton at the top of his class in 1864, at the age of 19, he earned money for graduate study by teaching for several terms at a local secondary school. By now he had decided that mathematics would not be his career. In 1865, he moved to New York City and enrolled at New York University's law school.

Root was admitted to the bar in 1867 and immediately went to work for a prominent law firm in the city. Two years later he opened his own law office and quickly became known as one of the leading corporate lawyers in New York. During the 1870s, Root married—his wife was the daughter of the editor of *Scientific American*—and became active in Republican politics. His first appointment to public office came in 1883, when he was named U.S. Attorney for the Southern District of New York. Root held this post for two years and distinguished himself for his fight against graft and corruption in city government. He then returned to his law practice while continuing as a leader in the local Republican party.

In 1898, Root was a leading supporter of the Republican candidate, Theodore Roosevelt, in his successful race for governor. Root's prominence in the party, combined with his legal expertise, led to his appointment in 1899 as Republican President William McKinley's Secretary of War. Root held this position for five years, serving both McKinley and his successor, Theodore Roosevelt. He proved to be a skilled administrator and reformed many of the War Department's operations; among his accomplishments was the creation of the Army War College in Washington, D.C.

In 1904, as Secretary of War, Root (seated, second from left) meets with U.S. Army generals. During his four years in that office, Root worked for peace in the Western Hemisphere.

As Secretary of War, Root also had a major effect on U.S. policy abroad. As a result of its victory in the Spanish-American War (1898), the United States had obtained several colonies formerly belonging to Spain, including the Philippines and Cuba. Root's responsibilities included overseeing the governance of these colonies, and he is credited with major contributions to their economic and social development, including improvements in education, sanitation, and labor conditions.

In 1904, Root left the cabinet to resume private law practice, but a year later he returned to Washington, D.C., as President Roosevelt's Secretary of State. The United States had now emerged as a world power, and Roosevelt believed that it had the responsibility of taking a leadership role in working for international peace. Root shared Roosevelt's views, and he carried out the President's wishes by acting as a conciliator—a person who tries to solve disagreements peacefully—in disputes that arose with other nations, rather than taking a hostile attitude that might result in the outbreak of war.

Root is credited with the peaceful settlement of many international disagreements. Among them were several differences between the United States and Great Britain over such issues as fishing rights in the North Atlantic, and border relations between the United States and Canada. In 1908, he negotiated the Root-Takahira Agreement, an important milestone in U.S.-Japanese relations in which both countries pledged their support for peaceful relations in the Far East.

In the western hemisphere, Root worked to promote better understanding between the United States and South America. At the third Pan-American Conference, held in Rio de Janeiro, Brazil, in 1906, Root made a widely praised speech in which he assured Latin American nations that the United States respected their independence and sovereignty. In 1907, at the Central American Peace Conference cosponsored by Mexico and the United States and held in Washington, D.C., Root proposed and saw the establishment of the Central American Court of Justice, a judicial body that applied international law to disputes between Central American countries.

After leaving the cabinet in 1909, Root continued to be active in public service while continuing his commitment to furthering the rule of international law. He was elected to the U.S. Senate in 1909 and served a six-year term. He was also appointed to the Hague Tribunal and later served a term as its president. During this period Root cofounded the American Society of International Law, and in 1910 he became president of the Carnegie Endowment for International Peace.

Root received the 1912 Nobel Peace Prize in recognition of his work for peaceful relations in the western hemisphere, for his contributions to U.S. colonies years earlier, and for his long commitment to the use of arbitration to resolve international disputes. In his acceptance address, Root offered his thoughts on the cause of war, which he said sprang from the uncivilized side of human nature. He maintained that no international body could impose and enforce peace. Rather, he believed that a peaceful world would evolve naturally as humankind became increasingly unwilling to tolerate the horrors and cruelty of war.

During World War I, Root continued to work for peace as president of the Carnegie Endowment. After the war, he supported the establishment of the League of Nations but failed to persuade American political leaders to approve U.S. membership in that organization.

Root finally retired from nearly a lifetime of public service in 1924, resigning as head of the Carnegie Endowment in his 80th year. He spent his retirement with his family, including children and grandchildren, in New York City and at the old Root home in Clinton. Although he was wealthy and socially prominent, Root lived simply

U.S. industrialist Andrew Carnegie used part of his considerable fortune to establish the Carnegie Endowment for International Peace in 1910, and he named his friend Elihu Root as its first director.

and in old age still counted nature study as one of his most enjoyable pastimes. He died in New York City in February 1937, eight days before his 92nd birthday.

FURTHER READING

Andrew Carnegie's Peace Endowment. 2 vols. New York: Carnegie Endowment for International Peace, 1985.

Carnegie, Andrew. *Autobiography of Andrew Carnegie.* 1920. Reprint, Boston: Northeastern University Press, 1986.

Harlow, Alvin F. *Andrew Carnegie.* New York: Julian Messner, 1953.

Jessup, Philip C. *Elihu Root.* 2 vols. 1938. Reprint. New York: Archon Books, 1964.

Leopold, Richard. *Elihu Root and the Conservative Tradition.* Boston: Little, Brown, 1954.

"Root, Elihu." In *Dictionary of American Biography.* Supplement 2. New York: Scribners, 1958.

Swetnam, George. *Andrew Carnegie.* New York: Twayne, 1980.

Elihu Root

BORN

February 15, 1845
Clinton, New York

DIED

February 7, 1937
New York, New York

EDUCATION

B.A., Hamilton College (1864);
J.D., New York University (1867)

OCCUPATION

Attorney; statesman

MAJOR ACCOMPLISHMENTS

U.S. Secretary of War (1899–1904); U.S. Secretary of State (1905–9); cofounder, Central American Court of Justice; U.S. Senator (1909–15); member and president, Hague Tribunal (1913); cofounder, American Society of International Law; president, Carnegie Endowment for International Peace (1910–24)

Henri
La Fontaine

1913

Henri La Fontaine believed that improved working conditions and expanded educational opportunities would lead to the establishment of world peace.

When the Nobel Peace Prize is awarded each fall, there is sometimes a "silent winner," someone whose own actions contributed to the achievements of the actual winner. Such was the case in 1913, when the Belgian politician Henri La Fontaine was named that year's Peace Prize recipient. La Fontaine certainly deserved the award, for by then he had been a leader of the peace movement for three decades. But La Fontaine might not have received the Peace Prize if it had not been for a man named Hodgson Pratt.

Pratt was one of England's leading pacifists in the second half of the 19th century. He traveled to Belgium in 1883 on a speaking tour to promote the cause of peace and to establish a branch of the International Arbitration and Peace Association, which he had cofounded in 1880. Henri La Fontaine, a young attorney with an interest in education, came to hear Pratt speak at a public forum one evening in Brussels. He was riveted by Pratt's speech—so much so that the peace movement commanded La Fontaine's attention for the rest of his life.

Henri La Fontaine was born in Brussels in 1854. His father was a high-ranking official in the finance department of the Belgian government. La Fontaine attended local elementary and secondary schools, then entered the city's Free University, where he studied law. After receiving a doctorate in 1877, he became an associate of the Brussels Court of Appeals. La Fontaine's interest in education led to his appointment a year later as an administrator at a new technical school for women in Brussels. While working as an attorney he also devoted considerable time to running the school, and the educational methods he devised became a model for similar schools elsewhere in Europe. La Fontaine was a lifelong supporter of women's rights and particularly of the admission of more women into the legal profession, and he served for a time as president of the Association for the Professional Education of Women.

Following his fateful encounter with Hodgson Pratt in 1883, La Fontaine did not give up his legal and educational career and interests. Instead, he made law and education the focus of his dedication to the peace movement. He became a specialist in international law, and cofounded the New University within the Free University for the purpose of study in international relations. When the Belgian branch of Pratt's International Arbitration and Peace Association was finally established in Brussels in the late 1880s, La Fontaine became its secretary-general.

La Fontaine became increasingly convinced that direct political action was needed to achieve international peace. Beginning in 1891, he became active in the Belgian Socialist party and cofounded the party journal, *La Justice*. In 1895, he was elected to the Belgian senate. He held this seat for nearly four decades, during which he also served as secretary and later vice president of the senate.

As a politician, La Fontaine supported the expansion of educational opportunity and improvements in working conditions. He believed that these domestic social reforms were necessary to create national stability—and that national stability would pave the way for eventual world peace. In foreign affairs, La Fontaine was an internationalist: he supported disarmament and arbitration, encouraged the formation of an economic union between Belgium and the tiny neighboring country of Luxembourg, and after World War I fully endorsed the League of Nations.

Despite his full-time work as a politician, La Fontaine also continued his peace-related activities in the field of education. As an expert in the creation and structure of world judicial bodies, or courts, La Fontaine was appointed professor of international law at the New University in 1893, and he held this post until 1940. He not only taught this subject at the university, but gave many public lectures on disarmament and other aspects of international relations.

In another effort to educate the public about international affairs, La Fontaine cofounded the House of Documentation in Brussels in 1895. This "peace library," funded by the Belgian government, included thousands of publications from all over the world on international issues. La Fontaine not only directed the collecting of these publications but also supervised their indexing and filing according to a classification system that he helped devise. The House of Documentation later compiled bibliographies on various topics in international relations and the peace movement.

In 1907, La Fontaine cofounded a publishing wing of the House of Documentation called the Union of International Associations. This organization, which La Fontaine directed until his death, published reference works

Henri La Fontaine

BORN
April 22, 1854
Brussels, Belgium

DIED
May 14, 1943
Brussels, Belgium

EDUCATION
Doctor of Jurisprudence, Free University, Brussels (1877)

OCCUPATION
Attorney, professor, politician

MAJOR ACCOMPLISHMENTS
Member, Belgian senate (1895–98, 1900–32, 1935–36); cofounder, House of Documentation, a major peace library in Brussels; cofounder, Union of International Associations, a publisher of peace literature; president, International Peace Bureau (1907); author of several important books on international relations, including *Histoire documentaire des arbitrages internationaux, 1794–1900* (1902) and *The Great Solution* (1916)

Hodgson Pratt (1824–1907), a prominent 19th-century British pacifist, converted many, including Henri La Fontaine, to the cause of peace through his speeches and writings. Though many members of the peace movement, including La Fontaine, believed he deserved the Nobel Peace Prize, Pratt never received the award.

relating to the peace movement, including directories, bibliographies, the periodical *La Vie Internationale* (*International Life*), and the *Yearbook of International Organizations*. The Union of International Associations became affiliated with the United Nations in 1951.

Also in 1907, La Fontaine succeeded Fredrik Bajer as president of the International Peace Bureau, and he became a delegate to the Interparliamentary Union. La Fontaine was named chairman of the union's judicial committee, and also served on commissions that drafted plans for a model world parliament and an international arbitration treaty.

La Fontaine wrote several books on international relations that became important documents of the peace movement. *Histoire documentaire des arbitrages internationaux, 1794–1900* (1902) is a history of every arbitration treaty in the Western world during a 106-year period. *Bibliographie de la paix et de l'arbitrage international* (*Bibliography of Peace and International Arbitration*, 1904) is a standard reference work containing more than 2,000 entries.

When he was awarded the Nobel Peace Prize in 1913, La Fontaine was considered the head of the popular peace movement in Europe. Worried about the approach of war, La Fontaine did not attend the ceremonies in Oslo. Several months later, his fears became reality when German troops invaded Belgium. La Fontaine fled to England and then the United States, where he settled in Washington, D.C.

La Fontaine spent the war years in America, where he wrote an important book in English, *The Great Solution*, published in Boston in 1916. The work is a guidebook that outlines the principles of peaceful international relations and describes how to set up international governing organizations; it was later used to create the framework of the League of Nations.

La Fontaine returned to Belgium after the war ended in 1918. The following year he served as a member of the Belgian delegation to the Paris Peace Conference, and in 1920 he joined his country's delegation to the first meeting of the League of Nations.

During the 1920s and 1930s, La Fontaine continued his work with the Interparliamentary Union and the House of Documentation, and he served in the Belgian senate until his retirement in 1936. Despite this busy schedule, La Fontaine—sometimes joined by his wife, whom he had married in 1903—also found time to pursue his longtime interest in mountain climbing (he served for a time as president of the Belgian Alpine Club). He also enjoyed painting and music, and he wrote and published poetry. La Fontaine died in May 1943 in Brussels at the age of 89. Sadly, his country was once again under German occupation, following its invasion by Nazi troops in 1940.

And what of Hodgson Pratt, the man who had turned Henri La Fontaine into a peace activist more than half a century earlier? Pratt continued his activities on behalf of peace, traveling widely in Europe and the United States and helping to found local peace and arbitration societies. He was even proposed as a candidate for the 1906 Nobel Peace Prize, but Theodore Roosevelt won instead. Pratt died a year later, at the age of 83, in London.

FURTHER READING

Davis, Hayne, ed. *Among the World's Peace-Makers*. 1907. Reprint, New York: Garland, 1972.

"La Fontaine, Henri." In *Biographical Dictionary of Modern Peace Leaders*. Edited by Harold Josephson. Westport, Conn.: Greenwood Press, 1985.

International Committee of the Red Cross

1917

The International Committee of the Red Cross grew out of the dream of a single person, Henri Dunant, the Swiss businessman whose book, *Un Souvenir de Solferino*, recounted the horrors he had witnessed during the bloody Battle of Solferino in 1859. Dunant had organized volunteers to treat the wounded after the battle, and in his book he called for a formally established relief effort that could be mobilized in future wars.

Dunant's book was widely read and evoked concern throughout the Western world for the treatment of war victims. A small charitable organization in his home city, the Geneva Public Welfare Society, decided to take action by appointing a committee, which included Dunant, to study his proposal and recommend further action. In October 1863, the committee sponsored an international conference in Geneva attended by representatives of 16 nations. These nations agreed to set up war relief organizations in their own countries and to have their efforts coordinated by a central committee, headquartered in Geneva, which they named

A Red Cross nurse treats a wounded German soldier at a temporary hospital in Abbeville, France, during World War I. Founded in 1863, the Red Cross developed into a major relief organization during the war, which lasted from 1914 to 1918.

Medical supplies are delivered to a Red Cross field station in Germany during World War I. From the outset, the Red Cross was a neutral organization that served victims on all sides of military conflicts.

the International Committee of the Red Cross. These efforts would be funded by both government and private contributions. As a symbol of their work, the new organization adopted the symbol of a red cross on a white background, a reversal of the colors on the Swiss flag. The organization, at both the national and international level, quickly became known simply as the Red Cross.

At the organizing conference, delegates had also drafted proposals for a treaty that would guarantee neutral status to war relief workers. In August 1864, representatives from 12 nations, called together by the Swiss government, gathered in Geneva to formally approve such a treaty. Its official title was "the Convention for the Amelioration of the Condition of the Wounded and Sick in Armed Forces in the

Field," but it became known as the 1864 Geneva Convention.

During a war between Denmark and Prussia in the first half of 1864—before the formal ratification of the Geneva Convention—several Red Cross–sponsored relief efforts had eased suffering on the battlefield. In various conflicts that erupted among European nations in the late 19th and early 20th centuries, the Red Cross continued its efforts, though they were often limited. The organization became stronger as more nations formed their own Red Cross chapters, including the United States, where Clara Barton founded the American Red Cross in 1881. In Muslim countries, chapters of the International Committee were called Red Crescent Societies. (For many centuries, Muslims have used the crescent as a religious and political symbol.)

The Red Cross developed into a major international relief society during World War I (1914–18). Much of this relief centered on medical aid. Volunteers from member nations around the world staffed hospitals, drove ambulances, prepared bandages and relief parcels, and performed countless other tasks to aid the wounded. A major accomplishment of the Red Cross during the war, however, was the work of a subunit set up by the International Committee in Geneva and known as the International Prisoners' Relief and Information Agency (IPRIA).

IPRIA was established soon after the war's outbreak in August 1914. Staffed by more than a thousand volunteers, this agency functioned as a clearinghouse for information on the status of missing soldiers. During the next four years, the agency traced and kept records on more than 7 million prisoners. It acted as a clearinghouse for messages between prisoners and their families, and distributed more than 2 million parcels containing food, clothing, and other personal items.

When agency volunteers traveled to prison camps to deliver messages and packages, they tried to determine whether or not prisoners were being treated humanely, in accordance with international agreements signed at the Second Hague Conference in 1907. These volunteers often had to force their way into the camps to inspect living conditions, but their persistence paid off: their reports on what they saw led to major improvements in the treatment of prisoners of war. Other agency efforts often secured the release of prisoners, either for repatriation—return to their home country—or for care in Switzerland, a neutral nation, until the war's end.

The work of IPRIA earned the Nobel Peace Prize for the International Committee of the Red Cross in 1917, a year before the war finally ended—and 16 years after its presentation to Henri Dunant, the founding father of the Red Cross. This was the only Peace Prize awarded during World War I.

The International Committee of the Red Cross was awarded the Nobel Peace Prize twice more, for the years 1944 and 1963. To read about its activities after World War I, see pages 118-19 and pages 176-77.

FURTHER READING

Burton, David H. *Clara Barton: In the Service of Humanity*. Westport, Conn.: Greenwood Press, 1995.

Durand, André. *From Sarajevo to Hiroshima: History of the International Committee of the Red Cross*. Geneva: Henri Dunant Institute, 1984.

Epstein, Beryl, and Sam Epstein. *The Story of the International Red Cross*. New York: Nelson, 1963.

Gumpert, Martin. *Dunant: The Story of the Red Cross*. Oxford: Oxford University Press, 1938.

Joyce, James A. *Red Cross International and the Strategy of Peace*. New York: Oceana, 1959.

Oates, Stephen B. *A Woman of Valor: Clara Barton and the Civil War*. New York: Free Press, 1994.

Stevenson, Augusta. *Clara Barton, Founder of the American Red Cross*. Indianapolis: Bobbs–Merrill, 1982.

Willemin, Georges, and Roger Heacock. *The International Committee of the Red Cross*. Groningen: Martinus Nijhoff, 1984.

International Committee of the Red Cross

FOUNDERS
Henri Dunant and the Geneva Public Welfare Society

FOUNDING
October 1863
Geneva, Switzerland

HEADQUARTERS
Geneva, Switzerland

PURPOSE
Founded to assist the sick and wounded during wartime; later expanded its efforts to caring for victims of natural disasters

MAJOR ACCOMPLISHMENTS, 1864–1917
Drafted the 1864 Geneva Convention, signed by 12 nations, guaranteeing neutral status to war relief workers; created the International Prisoners' Relief and Information Agency (IPRIA), a major prisoner-of-war relief organization during World War I (1914–18)

Woodrow Wilson

1919

As a child, Woodrow Wilson seemed rather backward. He was shy, spent much of his time daydreaming, and did not do well in school. In fact, the man who would grow up to be the head of a major university, a state governor, and President of the United States had a difficult time learning how to read, and speaking in public was agonizing for him.

He was born Thomas Woodrow Wilson in 1856 in the small town of Staunton, Virginia. For the rest of his life, Wilson would call himself a Virginian, but in fact he lived in that state only for brief periods. In 1858 the family moved to Augusta, Georgia, when Tommy Wilson's father, a Presbyterian minister, was called to serve the First Presbyterian Church. Twelve years later, when Tommy was 14, the family moved again, this time to Columbia, South Carolina, where Dr. Wilson became a professor at the local seminary.

Joseph Ruggles Wilson and his wife, Jessie, raised their children—Tommy, his two older sisters, and a younger brother—to be both pious and scholarly. There was love as well as discipline in the family, and the younger Wilsons knew that they were expected to meet two ideals in their lives: maintaining the highest standard of personal conduct and being of service to humanity.

Tommy Wilson worked hard to meet his parents' expectations, but he was a slow learner. Today historians believe that Wilson probably had dyslexia, a disorder of the nervous system that hinders the ability to read. Young Tommy was encouraged by the love and support of his family, and he developed concentration and self-discipline. At the center of his life was a deep religious faith that became even stronger as he grew older.

In college Wilson's talents began to emerge. For a year he attended a Presbyterian institution in North Carolina, where he received excellent grades, became a distinguished debater, and considered a career as a businessman. After a year off to help the family move again, this time to Wilmington, North Carolina, Wilson enrolled at the College of New Jersey—later renamed Princeton University—whose president was a family acquaintance. There he did well in his classes, especially history and economics, edited the college newspaper, polished his debating skills, and even helped coach the football team to a winning season. In his senior year, one of his essays on American government was accepted for publication in a well-known political journal, the *International Review.*

After graduating in 1879, Wilson entered the University of Virginia Law School, in Charlottesville. Although he withdrew before graduating, he was admitted to the bar in 1881 and moved to Atlanta, Georgia, to practice law. About this time, he stopped signing letters as "Thomas W. Wilson" and became known as "Woodrow Wilson." Wilson practiced law in Atlanta for two years, but he found he did not enjoy it. He decided that he wanted to study politics and history, and in the fall of 1883 he enrolled as a graduate student at Johns Hopkins University in Baltimore.

Wilson received his Ph.D. in 1886; his thesis was published in book form under the title *Congressional Government* and soon became a standard text. Wilson became a respected scholar and during the next three decades published a number of other major works on American history and politics, including *A History of the American People* (5 vols., 1902) and *Constitutional Government in the United States* (1908). After teaching at Bryn Mawr College and Wesleyan University, he returned to Princeton in 1890 as a professor of jurisprudence (law) and political economy. He quickly emerged as a popular member of the faculty, and in 1902 he was named president of the university.

As Princeton's president, Wilson became a reformer. During his eight years on the job, he improved the curriculum, replaced large classes with individual instruction and seminars, raised academic standards, and revised the honor system. However, in 1910 he got into a dispute with the university's board of trustees over how to spend several large donations, and the board asked for his resignation. Almost simultaneously, the state leaders of the Democratic party approached Wilson to run for governor of New Jersey. That fall he won the election with one of the largest majorities in the state's history.

Woodrow Wilson proved to be a reform-minded governor, too. Under his leadership, the state enacted laws to

overhaul primary elections, attack corruption, improve the workplace, and control public utilities. By 1912 Wilson had become a prominent politician in the Democratic party. That summer he was nominated to run for President, and in November he was elected.

As U.S. President, Wilson championed a program of reform that he named "the New Freedom." The goal of Wilson's program was the promotion and protection of free enterprise, with the federal government playing a prominent role. In response to Wilson's requests, Congress passed laws during the next four years that lowered tariffs, imposed income and inheritance taxes,

President Woodrow Wilson at work in the White House. Although Wilson was a longtime advocate of peace, he believed that the United States had to enter World War I in 1917 "to make the world safe for democracy."

Without the benefit of a microphone, Wilson addressed a crowd of 50,000 in San Diego, California, in late September 1920, trying to gain public support for the League of Nations. Overcome by strain, he collapsed a few days later and returned to Washington, D.C., a broken man. To his sorrow, the U.S. Senate refused to approve either the Treaty of Versailles or U.S. membership in the League of Nations.

established a national bank called the Federal Reserve, and regulated business and the railroads. Other legislation passed by Congress at Wilson's urging included the creation of a loan program for farmers and federal funding for the building of highways.

Wilson's foreign policy emphasized mutual respect and understanding between nations, and he often declared his opposition to imperialism—the extension of a country's power by gaining

control over another country. Wilson had joined the American Peace Society in 1908, and as President he declared that he intended to make the United States an advocate of world peace. To that end, he supported arms reduction and international arbitration.

Wilson was dismayed by the outbreak of World War I in August 1914, and he vowed to keep the United States from becoming involved in the conflict. Two years later he was elected to a second term as President, largely because of the truth of his campaign slogan: "He kept us out of war."

Wilson believed, however, that the United States should assume an active role in bringing the war to an end. With that goal in mind, he drew up a plan for the establishment of permanent world peace through the creation of an international government called the League of Nations, using the name proposed by French statesman Léon Bourgeois. Wilson presented the plan to Congress in January 1917. However, as Congress debated Wilson's proposal in the following months, German submarines torpedoed several American ships in the North Atlantic, and Wilson felt he had no choice but to ask Congress to declare war against Germany. Accordingly, on April 6, 1917, the United States officially entered World War I, on the side of England and France. In Wilson's words, this "war to end all wars" would be fought "to make the world safe for democracy."

As the war continued, Wilson maintained his belief that the United States should lead the nations of the world in establishing peace. In January 1918, he announced a 14-point plan that he had drawn up as the basis for peace. Its provisions included open diplomacy, freedom on the seas, equality in international trade, arms reduction, support for national self-determination, and the establishment of "a general association of nations."

The war ended in November 1918 when Germany requested an armistice, thereby acknowledging defeat. Early in 1919, Wilson traveled to Paris to meet with the prime ministers of France and England to draft a peace treaty, which became known as the Treaty of Versailles. In February 1919, a separate peace commission approved the covenant (a written agreement) for the establishment of the League of Nations. The covenant was added to the Treaty of Versailles, which was signed in June.

When Wilson returned to the United States, he found himself in political trouble. According to the U.S. Constitution, the U.S. Senate has to approve all treaties, and the Treaty of Versailles did not have the full support of a majority of senators. Although some senators approved of the treaty as written, others wanted it amended because they objected to some of its terms, including membership in the League of Nations; they were afraid that the United States would lose its sovereignty if it joined the League. Still other senators opposed the treaty in its entirety. Instead of trying to negotiate with the Senate—which was controlled by his opponents, members of the Republican party—Wilson declared that he was standing firm and would allow no changes.

Wilson decided to appeal directly to the American people for support of the Versailles Treaty. In early September of 1919, he left Washington, D.C., by train on a speechmaking tour of the western United States, where opposition to the treaty was strongest. The once-shy Wilson had become an accomplished orator, and he spoke movingly to crowds of thousands about his

hopes for peace. As the train headed farther west, however, his health began to fail, and in late September he collapsed in Colorado. He returned immediately to Washington, where he suffered a severe stroke in early October.

During his recuperation, the Senate prepared to vote on both the original Treaty of Versailles and an amended version. Wilson instructed Senate Democrats to vote only for the original treaty, and in November both versions were defeated. The following March, in response to demands by peace groups and private citizens, the Senate again considered the treaty. Wilson was urged by many to agree to changes in order to get the treaty passed but he refused, and again the treaty was defeated.

Wilson never fully recovered from the stroke, and his health deteriorated during his remaining months in office. His poor physical condition, however, was concealed from the public. In the fall of 1920, Wilson was notified that his peacemaking efforts had earned him the Nobel Peace Prize for 1919. The citation praised Wilson for "bringing a design for a fundamental law of humanity into present-day international politics." Although he felt honored to receive the award, he believed that getting the Treaty of Versailles ratified would have been a more impressive achievement. In November, the Republican party won the Presidential election, as well as a majority of seats in Congress, and Wilson realized that the Treaty of Versailles and the League of Nations would not be approved in his lifetime.

Wilson never gave up his hope for peace, and to the very end of his life he believed that the United States would someday become a member of the League of Nations. He made his last public statement on November 11, 1923, Armistice Day. In a radio address

Woodrow Wilson

BORN
December 28, 1856
Staunton, Virginia

DIED
February 3, 1924
Washington, D.C.

EDUCATION
B.A., Princeton University (1879); attended University of Virginia Law School (1879–81); Ph.D., Johns Hopkins University (1886)

OCCUPATION
University professor and president; politician; U.S. President

MAJOR ACCOMPLISHMENTS
President, Princeton University; author of major books about U.S. history, including *A History of the American People* (5 vols., 1902); governor of New Jersey (1911–12); President of the United States (1913–21); cofounder of the League of Nations

broadcast throughout the nation, he called upon all Americans "to put self-interest away and once more formulate and act upon the highest ideals and purposes of international policy."

In private life, Wilson was devoted to his family. He married his first wife, Ellen, in 1885, and had three daughters. After Ellen Wilson's death in 1915, he married Edith Bolling Galt. Wilson enjoyed playing golf for relaxation, but after his stroke he was confined to a wheelchair much of the time. He died in his sleep in early February, 1924, and was buried at the National Cathedral in Washington, D.C.

In the years since Wilson's death, historians have debated his role in the fate of the Treaty of Versailles. Many have concluded that his high-mindedness and his stubborn refusal to compromise led to the defeat of his goal. On the other hand, the Treaty of Versailles was flawed from the very beginning.

The treaty's provisions included extremely harsh treatment of Germany as the defeated nation—something that Wilson tried without success to oppose. The British and French governments insisted that Germany be forced to pay huge amounts of money, called reparations, to countries it had damaged during the war. But Germany was too poor to pay, and the provisions of the Versailles Treaty evoked anger and resentment among the German people. In the early 1930s, that anger and resentment led to the election of Adolf Hitler as Germany's leader. And in 1939, Hitler led his country into another world war.

Although the United States never became a member of the League of Nations, Woodrow Wilson's ideal lived on in the hearts and minds of millions of Americans. That ideal was formally adopted by the United States in 1945, when it joined with 50 other countries from around the world to create the United Nations.

Some historians continue to argue that Wilson himself played a role in the defeat of the League of Nations in the United States. However, other historians point out that U.S. participation would probably not have mattered in the long run; the European allies were determined to punish Germany, and their postwar treatment of that nation—independent of the League and the United States—inevitably led to World War II. Wilson's devotion to peace at any cost made him a man ahead of his time in U.S. politics.

For taking the necessary first steps to bring the United States into a world community of nations, Woodrow Wilson deserves to be called his nation's leading peacemaker.

FURTHER READING

Heckscher, August. *Woodrow Wilson: A Biography*. New York: Scribners, 1991.

Knock, Thomas. *To End All Wars: Woodrow Wilson and the Quest for a New World Order*. New York: Oxford University Press, 1992.

Link, Arthur. *Woodrow Wilson and the Progressive Era*. New York: Harper, 1954.

————, ed. *The Papers of Woodrow Wilson*. 69 vols. Princeton, N.J.: Princeton University Press, 1966–1996.

Randolph, Sallie. *Woodrow Wilson, President*. New York: Walker, 1992.

Steinberg, Alfred. *Woodrow Wilson*. New York: Putnam, 1961.

"Wilson, Thomas Woodrow." *Dictionary of American Biography*. Vol. 10, part 2. New York: Scribners, 1936.

Léon Bourgeois

1920

In the fall of 1920, two Nobel Peace Prizes were announced simultaneously: one for the present year and one, retroactively, for 1919. The 1919 winner was President Woodrow Wilson of the United States. The 1920 award went to Léon Bourgeois, a French statesman who had been active in the peace movement for many years.

Wilson and Bourgeois were acquainted with each other, for they had represented their respective countries at the Paris Peace Conference in 1919. But the two men had had major disagreements over the provisions of the Versailles Treaty. When Wilson heard about Bourgeois's award, the news reportedly made him unhappy, for it seemed to diminish the importance of his own Peace Prize.

Although Léon Bourgeois and Woodrow Wilson had their differences at the conference table, there were in fact similarities between the two statesmen. Both were reformers who wished to improve society. Both were guided by high ideals and a clear vision of what they wished to accomplish.

French statesman Léon Bourgeois was a founder of the League of Nations and the first president of its governing council. He dreamed of establishing an international peacekeeping force.

The opening session of the League of Nations in Geneva, Switzerland, on November 15, 1920.

And each was stubbornly convinced that his own view was correct. Perhaps it was their very similarities that made them enemies.

Their early lives, however, were very different. Unlike Wilson, Léon Bourgeois began his life in difficult circumstances. Born in Paris to a poor clockmaker in 1851, he knew poverty from an early age, and this made him sympathetic to radical politics as he grew older. As a child he was obviously gifted and loved to learn. Fortunately his brilliance was recognized by his teachers, who arranged for him to attend a distinguished secondary school in Paris. Not only did Bourgeois excel in his required subjects; he also learned Hindi and Sanskrit and became an accomplished musician and sculptor as well as a skilled draftsman. Everything in the world seemed to interest and delight him.

After graduation, Bourgeois served in an artillery regiment during the Franco-Prussian War (1870–71). At the war's end, he entered the University of Paris and earned a doctoral degree in jurisprudence (law). After practicing law for several years, Bourgeois became

a civil service employee of the French Ministry of Public Works in 1876, and he worked for the government for more than a decade. In 1887 he served briefly as the head of the Paris police.

Bourgeois had become increasingly involved in left-wing politics, and early in 1888 he was elected to the Chamber of Deputies as a Socialist-Radical, representing the working-class district of Châlons-sur-Marne. During the next five years, while serving as a deputy, Bourgeois also held various positions in several French cabinets. He was secretary of state for the interior (1888–89); minister of the interior (1890); minister of public instruction (1890–92), during which he introduced many popular reforms into the French educational system; and minister of justice (1892–93).

In November 1895, Bourgeois became the prime minister of France. He immediately established himself as a reformer and called for major economic and social changes to benefit the working class, including insurance and pension programs. To promote his ideas, he wrote a series of newspaper articles that were collected and published in book form as *Solidarité (Solidarity,* 1896). Bourgeois's program, however, was overwhelmingly defeated by the conservative French Senate. He resigned as prime minister in April 1896 but retained his seat in the Chamber of Deputies.

Two years later, in 1898, Bourgeois was again named minister of public instruction in the French cabinet. In 1899 he headed the French delegation, which also included Paul d'Estournelles de Constant, to the First Hague Conference. Bourgeois was chosen as chairman of the conference's Commission on Arbitration, and in that capacity he called for the establishment of an international court of arbitration to settle disputes between countries. The proposal was approved by the conference and led to the establishment of the

Permanent Court of Arbitration—the Hague Tribunal. Bourgeois was appointed to the tribunal in 1903.

In 1905, Bourgeois was elected to the French Senate and appointed minister of foreign affairs in the French cabinet. Two years later he represented France at the Second Hague Conference, where he headed a commission that examined various peaceful solutions to international conflict. Here the groundwork was laid for an organization of countries devoted to maintaining peace. In a 1908 speech, Bourgeois proclaimed that such an organization had been created at the conference, calling it La Société des Nations—the League of Nations.

The actual establishment of the League had yet to be accomplished, however, despite Bourgeois's efforts over the next few years. When world war broke out in 1914, Bourgeois pressed even harder for its creation, and three years later, his persistence paid off: he was named chairman of a French government commission to consider how to set up the League of Nations. The commission recommended that the League be established solely as an organization to preserve peace, and therefore to function only in times of crisis. It would have the authority to enforce compulsory arbitration on countries to settle disputes between them, and it would maintain an international army to enforce the settlements.

Bourgeois took this proposal to the Paris Peace Conference in 1919, where he served as a member of the French delegation. Here he encountered Woodrow Wilson and others who had also made proposals for a worldwide organization. Bourgeois insisted that an international peacekeeping army had to be part of the League of Nations, and that regular inspections had to be made to verify any disarmament agreements. Bourgeois's strident but unsuccessful attempts to have his point of view accepted caused considerable friction among the other delegates, especially Wilson. They believed that peace could not be established by military action, and Bourgeois could not convince them that some sort of enforcement mechanism was necessary to give the League authority.

Bourgeois's belief in the League of Nations continued despite his failure to see his ideas adopted, and he became his nation's chief representative to the League when it opened the following year in Geneva. He served both in the assembly and as first president of the council. When he was named winner of the 1920 Nobel Peace Prize later that year, he was cited for his longtime efforts to secure world peace through the use of arbitration.

In his final political role, Bourgeois served as president of the French Senate from 1920 to 1923, when he resigned because he was losing his sight. When he died two years later, at the age of 74, he was honored with a state funeral.

Bourgeois's proposal for an international peacekeeping force did not die, however. Twenty-five years later, it was proposed—and adopted—by the League of Nations' successor, the United Nations. And in 1988 the United Nations Peacekeeping Forces were awarded their own Nobel Peace Prize.

FURTHER READING

Abrams, Irwin. "Léon Bourgeois." In *The Nobel Peace Prize and the Laureates*. Boston: G. K. Hall, 1988.

Bonsal, Stephen. *Unfinished Business*. New York: Doubleday, Doran, 1944.

Earle, E. M., ed. *Modern France: Problems of the Third and Fourth Republics*. Princeton, N.J.: Princeton University Press, 1951.

Léon Bourgeois

BORN
May 29, 1851
Paris, France

DIED
September 29, 1925
Épernay, France

EDUCATION
Docteur en Droit, University of Paris (1875)

OCCUPATION
Attorney; statesman

MAJOR ACCOMPLISHMENTS
Prime minister of France (1895–96); cofounder and member, Hague Tribunal (1903); helped create the League of Nations; president, Council of the League of Nations (1920–21); president, French Senate (1920–23)

Karl Branting

Christian Lange

1921

arl Branting, cowinner of the 1921 Nobel Peace Prize, is one of only a handful of scientists who have received the award. Branting has an even greater distinction: to date, he is the only astronomer among the Nobel Peace laureates.

Even as a small boy, Branting was fascinated by the stars. Born in 1860, he was the only child of a prominent Stockholm educator and his wife; his father had developed the Swedish system of gymnastics. Recognizing their son's intelligence, the Brantings sent young Karl to the most prestigious school in Stockholm; one of his classmates was the future King Gustavus V.

Karl Branting entered the University of Uppsala in 1877 and prepared for a career in astronomy by majoring in mathe-

Karl Branting, an astronomer by training, turned his attention to politics and journalism in 1884. An advocate of peace, he later became prime minister of Sweden.

matics and natural science. Upon earning a degree in 1882, he joined the Stockholm Astronomical Society as its assistant director.

During his five years at the university, however, Branting's interests had broadened beyond science. At the same time that he was working toward his degree, he became involved in the liberal political movement then developing in Sweden. The new movement called for social change and the betterment of conditions for the working class. Encouraged by fellow members of the movement, Branting began writing for local periodicals on social issues. He made other contributions, too: when the Stockholm Workers' Institute ran out of funds to continue its educational programs, Branting gave his own money to keep the institute open.

In 1884 Branting decided to abandon astronomy as a career and to become a political journalist. He joined the staff of a liberal newspaper, *Tiden*, as a foreign correspondent, and traveled through Western Europe and Russia to report on progressive political movements. Branting became increasingly convinced that social problems could be solved only through socialism—a form of rule in which the government controls both the production and the distribution of goods and services.

In 1885 Branting succeeded Klas Arnoldson—who would win the Nobel Peace Prize in 1908—as the editor of *Tiden*. When the paper failed a year later, the Socialist party of Sweden hired Branting to edit its newly founded newspaper, *Social Demokraten* (*The Social Democrat*). Branting remained as head of the paper for more than three decades, turning it into one of the leading socialist periodicals. In addition to editing, he continued to write articles for the paper, including a regular report on the activities of the Swedish parliament. Branting also became a prominent member of the Socialist

party and worked actively on its behalf: he organized unions and supported strikes, helped settle disputes, and formed workers' clubs. His activities placed him in the forefront of the Swedish liberal movement.

In 1889 Branting broke away from the Socialist party to form the Social Democratic Labor party, which soon became a leading force in Swedish politics; he later served as president of the party for many years (1907–25). In 1896 Branting became the first Social Democrat to be elected to a seat in parliament, which he held until 1925. As a legislator, he strongly supported universal suffrage—the right of every citizen to vote—as well as programs to improve living conditions.

Branting had become a pacifist in his youth, and in parliament he fought with some success for a reduction in defense spending. He argued that the security of the country depended more on the health and well-being of its citizens than it did on armies and weapons, and money was thus better spent on social improvements than on armaments.

Branting joined with Klas Arnoldson to help bring about the peaceful separation of Norway from Sweden in 1905. His activities on behalf of peace increased during the next decade. He supported international arbitration to settle disputes between countries, and he backed the first proposals for a League of Nations. Branting was a strong supporter of Sweden's neutrality in World War I, although he personally sided with the Allied countries (Great Britain, France, and the United States) because of their liberal political institutions.

In 1917 Branting was named Swedish minister of justice in a new coalition government of the Liberal and Social Democratic parties. During the next few years constitutional changes introduced several social reforms, including suffrage for all male

PEACEMAKERS

Karl Branting

BORN
November 23, 1860
Stockholm, Sweden

DIED
February 24, 1925
Stockholm, Sweden

EDUCATION
Baccalaureate (1882) and graduate study in mathematics and natural science, University of Uppsala

OCCUPATION
Astronomer; journalist; politician

MAJOR ACCOMPLISHMENTS
Editor, *Social Demokraten* newspaper (1886–1914); founder (1889) and president (1907–25), Social Democratic Labor Party of Sweden; contributed to peaceful separation of Norway and Sweden (1905); member of Swedish parliament for 29 years (1896–1925); served as Sweden's minister of finance (1917–20), and first socialist prime minister (1920, 1921–23, 1924–25); delegate, League of Nations Council (1920–24), and codrafter of the Geneva Protocol (1924)

After serving for 10 years as secretary of the Norwegian Nobel Committee, Christian Lange became head of the Interparliamentary Union. His efforts on behalf of international disarmament earned him a share of the 1921 Nobel Peace Prize.

citizens. While serving as justice minister, Branting headed a committee that considered various proposals to end the world war, and in 1919 he attended the Paris Peace Conference as Sweden's representative. He successfully supported his country's membership in the League of Nations, and in 1920 he represented Sweden at the first meeting of the League Assembly. There Branting was a strong supporter of disarmament and arbitration and argued against using an international military force to enforce peace. In 1920 he also served briefly as Sweden's first socialist prime minister.

Branting was named cowinner of the 1921 Nobel Peace Prize for his support of the League of Nations as well as his contribution to the peaceful separation of Norway from Sweden. That same year he again became Sweden's prime minister, as well as foreign minister, and held both posts for two years. During his tenure, he led the successful effort in parliament to grant Swedish women the right to vote.

In 1923 Branting became a delegate to the League of Nations Council. A year later he was appointed to the council's disarmament committee, which drafted an international security agreement known as the Geneva Protocol. Also in 1924 he became Sweden's prime minister for the third and final time, but resigned early the following year when he became ill.

Branting, who had married in 1884—about the time that he decided to give up astronomy for journalism—died in Stockholm in February 1925, at the age of 64.

Like Karl Branting, with whom he shared the 1921 Nobel Peace Prize, Christian Lange began his professional life in one occupation and later changed to another. Lange's first occupation, however, was teaching history,

a subject to which he had been introduced by his paternal grandfather, a distinguished historian. As a member of a Norwegian family that wanted to see their country become independent from Sweden—which had controlled Norway since 1814—Christian Lange became aware of political and social issues at an early age.

Lange was born in 1869 in the port city of Stavanger, Norway, to an army officer and engineer and his wife. Like Branting, Lange excelled in school. He studied history and languages at the University of Oslo and received a graduate degree in 1893 with a thesis on internationalism. He then began a career as a secondary school teacher in Oslo. During summer vacations he traveled widely in Europe to increase his knowledge of foreign languages, and he also wrote a world history textbook that became popular. In addition, Lange began to take an active role in the Norwegian independence movement, which ended with the separation of Norway and Sweden in 1905.

In 1899 Lange was asked to become secretary of the arrangements committee when the Interparliamentary Union held its annual meeting that year in Oslo. The union had been founded in 1889 to promote the settlement of international disputes through arbitration. Lange performed his tasks efficiently and impressed the Norwegian host committee with his interest in the peaceful aims of the union. As a consequence, he was invited to serve as secretary of the newly created Norwegian Nobel Committee, which administered the Nobel Peace Prize. Thus, at the age of 30, Lange was launched in a new career, as an administrator of peace organizations.

Lange served as secretary of the Nobel Committee for 10 years. He resigned in 1909 to become secretary-general of the Interparliamentary Union at its headquarters in Brussels, but he continued to serve as an adviser to the Nobel Committee for many years. As secretary-general, he was the administrative head of the union: he traveled, lectured, raised money, and wrote and edited numerous publications.

When Germany invaded Belgium in the early days of World War I and seized the Union's funds, Lange moved its headquarters to neutral Norway. He kept the union alive by contributing his own money—which he earned by giving lectures at the Nobel Institute—and securing a loan from the Carnegie Endowment for International Peace.

During the war Lange participated in a Stockholm conference of neutral nations that was held to propose ways of ending the conflict; he was also active in a Dutch peace group working for similar ends. In addition, he wrote a lengthy report for the Carnegie Endowment on conditions in the warring nations of Europe.

When the war ended in November 1918, Lange set out to rebuild the Union. Despite enormous difficulties that included a lack of funds and conflicts between member nations, he succeeded in organizing the Union's first postwar conference, held in 1921 in Geneva, Switzerland. For his years of service to the Interparliamentary Union, Lange received a share of the 1921 Nobel Peace Prize.

Lange was a strong supporter of the newly founded League of Nations. He represented Norway at many League meetings and headed several League committees. At the Interparliamentary Union and in the League, Lange continued his advocacy of international disarmament. He wrote more articles and books on arms control and arbitration, and he made additional lecture tours, including one in the United States in 1925. During his lifetime, he gave more than 500 lectures on behalf of international peace.

In both his lectures and his writings, Lange used the word *internationalism* rather than *pacifism* to describe the world peace movement that he had so long supported. "Pacifism" meant only that one was opposed to war. Lange preferred "internationalism" because it suggested an active effort by nations to join together to establish peace.

Lange resigned as secretary-general of the Interparliamentary Union in 1934, at the age of 65. A year later he became an elected member of the Norwegian Nobel Committee. In 1938, several months before his death, Lange gave his last peace lecture, at a Quaker organization in London; it was later published in book form as *Imperialism and Peace*.

Lange, who married the daughter of an Oslo judge in 1894, had five children. One of his sons, Halvard Lange, became a prominent politician and served as Norway's foreign minister for a decade after World War II. Christian Lange died at his home in Oslo in December 1938 at the age of 69.

FURTHER READING

Abrams, Irwin. "Karl Branting." In *The Nobel Peace Prize and the Laureates*. Boston: G. K. Hall, 1988.

"Christian L. Lange and His Work for Peace." *American-Scandinavian Review*, Autumn 1969.

Derry, T. K. *A History of Modern Norway*. Oxford: Clarendon Press, 1973.

Falnes, O. J. *Norway and the Nobel Peace Prize*. 1938. Reprint, New York: AMS Press, 1967.

Jones, S. S. *The Scandinavian States and the League of Nations*. 1939. Reprint. Westport, Conn.: Greenwood Press, 1969.

Christian Lange

BORN

September 17, 1869
Stavanger, Norway

DIED

December 11, 1938
Oslo, Norway

EDUCATION

M.A., history and languages, University of Oslo (1893)

OCCUPATION

Teacher; administrator; writer

MAJOR ACCOMPLISHMENTS

Secretary-general, Interparliamentary Union (1909–34); author of numerous books and articles on internationalism and the peace movement, including *Imperialism and Peace* (1938)

Fridtjof Nansen

1922

In the nearly century-old history of the Nobel Peace Prize, Fridtjof Nansen, the 1922 winner, is unique: he is the only explorer to receive the award. Nansen had several occupations in the course of his life: he was also a prominent scientist, and in middle age he became a distinguished statesman and humanitarian. But the man who became one of the world's leading peacemakers first came to public attention for his feats in the Arctic.

Nansen was born in a small town near what is now Oslo, Norway, in 1861, one of several sons of a well-to-do lawyer and his wife. Like most Norwegians, the Nansen family enjoyed outdoor activities, including skiing, ice skating, hiking, and fishing. Fridtjof (pronounced *FREED-hoff*) Nansen loved nature and enjoyed camping trips with his brothers, and he decided at an early age that he would earn his living out of doors.

After completing secondary school, Nansen enrolled at the University of Oslo in 1880 as a student of zoology, a field he chose so that he could do fieldwork. In 1882 he joined the crew of a seal-hunting ship bound for the Arctic, and the journey took him past the coast of Greenland. Nansen's first glimpse of the island made him decide to cross it one day on foot, a feat that no one had been known to accomplish.

Over the next few years, Nansen held onto his dream while completing his doctorate in zoology. In 1888, a year after receiving his degree, he persuaded a Danish philanthropist to pay for the cost of the Greenland expedition. That summer he and five crew members set out on their journey. The actual crossing took 37 days, but weather forced the Nansen party to remain in Greenland for a year. When they returned to Norway in May 1889, Nansen was hailed as a hero and his exploit became known throughout the world.

During the next few years, Nansen worked as the curator of the University of Oslo's zoological collection while he wrote two books about his experience, *The First Crossing of Greenland* (1890) and *Eskimo Life* (1891). He also began making plans for his next Arctic expedition, this time to the North Pole, which no expedition had yet reached.

With financial help from the Norwegian government, Nansen built a special boat to float over ice, named the *Fram*. In the summer of 1893 he embarked with a 12-man crew and took the *Fram* to within 450 miles of the pole. Nansen and another crew member then continued on by dogsled. Although they did not find the pole, they did reach a latitude farther north than any previous expedition. When Nansen returned to Norway in 1896, he was once again

Fridtjof Nansen

Fridtjof Nansen (left) directs Red Cross famine relief operations in Russia in 1921. In this and other projects, including refugee resettlement and prisoner-of-war repatriation, Nansen helped millions of Europeans during the 1920s.

BORN
October 10, 1861
Store-Frøen, Norway

DIED
May 13, 1930
Oslo, Norway

EDUCATION
Dr. Philos., zoology, University of Oslo (1888)

OCCUPATION
Explorer; scientist; statesman

MAJOR ACCOMPLISHMENTS
Made first known crossing of Greenland (1888–89); later traveled farther north than any previous Arctic expedition (1893–96); professor of zoology and oceanography, University of Oslo (1908–30); invented the Nansen bottle, used to take samples of ocean water; Norwegian ambassador to Great Britain (1906–1908); led major war and hunger relief efforts for the League of Nations and the International Committee of the Red Cross; created the Nansen passport, an international travel document for refugees; Norwegian delegate, League of Nations Assembly (1920–30); author of four books about the Arctic

hailed for his exploits. A year later he published a two-volume account of the journey, *Farthest North.*

Nansen served as professor of zoology at the University of Oslo from 1896 until 1908, when he became professor of oceanography. Until 1917, Nansen devoted much of his time to scientific work. He cofounded the International Council for the Exploration of the Sea and directed its central laboratory in Oslo. He also wrote another book about the Arctic, *In Northern Mists* (1910–11). During this period Nansen participated in several scientific expeditions to the Arctic. Recognized by the turn of the century as the world's leading authority on polar exploration, he advised other explorers, including his fellow Norwegian Roald Amundsen, who reached the South Pole in 1911.

In the early 1900s, however, Nansen had begun pursuing an additional career, as a statesman. His widely publicized trips to Greenland and the North Pole had made him a public figure, and he became increasingly interested in national and international affairs. He participated in negotiations that secured Norway's independence from Sweden in 1905, and from 1906 to 1908 he served as Norway's ambassador to Great Britain.

During World War I, Nansen traveled to the United States to negotiate an agreement that gave Norway aid for the duration of the conflict. He became head of the Norwegian League of Nations Society, a group supporting the League, and led his country's delegation to the opening meeting of the League in 1920. At that meeting, the League Council appointed him high

Explorer-turned-statesman, Nansen served as a delegate to the League of Nations Assembly from its founding in 1920 until his death a decade later.

commissioner in charge of repatriating (resettling in their own country) some half million German and Austro-Hungarian prisoners of war who were being held in Russia.

Through personal negotiations with the Russian government—which did not recognize the League of Nations—Nansen secured the release of nearly all the prisoners over a two-year period. In August 1921, the International Committee of the Red Cross persuaded Nansen to take on an additional task in Russia: directing a relief effort for victims of a widespread famine. He accomplished this assignment by soliciting contributions from private donors as well as governments—the United States gave $20 million—and overseeing the operation from an office in Moscow. An estimated 10 million lives were saved as a direct result.

In a third humanitarian effort, Nansen helped resettle 1.5 million Russians who had fled their country after the 1917 revolution and were living in disease-ridden refugee camps across Western Europe. To help in their resettlement, he created a special travel document known as a Nansen passport, and he secured its approval by 52 nations.

In another effort to help refugees, Nansen arranged an exchange between Greece and Turkey following their war in 1922: one million Greeks living in Turkey were exchanged for half a million Turks living in Greece.

Nansen received the 1922 Nobel Peace Prize in recognition of his humanitarian efforts. The citation paid tribute to "his ability to stake his life time and time again on a single idea, on one thought, and to inspire others to follow him." Nansen donated the prize money to international relief work.

Nansen served in the League of Nations Assembly from 1920 until his sudden death 10 years later, following a rigorous ski trip. A few months afterwards, the League paid posthumous tribute to Nansen by creating a refugee relief organization in his name in Geneva. Eight years later that organization, the Nansen International Office for Refugees, was itself the recipient of the Nobel Peace Prize.

FURTHER READING

Denzel, Justin F. *Adventure North: The Story of Fridtjof Nansen*. New York: Abelard-Schumann, 1968.

Hall, Anna Gertrude. *Nansen*. New York: Viking, 1940.

Hoyer, Liv Nansen. *Nansen: A Family Portrait*. London: Longmans, Green, 1957.

Jacobs, Francine. *A Passion for Danger: Nansen's Arctic Adventures*. New York: Putnam: 1994.

Nansen, Fridtjof. *Norway and the Union with Sweden*. London: Macmillan, 1905.

———. *Russia and Peace*. London: Macmillan, 1924.

Nansen, Fridtjof, and Ludvig S. Dale. "Aspects of Peace." *North American Review*, November 1929, pp. 565–67.

"Rescuing Millions of War Victims from Disease and Starvation." *Current History*, July 1929, pp. 567–76.

Sorensen, Jon. *The Saga of Fridtjof Nansen*. New York: American–Scandinavian Foundation and W. W. Norton, 1932.

J. Austen Chamberlain

Charles G. Dawes

1925

T oday few people know of J. Austen Chamberlain, British politician and cowinner of the 1925 Nobel Peace Prize. It is his half-brother, Neville, a politician who became Britain's prime minister, who is famous—for actions that contributed to World War II. Yet for a time Neville honestly believed that *he* and not Austen would be celebrated by later generations as the leading peacemaker in the Chamberlain family. He was wrong.

Joseph Austen Chamberlain was born in Birmingham, England, in 1863, the first son of a wealthy manufacturer and politician whose surname was Joseph. His mother died while giving birth to him, and his father later remarried. When Austen was six, his half-brother, Neville, was born.

Austen was educated at Rugby, one of England's most prestigious boarding schools, and at Trinity College, Cambridge, where he received his undergraduate degree in 1885. After studying political science in France and Germany for several years, he returned to England to become personal secretary to his father, a member of Parliament.

From childhood on, J. Austen Chamberlain had been groomed for a political career by his father. In 1892 he ran successfully for Parliament as a Liberal Unionist Party candidate from the East Worcestershire district, near Birmingham. Chamberlain's first speech in Parliament following his election was greeted with high praise by many political leaders, including the prime minister, William Gladstone, who predicted a great career for the young man.

During the next few years, Chamberlain fulfilled these expectations. He was appointed to an increasingly important series of posts in quick succession: civil lord of the Admiralty in 1895; financial secretary of the Treasury Department, 1900; postmaster general in the cabinet, 1902; and chancellor of the Exchequer, 1903.

In 1906 Chamberlain's meteoric rise came to a halt when the Liberal Unionists were defeated by the Liberal party. But he continued to serve in Parliament with distinction, becoming a member of the Conservative party when it absorbed the Liberal Unionists in 1912. In the months preceding the outbreak of World War I, Chamberlain was one of several politicians who persuaded the British government to support France against the threat of German invasion. In 1915, when a coalition government that included the Conservatives came to power, Chamberlain returned to the cabinet as secretary of state for India and served in that post for two years.

In April 1918, Chamberlain became chancellor of the Exchequer in the coalition government of Prime Minister

British statesman Austen Chamberlain is less well-known than his younger half-brother, Neville, who became prime minister. But his accomplishments on behalf of peace far outshone Neville's and earned Austen Chamberlain a share of the Nobel Peace Prize in 1925.

David Lloyd George, the leader of the Liberal Party. During his two years of service, he accomplished the difficult task of finding ways to pay off the British government's enormous debt from World War I, which ended in November 1918. Although Chamberlain had long hoped to become prime minister someday, he alienated Conservative Party members by his unwavering support of Lloyd George in the coalition government and by championing independence for Ireland, which the Conservatives strongly opposed. At a party conference in 1922, Chamberlain was passed over in favor of another candidate for election as party leader. Since the party leader usually becomes prime minister when his party achieves a majority in Parliament, Chamberlain now realized that his goal would probably never be achieved.

In 1924, Conservative prime minister Stanley Baldwin appointed Chamberlain as secretary of foreign affairs. At the League of Nations in Geneva, the French government had recently proposed the adoption by League member nations of an arbitration agreement called the Geneva Protocol. Under this agreement, nations would promise to submit any disputes between them to a neutral body for resolution rather than going to war, and the Council of the League of Nations would have the authority to enforce compliance with the agreement. However, the British government was on record as opposing the Geneva Protocol because it was too sweeping in its authority, and Chamberlain had to reject Britain's participation in a speech to the Council in Geneva. In that speech, he proposed instead that the Council act as a peacemaker by dealing with international crises on a case-by-case basis.

Not long afterward, Chamberlain was able to participate in a major

peacemaking effort. The German foreign minister, Gustav Stresemann, approached both the British and French governments with a proposal for a nonaggression pact: Germany would guarantee that its postwar western boundary would remain along the Rhine River if France and Great Britain would sign a mutual peace agreement.

Under the auspices of the League of Nations, a series of meetings was held in Locarno, Switzerland, to negotiate the agreement. Representing their respective countries were Chamberlain, Stresemann, and the French foreign minister, Aristide Briand, as well as the foreign ministers of Belgium, Italy, Poland, and Czechoslovakia.

The final agreement, signed on October 16, 1925, was known as the Locarno Pact. Under its provisions, Germany was admitted to the League of Nations and its western border was guaranteed. All seven signers of the pact agreed to binding arbitration in the event of disputes between their countries, and they also pledged to work toward the goal of disarmament for all member nations within the League.

The Locarno Pact was hailed as a major milestone in the long quest for world peace. It removed much of the bad feeling that had persisted between France and Germany after the war, and it enabled the rebuilding of Western Europe to go forward. Chamberlain was widely applauded in Great Britain for the major role he played in negotiating the pact, and he was knighted by the grateful British king, George V. Chamberlain's contribution also earned him a share of the 1925 Nobel Peace Prize. Although Briand and Stresemann would share the award in the following year for various contributions to peace, Chamberlain was honored by being the only Locarno Pact participant to win the Peace Prize for 1925.

Chamberlain remained in office as foreign secretary until 1929. During those years he led British efforts to preserve peace in the Far and Middle East, and he supported the Kellogg-Briand Pact, a 1928 mutual peace agreement eventually signed by 65 nations, including the United States and Great Britain. In 1931 he served briefly as first lord of the admiralty.

In his remaining years in Parliament, Chamberlain supported the political career of his half-brother, Neville, who had been a member of Parliament since 1918. Neville Chamberlain had risen to prominence while holding several cabinet posts, and by the early 1930s it was clear that he would someday become prime minister.

In the years prior to his death, Austen Chamberlain warned against the Nazi government of Adolf Hitler and its threat to world peace. Beginning in the mid-1920s, Chamberlain was the author of half a dozen books on public affairs and the League of Nations, including *Down the Years* (1935), a series of profiles of prominent men he had known during his career.

Austen Chamberlain died in March 1937, at the age of 73, after suffering a stroke. Two months later, his half-brother became prime minister. In the fall of 1938, Neville Chamberlain joined leaders of several European nations in signing what they called a "peace agreement" with Hitler called the Munich Pact. Chamberlain returned to England in triumph, declaring that as a result of the agreement, there would now be "peace in our time." Neville Chamberlain was now associated with a peace pact, just as Austen had been.

But instead of preserving peace, as Austen Chamberlain's Locarno Pact

had done, the Munich Pact helped Hitler strengthen his government and its aggressive policies. Less than a year later, Hitler began World War II by invading Poland, and Neville Chamberlain's reputation as a peacemaker crumbled. He lasted as prime minister until May 1940 and died later that year, his name forever associated with the doomed Munich Pact.

Charles G. Dawes, the American banker and statesman who shared the 1925 Nobel Peace Prize with Austen Chamberlain, had a background very different from his cowinner. He also has the unique distinction of being the only Nobel Peace Prize winner to compose a tune that became a rock-and-roll hit.

Charles Gates Dawes was born in the town of Marietta, Ohio, in August 1865, just four months after the Civil War ended. His father, who had risen to the rank of general while serving in the Union Army during the war, owned a local mill and later served in Congress. Dawes was educated in local primary and secondary schools and graduated from Marietta College. He then enrolled at Cincinnati Law School.

After earning a law degree in 1886, Dawes moved to the rapidly growing city of Lincoln, Nebraska, to establish a career. There he founded a law firm with two partners and practiced for seven years, specializing in representing the claims of farmers against the railroad. Dawes married in 1889; he and his wife later had two children of their own and adopted two more. During his years in Lincoln, Dawes became a close friend of two Nebraskans who would rise to national prominence: the U.S. Senator and later U.S. Presidential candidate William Jennings Bryan, and army officer John J. Pershing, who would lead American military forces during World War I.

J. Austen Chamberlain

BORN
October 16, 1863
Birmingham, England

DIED
March 16, 1937
London, England

EDUCATION
B.A., Trinity College, Cambridge (1885)

OCCUPATION
Politician

MAJOR ACCOMPLISHMENTS
Member of Parliament (1892–1914); held several positions in the British cabinet; principal author of the Locarno Pact (1925)

Charles Dawes combined his skills as a banker, businessman, and attorney to create the Dawes Plan, a program that helped mend the German economy after World War I.

When a national financial depression occurred in the United States in 1893, Dawes went heavily into debt. To re-establish himself, he moved to Chicago and borrowed money to invest in gas and electric companies in Wisconsin and Illinois. These efforts were successful, and he was soon prosperous again. He also became active in Republican party politics and led his state's support for William McKinley in the 1896 Presidential election. McKinley expressed his gratitude by naming Dawes federal comptroller of the currency.

During his four years in that post, Dawes led a successful effort to reorganize the nation's banks. After McKinley's assassination in 1901, Dawes returned to private life as a businessman and banker. Back in Chicago, he founded the Central Trust Company, which became one of the largest banks in the Midwest.

In 1917, in his 52nd year, Dawes volunteered for service in the army after the United States entered World War I. His old friend General Pershing obtained a commission for Dawes as a major, and he served in France as manager of army supplies. Dawes's competence earned him several promotions, and in the course of the war he became a brigadier general. He was placed in charge of supplies for the entire Allied command and remained on duty for some months after the war ended in November 1918, to dispose of remaining military equipment.

In the years following the war, Dawes—unlike most of his fellow Republicans—was a strong advocate of U.S. participation in the League of Nations and was disappointed when the United States refused to join. His expertise in banking and economics led to his appointment in 1921 as the first director of the Bureau of the Budget, a federal agency created by the newly elected President Warren G. Harding. Dawes had been asked by Harding to become Secretary of the Treasury but had refused that appointment.

At the end of the war, Germany had been required by the Treaty of Versailles to pay huge sums, known as reparations, to countries it had damaged during the war, including France and Belgium. In 1923, when Germany was unable to pay these debts, French and Belgian troops moved in to occupy the Ruhr Valley, a German industrial area. An international committee of financial experts was formed to try to resolve this crisis. Representing the United States on this so-called Committee of Experts was Charles Dawes.

The committee's task was to find a way to help Germany become strong again economically so that it could pay its war debts, but not strong enough to threaten the future security of the Allied countries—France, Belgium, and other nations that it had attacked during World War I. Led by Dawes, the committee drew up a program known as the Dawes Plan, which proposed a sliding scale of payments for Germany, the reorganization of Germany's national bank under Allied supervision, a system of taxation that would give Germany the revenue to pay its debts, and a series of loans to the German government. The program was announced and ratified in London in April 1924 and went into effect the following September.

The immediate effect of the Dawes Plan was to stabilize German currency and re-establish the country's credit, and Dawes was hailed as the savior of Europe when he returned to the United States. His popularity earned him the nomination for Vice President on the Republican Presidential ticket headed by Calvin Coolidge. Coolidge and Dawes were elected in November 1924 and took office in March 1925.

Dawes was named cowinner of the 1925 Nobel Peace Prize for his role in developing the Dawes Plan, which remained in operation until the end of 1926. During that time, Germany did manage to pay some of its reparations and begin to rebuild its economy.

When Dawes's term as Vice President ended in 1929, he was appointed ambassador to Great Britain by newly elected President Herbert Hoover. He served in this post until 1932, when Hoover brought Dawes back to the United States to serve as head of the newly created Reconstruction Finance Corporation (RFC). The United States was now suffering from a major economic depression, and the RFC tried to stimulate the economy by making loans to various commercial enterprises.

Dawes had to leave the RFC after four months and return to Chicago, where he tried to rescue the failing Central Republic Bank and Trust Company, with which his own bank had merged. With a loan from the RFC, Dawes managed to save the bank and to stabilize the banking community in Chicago, and he later paid back the RFC in full.

During the last two decades of his life, Dawes concentrated on his business interests as well as philanthropy. One of his major projects was the creation of two homes for homeless men, one in Chicago and another in Boston, in memory of a son who had drowned in 1912. Dawes was also a founder of the Chicago Opera Association, which introduced grand opera to the city. For relaxation he enjoyed playing the piano and the flute, and writing music for both instruments.

Dawes died at his home in Evanston, Illinois, of a heart attack in April 1951, at the age of 85. His accomplishments were not over, however. Many years earlier, one of Dawes's musical compositions, "Melody in A," had been recorded by several musical groups and had become fairly popular. During the 1950s it was rediscovered by a songwriter named Carl Sigman, who wrote lyrics for the tune—and turned it into a rock hit called "It's All in the Game."

FURTHER READING

"Dawes, Charles G." In *Dictionary of American Biography*. Supplement 5. New York: Scribners, 1977.

Dutton, David. *Austen Chamberlain: Gentleman in Politics*. New Brunswick, N.J.: Transaction Books, 1987.

Petrie, Charles A. *The Life and Letters of the Right Hon. Sir Austen Chamberlain*. 2 vols. London: Cassell, 1939–40.

Timmons, Bascom N. *Portrait of an American: Charles G. Dawes*. New York: Holt, 1953.

Charles G. Dawes

BORN
August 27, 1865
Marietta, Ohio

DIED
April 23, 1951
Evanston, Illinois

EDUCATION
B.A., Marietta College (1884);
L.L.B., Cincinnati Law School (1886)

OCCUPATION
Lawyer; businessman; banker; diplomat; statesman

MAJOR ACCOMPLISHMENTS
Strengthened U.S. banking system as comptroller of the currency; Vice President of the United States (1925–29); principal author of the Dawes Plan (1924)

Aristide Briand

Gustav Stresemann

1926

W hen Aristide Briand was growing up in France, his parents must have often wondered if he would ever amount to anything. The future cowinner of the Nobel Peace Prize liked nothing better than to joke with his friends and was always in search of amusement. In adolescence he played cards and drank too much wine, and he did as little schoolwork as he could to get by. Even when the famous novelist Jules Verne took an interest in him, Aristide seemed unwilling to change his ways.

Aristide Briand (pronounced *Bree-OND*) was born in Nantes in 1862. His parents owned a profitable inn, and they gave their son advantages that they themselves had not had as children. Above all, the Briands believed in the value of education, and they sent Aristide to the best schools, including the Nantes secondary school, or *lycée*, which Verne had attended decades earlier. The French novelist, who had written *Twenty Thousand Leagues Under the Sea* and other fantasy classics, still had ties to his birthplace and school,

As a youth, Aristide Briand paid more attention to pleasure than to his studies, but in adulthood he developed an interest in politics—and eventually became prime minister of France.

and he liked to encourage bright students there.

Aristide Briand was obviously intelligent, witty, and personable, but classwork bored him to death. Verne's interest did not make him become a better student at the *lycée*, but it may have led him to go to Paris after graduation to study law. Verne himself had been a law student at the University of Paris before he became a writer.

Briand managed to earn a law degree despite his continuing fondness for having a good time. In the 1880s he established a law practice in the port city of St. Nazaire, near Nantes. It was never very successful, probably because Briand began to develop other interests—this time serious ones. He became increasingly drawn to politics and contributed articles on social and political topics to area journals; for a time he edited a local newspaper. He joined the Socialist party and became a strong supporter of trade unions, organizations of skilled workers who banded together to seek higher wages and better working conditions.

In 1894 Briand was elected secretary-general of the Socialist party. This new position led him to give up his law practice and enter politics full time. After running several times for a seat in the French Chamber of Deputies, he was finally elected in 1902. As a strong debater in the chamber, he led the successful fight for legislation that separated church and state in France. This led to his dual appointment in the spring of 1906 as minister of education and minister of religion in the French cabinet of the non-Socialist prime minister Jean-Marie Sarrien.

The Socialist party promptly expelled Briand for agreeing to be part of a non-Socialist cabinet. Briand, however, believed that he had done the right thing by giving the Socialist cause a voice in the government. Henceforth, Briand became skilled at working with coalitions, groups of politicians from different parties who come together to form a ruling majority. In the fall of 1906, when Sarrien was succeeded by Georges Clemenceau, Briand kept his two posts; two years later he added another: minister of justice. Finally, in the summer of 1909, Aristide Briand himself became prime minister. Although he had to step down from this post two years later, Briand was now launched on a formidable public career. In only seven years he had risen from private citizen to hold France's most important political office.

During the next 20 years, Briand would become prime minister on nine more occasions as various coalitions took control of the French government. Sometimes he also held an additional cabinet post simultaneously: during World War I, for example, he served for a time as both prime minister and minister of foreign affairs. He was out of office by the end of the war, however, and therefore did not participate in the 1919 Paris Peace Conference, which drew up the Versailles Treaty.

Briand was a strong supporter of the League of Nations, which was formally established by that treaty. However, he opposed other terms of the treaty, which he thought punished Germany too severely and would not establish long-lasting peace. This was not because Briand was sympathetic to the Germans; rather, he did not think the treaty provided a realistic way for Germany to pay the required reparations, payments to countries it had harmed. Briand was afraid that the Treaty of Versailles might in the long run lead to another war.

Although this view, sadly, proved to be correct, several efforts were undertaken during the 1920s to stabilize Germany and reduce the chances of war. One such effort was the Dawes Plan, negotiated in 1924 by the American banker and statesman Charles G. Dawes, which strengthened the

Aristide Briand

BORN
March 28, 1862
Nantes, France

DIED
March 7, 1932
Paris, France

EDUCATION
Diploma in law, University of Paris (1881)

OCCUPATION
Lawyer; politician; statesman

MAJOR ACCOMPLISHMENTS
Member, French Chamber of Deputies (1902–32); held various cabinet-level posts, including office of prime minister 10 times between 1909 and 1929; negotiated the Locarno Pact (1925) and the Kellogg-Briand Pact (1928)

GUSTAV STRESEMANN
HIS DIARIES, LETTERS, AND PAPERS

Edited and Translated by Eric Sutton

VOL. III

The title page of an English edition of Gustave Stresemann's writings bears his portrait. As German foreign minister during the 1920s, Stresemann cooperated with other European leaders to try to improve his country's economic and social situation after its devastating defeat in World War I.

German monetary system. The next effort was initiated by Germany itself.

Early in 1925, German foreign minister Gustav Stresemann—who would share the 1926 Nobel Peace Prize with Briand—approached the French and British governments with a proposal for a nonaggression pact. As a show of good faith, Germany was willing to guarantee its western boundary along the Rhine River, which divided Germany from France.

Shortly after Stresemann made his offer, Briand began another term as foreign minister of France. Briand and the British foreign minister, J. Austen Chamberlain, began secret negotiations with Stresemann. These led to a series of public meetings in Locarno, Switzerland, attended by Briand, Stresemann, and Chamberlain, as well as the foreign ministers of Belgium, Italy, Poland, and Czechoslovakia. At these meetings a peace agreement with Germany called the Locarno Pact was signed. Its terms included a pledge by the signing countries to work for international disarmament and to resolve future disputes through binding arbitration. The Locarno Pact also gave Germany membership in the League of Nations.

The Locarno Pact was hailed as a major contribution to the establishment of world peace, and it earned Briand a share of the 1926 Nobel Peace Prize. His peacemaking efforts were not over, however.

In 1926 Briand was privately encouraged by the American educator and statesman Nicholas Murray Butler, head of the Carnegie Endowment for International Peace, to propose a treaty of friendship between France and the United States. Briand waited until he had found an appropriate time for such a proposal, which turned out to be April 6, 1927, the 10th anniversary of the entry of United States into World War I. On that date, he sent a formal note to the U.S. Secretary of State, Frank B. Kellogg, proposing such a treaty.

Kellogg responded by suggesting that the two nations invite other nations to join with them in a pact "renouncing war as an instrument of national policy." After a series of negotiations lasting more than a year, the Kellogg-Briand Pact, also known as the Pact of Paris, was signed in Paris on August 17, 1928, by representatives of 15 nations. Eventually a total of 65 countries signed the pact.

The Kellogg-Briand Pact further enhanced Briand's international prestige. He continued to support the League of Nations and in 1930 sent the League a proposal for the creation of a United States of Europe. That proposal was dismissed by the League—but nearly four decades later became a reality with the creation of the European Community (now the European Union).

Briand was an international hero, but in France his political power had declined. He retired in 1931, after failing to win election as president of France, and died in Paris in March 1932, several weeks before his 70th birthday.

Like Aristide Briand, Gustav Stresemann, cowinner of the 1926 Nobel Peace Prize, was born into a family that had made itself prosperous through hard work, and without the benefit of education. Unlike Aristide Briand, young Gustav enjoyed school and was always a serious and excellent student.

Gustav Stresemann (pronounced STRAYZ-ah-monn) was born and raised in Berlin, where his father owned a prosperous tavern and a beer distributorship. Everyone worked in the family business, including Gustav, who became the only family member to attend high school. After graduation, he studied literature and politics at the University of Berlin, then attended the University of Leipzig, where he earned a doctorate in social science in 1902.

Instead of becoming a university professor, however, Stresemann decided to remain a businessman. He moved to Dresden to become an executive with an association of German chocolate manufacturers. His success in that job led to his appointment as director of the Saxon Industrialists' Union, where he also edited the organization's newspaper. Stresemann married in 1906; he and his wife later had two sons.

Stresemann entered politics in 1907, winning election to the Reichstag, the German parliament, on the National Liberal party ticket. Despite its name, the party was conservative; it supported the monarchy and the ideal of German cultural and military superiority. Stresemann quickly became a leader of the Liberal party in the Reichstag, where he was a strong supporter of the German navy.

Stresemann was not eligible for military service because he had a heart ailment, but he served his country during World War I by leading parliamentary support for Germany's military efforts. At the same time, Stresemann urged his colleagues to be prepared to make peace with the Allies—those nations, including France, with whom Germany was fighting.

In November 1918, the German government requested an armistice—a halt in the fighting—and shortly afterward the German emperor, Kaiser Wilhelm II, abdicated and left the country. The following May, while the peace conference was being held in Versailles, Stresemann and other German officials met in the city of Weimar to draw up a constitution for a new German government, which was named the Weimar Republic. A year later, Stresemann became a member of the new Reichstag, and in 1923 he was elected chancellor (the equivalent of prime minister). Although he served only four months in this office, Stresemann was able to put down several revolts in the country and make efforts to stabilize German currency. When the government was reorganized later that year, Stresemann became foreign minister and held that post until his death.

As foreign minister, Stresemann led the German government in carrying out the provisions of the Dawes Plan, the agreement signed in 1924 that helped Germany fulfill its financial obligations called for in the Treaty of Versailles. A year later, he made his peace proposal to Aristide Briand and J. Austen Chamberlain, paving the way for the Locarno Pact. In 1926, Stresemann continued his peacemaking efforts by negotiating a neutrality treaty with the Soviet Union. Later that year he was named cowinner with Briand of the Nobel Peace Prize, largely for his efforts on behalf of the Locarno Pact.

Stresemann continued to work for German recovery despite his poor health. Still in office as foreign minister, he died in Berlin in October 1929 after suffering a stroke. After his death, the German government became increasingly nationalistic and ultraconservative, paving the way for the collapse of the Weimar Republic and the ascendancy of Adolf Hitler and the Nazi party in 1933.

FURTHER READING

Ferrell, Robert H. Ferrell. *Peace in Their Time: The Origins of the Kellogg-Briand Pact.* New Haven: Yale University Press, 1952.

Olden, Rudolf. *Stresemann.* New York: E. P. Dutton, 1930.

Miller, David H. *The Peace Pact of Paris: A Study of the Briand-Kellogg Treaty.* New York: Putnam, 1928.

Thomson, Valentine. *Briand: Man of Peace.* New York: Covici-Friede, 1930.

Turner, Henry Ashby. *Stresemann and the Politics of the Weimar Republic.* Princeton, N.J.: Princeton University Press, 1963.

Vallentin, Antonia. *Stresemann.* Foreword by Albert Einstein. New York: R. R. Smith, 1931.

Gustav Stresemann

BORN
May 10, 1878
Berlin, Germany

DIED
October 3, 1929
Berlin, Germany

EDUCATION
Attended the University of Berlin; Ph.D., social science, University of Leipzig (1902)

OCCUPATION
Businessman; statesman

MAJOR ACCOMPLISHMENTS
Foreign minister of Germany (1923–29); negotiated the Locarno Pact (1925)

Ferdinand Buisson

Ludwig Quidde

1927

Until Ferdinand Buisson was nearly 60 years old, he devoted most of his attention to education. He had became interested in the European peace movement as a younger man, had helped to create an international peace organization, and had written many articles on the relationship of education to peace. But when Buisson was in his 50s, a famous trial occurred in Paris that caused him to become involved in politics. That involvement led to his election to the French parliament, and his later activities as a member of parliament led to his receipt of the 1927 Nobel Peace Prize.

Ferdinand Buisson (pronounced *Bwee-SAWN*) was the eldest son of a prominent Protestant family in Paris; his father was a judge who died when Ferdinand was a teenager. The Buissons were not especially well-to-do, and Ferdinand had to go to work as a tutor to help support his mother and siblings. While holding down this job, Ferdinand managed to complete his secondary education and to study philosophy at the University of Paris.

In his 80s, prominent French educator Ferdinand Buisson became a one-man peace movement, working tirelessly to improve relations between his country and Germany.

Buisson enjoyed teaching, and he hoped to continue that career in France. After receiving his doctoral degree in the early 1860s, he took and passed the government licensing examination. However, in order to receive the license, he had to swear allegiance to the French emperor, Napoleon III. Buisson disliked the emperor's policies, refused to sign the loyalty oath, and therefore had to leave France to find a teaching position. In 1866 he moved to Neuchâtel, Switzerland, and taught at a college there.

During his five years in Switzerland, Buisson was attracted to the peace movement, which had its roots in that country. As a philosopher, he had long been interested in ethical and moral issues; in his first book, *Le Christianisme liberal* (*Liberal Christianity*), published in 1865, he had argued that church and state had to be separated, and that organized religion should be replaced by a personal moral code.

In 1867 Buisson attended a peace conference in Paris, and there he joined with Frédéric Passy and others in founding the International League for Peace and Freedom. Buisson was now convinced that lasting world peace could be achieved only through education, and he devoted his spare time to writing articles on that topic for various journals.

When Napoleon III abdicated in 1871 following France's defeat by the Germans in the Franco-Prussian War, Buisson returned to Paris, where he established a home for war orphans. He was then invited to become minister of public instruction in the new government, called the Third Republic. Despite the liberalism of the regime, the Catholic Church still controlled the French educational system. In his new post, Buisson immediately began a campaign to remove the public schools from Catholic domination. His views met with intense opposition, however, and he was forced to resign.

Out of office, Buisson continued to work for this goal while supporting himself by teaching and writing. During the 1870s, his idea gradually gained acceptance, and in 1879 he was reappointed to another post within the education ministry, this time as director of primary education. In this position Buisson achieved a partial victory: he helped draw up legislation that guaranteed free, compulsory, and nondenominational (not controlled by the Church) primary school education throughout the country.

During his 17 years in office Buisson also edited an education journal and compiled the *Dictionnaire de pedagogie et d'instruction primaire* (*Dictionary of Pedagogy and Primary Instruction*, 4 vols., 1878–87). In 1896 he resigned his ministry post to become a professor of education at the University of Paris.

In the 1890s a notorious trial took place in Paris. The defendant was a French army captain named Alfred Dreyfus (pronounced *DRAY-fuss*) who was accused and eventually convicted of treason, or betraying the government. It was later discovered, however, that Dreyfus had been wrongly accused and convicted; the real culprits were high-ranking military officers who had used Dreyfus as a scapegoat to cover up their own crimes. Dreyfus was Jewish, and it was clear that anti-Semitism—prejudice against Jews—had played a major role in his conviction.

Many prominent men and women, not only in France but from other nations, came to Dreyfus's defense and urged the French government to release him from prison. In 1898 Buisson helped found a civil liberties association called the League of the Rights of Man, whose goal was not only to free Dreyfus but to fight on behalf of all victims of injustice. (Dreyfus was eventually released from prison in 1906.)

In 1902, Buisson's increasing political involvement led him to seek election to the Chamber of Deputies, the

Ferdinand Buisson

BORN
December 20, 1841
Paris, France

DIED
February 16, 1932
Thieuloy-Saint-Antoine, France

EDUCATION
Doctorate of Letters, University of Paris (1891)

OCCUPATION
Educator; politician

MAJOR ACCOMPLISHMENTS
Director of primary education in France, where he helped end Church control of primary schools; cofounder, League of the Rights of Man; undertook personal campaign in 1923–24 to establish peaceful relations between France and Germany

Historian Ludwig Quidde, a leader of the German peace movement, was dismayed by his country's militarism and led a campaign to support disarmament.

lower house of the French parliament, as a member of the Radical-Socialist party. He won that election and held the seat from 1902 until 1914. During these years in parliament Buisson continued his activities on behalf of peace. He lost his bid for re-election in 1914, when world war was erupting, but as a private citizen and university professor he wholeheartedly supported the French war effort during the next four years, and he became an early supporter of Woodrow Wilson's proposal for a League of Nations.

Buisson was re-elected to his old seat in parliament in 1919, the same year that the Treaty of Versailles, ending World War I, was drawn up. Buisson strongly opposed the terms of the treaty, which he thought were too harsh to Germany and would only cause bitter feelings rather than establish lasting peace. During the next few years he worked behind the scenes to improve relations between France and Germany, and in 1923 a major opportunity for peacemaking arose.

Early in January, troops from France and Belgium marched into Germany to occupy the Ruhr Valley, the country's industrial center, when Germany was unable to pay its reparations, or war debts. Buisson responded to the crisis by making himself a public spokesman for peace between France and Germany. At great personal risk, the 82-year-old Frenchman made speaking tours of both countries, and organized lectures in Paris by leading pacifists. Although Buisson's efforts were not connected to the 1925 Dawes Plan, which ultimately ended the crisis, they did contribute to an easing of tensions between the two nations, which made the plan's acceptance possible.

Buisson retired from parliament in 1924. That same year he was named by the French government as a grand officer of the Legion of Honor, France's highest award. For his many efforts on behalf of peace, Ferdinand Buisson, in

his 86th year, was named cowinner of the 1927 Nobel Peace Prize; he donated the prize money to several pacifist organizations.

Now a widower with three grown children, Buisson devoted his remaining years to promoting international teacher exchanges. He died at the age of 90 in February 1932, at his home near Paris.

Ludwig Quidde, the German pacifist who shared the 1927 Nobel Peace Prize with Ferdinand Buisson, knew from an early age that he would never have to earn his own living. Independent wealth gave Quidde the leisure to do as he wished with his time. But instead of pursuing pleasure, Quidde chose to devote both his money and his life to the cause of peace.

Quidde (pronounced *KVID-duh*) was the eldest son of a rich merchant in Bremen, Germany. He excelled at his studies, and after graduating from secondary school went on to do graduate work in medieval history. He attended the universities of Strasbourg and Göttingen, and received a doctorate from the latter in the mid-1880s.

For a while, Quidde devoted himself to scholarly studies. He first helped prepare a series of medieval documents for the German government, then founded and edited a journal of German history. In the early 1890s he served as secretary of the Prussian Historical Institute in Rome. During this time Quidde had become a pacifist through the influence of his wife, whom he had married in 1882, and through extensive reading on the history of warfare.

Quidde became active in the peace movement beginning in 1892, when he joined Alfred Fried's newly founded German Peace Society. The following year he published anonymously a widely read pamphlet that attacked the growth of militarism in Germany. In 1894, Quidde published another pamphlet, this time under his own name, which satirized the German kaiser, or emperor, Wilhelm II. Quidde was accused of libel, convicted, and sentenced to prison for three months.

Upon his release, Quidde formed an antiwar group in Munich to promote pacifist ideals. He also helped reorganize the antimilitarist German People's Party and began making political speeches calling for disarmament. In 1896 he was convicted of treason and was again sentenced to serve three months in prison.

During the late 1890s Quidde participated in a variety of peace-related activities, including several peace congresses, and became recognized as a leader of the international pacifist movement. He was elected to the council of the International Peace Bureau, and in 1901 he served as chairman of the World Peace Congress, held in Glasgow. Six years later he organized the World Peace Congress in Munich. Quidde's other activities at this time included an attempt, with Frédéric Passy, to draw up a peace agreement between Germany and France.

Quidde held elective office in Germany twice during this period. He served for a time on the Munich City Council and in 1907 was elected to the Bavarian parliament, where he held a seat for one year. In the years leading up to World War I, he devoted much of his time to the cause of disarmament. When Germany began the war in August 1914, Quidde left the country.

For the next four years Quidde's exact whereabouts were often unknown. He probably spent much of his time in Switzerland and the Netherlands, and he is known to have attended a peace conference at The Hague in 1915. During this time he also wrote several pamphlets that offered proposals for establishing world peace.

After the war ended in November 1918, Quidde returned to Germany, where he tried to reorganize the peace movement there. He became head of the German Peace Cartel, an association of more than 20 peace groups. In 1919, after the monarchy ended and the Weimar Republic was established as the legitimate German government, Quidde won election to the new parliament that replaced the Reichstag.

Quidde supported the League of Nations, which was established by the Versailles peace treaty, but he was opposed to the treaty itself because of its harshness toward Germany. At the same time, he believed that Germany should not be allowed to rearm itself. Although this was expressly forbidden by the treaty, there were rumors that Germany was secretly building an air force and recruiting an army. In 1924 Quidde wrote a series of newspaper articles accusing Germany of these actions—and for a third time was sent to prison briefly, again for treason.

Like Ferdinand Buisson, Quidde won a share of the 1927 Nobel Peace Prize for his longtime effort to make his countrymen support peace. In the next six years, Quidde continued that effort, but he realized that the chances for its success were diminishing as the ultra-right-wing and militaristic Nazi party gained increasing power.

When the Nazis took over the government in 1933 and Adolf Hitler became chancellor, Quidde again left Germany, and settled in Geneva, Switzerland. There he remained active in the pacifist movement until his death eight years later, in his 83rd year.

FURTHER READING

"Buisson, Ferdinand" and "Quidde, Ludwig." In *Biographical Dictionary of Modern Peace Leaders*. Edited by Harold Josephson. Westport, Conn.: Greenwood Press, 1985.

Chickering, Roger. *Imperial Germany and a World Without War: The Peace Movement and German Society 1892–1914*. Princeton, N.J.: Princeton University Press, 1975.

Quidde, Ludwig. "The Future of Germany." *Living Age*, April 5, 1924, pp. 635–38.

Ludwig Quidde

BORN
March 23, 1858
Bremen, Germany

DIED
March 4, 1941
Geneva, Switzerland

EDUCATION
Ph.D., medieval history, University of Göttingen

OCCUPATION
Historian; peace activist

MAJOR ACCOMPLISHMENTS
Head of World Peace Congress, Glasgow (1901); organized World Peace Congress, Munich (1907); author of numerous articles and pamphlets advocating pacifism

Frank B. Kellogg

1929

M ost people associate the name "Kellogg" with breakfast cereals, but it is also the surname of a prominent American statesman and peacemaker named Frank B. Kellogg. Kellogg, a self-educated lawyer who won the Nobel Peace Prize in 1929, was distantly related to W. K. Kellogg, the cereal magnate, and in the earlier part of this century he was just as famous.

Frank Billings Kellogg was born in the small farming community of Potsdam, New York, in 1856. When the Civil War ended in 1865, the Kellogg family headed west and settled on a wheat farm near Elgin, Minnesota. Young Frank attended school whenever he could take time away from farm chores. Finally, at the age of 14, he left school to help manage the farm full time.

Kellogg did not want to become a farmer, however. His ambition was to practice law. In 1875, after his younger brother had become old enough to take over, he left the farm and moved to Rochester, Minnesota, to pursue his

Largely self-educated, Frank Kellogg rose from Minnesota farm boy to a distinguished career as a corporate lawyer, U.S. senator, diplomat, and secretary of state.

dream. He took a job without pay as a clerk in a law office while he supported himself as a handyman. He also embarked on a program of self-education, teaching himself not only law but also history, Latin, and German. By 1877, he had learned enough law to pass the Minnesota bar examination.

Kellogg opened a law practice with another young attorney in Rochester, but they attracted only a few clients. Kellogg increased his income by going into Republican politics, winning election as city attorney and then as district attorney. In this position, which he held from 1881 to 1886, Kellogg made a name for himself by successfully representing several small communities in a lawsuit against a railway company.

In 1887, a year after he married, Kellogg joined two other attorneys to form a new law firm, Davis, Kellogg, and Severance, specializing in corporation law. In the following decade it became one of the most successful in the region by representing clients in their claims against railroad, mining, and other companies. In 1900 Kellogg rose to national prominence when he won a case for a major St. Paul newspaper against a large Minnesota paper company. Four years later, President Theodore Roosevelt named him special counsel to the U.S. Attorney General, specializing in antitrust cases. (A trust is a group of corporations that have joined together to increase profits by creating a monopoly and thus eliminating competition.)

As special counsel, Kellogg played an important role in the prosecution of several antitrust cases, including *Standard Oil Company* v. *United States* in 1911. He also served as special counsel to the Interstate Commerce Commission, and in that capacity he investigated the business practices of U.S. railroads. During his years of service in Washington, D.C., Kellogg continued to practice law as a partner in his Rochester firm. His prominence as an

attorney led to his election in 1912 as president of the American Bar Association, the national professional organization for lawyers.

Kellogg was active in Republican party politics in Minnesota and served as a state delegate to the Republican National Convention in 1904, 1908, and 1912. In 1916 he was elected to the U.S. Senate, where he was one of only a few Republicans to support the League of Nations. After he lost his campaign for re-election and left the Senate in 1923, he served as U.S. delegate to the fifth Pan-American Conference in Chile.

In 1924 President Calvin Coolidge appointed Kellogg U.S. ambassador to Great Britain. In that post, he persuaded the British to support the Dawes Plan, a program to help Germany pay off its war debts that had been devised by the American banker and statesman Charles G. Dawes. After his return to the United States in 1925, Coolidge named Kellogg to his cabinet as Secretary of State. During the following four years, Kellogg's duties and accomplishments included the negotiation of more than 80 treaties between the United States and foreign governments.

The best known of these treaties was the Kellogg-Briand Pact of 1928. The treaty, also known as the Pact of Paris, had initially been proposed by French foreign minister Aristide Briand as an alliance between France and the United States. The U.S. government was wary of such an agreement, fearing that it might draw American forces into future conflicts. Kellogg proposed an alternative: the United States and France would invite other nations to join in a declaration that warfare would no longer be used as an instrument of national policy.

The Kellogg-Briand Pact was initially signed by 15 nations on August 17, 1928; eventually 65 countries agreed to the pact. The U.S. Senate—

Frank B. Kellogg

BORN
December 22, 1856
Potsdam, New York

DIED
December 21, 1937
Minneapolis, Minnesota

EDUCATION
Attended elementary school for five years

OCCUPATION
Attorney; statesman

MAJOR ACCOMPLISHMENTS
U.S. Senator (1917–23); U.S. ambassador to Great Britain (1924–25); U.S. Secretary of State (1925–29); sponsor and negotiator of the Kellogg-Briand Pact (1928); member, Hague Tribunal (1930–35)

U.S. Secretary of State Frank Kellogg (left) and Italian representative Nobile Giacomo de Martini sign the Kellogg-Briand Pact. Aristide Briand, coauthor of the pact, won the Nobel Peace Prize in 1928, the year the pact was signed.

which has to approve all treaties of the U.S. government—ratified the agreement with only one opposing vote.

Hailed as a major milestone on the road to world peace, the Kellogg-Briand Pact was likened to "an international kiss." Thus there was little surprise when the 1929 Nobel Peace Prize was awarded to Frank Kellogg for his role in negotiating the pact; Briand had won the Peace Prize the year before.

The 1929 prize was announced in 1930, and later that year Kellogg received another honor when he was appointed to the Hague Tribunal, the court of international justice in the Netherlands. He served for five years, retiring in 1935 because of poor health.

Not long before his death, Kellogg announced that he was donating half a million dollars to Carleton College in Northfield, Minnesota, for the establishment of an institute of international relations. After suffering a stroke, Frank Kellogg died in Minneapolis in December 1937, the day before his 81st birthday.

FURTHER READING

Bryn-Jones, David. *Frank B. Kellogg: A Biography*. New York: Putnam, 1937.

Ferrell, Robert H. *Peace in Their Time: The Origins of the Kellogg-Briand Pact*. New Haven: Yale University Press, 1952.

"Kellogg, Frank Billings." In *Dictionary of American Biography*. Supplement 2. New York: Scribners, 1958.

Miller, David H. *The Peace Pact of Paris: A Study of the Briand-Kellogg Treaty*. New York: Putnam, 1928.

Nathan Söderblom

1930

From the time he was a small child, Nathan Söderblom knew that he wanted to become a clergyman. His father was a minister, and in his mother's family there were clergymen, too. Nathan thought that he would be like his father and grow up to lead a congregation in a small Swedish town. However, when he was a young man, he had an experience that made him aspire to a larger role in the world. Four decades later, that experience led to a unique achievement: in 1930 Nathan Söderblom became the first member of the clergy to receive the Nobel Peace Prize.

Söderblom was born in 1866 in the provincial community of Trönö, Sweden, about a hundred miles north of Stockholm. Both religion and learning were important to his parents, and young Nathan's father took over his education at an early age, beginning Latin lessons when Nathan was five. Nathan Söderblom attended local schools and then enrolled at Uppsala University, which his father had attended, in 1883, at the age of 17.

Söderblom studied classical languages at the university and received his undergraduate degree with honors in Greek. He went on to study theology and gained respect and admiration from both his professors and his fellow students, who elected him president of the student body.

A medal commemorating the elevation in 1914 of Nathan Söderblom to archbishop of the Swedish Lutheran Church. Söderblom devoted his life to interdenominational cooperation.

Archbishop Nathan Söderblom believed ecumenism and peace are inseperable. To promote his goal of ecumenism, he reached out to Christian religious leaders throughout the world.

In 1890, two years before he received his doctorate, Söderblom was invited to become a delegate to a world Christian student conference sponsored by Yale University in New Haven, Connecticut. The conference had been called as part of a growing ecumenical movement, or movement for unity, among the various Christian denominations. Söderblom was stirred by the conference and its mission, and he de-

cided that henceforth he would devote his life to the goal of ecumenism—Christian unity.

After receiving his degree in theology in 1892, Söderblom was ordained in the Swedish Lutheran Church, the state church of Sweden. That same year he published his first book, a study of Martin Luther, the 16th-century founder of Lutheranism. Söderblom worked briefly as the chaplain of a mental hospital in Uppsala, and was then appointed minister of the Swedish church in Paris. The church served diplomats, businessmen, students, and other Swedes who were living in the French city. Among the members of the congregation was Alfred Nobel, a major financial supporter of the church. When Nobel died in 1896, Söderblom conducted the memorial service.

In 1897, Söderblom married Anna Forsell, a fellow student at the University of Uppsala who later collaborated with him on his writings; the couple eventually had 10 children. During his seven years in France, he earned a doctoral degree in theology and the history of religions at the University of Paris.

Söderblom and his family returned in 1901 to Uppsala, where he became professor of theology. He remained in this post for 13 years, and during this period also taught for a time at the University of Leipzig in Germany. Focusing on comparative religion and the philosophy of Martin Luther, Söderblom was a dynamic teacher who is credited with inspiring a religious revival in Sweden. Söderblom left his position at the University of Uppsala in 1914 to become archbishop of the Swedish Lutheran Church.

Pursuing his goal of ecumenism, Söderblom became the principal founder of the General World Union of Churches for International Understanding, a group of like-minded clergymen from around the world. Members gathered in Konstanz, Germany, in the summer of 1914 for a conference, but the outbreak of war in August ended their meeting ahead of schedule. Three years later, Söderblom organized another ecumenical conference, this time in Sweden, but because of the ongoing war only representatives from five neutral nations attended. At the conference Söderblom and other delegates issued a proclamation calling for all churches to work for the settlement of international disputes through mediation and arbitration.

In the years following the end of World War I in 1918, Söderblom continued to be an advocate of both ecumenism and peace, which he believed were inseparable. He wrote many articles and a number of books on this subject as well as other religious topics; many of them were translated into other languages, including English.

In 1925 Söderblom led the General World Union of Churches in sponsoring an international religious gathering, the Universal Christian Conference on Life and Work, which was held in Stockholm. More than 600 delegates from 37 countries attended; they represented not only most Protestant denominations but also the Eastern Orthodox Church. Söderblom presided over the conference meetings, which proclaimed the need for Christian unity as a basis for establishing world peace.

Nathan Söderblom was awarded the 1930 Nobel Peace Prize for his longtime commitment to the achievement of world peace through religious unity. In his acceptance speech, Söderblom announced that a second world ecumenical conference would be held in London in 1935. Unfortunately, he did not live long enough to attend.

In the late spring of 1931, several months after receiving the Nobel Peace Prize, Söderblom traveled to the University of Edinburgh in Scotland to give the Gifford Lectures, a prestigious annual series on the subject of religion. In June, after completing some of the lectures, he became ill and returned to Sweden. He died of a heart attack in Uppsala several weeks later at the age of 65.

Nathan Söderblom's sudden death did not end his influence as a peacemaker, however. The 1935 ecumenical conference in London was one of several similar events that grew out of the organization he had founded in 1914 and the ecumenical conference he had organized in 1925. The dual goal of ecumenism and peace remained alive during the late 1930s and 1940s, despite the outbreak of World War II, and in 1948 the World Council of Churches was founded as a permanent organization to pursue those goals. It continues its work today—thanks to the vision of Nathan Söderblom.

FURTHER READING

Curtis, C. J. *Söderblom: Ecumenical Pioneer.* Minneapolis: Augsburg, 1967.

Sundkler, Bengt. *Nathan Söderblom: His Life and Work.* Malmö: Gleerups, 1968.

Nathan Söderblom

BORN
January 15, 1866
Trönö, Sweden

DIED
July 12, 1931
Uppsala, Sweden

EDUCATION
B.A., University of Uppsala (1886); Doctor of Theology, University of Paris (1901)

OCCUPATION
Clergyman

MAJOR ACCOMPLISHMENTS
Professor of theology and comparative religion, University of Uppsala (1901–14); archbishop, Swedish Lutheran Church (1914–31); inspired religious revival in Sweden; led world ecumenical movement; founder, General World Union of Churches; chairman, Universal Christian Conference on Life and Work (1925); author of numerous articles and books on religious issues, in particular ecumenism and peace, including *Christian Fellowship* (1923) and *The Church and Peace* (1929)

Jane Addams

Nicholas Murray Butler

1931

In December 1887 a young American woman named Jane Addams and her best friend, Ellen Gates Starr, sailed from New York en route to England. Jane Addams was 27 years old, had health problems, and knew that she would probably never marry. She had tried to pursue a career in medicine, but illness had ended that dream. Now, on her second visit abroad, she was taking a vacation in England and hoping that this trip would help her decide what to do with her life.

Jane Addams came from a wealthy family, but her life so far had not been happy. Born in 1860 in Cedarville, Illinois, a small town in the northern part of the state, Jane was the eighth of nine children. Her father was a prosperous businessman, banker, and state senator. Her mother died before Jane's third birthday, and her father remarried five years later.

Jane was a lonely, shy child with a spinal deformity. She was close to her father, and her stepmother encouraged her reading and schooling; nevertheless, Jane grew up uncertain of her place in the world.

After graduating from local public schools, Jane Addams entered Rockford Female Seminary in 1877. The seminary,

Jane Addams is remembered as a pioneering social worker, but during her lifetime she was equally famous as a leader of the international peace movement.

located in the nearby town of Rockford, Illinois, was one of only a few institutions in the Midwest to offer college-level classes to women, and it encouraged an interest in women's rights. During Addams's years there, the seminary became accredited as Rockford College, and she received a bachelor of arts degree in 1882.

Addams assumed that her deformity and other ailments, which meant that she could not have children, made her unsuitable for marriage. Although she could have remained at her parents' home, as most unmarried women did in the 19th century, she decided to pursue a career as a physician. Her family supported her in this choice and allowed her to enroll at one of the few medical schools in the nation then open to women, the Woman's Medical College of Philadelphia. After only a few months of study there, however, her poor health forced her to withdraw.

For some time afterward, Jane Addams searched for another occupation to engage her and use her abilities. Like many other wealthy women of her time, she traveled to Europe and spent several years there studying languages, fine arts, philosophy, and history. Then she returned to the family home in Cedarville for a few years, brooding and unhappy. Finally, in 1887, she decided to make another trip abroad, this time to England.

While Addams and her friend Ellen Starr were in London, they visited Toynbee Hall, a settlement house in a poor district. Settlement houses—community centers for the underprivileged—had recently been established in several English cities. Addams was impressed by what she saw, and tried to learn as much as she could about social reform movements. When she returned to the United States in late 1888, she knew what she wanted to do with her life: establish a settlement house.

The nearest large city to Addams's hometown was Chicago. She decided to found her settlement house in that city's poorest neighborhood, an area on the South Side whose main thoroughfare was Halsted Street. With Ellen Starr, Addams rented part of a once-grand mansion on Halsted that was owned by a family named Hull. The two women moved there in September 1889 and established what became known as Hull-House.

During the next few years, Hull-House developed into a busy community center that served scores of neighborhood residents—men, women, and children—every day. Using her own money as well as donations from friends, and with the assistance of Starr, Addams was able to buy the mansion. In the following decades, donations from wealthy Chicago businessmen enabled her to expand Hull-House into a complex of 13 buildings.

Hull-House included a day nursery, bookbindery, library, gym, community kitchen, small museum, an art studio, and a boardinghouse for young working women. Hull-House provided lessons in literature, art, cooking, sewing, English, music, and drama, and various social clubs offered recreation. During Addams's lifetime, Hull-House served thousands of people of all ages. Its success was due in large part not only to Addams's organizational ability and total commitment to her goal, but also to her warm personality and her obvious love for the people, especially children, whom she served.

Addams's work with the poor drew her into other areas of social reform. She supported laws to restrict child labor, protect female employees, establish safety regulations in factories, and make school attendance mandatory. She also became a prominent supporter of woman suffrage, the right of women to vote.

Beginning in the early 1900s, Addams devoted an increasing amount of attention to the peace movement. Raised in a Quaker environment,

Jane Addams

BORN
September 6, 1860
Cedarville, Illinois

DIED
May 21, 1935
Chicago, Illinois

EDUCATION
B.A., Rockford College (1882)

OCCUPATION
Social worker

MAJOR ACCOMPLISHMENTS
Founder, Hull-House (1889); founder and president, Women's International League for Peace and Freedom (1919); author of numerous articles and 11 books on peace and social reform, including *Newer Ideals of Peace* (1907) and *Twenty Years at Hull-House* (1910)

During a visit to Japan in 1923, Jane Addams is welcomed by flag-waving school-children. Addams traveled throughout the world on behalf of the peace movement and often made women and children the focus of her efforts to promote peace.

Addams had always been opposed to war. (Quakers are members of the Society of Friends, a religious sect founded in England in the 17th century. The sect has always opposed warfare.) However, she had become increasingly convinced that true peace was not simply the absence of war. Rather, she defined it as "the nurture of human life."

Addams made several major contributions to the peace movement. In 1915 she helped create the Woman's Peace Party and became its first chairperson. Several parts of the party's platform, which she wrote, were later used by President Woodrow Wilson in his proposal for the League of Nations. Also in 1915, Addams was elected president of the International Congress of Women, which was held at The Hague, in the Netherlands. The congress had been organized to draft a peace plan to end World War I, which had begun in August 1914.

During the remaining years of the war, Addams continued to work for world peace through her writings and lectures. Many people learned about Addams through her many articles and 11 books, some of which became best-sellers. As a pacifist, she was totally opposed to U.S. entry in the war in April 1917, and this stance led many to criti-cize her as a traitor. The Daughters of the American Revolution, a patriotic group, expelled her from membership for her pacifist views.

In the years following the war, which ended in 1918, Addams was active in relief efforts that brought food to European women and children, including those in former enemy countries. She helped establish national women's organizations in Europe, and founded and led a worldwide peace organization, the Women's International League for Peace and Freedom (WILPF), an outgrowth of the Hague conference of 1915. Addams was also a founder of the American Civil Liberties Union, a group that defends the constitutional rights of all citizens.

In the final decade of her life, Addams channeled her activities for peace through WILPF, a private organization whose goals included disarmament and the abolition of compulsory military service. Although she developed a serious heart ailment in 1926, she continued her peacemaking efforts. In 1931 those efforts earned her a share of that year's Nobel Peace Prize. Jane Addams thus became the first American woman to receive the award.

In the early 1930s Addams developed cancer. When she died in May 1935, following an operation for the disease, she was mourned throughout the world and lauded for her lifetime of service to humanity. Following a funeral service at Hull-House, Jane Addams was buried in her hometown of Cedarville, Illinois. The famous institution that she founded continued to serve the people of Chicago until the 1960s. It is now a public museum dedicated to the memory of Jane Addams and her many accomplishments.

Nicholas Murray Butler, the American educator who shared the 1931 Nobel Peace Prize with Jane Addams, was also a reformer. Butler was born in Elizabeth, New Jersey, in 1862, the eldest of five children of a wealthy textile importer and his wife. He was educated at public and private schools in New Jersey before entering Columbia University in New York City in 1878 to study law.

Midway through his undergraduate years, Butler decided that he was more interested in becoming an educator. He graduated with honors in philosophy in 1882, then went on to earn master's and doctoral degrees in that subject at the university.

After spending a year studying in Berlin and Paris, Butler returned to Columbia in 1885 as an assistant professor of philosophy. While teaching at the university, he became interested in other forms of education, including vocational, or job-oriented, training. In 1887 Butler became president of the Industrial Education Association, an organization that promoted the teaching of manual arts (metalworking, carpentry, and similar skills) and domestic skills (sewing, cooking, and nursing) in public schools. Under his leadership, the association established the New York College for the Training of Teachers in 1889. It was renamed Teachers College in 1892 and nine years later became part of Columbia University.

In 1890 Butler became professor of philosophy, ethics, and psychology at the university. Soon afterward, he began introducing a series of teaching reforms in the university curriculum and established education as an academic discipline at Columbia. During the 1890s he successfully advocated reforms in public school education in both New Jersey and the state of New York, including teacher certification and the removal of school boards from political control.

Butler's accomplishments during this period were astounding. While continuing his professorial duties at Columbia, he founded a scholarly journal, *Educational Review*; headed the National Education Association, a teachers' organization; and was a co-

founder of the College Entrance Examination Board. In 1902 he became president of the university.

As the head of Columbia University for 43 years, Butler turned it into one of the leading institutions of its kind in the world. He founded its schools of journalism and dentistry and expanded other graduate departments. In addition, he attracted many famous scholars in the humanities and natural sciences to its faculty.

Butler was also active in politics. A lifelong member of the Republican party, he attended national party conventions, helped determine party policy, and in 1920 even sought—unsuccessfully—the Republican nomination for President. But in addition to his work in the fields of education and politics, Butler is remembered today for his longtime commitment to the cause of peace.

Butler first became interested in the peace movement in the 1880s, while traveling in Europe. He became a friend of the French peace leader Paul d'Estournelles de Constant and other European statesmen, and maintained these friendships through correspondence and on subsequent trips abroad. As a consequence, Butler became an advocate of arms limitation, arbitration, and the establishment of a world court to settle international disputes. In 1907 he presided at an international arbitration conference held in New York State, and during the next few years gave a series of lectures on arbitration and other peace issues. These were later published in book form as *The Internationalist Mind* (1912) and were widely read.

In 1910 Butler persuaded the industrialist Andrew Carnegie to donate $10 million for the creation of a private organization called the Carnegie Endowment for International Peace. Butler became head of the Endowment's division of education and held that post until 1925. In that year he

Nicholas Murray Butler

BORN
April 2, 1862
Elizabeth, New Jersey

DIED
December 7, 1947
New York, New York

EDUCATION
A.B. (1882), A.M. (1883), Ph.D. (1884), Columbia University

OCCUPATION
Educator

MAJOR ACCOMPLISHMENTS
Founded Columbia Teachers College; president, Columbia University (1902–45); founder and president, Carnegie Endowment for International Peace; initiated Kellogg-Briand Pact (1928); author of numerous books and articles on education and peace

During his 43-year tenure as president of Columbia University, Nicholas Murray Butler was also active in the peace movement. In 1910 he encouraged a friend, industrialist Andrew Carnegie, to establish the Carnegie Endowment for International Peace. Butler succeeded Elihu Root as head of the Endowment in 1925.

succeeded Elihu Root as president of the organization. As the head of the Carnegie Endowment, Butler directed its peacemaking activities around the world, which included rebuilding libraries in Europe that had been damaged or destroyed during World War I, sponsoring cultural exchanges between countries, and making grants to colleges for the establishment of courses in international relations.

One of Butler's major contributions to peace was his initiation and support of a major international peace treaty, the Kellogg-Briand Pact. The pact had its origins in a conversation that Butler had in 1926 with the French statesman Aristide Briand, during which Butler suggested that the United States would be responsive to a peace offer from France. That suggestion led to the creation in 1928 of the Kellogg-Briand Pact, and Butler worked hard to mobilize public opinion in support of the plan. It was eventually signed by 65 countries, including the United States.

For his work with the Carnegie Endowment and his role in creating the Kellogg-Briand Pact, Nicholas Murray Butler was named cowinner of the 1931 Nobel Peace Prize. In the years leading up to World War II, Butler continued to work for peace through the cultural and educational programs of the Carnegie Endowment. He believed that war could be averted through the establishment of a European economic union—an idea that became a reality only after the war with the creation of the European Common Market in 1958. Although Butler was opposed to war, he strongly supported U.S. entry into World War II after its outbreak in 1939.

Butler wrote more than a dozen books on education and international relations during his long career; the last, a collection of his essays and speeches, was published in 1946. Although he had a distinguished public life, Butler's personal life was far from happy. His first wife, whom he married in 1887 and with whom he had a daughter, died in 1903. Four years later he remarried, but unhappily, and his daughter died young.

Butler planned to remain as Columbia's president until his own death, but during the 1940s he gradually lost his eyesight and became deaf. Finally, in 1945, he resigned. He died two years later, in December 1947, of pneumonia.

FURTHER READING

Addams, Jane. *A Centennial Reader.* New York: Macmillan, 1960.

———. *Twenty Years at Hull-House.* 1910. Reprint, New York: New American Library, 1981.

———. *The Second Twenty Years at Hull-House.* New York: Macmillan, 1930.

Butler, Nicholas Murray. *Across the Busy Years.* 2 vols. New York: Scribners, 1939, 1940.

"Butler, Nicholas Murray." In *Dictionary of American Biography.* Supplement 4. New York: Scribners, 1974.

Davis, Allen F. *American Heroine: The Life and Legend of Jane Addams.* New York: Oxford University Press, 1973.

———, ed. *Jane Addams on Peace, War, and International Understanding, 1899–1932.* New York: Garland, 1976.

De Benedetti, Charles. *Origins of the Modern American Peace Movement.* Millwood, N.Y.: KTO Press, 1978.

Farrell, J. C. *Beloved Lady: A History of Jane Addams's Ideas on Reform and Peace.* Baltimore: Johns Hopkins University Press, 1967.

Lasch, Christopher, ed. *The Social Thought of Jane Addams.* Indianapolis: Bobbs-Merrill, 1975.

Marrin, Albert. *Nicholas Murray Butler.* New York: Twayne, 1976.

Wheeler, Leslie. *Jane Addams.* Morristown, N.J.: Silver Burdett Press, 1990.

Norman Angell

1933

In the early 1890s, an Englishman still in his teens came to the United States, hoping to make his fortune in the West. Like many young men who left their homelands for America in the 19th century, he thought that the New World would give him opportunities for a fresh start. He had tried his hand at journalism before coming to the United States, and had decided it held no future for him.

Soon after arriving out West, the young man began a series of rigorous outdoor jobs. Eventually, he decided to settle in California as a gold prospector. He staked a claim, but for some reason the claim was denied. Frustrated, and tired of manual labor, the young man returned to journalism. The loss of his homestead had a then-unforeseen effect on the young man: a writer with pacifist sympathies, he set out on a path that would lead to the Nobel Peace Prize some four decades later.

When Norman Angell was awarded the 1933 Peace Prize, he had been known by that name for more than 20

Norman Angell's pacifist sympathies led him to a career as a writer of articles and best-selling books that promoted internationalism by describing the terrible costs of warfare.

years. But he was born Ralph Norman Lane in December 1873 in Holbeach, England, to a wealthy landowner and local merchant named Thomas Angell Lane and his wife. Young Norman was bright but restless, and after attending an English boarding school he was sent to a preparatory school in France, where his parents hoped he would mature.

In France, Norman became drawn to radical political ideas, and he left school at the age of 15 and moved to Geneva, Switzerland. There he became part of the city's international community, which included revolutionaries and political refugees. Despite his youth, he was hired as an editor of an English-language newspaper, and while earning his living at the newspaper he attended lectures at the University of Geneva. But after three years, Norman became restless and returned to England. He lived at home for a while, without much sense of direction, until his father gave him 50 pounds and encouraged him to find a future for himself in America.

Norman Lane spent seven years in the West working successively as a cowboy, laborer, prospector, and mail carrier. In 1898, his homestead claim denied, he applied for a newspaper job and was hired. His career as an American journalist did not last long, however. Later that year he was called home to England on family business. While he was in the United States, Norman Lane married an American woman, but there were apparently difficulties in the marriage, and at some point the couple separated.

When his family business was finished, Norman Lane decided not to return to the United States. Convinced that he could now earn a living by writing, he moved to Paris and resumed his career in journalism. He worked briefly as a freelance correspondent for American newspapers, and then in 1899 became editor of the Paris *Daily Messenger*, an English-language newspaper. He also contributed essays on current events and politics to the newspaper. On the side, he began writing a book on the contemporary scene; it was published in 1903 as *Patriotism Under Three Flags*. Norman Lane's first book attracted wide attention and led to his appointment in 1904 as editor of the Paris edition of a leading London newspaper, the *Daily Mail*.

In the early 1900s, Norman Lane gradually became committed to the goal of international cooperation and decided that he would focus his writing on aspects of that topic. His second book, *Europe's Optical Illusion*, published in 1909, addressed the economic basis of war. So convinced was Lane of the book's importance that he paid for its first publication himself. An English historian named Lord Esher was impressed by *Europe's Optical Illusion*, and he distributed several hundred copies to prominent Europeans. Their response was overwhelmingly favorable, and the book's popularity led to its reprinting in 1910 under a new title, *The Great Illusion*. The author, too, appeared under a new name: in the preceding year, Norman Lane had changed his surname to his father's middle name, and was henceforth known as Norman Angell.

In *The Great Illusion* Angell argued against war, saying that it was never profitable and that it hurt both the victors and those whom they had defeated. The book became a best-seller: it sold 2 million copies and was translated into more than two dozen languages. Angell left the *Daily Mail* in 1912 to edit a new journal of public affairs, *War and Peace*. During the next decade he also became a contributor to leading American periodicals.

Following the outbreak of World War I in 1914, Angell joined with several British political leaders to found the Union of Democratic Control, an organization that called for greater public control over the British government's foreign policy. He also drew up a proposal for a permanent association of nations that would ensure international peace after the war ended. Angell's proposal, which he discussed in articles and lectures, was read with interest by U.S. President Woodrow Wilson, who incorporated some of Angell's ideas into his own proposal for the League of Nations.

After the war ended in 1918, Angell attended the Paris Peace Conference as a journalist. He was critical of the harsh terms of the resulting Versailles Peace Treaty, which required Germany to pay enormous amounts of money to countries it had harmed during the war. However, he approved of the League of Nations, which was created by the treaty. During the next few years, while he continued working as a journalist, Angell was active in war relief associations. He founded one of them himself: Fight the Famine, an organization that provided food, medical supplies, and clothing to children in war-torn Central Europe.

In addition to working full time as a journalist and nearly full time as a humanitarian, Angell continued to write books on world affairs and the quest for peace. During the 1920s, he ran for Parliament several times before finally winning election in 1929 to the House of Commons on the Labour Party ticket. He served only two years, however; he resigned in 1931, believing that he could serve the cause of world peace more effectively as a writer than as a politician. That same year, he was knighted by King George V of England.

Another honor came to Norman Angell in 1934, when he was named the winner of the 1933 Nobel Peace Prize. By this time, Angell had written hundreds of articles and more than two dozen books on current affairs, many of them about disarmament and the abolition of war. The citation accompanying the award focused on that accomplishment by praising Angell as a "peace educator," but his humanitarian service during nearly three decades was also noted approvingly.

During the 1930s, as the likelihood of another world war grew, Angell was an outspoken critic of Adolf Hitler and Nazi Germany. Although Angell was opposed to war and was sympathetic to pacifism, he himself was not a pacifist. While he hoped that international disarmament would someday occur, he was realistic about the present situation. Hitler, he believed, was an enemy of the common good and had to be fought.

In the late 1930s, as Nazi persecution of Jews increased, Angell urged the British government to admit Jewish refugees. He himself sheltered some of them at his home in rural England. When his country went to war with Germany in September 1939, Angell joined the Ministry of Information, a government agency that rallied support for the war effort. In this capacity he traveled to the United States in 1940 to seek American help for Great Britain. After the United States entered the war in December 1941, Angell stayed on in New York City, where he lived for 10 years. He continued to work as a journalist, write books, and give lectures. During this time he became a leading advocate of world government under the United Nations, founded in 1945 as the successor to the League of Nations.

Angell returned to England in 1951 and settled in rural Surrey. That year he published an autobiography, *After All*. He continued to lecture and write articles on world affairs—in particular, colonialism, the growth of Third World nations, and tensions between Israel and its Arab neighbors. As he grew older, Angell's health began to decline and he was forced to make fewer and fewer public appearances. He wrote his 35th and last book in 1958.

During the 1960s, Angell made several more trips to the United States. The last occurred in 1966, when he donated his personal papers to Ball State University in Muncie, Indiana, and received an honorary degree from the university. He died a year later, in October 1967, at a nursing home in Surrey, England, at the age of 93.

FURTHER READING

Angell, Norman. *After All: The Autobiography of Norman Angell*. London: Hamish Hamilton, 1951.

Ceadel, M. *Pacifism in Britain, 1914–1945*. Oxford: Clarendon Press, 1980.

Marrin, Albert. *Sir Norman Angell*. New York: Twayne, 1979.

Miller, J. D. B. *Norman Angell and the Futility of War*. New York: St. Martin's, 1986.

Norman Angell

BORN
December 26, 1873
Holbeach, England

DIED
October 7, 1967
Surrey, England

EDUCATION
Attended preparatory school in England and France; briefly attended University of Geneva

OCCUPATION
Writer

MAJOR ACCOMPLISHMENTS
Wrote numerous articles and books on international cooperation and how it can be achieved, beginning with *The Great Illusion* (1909); editor, *War and Peace* (periodical); founder, Fight the Famine

Arthur Henderson

1934

I n 1875 no one would have predicted a great future for Arthur Henderson. He had left school three years earlier, at the age of nine, to work at a series of menial jobs. Now he was 12, and apprenticed to an iron molder. If he did well at his assigned tasks, he could hope to remain and to eke out a bare living—unless he fell victim to an accident on the job, which happened often to boys his age who were forced to earn their living as skilled laborers.

But Arthur stuck it out, and four years later he reached an important milestone in his personal life. At the age of 16, he converted to Methodism, a branch of Protestant Christianity. As a follower of the Methodist Church, he gained self-esteem and confidence in his abilities, became a leader of working men and women and a leading advocate of world peace—and won the Nobel Peace Prize.

Arthur Henderson was born in Glasgow, Scotland, in 1863 to a poor cotton-factory worker and his wife. Arthur's

Arthur Henderson's Methodist beliefs inspired him to become a trade union leader, cofounder of the British Labour party, and an internationally known disarmament advocate.

father died when he was nine, and he had to leave primary school and go to work to help support the destitute family. Three years later his life improved somewhat when his mother remarried and moved to Newcastle-upon-Tyne. In this industrial city in northeastern England, where there was a high level of unemployment, Arthur was fortunate to find an apprenticeship. The work was arduous, but he was bright and applied himself.

The Methodist Church, which Arthur Henderson joined in 1879, provided a set of values that would guide him for the rest of his life. The church encouraged its members to work hard at their jobs, to remain fit and sober, and to perform acts of service for their fellow human beings. Henderson eventually married a fellow Methodist and became a lay preacher in the church. (A lay, or layman, preacher is a church member who is not an ordained clergyman but has permission from church authorities to preach.) In this capacity, he grew skilled as a public speaker, and he further developed this ability by joining a local debating society.

At the age of 18, Henderson completed his apprenticeship and became a journeyman, the next level in his trade. He joined the ironfounders' labor union and soon became one of its acknowledged leaders. Henderson now knew that the labor movement would be his life's work. During the next few years, he served as a union official, and in 1892 he entered politics as a city councilor in Newcastle.

In 1896 Henderson moved to Darlington, a manufacturing town not far from Newcastle, and was elected to the county council. He was now a full-time employee of the labor union and had become nationally known among trade unionists. In 1900 he cofounded the Labour Representation Committee, which became the forerunner of the Labour political party in England. Three years later he was elected mayor of Darlington and member of Parliament on the Labour party ticket.

Henderson served as chairman of the first Labour party conference, held in 1906. Later that year, Henderson was re-elected to Parliament, and 28 other Labour party candidates were also elected. Henderson led his fellow Labourites in Parliament and in 1911 became the secretary of the party; he held this post for more than two decades.

Henderson supported Great Britain's entry into World War I in August 1914, but the Labour party leader, Ramsay MacDonald, did not. When MacDonald resigned because of his disagreement with the government's war policy, Henderson succeeded him as the leader of the party. In 1915 Henderson was named to head the British board of education as a member of a coalition government (a government in which the leaders of two or more political parties share power). A year later he became the first Labour party member to join the British cabinet when he was appointed postmaster general.

In 1917, as a minister-without-portfolio in the coalition government led by Prime Minister David Lloyd George, Henderson traveled to Russia—whose czar had just been overthrown in the Russian Revolution—to persuade the new government there to remain in the war on the side of Great Britain. He left the cabinet shortly afterward following a disagreement with Lloyd George.

Henderson now assumed the task of reorganizing and strengthening the Labour party. He drew up a list of foreign policy objectives for the party, which included the establishment of an international organization to settle disputes between nations peacefully. Henderson also helped draft a party constitution, which extended Labour party membership to members of the middle class as well as the working class.

Arthur Henderson

BORN
September 13, 1863
Glasgow, Scotland

DIED
October 20, 1935
London, England

EDUCATION
Primary school

OCCUPATION
Labor leader; statesman

MAJOR ACCOMPLISHMENTS
Cofounder, British Labour Party (1906); British foreign minister (1929–31); worked for disarmament as a leader of the League of Nations Assembly; chairman, World Disarmament Conference (1932–34)

Newly elected member of Parliament Arthur Henderson (center) walks to the House of Commons on March 13, 1924, accompanied by his two sons, William (left) and Arthur, Jr. Henderson achieved a historic "first" on that date when he became the first member of Parliament to be welcomed into that body by his previously elected sons.

In 1919 Henderson persuaded fellow Labourites in Parliament to support the League of Nations, which had been created by the Versailles Peace Treaty. He continued as a party leader in Parliament in the early 1920s. In 1924, when the first Labour government in British history was elected, he became a member of the cabinet as home secretary. Henderson's new responsibilities involved domestic issues, but he continued to take an active interest in foreign affairs. Although World War I had not made Henderson a pacifist, it had convinced him that warfare posed the greatest danger to humanity and had to be opposed. The intensity of his feeling on this issue may have been explained in part by a personal tragedy: his eldest son had been killed in the war.

During the 1920s, Henderson served as a delegate to the Assembly of the League of Nations. There he helped draft the international security agreement of 1924 known as the Geneva Protocol, which called for the settlement of international disputes by arbitration. Five years later, in 1929,

Labour prime minister Ramsay MacDonald named Henderson foreign secretary. Henderson used this position to continue efforts to ensure security among the nations of Europe.

That same year Henderson was a prominent delegate to the Tenth Assembly of the League of Nations in Geneva. On behalf of Great Britain, he signed an agreement committing his nation to compulsory arbitration in settling disputes. In so doing, he set an example that was followed by more than 40 other nations. Henderson also spoke out on behalf of disarmament and called for an international agreement to reduce the supply of weapons.

Henderson's support for disarmament led to his appointment in 1931 as chairman of the World Disarmament Conference, sponsored by the League and held in Geneva beginning in 1932. Henderson faced a number of problems in this role: he was in poor health, the Labour government had been removed from office in Britain, a worldwide economic depression had begun, and Japan and Germany were both showing signs of aggression. Yet he persisted in convening conference sessions for nearly three years, until the growing threat of Nazi Germany and its leader, Adolf Hitler, led to the collapse of the conference in 1934.

Henderson's determined support of disarmament in the face of overwhelming odds earned him the 1934 Nobel Peace Prize. In his acceptance speech, he voiced optimism for the future creation of "nothing less than a world commonwealth." Henderson was unable to continue working for that goal, however. In the remaining year of his life, ill health forced his gradual withdrawal from politics. He died in London in October 1935, at the age of 71.

FURTHER READING

Hamilton, Mary Agnes. *Arthur Henderson*. London: Heinemann, 1938.

Carl von Ossietzky

1935

oday, in Berlin, Germany, few people remember why a street in the eastern part of the city is called Ossietzky-Strasse. But earlier in this century, the man for whom it is named was celebrated as a hero throughout the world—everywhere, in fact, but in his native Germany. Only some years after his death—and after the end of the terrible war he had tried to stop—did the citizens of Berlin pay belated tribute to Carl von Ossietzky by naming a street after him.

Carl von Ossietzky was born in the German port city of Hamburg in 1889. His father, an unsuccessful merchant, died when Carl was two years old, and seven years later his mother remarried. Carl's stepfather was a prominent member of the Social Democratic party, a liberal political group that supported social reform and opposed Germany's increasing militarism, and young Carl was strongly influenced by his views. When he completed secondary school he decided that

Carl von Ossietzky gave his life for the cause of peace. He died a martyr in a German prison hospital in 1938 as Adolf Hitler prepared for the war that Ossietzky had tried so hard to prevent.

instead of enrolling in a university he would become a writer.

By his early 20s Ossietzky had contributed political articles as well as poetry to several periodicals. He also became part of the peace movement and cofounded the Hamburg branch of the German Peace Society in 1912. Not long afterward, Ossietzky had his first negative encounter with the government: he was fined for writing an article in a local newspaper that was critical of the military.

Ossietzky was dismayed when his country began World War I in 1914, and two years later he entered the army reluctantly after being drafted. His experience fighting in eastern France turned him virtually overnight into a pacifist. He had long believed that there was nothing heroic about war. Now he was convinced that it brought only terror and misery to humankind.

After Germany's defeat in November 1918, Ossietzky returned to Hamburg to resume his career as a writer and to work for peace. After serving briefly as president of the local chapter of the German Peace Society, he moved to Berlin in 1920 to become secretary of the national organization. During the next few years he also continued to write political articles and cofounded an antiwar movement called Nie Wieder Krieg (No More War).

In 1924 Ossietzky resigned as secretary of the German Peace Society to become foreign editor of a liberal Berlin newspaper, the *Volkszeitung*. Two years later he joined the staff of another paper, *Die Weltbühne*, and in 1927 he became that paper's editor-in-chief. That same year, under Ossietzky's editorship, *Die Weltbühne* published an article that criticized the government for not opposing paramilitary groups in Germany. (Under the terms of the Versailles Peace Treaty, which ended World War I, Germany was not allowed to maintain an official army. During the 1920s, a number of paramilitary groups—private military organizations—sprang up and trained regularly. They were composed of men and boys who were unhappy about Germany's loss.) For publishing his article, Ossietzky was convicted of libel against the government and sentenced to a month in prison.

In 1929 Ossietzky again came into conflict with the German government when he published an article in *Die Weltbühne* that described its secret building of warplanes, again in violation of the Versailles Treaty. Ossietzky and the article's author, Walter Kreiser, were arrested on a charge of treason, but the trial was not held until 1931. In the meantime, in a national election in 1930, the militaristic National Socialist (Nazi) Party, led by Adolf Hitler, won more than 100 seats in the Reichstag, the German legislature. In his newspaper, Ossietzky vigorously protested the Nazi victory and warned against the party's growing power.

At the trial of Ossietzky and Kreiser in 1931, both men were convicted and sentenced to 18 months in prison. Many prominent liberals protested the conviction, including the scientist Albert Einstein, and both Ossietzky and Kreiser were urged by their supporters to flee the country before they could be jailed. Kreiser took their advice and moved to Paris, but Ossietzky vowed to remain in order to fight what he called the "rottenness" in his nation.

Carl von Ossietzky

Ossietzky went to prison in the spring of 1932 and served seven months of his sentence; he was released that December as part of a Christmas amnesty declared by the government. Weeks later, in January 1933, Hitler became chancellor of Germany. In February a mysterious fire swept through the building that housed the Reichstag. Hitler used the fire—which may have been set by his fellow Nazis—as an excuse to round up all political opponents of the Nazi regime, including Ossietzky. He was imprisoned for a while in Berlin, then sent to concentration camps—first Sonnenburg, then Esterwegen.

Ossietzky suffered terribly during his years of internment. His longtime heart ailment grew worse, and he developed severe tuberculosis—perhaps through a deliberate injection of the bacilli by a prison camp doctor. His plight did not go unnoticed, however. Leading peace activists from around the world, including Jane Addams of the United States and Norman Angell and Bertrand Russell of Great Britain, protested to the German government. At the same time, they and other prominent men and women, including Albert Einstein and the German novelist Thomas Mann, wrote to the Nobel Peace Prize committee, recommending that Ossietzky receive the award.

In 1936 Carl von Ossietzky was named the winner of the 1935 Nobel Peace Prize for his courageous stand against the threat of militarism and his "burning love for freedom of thought." Hitler was infuriated, and he prevented Ossietzky from receiving the prize. Ossietzky himself was now too ill to travel and had been moved from the Esterwegen camp to a prison hospital in Berlin. Nevertheless, he received telegrams and letters of congratulation from around the world. In many countries he was publicly celebrated as a hero, and rallies of support were held for him. In New York City, Columbia University president and previous Nobel winner Nicholas Murray Butler organized a mass meeting in December 1936 to honor Ossietzky for his commitment to "ideals of peace and . . . the public policies which make for peace."

Ossietzky never left the prison hospital in Berlin. He died there in May 1938, at the age of 48. He was survived by his wife, an English nurse whom he had married in 1913, and their young daughter. The German government, under Adolf Hitler, went on to fight, and lose, World War II—the conflict that Ossietzky had warned against and had given his life to prevent. In 1946, a year after the war ended, Ossietzky's heroism was finally acknowledged in his adopted city with the renaming of a street in his honor.

FURTHER READING

Abrams, Irwin. "Carl von Ossietzky." In *The Nobel Peace Prize and the Laureates*. Boston: G. K. Hall, 1988.

La Fontaine, Henri. "Ossietzky." *Nation*, October 9, 1937, p. 388.

"Martyr to Militarism." *Christian Century*, May 25, 1938, pp. 653–56.

BORN
October 3, 1889
Hamburg, Germany

DIED
May 4, 1938
Berlin, Germany

EDUCATION
Secondary school

OCCUPATION
Writer

MAJOR ACCOMPLISHMENTS
Secretary, German Peace Society; editor-in-chief, *Die Weltbühne*; co-founder of the antiwar movement Nie Wieder Krieg; outspoken critic of German militarism; early and persistent opponent of Adolf Hitler and the Nazi party

Carlos Saavedra Lamas

1936

In 1936 the Argentinian statesman Carlos Saavedra Lamas became the first South American to win the Nobel Peace Prize. Furthermore, he received the award for acting as a peacemaker in a war between two South American nations, Bolivia and Paraguay. But Saavedra Lamas's accomplishments extended far beyond his own continent and earned him praise and admiration throughout the world.

Carlos Saavedra Lamas was born in Buenos Aires in 1878 to wealthy parents. He was educated by private tutors and later attended a Roman Catholic secondary school and college. He then studied for a doctorate in law at the University of Buenos Aires and graduated in 1903 with highest honors.

Saavedra Lamas did postgraduate study in Paris, then returned to Argentina to become professor of law at the University of La Plata. After several years he joined the law faculty of the University of Buenos Aires and taught there until 1946. Early on, Saavedra Lamas developed specialties in labor law and international law, and he pursued these interests throughout his scholarly career.

Along with his university appointment, Saavedra Lamas also had a career in government service. During the following decades he served in a series of government posts related to education, justice, and foreign affairs, and was elected to two terms in the national legislature.

Beginning in the 1920s Saavedra Lamas became a treaty adviser to the Foreign Ministry, and in 1928 he was named president of the International Labor Conference, under the auspices of the League of Nations in Geneva, Switzerland. At this time, however, Argentina was not part of the League; it had withdrawn in 1920 in a dispute over the election of new member nations.

In 1932 Saavedra Lamas was appointed foreign minister of Argentina. In his new position he decided to take an active role in trying to solve a long-standing dispute between two other South American nations, Bolivia and Paraguay, which bordered Argentina on the north.

At issue was a territory called Chaco, which lay between Bolivia and Paraguay. Chaco had been claimed and settled by Paraguay in the early 19th century, but actual ownership had always been in dispute between Paraguay and Bolivia. That dispute intensified in the 1920s, when oil was discovered in Bolivia. In order to ship its oil, landlocked Bolivia decided to press its claims to Chaco in order to gain access to the Atlantic Ocean via the Paraguay River.

In 1928 fighting erupted between the two nations when Paraguay refused to cede Chaco to Bolivia, but a cease-fire

Carlos Saavedra Lamas

Argentinian statesman Carlos Saavedra Lamas was awarded the 1936 Nobel Peace Prize for his successful efforts to end the Chaco War between Bolivia and Paraguay.

BORN
November 1, 1878
Buenos Aires, Argentina

DIED
May 5, 1959
Buenos Aires, Argentina

EDUCATION
Doctorate of Laws, University of Buenos Aires (1903)

OCCUPATION
University professor; statesman

MAJOR ACCOMPLISHMENTS
Professor (1910–46) and president (1942–44), University of Buenos Aires; president, International Labor Conference (1928); foreign minister of Argentina (1932–1938); formulated the Declaration of August 3 (1932); proposed and wrote the South American Antiwar Pact (1933); formed commission (1935) that ended the Chaco War; president, Assembly of the League of Nations (1936)

was established that lasted four years. Soon after Saavedra Lamas became foreign minister in 1932, bloody warfare resumed between Bolivia and Paraguay. In his role as peacemaker, Saavedra Lamas took a series of steps to resolve the conflict. He began by successfully proposing a broad resolution, called the Declaration of August 3. According to this resolution, all South American nations agreed that they would not recognize any national boundaries that had been changed by war.

Saavedra Lamas's next step was the creation of the South American Antiwar Pact. This pact, signed by all South American nations, had three major provisions: First, the nations agreed to renounce wars of aggression—that is, they said they would not invade other countries. Second, they agreed to recognize only those national boundaries created by peaceful means. Third, sanctions (peaceful punishments such as blockades and denial of trade) would be imposed against aggressor nations, and efforts would be made to conciliate (make peace with) these aggressor nations.

The Antiwar Pact of 1933 won international praise for both Saavedra Lamas and the nation of Argentina as leaders in the quest for peace. Through his efforts, Argentina was readmitted to the League of Nations that same year. Later the pact was submitted to the League Assembly and was signed by 11 European nations.

By now, Saavedra Lamas had become known as South America's leading statesman. In that role he was approached by newly elected U.S. President Franklin D. Roosevelt to reinforce friendly relations between Latin America and the United States. As a consequence, Saavedra Lamas and his nation became active in the Pan-American Union, an intercontinental organization that promoted cooperation among the countries of North, Central, and South America.

Although Paraguay and Bolivia had signed both the Declaration of August 3 and the Antiwar Pact, the Chaco War continued to rage. Saavedra Lamas had not given up his attempts to end the war, however. He believed that his accomplishments in the field of international relations would eventually enable him to settle the dispute—and he was correct.

By 1935, Saavedra Lamas's prestige allowed him to intervene and to be accepted as a peacemaker by both Bolivia and Paraguay. He then formed a commission composed of representatives from six then-neutral nations in North and South America—Brazil, Chile, Peru, Uruguay, Argentina, and the United States—to mediate an end to the war, which had killed more than 100,000 people since its outbreak in 1932.

On June 12, 1935, the commission announced a cease-fire and the beginning of negotiations between Paraguay and Bolivia to resolve the boundary dispute. A year later, Saavedra Lamas was named the winner of the 1936 Nobel Peace Prize for leading the effort to end the Chaco War. Some months before the award was announced, Saavedra Lamas had been accorded another honor: election to the presidency of the League of Nations Assembly in Geneva.

Saavedra Lamas retired as Argentina's foreign minister in 1938, the same year that a treaty ending the Chaco War was signed. The treaty gave three-fourths of the disputed Chaco territory to Paraguay; the remaining one-fourth went to Bolivia, which also received access rights to the Paraguay River and to the Paraguayan river port city of Puerto Casado.

In the early 1940s Saavedra Lamas served as president of the University of Buenos Aires while continuing as a member of the law faculty. In the course of his career, he received awards from 11 nations, including the German Iron Cross and the French Legion of Honor. Saavedra Lamas retired from the university in 1946 and spent his remaining years in Buenos Aires, where he lived with his wife and son. He died at his home in May 1959 at the age of 80 after suffering a brain hemorrhage.

FURTHER READING

Abrams, Irwin. "Carlos Saavedra Lamas." In *The Nobel Peace Prize and the Laureates*. Boston: G. K. Hall, 1988.

Robert Cecil
(Viscount Cecil of Chelwood)

1937

Even as a very young man, growing up in England in the second half of the 19th century, Robert Cecil was known for his progressive views, especially his support of women's right to vote. As a grown man, serving in Parliament, he became firmly committed to the cause of international cooperation, and in late middle age he helped to create the League of Nations. His untiring support of the League earned him the 1937 Nobel Peace Prize.

Edgar Algernon Robert Gascoyne Cecil was born into an aristocratic family in London in 1864. He was the third of five sons of Lord Cecil, the 3rd Marquess of Salisbury, who later in the century served as prime minister of Great Britain. Young Robert, as he was called, grew up in a household of enormous wealth and privilege. He was educated at home until the age of 13, and was then sent to Eton, a distinguished secondary school. After completing course work there, he studied law at Oxford University and graduated in 1886.

During the next two decades, Robert Cecil practiced law in London, where he lived with his wife, whom he had married in 1889. (The couple had no children.) Cecil seemed

In 1931, Robert Cecil addresses a meeting of peace advocates from 17 nations and 170 organizations in Paris. For two decades, Cecil worked to strengthen the League of Nations and supported its efforts to prevent war.

destined to make the legal field his career, and even coauthored a well-respected textbook on commercial law. He had always been interested in politics, however, and in 1906, three years after the death of his father, he was elected to Parliament as a Conservative. His father had been a lifelong member of the Conservative party, but Robert Cecil soon discovered that the party was not sympathetic to his reformist views. He broke with the Conservatives, declared himself an independent, and after several tries was re-elected to Parliament from another district.

Following Great Britain's entry into World War I in 1914, when Cecil was 50, he was disappointed to learn that he was too old for military service. As an alternative, he became a volunteer with the International Committee of the Red Cross and worked for a year both in London and abroad on the organization's behalf. Midway through the war, Cecil was appointed to the British cabinet as undersecretary of foreign affairs and masterminded the blockade against Germany during the conflict.

The war had a deep and long-lasting effect on Cecil, and he determined to do all that he could to establish lasting peace once the fighting ended. In 1916 he drew up a memo that proposed setting up a postwar international commission to further that goal. The memo was sent to his fellow cabinet members and ultimately endorsed by them. It later became part of Great Britain's draft of the Covenant of the League of Nations.

Early in 1919 Cecil traveled to France as a member of the British delegation to the Paris Peace Conference. He strongly supported the admission to the League of Nations of Germany and countries that had supported it during the war, and he was disappointed when that proposal was rejected by the Allied—victorious—nations, including Great Britain. That rejection, he believed, sowed the seeds of future conflict.

Nevertheless, Cecil became a firm supporter of the newly created League. He played an active role in persuading many neutral nations to join the organization, and after resigning from the British government in 1920, he represented South Africa—then part of the British Empire—for several years in the League Assembly. (Cecil had been appointed by his friend and fellow League supporter Jan Smuts, then the South African prime minister.)

In 1923, the British government gave Cecil the title Viscount Cecil of Chelwood. This new title gave him a permanent seat in the House of Lords, the upper house of Parliament. In this capacity, he was assigned responsibility for Great Britain's relationship with the League of Nations. Devoting himself full time to the League, Cecil had to deal with the growing threat of militarism in the years following his appointment, in particular the aggressive actions of the Italian dictator Benito Mussolini. During this period he wrote several books on internationalism and the League, and also served as chancellor of the University of Birmingham, a post to which he had been appointed at the end of World War I.

Cecil was often frustrated in acting as an intermediary between his government and the League. Great Britain refused to participate in many League efforts that he supported, including the Geneva Protocol, which required participating countries to submit international disputes to a world court. As Britain's representative to a League-sponsored naval disarmament conference in Geneva in 1927, Cecil was dismayed when his government did not agree to terms proposed by the United States. When the conference collapsed as a consequence—a serious setback for the League of Nations—Cecil resigned from his official position as Britain's liaison officer with the League.

As a private citizen Cecil continued to muster public support for the League of Nations. In this capacity he served as president of the International Federation of League of Nations Societies, an organization of private League support groups around the world. In 1932 he had the satisfaction of seeing many of his proposals for disarmament incorporated in a peace plan proposed by U.S. President Herbert Hoover, although this plan also failed because of official British opposition. In 1934, Cecil launched another effort, called the Peace Ballot. This was a national referendum in which 10 million Britons expressed their support for the League of Nations and 9 million called for the abolition of military air forces.

Despite this show of public support in England and in other member countries, the League of Nations continued to lose authority during the 1930s as it seemed powerless to control increasing militancy in Germany and Italy. In the face of this growing dilemma, Cecil made yet another attempt to save the organization. In 1936 he founded the International Peace Campaign, a group dedicated to the achievement of world disarmament and to strengthening the League's authority to resolve conflicts between nations.

Robert Cecil's tireless efforts on behalf of the League of Nations earned him the 1937 Nobel Peace Prize. In his acceptance address, he warned of the imminent danger of another world war, and he pleaded with world leaders to support the League of Nations "before Europe has been again plunged into a fresh bloodbath."

Despite those warnings, World War II began in September 1939. Cecil, now approaching 80, spent the war years in semi-retirement. His book *A Great Experiment*, which described his experiences with the League, was published in 1941. When the war ended in 1945, Cecil attended the final meeting of the League of Nations in Geneva as it made way for its successor organization, the United Nations. He was later named honorary president for life of the United Nations Association. In 1949 his autobiography, *All the Way*, was published.

Cecil spent his remaining years with his wife at their home in Tunbridge Wells. He died there in November 1958 at the age of 94.

FURTHER READING

"Cecil, Edgar Algernon Robert Gascoyne, Viscount Cecil of Chelwood." In *Dictionary of National Biography, 1951–1960*. Oxford: Oxford University Press, 1971.

Robert Cecil
(Viscount Cecil of Chelwood)

BORN
September 14, 1864
London, England

DIED
November 24, 1958
Tunbridge Wells, England

EDUCATION
A.B. (1884), L.L.D. (1886), Oxford University

OCCUPATION
Attorney; statesman

MAJOR ACCOMPLISHMENTS
Member of Parliament (1906–27); president, International Federation of League of Nations Societies (1927–39); initiated the Peace Ballot (1934), a referendum in support of disarmament and the League; founded the International Peace Campaign (1936)

Nansen International Office for Refugees

1938

I n 1921 the newly created League of Nations established an organization at its headquarters in Geneva, Switzerland, to coordinate the resettlement of millions of refugees, primarily in Europe, who had been uprooted from their homes during World War I (1914–18). They named that organization the High Commission for Refugees. As its first director, called the high commissioner for refugees, the League appointed the Norwegian explorer, scientist, and humanitarian Fridtjof Nansen.

As high commissioner, Nansen helped resettle millions of refugees who had fled Russia following the Revolution of 1917. He also repatriated (returned to their home countries) half a million prisoners of war being held in Russia and brought aid to millions in that country who were victims of a widespread famine. In addition, he led resettlement efforts of refugees in Greece and Turkey. Because most refugees lacked proper travel papers, Nansen created a special document known as the Nansen passport that was ultimately accepted by 52 nations.

When Nansen's work as high commissioner earned him the Nobel Peace Prize for 1922, he donated his award money to refugee assistance programs. Nansen died eight years later, in May 1930. That fall, the League of Nations created a new refugee organization as a successor to the High Commission. They named it the Nansen International Office for Refugees, in honor of Fridtjof Nansen, and it began operations in Geneva in April 1931.

One of the major tasks accomplished by the Nansen Office was finding homes in the Middle East for more than

More than 50,000 Armenian refugees like these, an unwelcome minority in Turkey, were resettled in the Middle East in the 1930s by the Nansen Office.

Fearing Nazi persecution, Austrian Jews gather at a foreign consulate in Vienna in the late 1930s, hoping to receive visas so they can leave the country. Both the Nansen International Office for Refugees and its sister organization, the High Commission on Refugees from Germany, aided Jews fleeing Nazi persecution in the years before World War II.

Nansen International Office for Refugees

FOUNDING

Created by the League of Nations in the fall of 1930; began operations on April 1, 1931, Geneva, Switzerland

HEADQUARTERS

Geneva, Switzerland

PURPOSE

Refugee resettlement

MAJOR ACCOMPLISHMENTS

During its eight-year existence (1931–39), resettled and gave financial and other assistance to more than 800,000 refugees; led support for the Refugee Convention of 1933

50,000 Armenians who were an unwelcome resident minority in Turkey. In another successful relocation effort, the organization persuaded the South American nation of Paraguay to accept 4,000 former residents of the Saar, a long-disputed European territory that was given to Germany in 1935.

The Nansen Office not only relocated refugees, however; its main responsibility was to help them settle in their new homelands by giving them financial aid, acting as a liaison between the refugees and the host nation governments, and assisting them with other problems that arose. The Nansen Office was self-supporting—funded by Fridtjof Nansen's estate and by a small surcharge on each Nansen passport.

In the fall of 1938 the Nansen International Office for Refugees was awarded that year's Nobel Peace Prize for its years of humanitarian assistance and its resettlement of some 800,000 refugees. The Nansen Office was also cited for the leading role it played in the adoption of the Refugee Convention of 1933, an international agreement signed by 14 nations that guaranteed basic human rights to refugees.

At its founding in 1930, the Nansen Office was set up to operate for 10

years. In 1933 an additional refugee organization, called the High Commission on Refugees from Germany, was established by the League of Nations to deal with the sudden rush of Jewish refugees who were fleeing persecution in Nazi Germany. By 1935 plans were under way to merge both of these refugee organizations into a single unit. This merger was finally completed on January 1, 1939, when the new organization, the High Commission for All Refugees under League of Nations Protection, opened its office in London, England.

The High Commission remained headquartered in London during World War II, which began in September 1939 and ended six years later. When its parent organization, the League of Nations, was dissolved in 1945 and replaced by the United Nations, a new refugee organization was created under UN auspices: the Office of the UN High Commissioner for Refugees. Nine years later, it also won the Nobel Peace Prize.

FURTHER READING

"Nansen International Office for Refugees." In *Nobel Prize Winners*. New York: H. W. Wilson, 1987.

International Committee of the Red Cross

1944

French prisoners of war in Germany receive Red Cross food parcels during World War II. These and other humanitarian efforts earned the Red Cross a second Nobel Peace Prize.

he International Committee of the Red Cross (ICRC), which received the 1917 Nobel Peace Prize for its efforts to aid prisoners of war during World War I (1914–18), greatly expanded its relief efforts in the following decade. The ICRC's first responsibility after the war ended was to assist international efforts—including those of the League of Nations—to repatriate (return to their homelands) millions of refugees who had fled their countries during the fighting. This was accomplished through the cooperation of many national Red Cross and Red Crescent societies, which had worked separately during the war. (Red Crescent was the name given to Red Cross societies in Muslim countries beginning in 1906.)

In 1919, with the encouragement and approval of the ICRC, these national Red Cross and Red Crescent societies from around the world joined together to form the League of Red Cross Societies. This new umbrella organization was created to encourage and coordinate the efforts of national Red Cross and Red Crescent societies in peacetime. The name "Red Cross" now comprised multiple organizations: the ICRC, the League of Red Cross Societies, and the many national Red Cross and Red Crescent societies. They became known collectively as the International Red Cross.

During the 1920s, the various Red Cross organizations turned their attention to peacetime humanitarian efforts. They began to provide relief for victims of natural disasters and gradually expanded their activities to include the teaching of first aid and accident prevention, water safety, nurses' training, and the maintenance of blood banks.

In Geneva, the ICRC focused on improving international guidelines for dealing with prisoners of war. It is credited with creating and marshaling support for the 1929 Geneva Convention, an agreement that specified guidelines for humane treatment of prisoners of war. The convention was signed by every major nation in the world except Japan and the Soviet Union. During the 1930s, the ICRC sponsored relief efforts in several regional conflicts, including the Italian-Ethiopian War and the Spanish Civil War.

In 1939, following the outbreak of World War II, the ICRC established the Central Prisoners of War Agency (CPWA). This was modeled on its World War I agency, IPRIA, and performed the same services, but on an even larger scale: keeping records on millions of prisoners, acting as a clearinghouse for messages between prisoners and their families, distributing gift parcels, and monitoring conditions in prison camps. CPWA workers even gained admission

The contents of a standard Red Cross food parcel distributed to U.S. prisoners of war during World War II. Such parcels were a welcome—and often lifesaving—addition to a meager prison diet.

to several Japanese camps, although Japan had refused to sign the 1929 convention.

Together with the League of Red Cross Societies, the ICRC delivered food and clothing in the war-torn countries of Europe. Despite strong opposition from the Nazi government, the ICRC was able to distribute relief packages in several German concentration camps. It also issued travel documents to more than 30,000 Jewish refugees escaping from Nazi persecution in German-occupied countries.

At the end of the war in 1945, the ICRC was named the winner of the 1944 Nobel Peace Prize for its humanitarian efforts on behalf of victims of the war. The citation commended the ICRC for holding "aloft the fundamental conceptions of the solidarity of the human race . . . and the need for true understanding and reconciliation, if peace is ever to be brought about."

Note: The International Committee of the Red Cross was awarded the Nobel Peace Prize a third time, in 1963. To read about its activities after World War II, please turn to pages 176–77.

FURTHER READING

Durand, André. *From Sarajevo to Hiroshima: History of the International Committee of the Red Cross*. Geneva: Henri Dunant Institute, 1984.

Epstein, Beryl, and Sam Epstein. *The Story of the International Red Cross*. New York: Nelson, 1963.

Gumpert, Martin. *Dunant: The Story of the Red Cross*. Oxford: Oxford University Press, 1938.

Joyce, James A. *Red Cross International and the Strategy of Peace*. New York: Oceana, 1959.

Willemin, Georges, and Roger Heacock. *The International Committee of the Red Cross*. Groningen: Martinus Nijhoff, 1984.

International Committee of the Red Cross

FOUNDERS

Henri Dunant and the Geneva Public Welfare Society

FOUNDING

October 1863
Geneva, Switzerland

HEADQUARTERS

Geneva, Switzerland

PURPOSE

Founded to assist the sick and wounded during wartime; after World War I expanded its efforts to caring for victims of natural disasters and to other humanitarian relief

MAJOR ACCOMPLISHMENTS, 1918–44

Helped repatriate millions of refugees after World War I; encouraged the creation of the League of Red Cross Societies; led effort to create the 1929 Prisoner of War Convention; sponsored relief efforts during the Italian-Ethiopian War (1935–36) and the Spanish Civil War (1936–39); established and directed the Central Prisoners of War Agency (CPWA) during World War II (1939–45)

Cordell Hull

1945

Cordell Hull, the winner of the 1945 Nobel Peace Prize, had already earned another distinction a year earlier: in 1944 he concluded nearly 12 years as U.S. Secretary of State, thus serving longer than anyone else in that cabinet post. Hull's efforts on behalf of international peace during those years made him known around the world and led him to become a Nobel winner. Those efforts, however, had been inspired decades earlier by his interest in Latin American affairs—an interest that was born when Hull served as a soldier in Cuba.

Hull's early life hardly prepared him to become a prominent statesman. He was born in near-poverty in a log cabin in rural Tennessee in 1871—some six years after the death of Abraham Lincoln, another American who came into the world in similar circumstances. The log cabin did not even belong to the Hull family; it had been rented by his father, a farmer who was trying to set up a lumber business. When they were old enough, Cordell and his four brothers began to work in the business, which gradually prospered.

Cordell Hull decided as a teenager, however, that he did not want to be a lumberman. He was doing well in the local schools he attended, and for a while he thought he would become a teacher. Hull briefly attended teacher-training schools in Tennessee, Kentucky, and Ohio in the late 1880s before deciding on a career in law and politics. He studied for five months at a small law institute in Tennessee, then worked as an apprentice at several law firms in and near Nashville while he became involved in local Democratic party politics.

Hull opened his own law practice in 1892, and that same year was elected to the Tennessee legislature, his first political office. He left his home state briefly in 1898 to serve as a captain with a volunteer military company during the Spanish-American War. Although the fighting had ended by the time Hull arrived in Cuba, he remained there for several months as part of the occupying forces. This brief episode in Hull's life apparently had a significant effect on him: as a quiet young man from the backwoods, he was forced to turn his attention to the outside world for the first time. Hull learned Spanish during his stay in Cuba, and he returned to Tennessee with the desire to play a larger role in his nation's political affairs.

Hull continued to practice law while remaining active in politics. He became a circuit court judge in 1903, and three years later he seized the opportunity to serve in the national government by running successfully for the U.S.

House of Representatives. Taking office in 1907, he served in the House for nearly two decades. Hull rose to prominence after the election of the Democratic party candidate, Woodrow Wilson, as President in 1912. During Wilson's two terms in office, Hull was a leading House supporter of the President's policies, in particular his various financial reform measures.

Following World War I (1914–18), when Wilson helped create the League of Nations as part of the Versailles Peace Treaty of 1919, Hull became the League's vigorous defender. He was therefore dismayed when the Senate rejected both the treaty and U.S. membership in the League. When the Democratic party lost the national elections in 1920, Hull resigned briefly from the House of Representatives to serve for several years as chairman of the Democratic National Committee, the party's governing organization.

Hull returned to the House in 1924, where he continued to concentrate on financial legislation. During his years in the House under Wilson, Hull had become convinced that a nation's economic policy and its foreign policy were intertwined. In particular, he firmly believed that war was caused by economic nationalism—by nations trying to gain supremacy over one another in international markets rather than learning to cooperate for mutual economic benefit. As a consequence of this belief, Hull had always opposed high tariffs—the taxes that a nation levied on goods that were imported from another nation—and he worked for the passage of fair international trading treaties.

In 1930 Hull realized a longtime dream when he was elected to the U.S. Senate. He did not serve out his six-year term, however, for in 1933 the newly elected Democratic President, Franklin D. Roosevelt, named Hull Secretary of State. Many people, in-

cluding Hull himself, were surprised by the appointment, because that cabinet post had been held in the past by men who were more experienced in international affairs. However, the United States and other industrialized countries around the world were in the grip of a major economic slump—what would later be called the Great Depression. It was already apparent that during the next decade, world affairs would be centered largely on economic issues—and Hull had already demonstrated that he had a clear understanding of international economics.

Hull proved to be an outstanding Secretary of State. Not only was he knowledgeable, but he also looked the part of a statesman—tall, silver-haired, with a dignified bearing and a manner of gentle but firm authority. One of his first actions in his new post was to carry out one of Roosevelt's major foreign policy objectives—the so-called Good Neighbor policy, which worked to strengthen ties between the United States and Latin American nations. Remembering his Cuban experience, Hull had been able to offer support from the sidelines when Woodrow Wilson pursued a similar policy toward Latin America; now he was in charge, and he fulfilled his role with enthusiasm.

He began by convening the seventh Pan-American Conference, held in Montevideo, Uruguay, in December 1933. Hull led the U.S. delegation to the conference, where he proclaimed his country's commitment to stay out of domestic affairs in Latin America. This proclamation had several immediate effects: U.S. troops, which were then occupying Haiti, were withdrawn, and the U.S. Congress ratified a new treaty with Cuba that ended North American intervention there.

Hull continued to pursue the Good Neighbor policy throughout the decade. In 1936 he led the U.S.

Cordell Hull served as U.S. Secretary of State longer than any man in history. His peacemaking accomplishments during his tenure included successsful efforts to establish the United Nations.

At the Dumbarton Oaks Conference, held in Washington, D.C., in 1944, Hull and representatives of three other Allied powers—Great Britain, China, and the Soviet Union—laid the groundwork for the creation of the United Nations.

delegation to the Conference for the Maintenance of Peace, an official gathering in Buenos Aires, Argentina, of representatives from western hemisphere nations. At this conference, held as war clouds began to gather over Europe, the participants pledged to consult one another before taking military action if hemispheric security was threatened.

Hull was also a leader of the eighth Pan-American Conference, held in Lima, Peru, in 1938. Germany had recently taken control over Austria, and war in Europe seemed closer than ever. At this conference, Hull proposed and led support for a resolution proclaiming that a threat to any republic in the Americas would be regarded as a threat to them all.

During World War II (1939–45), the attention of the United States in foreign affairs shifted from Latin America to Europe and the Pacific, where the war was being fought. Dividing up responsibility after the war began in 1939, Roosevelt concentrated on Europe and gave Hull much of the policymaking authority for Asian affairs. In the two years between the outbreak of the war and U.S. entry

into the conflict in 1941, Hull worked hard but without success to persuade Japan to end its ongoing war with China and its military actions in Indochina.

World War II signaled the final failure of the League of Nations, which had been founded two decades earlier to put an end to warfare for all time. Not long after this second international conflict erupted, Hull proposed that a new world organization—with the United States as an active participant—be created as soon as the war ended. Toward this end, he formed the Advisory Committee on Postwar Foreign Policy in 1941.

Hull—and many other observers—believed that the League of Nations had failed to win U.S. support because Wilson had made its acceptance a political issue. Hull was determined to acquire the backing of both major political parties for the new world organization that he proposed. He therefore invited both Democrats and Republicans to serve on the committee, and he encouraged committee discussions that focused on the goal rather than on party disagreements on foreign policy.

During the next few years, as the committee met periodically, different proposals for the new organization were discussed. Hull strongly supported a single international group rather than an alliance of regional groups, and his plan was eventually agreed upon. Under his leadership, the State Department drafted a document called the Charter of the United Nations. This document became the centerpiece of the U.S. proposal at the Dumbarton Oaks Conference, a gathering held in Washington, D.C., in October 1944 that formally proposed the establishment of the United Nations.

Cordell Hull

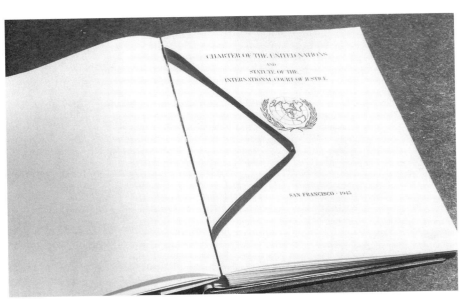

The Charter of the United Nations. A preliminary version of the charter was drafted by Hull and his staff from the U.S. State Department and adopted by delegates to the Dumbarton Oaks Conference.

BORN

October 2, 1871
Overton County, Tennessee

DIED

July 23, 1955
Bethesda, Maryland

EDUCATION

Briefly attended teacher-training schools in Tennessee, Kentucky, and Ohio, and a law institute in Tennessee

OCCUPATION

Attorney; statesman

MAJOR ACCOMPLISHMENTS

Member, U.S. House of Representatives (1907–31); member, U.S. Senate (1931–33); Secretary of State (1933–44); leading proponent of U.S. Good Neighbor policy with Latin America; led U.S. effort to establish the United Nations

Dumbarton Oaks was Cordell Hull's triumph—and it also signaled the end of his career. Now in his early 70s, he was in failing health, and illness forced his resignation as Secretary of State in late November 1944. Hull was named a delegate to the San Francisco Conference, held in the spring of 1945 to draw up the official UN Charter, but he was still ill and could not attend.

Later that year Cordell Hull was named the winner of the 1945 Nobel Peace Prize for his work on behalf of hemispheric cooperation, international trade, and the United Nations. Hull remained in frail health during the final decade of his life. He did manage, however, to write his memoirs, which were published in two volumes in 1948.

After Hull's wife, whom he had married in 1917, died in 1954, his health deteriorated rapidly. Following a series of strokes and heart attacks, he was hospitalized in the spring of 1955 at the U.S. naval hospital in Bethesda, Maryland. He died there several months later, at the age of 83.

FURTHER READING

Hinton, Harold B. *Cordell Hull: A Biography*. New York: Doubleday, Doran, 1942.

"Hull, Cordell." In *Dictionary of American Biography*. Supplement 5. New York: Scribners, 1977.

Hull, Cordell. *The Memoirs of Cordell Hull*. 2 vols. New York: Macmillan, 1948.

Emily
Greene Balch

John R. Mott

1946

W hen economist and social reformer Emily Greene Balch was named cowinner of the 1946 Nobel Peace Prize in her 80th year, the still-vigorous Balch was asked to explain how she was able to stay so active despite her age. In reply, she quoted a favorite saying of her grandfather's: "An old woman is as tough as a boiled owl."

Emily Greene Balch was "tough"—forceful and determined—even as a small child, but she also learned to support peaceful change at an early age. The daughter of a lawyer and his wife, she was born in 1867 in Jamaica Plain, Massachusetts, then a small community on the outskirts of Boston. Her family had been active abolitionists—opponents of slavery—before the Civil War, and her father had served for a time as an aide to Senator Charles Sumner of Massachusetts, a leading abolitionist and pacifist.

A major influence on Balch was the family's membership in the Unitarian Church. Unitarianism, a Protestant

Economist and social worker Emily Greene Balch began her long career as a peace activist when she attended the first International Congress of Women during World War I.

sect, had been founded in New England in the early 19th century. Unitarians believed strongly in social reform and in the duty of everyone to improve the lives of the less fortunate. They also believed in women's rights, and Balch grew up in an atmosphere that encouraged her to get as much education as she could.

After attending private primary and secondary schools, Balch enrolled in 1886 at the recently founded Bryn Mawr College, an institution for women near Philadelphia. Bryn Mawr was affiliated with the Society of Friends, or Quakers, a religious denomination that practiced pacifism, and the teachings of the Friends also influenced her. Balch completed the four-year curriculum in three years, majoring in Latin and Greek, and graduated with the first class in 1889.

At Bryn Mawr Balch had become interested in the work of Jacob Riis, a journalist who publicized slum conditions in American cities and urged reform. Inspired by Riis, she decided to do graduate work in social science. After studying privately for a while with a prominent American sociologist named Franklin H. Giddings, she enrolled at the University of Paris on a fellowship from Bryn Mawr. There she made a study of the French system of relief for the poor and attended classes in economics. Her first book, *Public Assistance of the Poor in France* (1893), was based on her work in Paris.

Balch returned to the United States in 1891 and settled in Boston, where she became a social worker with the Children's Aid Society. A year later, with her friend Vida Scudder, she helped found the Denison House Settlement, a community organization to serve the inner-city poor, and she served as head of the settlement in 1892–93. In Boston she became interested in the trade labor union movement, joined the American Federation of Labor, and cofounded the Women's

Trade Union League. In the early 1890s Balch also became active in the Consumers' League and helped draft a minimum-wage bill for presentation to the Massachusetts state legislature—the first such bill ever presented to an American legislative body.

Despite these accomplishments, Balch felt that she needed to do more in order to be "of use" to society. She decided to become a college teacher so that she could inspire other women to work for social improvement. Choosing economics as her field, Balch studied at the Harvard Annex (later Radcliffe College), the University of Chicago, and the University of Berlin, where she received a doctorate in social science in 1896. That fall she joined the economics faculty of Wellesley College, a women's institution near Boston, as an assistant instructor; seven years later she was named an associate professor. In 1913 Balch was appointed to a full professorship in economics, political science, and social science and became head of the department of economics and sociology.

Balch's friend Vida Scudder taught in the English department at Wellesley, and in her classes she emphasized social issues in literature. Students were often inspired by Scudder's lectures to enroll in Balch's courses, in order to learn more about the economic and political basis of social conditions. During more than 20 years of teaching at Wellesley, Balch became one of the most widely liked and respected members of the faculty.

In addition to her teaching career, Balch continued to work for social improvement. She served as a board member of the municipal child welfare agency in Boston and the city planning commission; she also served on the boards of state commissions on industrial education and immigration. Balch pursued her interest in immigration by traveling to Austria-Hungary in the early 1900s and studying the emigra-

Emily Greene Balch

BORN

January 8, 1867
Jamaica Plain, Massachusetts

DIED

January 9, 1961
Cambridge, Massachusetts

EDUCATION

B.A., Bryn Mawr College (1889); graduate study at the University of Paris (1890–91) and at the Harvard Annex (1893) and the University of Chicago (1895); Ph.D., University of Berlin (1896)

OCCUPATION

Economist; social reformer

MAJOR ACCOMPLISHMENTS

Professor of economics, Wellesley College; cofounder and longtime executive of the Women's International League for Peace and Freedom (WILPF)

U.S. delegates to the first International Congress of Women in 1915 included Jane Addams (front row, second from left), who helped organize the congress. Emily Greene Balch is on the far left in the third row, wearing a large hat with flowers.

tion patterns of Austro-Hungarians in the United States. Her second book, *Our Slavic Fellow Citizens* (1910), was a study of their communities in major American cities.

Balch had long been interested in the peace movement, and she became an active partipant in 1915 when she joined the American delegation, led by Jane Addams, to the International Congress of Women. Held at The Hague, the capital of the Netherlands, this peace congress met to propose ways to end the world war that had broken out in August 1914. Once again, Balch decided that she had found another appropriate outlet for her energies and interests: the cause of international pacifism. When the congress ended, Balch traveled with several other delegates to the Scandinavian countries and Russia to plead the cause of peace. Later, with Jane Addams and Alice Hamilton, she coauthored a book about the congress (*Women at the Hague*, 1915), and she also edited the congress's official proceedings.

After returning to the United States, Balch took a leave of absence from Wellesley to promote the pacifist

cause, and her efforts intensified after the United States entered the war in April 1917. While on leave, she contributed articles to the *Nation*, a leading liberal periodical, that expressed opposition to the war, compulsory military service, and legislation that restricted antiwar activities. She also participated in demonstrations that supported conscientious objectors—those who refused to serve in the military because they opposed war and who were usually imprisoned as a consequence.

Balch's political activities were looked upon with disapproval by the administrators of Wellesley, and in 1918 the college's board of trustees fired her for "her outspoken views on pacifism and economics." Balch was apparently not too disturbed by this event, for it meant that she was now able to devote her full attention to the peace cause. That same year she published her second book, *Approaches to the Great Settlement*, a discussion of peace terms then being proposed for ending the war. British peace activist Norman Angell wrote the foreword to the book.

In 1919, as a delegate to the second International Congress of Women, held in Zurich, Switzerland, Balch helped found an important pacifist organization, the Women's International League for Peace and Freedom (WILPF), which was led for many years by Jane Addams. Working much of the time from WILPF headquarters in Geneva, Switzerland, Balch served as the organization's treasurer until 1922.

WILPF continued to be the focus of Balch's pacifist activities for the rest of her life. Her commitment to pacifism had been reinforced further in 1921, when she left the Unitarian church to become a member of the Society of Friends. During the next two decades, Balch served in various administrative positions with WILPF. In these roles she worked closely with the League of Nations, which WILPF strongly supported, by helping the League Secretariat to organize conferences on specific international problems, including disarmament.

As a representative of WILPF, Balch earned wide recognition when she made an investigative study of Haiti, long occupied by the U.S. Marines. Her subsequent report offered recommendations to improve conditions there that were later adopted by the U.S. government. Balch's numerous efforts on behalf of WILPF also included the establishment of international summer schools, held on college campuses, to promote peace. During the 1930s, she aided dozens of Jewish refugees fleeing persecution in Nazi Germany and helped to resettle them in the United States.

Perhaps Balch's most important role at WILPF, however, was an unofficial one: in every activity that she undertook, Balch earned a reputation as a reconciler, someone who could resolve differences that arose among members from different regions around the world. By working cooperatively, Balch believed that she was creating a model for international cooperation—and ultimately lasting peace.

Although Balch initially opposed World War II, which began in September 1939, she departed from her pacifist views to support U.S. entry into the war in December 1941, after the Japanese attack on Pearl Harbor. She continued, however, to work for international peace through WILPF. With this goal in mind, she developed proposals for postwar internationalization of defense bases, the polar regions, and major world waterways. Beginning in 1942, she helped resettle many Japanese Americans who had been detained in holding camps by the U.S. government. In 1944, again on behalf of WILPF, Balch drew up a series of peace proposals and presented them to President Franklin D. Roosevelt.

In August 1946, a year after the war ended, Balch led the U.S. delegation to WILPF's 10th international conference, held in Luxembourg. Three months later she was named cowinner of the 1946 Nobel Peace Prize—15 years after her friend Jane Addams had won the award. As the second American woman to win the Peace Prize, Balch was cited for her "lifelong, indefatigable work for the cause of peace." Interestingly, Balch had been strongly recommended for the award by the president of Wellesley College; 11 years earlier, the college and Balch had become reconciled when she was asked to speak at Wellesley's Armistice Day ceremonies.

Like Emily Greene Balch, John R. Mott, who shared the 1946 Nobel Peace Prize with her, became committed to pacifism as a consequence of his religious beliefs. Born in 1865 in rural New York State, Mott and his two older sisters moved with their parents two years later to Postville, Iowa. There his father became a prosperous lumber dealer and was later elected mayor.

When John Mott was 13, the family was converted to Methodism by a traveling evangelist. As part of their religious faith, Methodists believed in working hard and helping their fellow human beings, and these values were stressed in the Mott household. Mott's parents also valued education, and at the age of 16 John was sent to Upper Iowa University, a Methodist preparatory school and college in nearby Fayette.

Mott excelled there in his classwork, became a champion debater, and showed an outstanding talent in dramatics. His professors encouraged him to pursue a career in law and politics and suggested that he transfer to a more prestigious university in the eastern United States. Mott chose Cornell, in his native New York State, and enrolled there in 1885 as a member of the sophomore class.

As the head of the American and World YMCAs, and cofounder of the World Council of Churches, John Mott was an internationally known advocate of peace.

Italian prisoners of war play a game of volleyball organized by YMCA workers during World War II. Like the Red Cross, the YMCA provided aid to victims on both sides of the conflict.

At Cornell Mott was an outstanding student and athlete, but not especially religious. Midway through his first year there, however, he had an experience that changed his life. In January 1886 he decided to attend a lecture by J. K. Studd, who had become famous as a cricket player at Cambridge University in England. Studd was touring American colleges and making inspirational speeches at the invitation of Dwight Moody, a leading American religious leader. Mott arrived at the lecture hall at the end of the speech—just in time to hear Studd's last words: "Seekest thou great things for thyself? Seek them not. Seek ye first the Kingdom of God."

Convinced that these words were meant for him to hear, Mott returned to his dormitory and spent a sleepless night. The next day, following a personal meeting with Studd, he decided to pursue a career in religion. He began to study the Bible and visited prisoners in the local jail to share his faith with them. Long a member of the YMCA (the Young Men's Christian Association), a Protestant social and religious organization that promoted Christian fellowship and public service, Mott became active in the Cornell chapter.

In the summer of 1886, Mott represented Cornell at the first Christian Student Conference, a gathering of several hundred young men from U.S. and Canadian colleges that had been organized by Dwight Moody. Inspired by the conference, he returned to Cornell to become president of the campus YMCA. As a result of his efforts, membership increased threefold, making the Cornell chapter the largest student Y in the world.

Mott graduated from Cornell in 1888 with two bachelor's degrees, one in philosophy and the other in history and political science. He was also elected to Phi Beta Kappa, the national scholastic honor society. Following graduation, Mott agreed to serve for one year as student secretary of the YMCA's International Committee. However, he enjoyed the work so much—traveling to college campuses and helping student leaders plan Y-related activities—that he remained in the job until 1915, a total of 27 years.

During this time, Mott became known internationally for his activities on behalf of Christian evangelism, a movement that stressed personal religious conversion, and ecumenism, an international effort to unite the various Christian denominations. A born organizer, Mott believed that his life's work lay, in his words, in "weaving together Christian forces all over the world." One of his first actions on behalf of that goal was the founding in 1893 of the Foreign Missions Conference of North America, an organization that united and coordinated the activities of Protestant missionary groups throughout the North American continent; Mott served as an executive of this group until the early 1940s.

In 1895 Mott cofounded the World's Student Christian Federation at a conference in Sweden and served as its general secretary for two years. He remained active in the federation until the mid-1920s, and during this time organized national student religious movements throughout the world whose membership eventually totaled more than 300,000 men and women.

Another major milestone in Mott's professional life occurred in 1910, when he was chosen to preside over the World Missionary Conference, held in Edinburgh, Scotland. Following the conference, he remained active in its so-called continuation committee, formed to organize future world missionary conferences, and later served as the committee's leader. In this capacity he traveled throughout the Far East, organizing missionary councils in every major Asian country. When the continuation committee became the International Missionary Council in 1921, Mott became its chairman and served in that post until 1942, when he was named honorary chairman.

Beginning in the late 1890s, Mott also helped reactivate the Student Volunteer Movement for Foreign Missions, another department of the YMCA, and served as chairman of its executive committee until 1928. In this capacity Mott oversaw the recruitment of more than 10,000 U.S. and Canadian student volunteers to serve as Protestant missionaries abroad. Mott held other offices in the American YMCA as well, including the general secretaryship from 1915 to 1928. Two years earlier, he had also been named head of the World YMCA, and he remained in that post until his retirement in 1947.

During both World War I (1914–18) and World War II (1939–45), the YMCA was active in war relief efforts, and Mott played a major role in that work. During World War I, he served as general secretary of the National War Work Council and led the United War Work Campaign, which raised nearly $200 million for war relief. He also traveled to Russia as part of a diplomatic peace mission. Mott received the Distinguished Service Medal from President Woodrow Wilson for these various peace-related efforts, as well as awards from two dozen other countries. After the war, he attended the Paris Peace Conference in 1919 to make a plea for religious freedom.

During World War II, despite his advanced age, Mott led several fund-raising campaigns to support various Y-sponsored relief efforts, including a program for prisoners of war. He also led American efforts during the war years to establish what later became the World Council of Churches.

When John Mott was named cowinner of the 1946 Nobel Peace Prize, he was cited for being "a tireless fighter in the service of Christ, opening young minds to the light which he thinks can lead the world to peace and bring men together in understanding and goodwill."

Mott was the author of 16 books on religious topics, published between 1897 and 1947. In addition to his numerous honors from governments throughout the world, Mott received honorary degrees from more than a dozen universities. In 1948, when the World Council of Churches was formed, Mott was named its honorary president.

Mott was married in 1891 and had four children by his first wife; following her death in 1952 he remarried. He died at his retirement home in Orlando, Florida, in January 1955 at the age of 89.

FURTHER READING

"Balch, Emily Greene." In *Dictionary of American Biography*, Supplement 7. New York: Scribners, 1981.

Hopkins, Charles H. *John R. Mott, 1865–1955: A Biography*. Grand Rapids, Mich.: Eerdmans, 1979

Mathews, Basil. *John R. Mott: World Citizen*. New York: Harper, 1934.

"Mott, John R." In *Dictionary of American Biography*, Supplement 5. New York: Scribners, 1977.

Randall, Mercedes M. *Improper Bostonian: Emily Greene Balch*. New York: Twayne, 1964.

John R. Mott

BORN
May 25, 1865
Livingston Manor, New York

DIED
January 31, 1955
Orlando, Florida

EDUCATION
Earned two bachelor's degrees at Cornell University (1888)

OCCUPATION
Religious leader

MAJOR ACCOMPLISHMENTS
Founder, Foreign Missions Conference of North America; cofounder, World's Student Christian Federation; chairman, International Missionary Council; head of the American and World YMCAs; cofounder, World Council of Churches

American Friends Service Committee

Friends Service Council

1947

I n 1947 the Nobel Peace Prize Committee decided to present that year's award to two separate organizations—one American, the other British—with a common origin: the American Friends Service Committee and the Friends Service Council. Both of these groups were social service organizations that had been founded by Quakers—members of a religious denomination called the Society of Friends. And that denomination itself had a long history of working on behalf of peace, going back to its founding three centuries earlier.

The Society of Friends grew out of the beliefs of a simple English shoemaker named George Fox. Born in 1624, Fox developed a strong interest in religion as a child. In his teens, he became increasingly troubled by the wide gulf that he saw between the teachings of Christianity and the lives of those who called themselves Christians. Fox believed that every person had an "inner light" of divinity, and that if people became aware of that inner light, they could call it forth and thus allow God to direct their lives. In so doing, they would be able to carry out the teachings of Christ, in particular the Christian commandment to love one's fellow men and women.

In 1643, at the age of 19, Fox began to preach his philosophy, which emphasized brotherhood and equality and renounced warfare and violence. He soon attracted many followers, and their numbers grew in spite of persecution by other Protestants. In 1668 Fox established his movement as a separate denomination, which he called the Society of Friends. Opponents poked fun at the group by calling them "Quakers" because of the rocking movement that some of them made during their religious gatherings, called "meetings." However, the term gradually came into general use and was eventually used by members themselves.

In the late 1600s, Quakers came to the New World, where they settled in several American colonies. A Quaker named William Penn founded his own colony, Pennsylvania, and its principal city, Philadelphia, which means "City of Brotherly Love." Philadelphia soon became the center of Quakerism in the New World, although Quakers also settled in the other 12 colonies.

From the time of its founding, the Society of Friends encouraged its members to practice their philosophy of brotherhood and equality by helping anyone in need. Following the teachings of George Fox, the Society of Friends also opposed slavery. As the abolitionist movement—the movement to end slavery—grew in America in the 18th century, Quakers throughout the colonies became its most vigorous supporters. After the Revolution, as slavery continued in

American Friends Service Committee workers unload building materials in France in 1946. In the aftermath of World War II, AFSC and Friends Service Council volunteers helped to rebuild many bombed-out areas of Europe.

American Friends Service Committee

FOUNDERS
Members of the Society of Friends (Quakers) of Philadelphia

FOUNDING
1917
Philadelphia, Pennsylvania

HEADQUARTERS
Philadelphia, Pennsylvania

PURPOSE
Initially founded to offer service alternatives to combat during World War I (1914–18); later expanded its efforts to include various humanitarian activities and to promote peace in the world

MAJOR ACCOMPLISHMENTS
Provided major humanitarian relief in France during World War I, and in Germany and Russia after the war; aided victims of Spanish Civil War (1936–39); rescued Jews from Nazi Germany; during World War II, sponsored work camps for conscientious objectors in the United States; after the war, aided refugees throughout the world

the new United States, Quakers continued to protest through public meetings, numerous publications, and appearances before the national and state legislative bodies. These protests continued until the Emancipation Proclamation, issued by President Abraham Lincoln in 1863, freed American slaves.

Quakers in Great Britain conducted a similar campaign against slavery, which succeeded earlier there than in the United States: the British government banned slavery throughout its empire in 1807. Beginning in the late 1700s, British and American Quakers became involved in various forms of social service, establishing retreats for the insane, working for the improvement of prison conditions, and feeding the hungry. They also supported woman suffrage—the right of women to vote—and opposed capital punishment. British Quakers played a major role in aiding Irish famine victims in the 1840s, and a decade later, during the Crimean War (1853–56), they brought medical supplies and helped wounded soldiers on the battlefield.

In 1868 British Quakers founded the Friends Foreign Mission Associa-

tion (FFMA) to coordinate and expand their overseas humanitarian activities by sending Quaker missionaries to Asia and Africa to establish schools and hospitals. Two years later, in 1870, British Quakers formed the Friends War Victims Relief Committee, which brought aid to towns in France and Germany hard hit by the Franco-Prussian War.

In both the United States and Great Britain, the Society of Friends advocated pacifism. In 1828, Quakers had helped to found the first pacifist organization in North America, the American Peace Society. British Quakers were active in the peace movement that developed in Europe during the second half of the 19th century.

When the United States entered World War I in April 1917, a small group of Quakers in Philadelphia publicly offered to serve the government in a nonmilitary capacity. They declared their willingness to participate "in any constructive work in which we can conscientiously serve humanity." Under the leadership of Rufus M. Jones, a philosophy professor at Haverford College, a Quaker institution near

AFSC worker Roger Craven talks with a family in St. Nazaire, France, living in a house built by Quaker volunteers.

Philadelphia, the group established permanent headquarters in that city and called themselves the American Friends Service Committee (AFSC).

Jones received permission from President Woodrow Wilson to send AFSC members to France to perform various kinds of relief work. From the summer of 1917 until the war's end in November 1918, more than 100 AFSC volunteers worked side by side with French civilians. They built and staffed a surgical hospital and a tuberculosis sanitarium, assisted at a maternity hospital, planted and harvested crops, joined factory assembly lines, built housing, and helped to evacuate and treat war victims.

After the war, the AFSC volunteers went to defeated Germany, where they distributed food and clothing. In 1919 the AFSC was given specific re-

sponsibility by the American government to raise funds for and to administer a program to feed needy German children; after it was successfully established in Germany, the program was extended to Poland, Serbia, and Austria. Under the leadership of Rufus Jones, the AFSC also aided victims of a widespread postwar famine in Russia; between December 1921 and April 1923 AFSC volunteers provided food every day for more than 50,000 Russians.

While the war was still being fought, a British Quaker named Carl Heath had proposed the establishment of peace centers throughout the world. His plan was adopted by a group of London Quakers, who in 1919 founded the Council for International Service (CIS) to accomplish that goal. Working with the American Friends Service

Committee, the CIS set up Quaker International Centers throughout Europe to promote the cause of peace. These centers performed varied services, depending on where they were located. The activities of the Quaker International Center in Geneva, where the League of Nations had its headquarters, included assisting the League in its efforts to help refugees.

In 1927 the Friends Foreign Mission Association (FFMA) and the Council for International Service (CIS) merged to become the Friends Service Council (FSC). The FSC established its headquarters in London and announced that it would concentrate on what it called "the ministry of reconciliation." Under the FSC, Quakers worked to help refugees, persecuted minorities, and political prisoners in various European countries. Quaker International Centers continued to perform their services under the FSC.

During the 1920s, the American Friends Service Committee reorganized itself into four divisions—Foreign, Interracial, Peace, and Home Service— and offered peacetime humanitarian service throughout the world in the years that followed. During the Spanish Civil War (1936–39), AFSC volunteers offered aid to victims on both sides of the conflict. When persecution of Jews in Nazi Germany intensified in 1938, Rufus Jones led an AFSC delegation to Berlin, where they persuaded German officials to allow many Jews to emigrate to the United States and other countries.

When the United States entered World War II in December 1941, Quakers and other pacifists registered as so-called conscientious objectors to avoid having to fight. The government barred conscientious objectors from serving abroad during the war, so the AFSC established public service camps for them throughout the United States. There they worked as foresters, firefighters, and soil conservationists. Dur-

Rufus Jones (1863–1948), a Quaker and a college philosophy professor, founded the American Friends Service Committee in Philadelphia in 1917 to offer humanitarian aid to victims of World War I. He led the organization for many years, retiring in 1944 at the age of 81.

ing the war the AFSC was also allowed by the government to sponsor relief efforts in countries not occupied by the Axis powers (Germany and Japan and their allies). After the war ended in 1945, the AFSC aided refugees throughout the world, distributing food, clothing, and medical supplies.

In Great Britain, the Friends Service Council reactivated the Friends War Victims Relief Committee in 1940; the name was changed to the Friends Relief Service three years later. From 1940 until 1948 this relief group operated in France, the Netherlands, Greece, Germany, Austria, and Poland, as well as Great Britain, offering various humanitarian services: volunteers drove ambulances, distributed food and clothing, and established refugee camps.

For their humanitarian efforts, the American Friends Service Committee and the Friends Service Council shared

Friends Service Council

FOUNDERS
Members of the Society of Friends (Quakers) of London

FOUNDING
1927
London, England

HEADQUARTERS
London, England

PURPOSE
To coordinate missionary and relief work conducted by the British Society of Friends, principally through Quaker International Centers and the Friends War Victims Relief Committee

MAJOR ACCOMPLISHMENTS
Prior to World War II, aided refugees, persecuted minorities, and political prisoners throughout Europe, and sponsored peace education programs; from 1940 to 1948, offered major humanitarian assistance in Western Europe

A Friends Service Council worker distributes food to refugee children in Marseilles, France, in 1945.

the 1947 Nobel Peace Prize. In the citation accompanying the joint award, the Society of Friends—the parent of both organizations—was singled out for praise: "The Quakers have shown us that it is possible to translate into action what lies deep in the hearts of many: compassion for others and the desire to help them."

Today both the AFSC and the FSC continue their humanitarian efforts throughout the world. As representatives of these organizations, thousands of volunteers work to feed the hungry, heal the sick, improve public health, defend human rights, and bring relief to victims of both warfare and natural disasters. They also continue their historic commitment to the establishment of world peace by supporting disarmament and the international peace movement, and through the sponsorship of major peace education programs.

FURTHER READING

Bowden, James. *The History of the Society of Friends in America.* 1850–54. 2 vols. Reprint, New York: Arno, 1972.

Forbes, J. *The Quaker Star Under Seven Flags.* Philadelphia: University of Pennsylvania Press, 1962.

Ingle, H. Larry. *First Among Friends: George Fox and the Creation of Quakerism.* Oxford and New York: Oxford University Press, 1994.

Isichei, Elizabeth A. *Victorian Quakers.* Oxford: Oxford University Press, 1970.

Jones, Mary Hoxie. *Swords into Ploughshares: An Account of the American Friends Service Committee, 1917–1937.* New York: Macmillan, 1937.

"Jones, Rufus Matthew." In *Dictionary of American Biography.* Supplement 4. New York: Scribners, 1974.

Jones, Rufus M. *A Small-Town Boy.* New York: Macmillan, 1941.

Yarrow, C. H. M. *Quaker Experiences in International Conciliation.* New Haven: Yale University Press, 1978.

Yolen, Jane. *Friend: The Story of George Fox and the Quakers.* New York: Seabury, 1972.

John Boyd Orr

1949

"T here can be no peace in the world so long as a large proportion of the population lack the necessities of life and believe that a change of the political and economic system will make them available. World peace must be based on world plenty."

With those words, Sir John Boyd Orr, fellow of the Royal Society, recipient of the Military Cross, member of the Distinguished Service Order and of the French Legion of Honor, accepted his latest honor, the 1949 Nobel Peace Prize. Boyd Orr was a scientist, with degrees in chemistry and medicine, who had spent nearly 40 years working in the field of nutrition. But he was also a humanitarian who devoted his career to finding ways of feeding millions of hungry people. A well-fed world, Boyd Orr firmly believed, was the basis for lasting peace.

Boyd Orr did not develop an interest in nutrition, however, until he was 30. And he had little curiosity about

Scientist John Boyd Orr, shown here with his wife, improved the diets of millions worldwide, working first with the League of Nations and later with its successor, the UN.

science until he was nearly 20. In fact, as a child he seemed to resist education. Born in 1880 in Kilmaurs, Scotland, where his father owned a small quarry, John Boyd Orr and his six brothers and sisters received their early lessons at home from their mother and grandmother. At the age of 13, Boyd Orr enrolled at a nearby boarding school but was such an indifferent student that he was asked to leave. Back home, he spent the rest of his teenage years working in his father's quarry while reluctantly attending classes at the local village school. During this time he became interested in books and began to read extensively.

The Boyd Orrs were very religious—the family belonged to the Free Church of Scotland, an evangelical sect—and when John, now 19, said that he wanted to do something else with his life besides work in a stone quarry, they suggested a career in the ministry. Taking their advice, he applied for and received a scholarship to study theology at the University of Glasgow, and enrolled there in 1899.

One day during his first year at Glasgow, Boyd Orr wandered into a zoology class by chance. The professor was lecturing on the theories of Charles Darwin, the 19th-century scientist who had proposed a revolutionary theory of evolution. Boyd Orr was so fascinated by the lecture that he enrolled in several science courses—and did so well in them that he changed his career plans and decided to become a science teacher.

After completing his university studies with a concentration in chemistry in the early 1900s, Boyd Orr taught in slum areas in and around Glasgow for four years to satisfy the terms of his university scholarship. He

was appalled by the physical condition of his students, who were frequently ill and obviously malnourished, and that experience led him to study medicine.

After Boyd Orr received his medical degree with honors from the University of Glasgow in 1914, he accepted an appointment as director of the Animal Nutrition Research Laboratory, which had just been founded at the University of Aberdeen. Finding that the facility was limited, he began a large-scale fund-raising campaign to build a large laboratory as World War I was breaking out in the late summer of 1914. Boyd Orr took a leave of absence and volunteered for service in the British army as a doctor. During the next four years, he served in France with distinction and won several prestigious decorations, including the Military Cross and the Distinguished Service award.

When the war ended in the fall of 1918, Boyd Orr went back to Aberdeen. There he resumed fund-raising and eventually built a large laboratory, together with an extensive science complex that included the Rowett Research Institute for nutritional studies; the Strathcona House Nutrition Center, which drew nutritionists from around the world; a library; and an experimental farm. During the next decade, Boyd Orr's extensive studies at the Rowett Institute on nutrition in farm and dairy animals made him widely known.

Boyd Orr also investigated human nutrition, in particular the diets of several tribes in Africa that he studied in 1925, and he became convinced that the discoveries being made about animals at Rowett could be used to improve the health of human beings. He undertook an extensive study of cow's milk—which at that time was not widely drunk by the British population—and proved that children who included milk in their daily diets had considerably better health than those who did not. Boyd Orr's findings led the British government to pass legislation that provided free or inexpensive milk to all schoolchildren.

Boyd Orr continued his studies of human nutrition during the 1930s and found evidence that a large portion of the British population—more than half—was unable to afford an adequate diet and that 10 percent of the population was severely malnourished. He discussed those findings in his book *Food, Health, and Income,* published in 1936, which also urged the British government to adopt a national food program. During this time Boyd Orr also served on the League of Nations Technical Commission on Nutrition, where he helped draft a list of international dietary standards and worked on a proposal to bring worldwide agricultural production into closer harmony with nutritional needs.

Following the outbreak of World War II in September 1939, Boyd Orr began work on a book called *Feeding the People in War Time.* Coauthored with David Lubbock and published the following year, the book described simple and inexpensive diets based on foods produced at home. It also outlined a food policy for the government that included rationing, price controls, and the regulation of agricultural production. The book was widely read by the British public, and many of its proposals were adopted by the British government.

Boyd Orr made two visits to the United States during the war. In 1942 he met with U.S. Vice President Henry Wallace and other government officials in Washington, D.C., to discuss the development of a world food policy. A year later he attended a conference on "Freedom from Want" hosted by President Franklin D. Roosevelt in Hot Springs, Virginia, and attended by representatives from other Allied nations—those nations, including Great Britain, France, and the United States, that were fighting Nazi Germany in the war. Boyd Orr was not an official British delegate, however, because the government did not agree with some of his proposals for international regulation of agricultural production and trade. The government feared that the adoption of such proposals might hurt Great Britain economically.

Boyd Orr retired from the Rowett Research Institute in 1945, the same year that the war ended. He was then elected to a seat in Parliament as a representative of all the universities of Scotland. At this time he also became rector of the University of Glasgow.

In the fall of 1945, Boyd Orr attended a meeting in Quebec of the newly founded Food and Agriculture Organization (FAO), an agency of the United Nations, as an unofficial adviser to the head of the British delegation, Philip J. Noel-Baker. At the invitation of Canadian statesman Lester B. Pearson, Boyd Orr addressed the conference and made a strong plea for the new agency to have broad authority. Although he had assumed that the speech would not be well received, the delegates were impressed, and Boyd Orr was chosen unanimously to serve as the first director-general of the FAO.

During his years in office, Boyd Orr led the FAO's development into a major arm of the UN. His greatest accomplishment was the establishment of

John Boyd Orr

BORN
September 23, 1880
Kilmaurs, Scotland

DIED
June 25, 1971
Brechin, Scotland

EDUCATION
Ch.B. (1902), M.B. (1912), M.D. (1914), D.Sci. (1920), University of Glasgow

OCCUPATION
Scientist; educator

MAJOR ACCOMPLISHMENTS
Founded the Rowett Research Institute, University of Aberdeen; member of Parliament; director-general, UN Food and Agriculture Organization; author of numerous books and articles on nutrition, food distribution, and agricultural production

the International Emergency Food Council, which prevented widespread famine from occurring in Europe in the difficult postwar years by coordinating food distribution and imposing rationing. While in office, he also worked—without success—for the establishment of a so-called world food board, under UN auspices, to prevent widespread hunger as the world's population rapidly increased.

After he left office in 1948, Boyd Orr continued to call for the creation of a "food board," and in numerous speeches and articles he asked the more developed nations to take responsibility for ending world hunger. On his frequent speechmaking trips through Europe, Boyd Orr also advocated the creation of a permanent world government that would have the authority to prevent war. Many countries, including his own, were hostile to his proposals because they threatened national sovereignty. One country that responded positively to Boyd Orr was India, where he served in 1949 as an adviser to the government on agricultural development and food distribution.

John Boyd Orr's work "to free mankind from want," which "clearly paves the way for peace"—in the words of the Nobel citation—earned him the 1949 Peace Prize. This was one of many awards that Boyd Orr received in his lifetime. Knighted by King George V in 1935, he was made a peer by King George VI in 1948. Boyd Orr was also a fellow of the Royal Society, a member of the French Legion of Honor, and an honorary member of the New York Academy of Sciences and the American Public Health Association, which honored him with its Lasker Award for distinguished service to humanity. In addition, he received more than a dozen honorary degrees from universities around the world.

For more than a decade after receiving the Nobel Prize, Boyd Orr continued to be active in the fight against world hunger. He helped Pakistan set up a food distribution program in 1951, attended an economic conference in Moscow as a British delegate the following year, and later toured China and Cuba. He also took part in several scientific and economic exchanges with countries in Eastern Europe.

A frequent collaborator with Boyd Orr in his work was his wife, Elizabeth Callum Boyd Orr, whom he married in 1915. The couple had three children; their only son was killed in World War II.

Boyd Orr retired from professional life in the 1960s but remained physically active at his home in rural Scotland. He also wrote several more books, including a volume of memoirs, *As I Recall*, published in 1966. (During his lifetime, 16 books by Boyd Orr—two of them coauthored by him—were published.) For exercise he loved to take long walks in the countryside and to participate in the sport of curling, and he also liked to perform traditional Scottish dances. Boyd Orr died in June 1971, several months before his 91st birthday.

FURTHER READING

Boyd Orr, John. *As I Recall*. New York: Doubleday, 1967.

Hambidge, Gove. *The Story of FAO*. New York: Van Nostrand, 1955.

Lamartine Yates, Paul. *So Bold an Aim: Ten Years of International Cooperation Toward Freedom from Want*. Rome: Food and Agriculture Organization, 1955.

Ralph J. Bunche

1950

Diplomat Ralph Bunche was the first African American to win the Nobel Peace Prize. He earned the award for his efforts to achieve peace between Israelis and Arabs in the Middle East.

W hen 23-year-old Ralph J. Bunche headed east from Los Angeles in the late summer of 1927, the family members, friends, and other well-wishers who gathered at the train station to see him off had reason to be proud. In fact, they were so proud of him that they had raised $1,000 to help him with living expenses as he began his first year of graduate study at Harvard University, in Cambridge, Massachusetts. They knew that Bunche, an outstanding student and athlete who had recently graduated with highest honors from the University of California at Los Angeles, had a distinguished fu-

During the Arab-Israeli War in 1948, United Nations mediator Ralph Bunche meets with UN officials during a break in negotiations between the two sides in the conflict.

ture ahead of him—if only he could continue to overcome the racial prejudice that kept most African-Americans from personal achievement.

Ralph Bunche, the grandson of a slave, fulfilled his supporters' dreams, and his own, by becoming an outstanding educator and statesman. He also became the first black man to win the Nobel Peace Prize.

Ralph Johnson Bunche was born in Detroit, Michigan, in 1904 to a poor barber and his wife. When Ralph was 10, he and his younger sister moved with their parents to Albuquerque, New Mexico, because a doctor had recommended a drier climate for his ailing mother. However, both parents died less than two years later, and the two children went to live with their maternal grandmother in Los Angeles.

"Nana" Johnson ran a strict but affectionate household, and she made sure that her grandson attended both church and school and did his homework. Her attention was repaid: Ralph Bunche graduated from high school in 1922 at the top of his class. With scholarship assistance, he enrolled at UCLA. There he became an outstanding student and athlete while working as a janitor, carpet layer, and busboy. He also excelled in debate, which sparked his interest in current affairs. Majoring in international relations, Bunche graduated with highest honors in 1927.

After a year of graduate study at Harvard University, Bunche earned a master's degree in government. He then began his teaching career at Howard University, an all-black institution in Washington, D.C., where he rose from the rank of instructor to tenured professor and chairman of the political science department in nine years. In 1932–34 he was on leave from Howard while he studied for a doctorate in government at Harvard. For his dissertation—a comparative study of Dahomey, a West African French colony, and French Togoland, a country administered by the League of Nations—Bunche traveled to Africa with the aid of a small fellowship. In 1934 the dissertation earned him both the Ph.D. and a prize for the most outstanding essay in the social sciences written at Harvard that year.

In the mid-1930s, Bunche took another leave from Howard when he received a fellowship from the Social Science Research Council to continue his study of colonialism. The fellowship enabled Bunche to do research at several universities, including the University of Capetown in South Africa. During this period he wrote a pamphlet called A World View of Race (1936) that was widely read, and he served as codirector of a race relations institute at Swarthmore College. Beginning in 1928 and continuing into the 1940s, Bunche also wrote numerous articles for professional and popular journals on race relations and colonialism. Following a trip around the world to study colonial conditions, he took another leave from Howard to join the staff of the Carnegie Corporation, a public policy research institution in New York City, in 1938.

During his two years on the Carnegie staff, Bunche served as the principal aide to a prominent Swedish sociologist named Gunnar Myrdal. At that time Myrdal was doing research for a book on racial prejudice against black Americans, and Bunche accom-panied him on his travels around the country. In more than a few instances, Bunche experienced discrimination personally on these travels, and he and Myrdal were literally run out of several towns in the South, where race prejudice was especially strong. (The resulting book, An American Dilemma, was published in 1944 and is considered a classic study of prejudice.)

Bunche returned to Howard in 1940. A year later, when the United States entered World War II, Bunche tried to enlist in the military. When he was rejected because of a physical disability, he took another leave of absence from Howard and offered his services to the U.S. government. Bunche was assigned to the staff of the Office of the Coordinator of Information— later renamed the Office of Strategic Services (OSS)—as a policy analyst for Africa and the Far East.

In 1944 Bunche transferred to the staff of the State Department as an expert on colonial problems. He later served in the department as a specialist on Africa and in 1945 became deputy head of the Division of Dependent Area Affairs, a position he held until 1947. For part of this time he was acting head of the division—the first black person to hold that office.

During this period Bunche attended several important international gatherings as an adviser to the U.S. delegation, including the founding conference of the United Nations in San Francisco in 1945. A year earlier, Bunche had helped draw up a part of the United Nations Charter that concerned non-self-governing and trusteeship territories. In the spring of 1946, on leave from the State Department, Bunche became director of the Trusteeship Division of the UN Secretariat, which he had helped to set up.

Ralph J. Bunche

BORN
August 7, 1904
Detroit, Michigan

DIED
December 9, 1971
New York City

EDUCATION
B.A., international relations, University of California, Los Angeles (1927); M.A. (1928), Ph.D. (1934), government, Harvard University

OCCUPATION
Educator; statesman

MAJOR ACCOMPLISHMENTS
Instructor and later professor of political science, Howard University (1928–41); principal negotiator, United Nations Palestine Commission (1948–49); under secretary-general, United Nations (1967–71)

During 1947 Bunche worked closely with the UN Special Committee on Palestine, a Middle Eastern territory under UN supervision. After a lengthy study, the committee recommended that the territory be partitioned into Jewish and Arab states, and Bunche was largely responsible for drafting the committee report. In December 1947 he was named principal secretary of the UN Palestine Commission, which was to oversee the partition of the territory. Conflict between Arabs and Israelis broke out several months later, following the establishment of the nation of Israel, and the United Nations appointed Count Folke Bernadotte of Sweden to mediate the dispute, with Bunche acting as his assistant. When Bernadotte was assassinated by an Israeli terrorist in September 1948, the UN put Bunche in charge of the negotiations.

In the face of overwhelming difficulties, Bunche negotiated an armistice between the Arabs and the Israelis by patiently securing four separate agreements in 1949 between Israel and the Mideast nations of Egypt, Lebanon, Jordan, and Syria. For these efforts Bunche was awarded the 1950 Nobel Peace Prize. The accompanying citation praised Bunche for his "unfailing sense of optimism" and his "infinite patience" during the negotiations. It also noted that while the victory belonged to the United Nations, "it was one individual's efforts that made victory possible."

Bunche devoted the rest of his professional life to the United Nations. He served as under secretary for special political affairs from 1955 until 1967, when he became under secretary-general. In these positions Bunche was called upon to be a peacemaker in several major crises: In 1956, when Egypt attempted to nationalize the Suez Canal, he directed the UN Emergency Force that ultimately ended the dispute. Four years later Bunche headed a UN operation to establish peace in the Congo, an African nation that had recently gained independence from Belgium. In 1964 Bunche led the establishment of a UN peacekeeping force to deal with a civil war in Cyprus, and a year later he helped bring about a cease-fire in a dispute between India and Pakistan.

During the 1960s Bunche also became a public supporter of the civil rights movement that sought equality for African Americans. As part of that support, he joined the Reverend Martin Luther King, Jr., in the civil rights march in Montgomery, Alabama, in 1965.

In the late 1960s, Bunche became an adviser to the United Nations secretary-general, U Thant. He also continued to speak out against racism in the United States and actively opposed the Vietnam War, arguing that the money spent on the fighting could be better employed in improving the lives of inner-city African Americans.

When Bunche retired in 1971, he looked forward to enjoying some leisure time with his wife, whom he had married in 1930, their three children, and grandchildren. His retirement was brief, however: he died in New York City only a few months after leaving office.

FURTHER READING

Haskins, Jim. *Ralph Bunche: A Most Reluctant Hero*. New York: Hawthorn, 1974.

Kugelmass, J. Alvin. *Ralph J. Bunche: Fighter for Peace*. New York: Julian Messner, 1962.

Mann, Peggy. *Ralph Bunche, UN Peacekeeper*. New York: Coward, McCann, 1975.

Urquhart, Brian. *Ralph Bunche: An American Life*. New York: Norton, 1993.

Léon Jouhaux

1951

W hen he was 11 years old, Léon Jouhaux was forced to leave the Paris elementary school he attended and go to work to help support the family. The reason? His father, a laborer in a match factory, had gone on strike and thus lost his income. Young Léon, who had dreamed of one day becoming a mechanical engineer, was later able to return to school briefly, but the family's poverty kept him from ever becoming a full-time student again.

The bitter memory of having to give up formal education stayed with Jouhaux throughout his life, and it influenced his decision as an adult to fight for better living conditions for working men and women. Out of bitterness came enormous accomplishment—and the honor of winning the 1951 Nobel Peace Prize.

Léon Jouhaux (pronounced *Joo-OH*) was born in 1879 in Paris to a slaughterhouse laborer and his wife. When Léon was two years old, his father got a job at the match factory, and Léon later worked there, too, after a series of jobs at a

Léon Jouhaux addresses an international labor conference sponsored by the League of Nations and held at League headquarters in Geneva, Switzerland, in 1928.

During World War II, the headquarters of the International Labor Organization, which had been founded in 1919 as an agency of the League of Nations, were moved temporarily to this college in Montreal, Canada. The ILO returned to Geneva after the war when it became part of the newly founded United Nations.

locksmith shop and in soap and wallpaper factories. Between jobs, and before going to the match factory, Léon was able to complete a term at each of two French secondary schools, or *lycées*, on a scholarship, but he had to withdraw and go back to work because the family needed his wages.

At the match factory, Jouhaux rose to a semi-skilled position. In 1897, at the age of 18, he went on leave when he was called up for military service. Sent to Algeria, a French colony in North Africa, with a unit of the French army, he served for three years. He was discharged from the army in 1900 to help his father, who had become blind.

The senior Jouhaux's blindness had been caused by years of exposure to white phosphorus in the match factory. The industrial use of white phosphorus was controversial because it was dangerous to health, and many companies had banned it for this reason. Outraged by his father's disability, Léon Jouhaux

returned to Paris and led a protest strike against the match factory, calling on the management to stop using white phosphorus. The strike was successful, but Jouhaux was fired for his role. He did not get his job back until six years later, after a lengthy effort by his labor union.

During those six years, Jouhaux worked as a laborer on the docks and in a fertilizer plant and a sugar refinery. He also began a program of self-education, attending free lectures at several schools in Paris and reading widely. The end of that period also saw the beginning of Jouhaux's career in the labor movement: in 1906, following his reinstatement at the match factory, the matchworkers' union chose him as its representative to France's national federation of labor unions, the Confédération Générale du Travail (General Confederation of Labor), commonly referred to as the CGT.

Jouhaux became a prominent member of the CGT and in 1909 was elected secretary-general. During the next few years he was the organization's leading spokesman, traveling around France to give speeches and editing the CGT newspaper, *La Bataille syndicaliste* (*The Syndicalist Battle*). In the months preceding World War I, Jouhaux led CGT opposition to the war and made an unsuccessful personal appeal to the head of the German labor federation, asking that it organize an antiwar movement.

After war was declared in August 1914, Jouhaux helped his country by serving on several government committees that oversaw the production of defense goods. Three years later, Jouhaux led the French delegation at an important labor conference in Leeds, England, attended by trade unionists from the Allied nations (those that were fighting Germany, including France, Great Britain, and the United States). There he voiced hope for political liberty, economic harmony, disarmament, and compulsory international arbitration when the war ended. At the Versailles Peace Conference in 1919, Jouhaux joined other labor leaders in creating the International Labor Organization (ILO) as part of the newly formed League of Nations.

During the next two decades, Jouhaux remained active as head of the CGT; in the early 1920s he led efforts that prevented a Communist takeover of the organization. He also served as an official of the ILO and as a member of the French delegation to the League of Nations, where he helped draft proposals for arms control. As both a labor leader and a League representative, Jouhaux was an active delegate to international conferences during the early 1930s on unemployment and arms reduction.

As another world war loomed in the late 1930s—and the League of Nations seemed powerless to stop it—Jouhaux became a leading spokesman for peace. He publicly opposed Italy's invasion of Ethiopia in 1935, the outbreak of the Spanish Civil War (1936), and the takeover by Nazi Germany of Czechoslovakia and Austria (1938). In 1938 he traveled to the United States to make a personal appeal to President Franklin D. Roosevelt to take action against Germany.

Despite Jouhaux's efforts, World War II began in September 1939. Less than a year later France fell to the German army, and at that point the CGT was dissolved. Jouhaux fled to the south of France, where he worked for the Resistance, a secret organization fighting to end Nazi occupation. He was arrested in Marseilles in December 1941, and he and his wife spent two years under house arrest. In 1943 they were deported to a German concentration camp in Buchenwald, and despite the horrible conditions there they survived until the camp was liberated by Allied troops in 1945.

Jouhaux returned to Paris and resumed his work with the International Labor Organization and the reactivated CGT. He also became an official of the postwar French government as president of the French Economic Council. In 1947 he ended his association with the CGT when it refused to approve the European Recovery Program, a plan to rebuild wartorn Europe that was devised by George C. Marshall. He went on to form and become president of a new organization, the CGT-Force Ouvrière (CGT-Work Force), which sought to unify France and other continental nations into the United States of Europe. He also encouraged the formation of an all-Europe labor movement and the improvement of living and working conditions for the European labor force.

Jouhaux's longtime efforts on behalf of peace earned him the Nobel Peace Prize for 1951. The accompanying citation praised him for his long effort "to lay the foundations of a world which could belong to all men alike, a world where peace would prevail." Jouhaux was apparently surprised by the award, and in his acceptance address he emphasized his belief that it belonged not to him alone but to "all those in the trade union movement."

Jouhaux remained active in both the French Economic Council and the CGT-Force Ouvrière during the next few years, although he was now in his 70s. He died in Paris in the spring of 1954 after suffering a heart attack.

FURTHER READING

"Jouhaux, Léon." In *Current Biography Yearbook 1948*. New York: H. W. Wilson, 1949.

Lorwin, L. L. *The International Labor Movement*. New York: Harper, 1953.

Léon Jouhaux

BORN
July 1, 1879
Paris, France

DIED
April 28, 1954
Paris, France

EDUCATION
Briefly attended a secondary school

OCCUPATION
Labor leader

MAJOR ACCOMPLISHMENTS
Secretary-general, Confédération Générale du Travail (CGT) (1909–40); cofounder and vice president, International Labor Organization; president, French Economic Council; founder and president, CGT-Force Ouvrière (1947–54)

Albert Schweitzer

1952

I n 1905, 30-year-old Albert Schweitzer, a prominent resident of Strassburg, Germany, turned his back on a promising career as a scholar in the fields of both religion and music. That fall he entered medical school to prepare himself for a new career as a medical missionary in Africa. Even if he had not chosen this new occupation, it is likely that Schweitzer would have become well known, at least in religious and musical circles. But his decision to devote his life to helping native Africans led him to become celebrated as a leading hero of the 20th century—and to win the Nobel Peace Prize.

Schweitzer was born to French parents in 1875 in the small town of Kaysersberg, where his father was a Lutheran pastor. Kaysersberg was part of the province of Alsace, which had belonged to France until 1871, when it was taken over by Germany as part of the settlement that ended the two-year Franco-Prussian War. When Albert was still an infant, the family moved to Günsbach, another town in Alsace,

Celebrated as a great humanitarian when he won the Nobel Peace Prize in 1952, musician, scholar, and physician Albert Schweitzer spent the last decade of his life campaigning against nuclear waste.

where his father became pastor of the local Lutheran church. Albert, like the other four children in the family, grew up speaking both French and German. From the age of five he was taught by his father to play the piano and the organ.

Like his father and two grandfathers, Albert Schweitzer quickly became a skilled organist; by the age of nine he was playing for services at his father's church. After attending local elementary schools, he was sent to a secondary school in the Alsatian city of Mulhouse. There he also continued his organ studies with a private teacher while he lived with a strict great-uncle who allowed him music as his only leisure activity.

After graduation, Schweitzer entered the University of Strassburg in the fall of 1893 to study theology, with the intention of becoming a Lutheran minister like his father. (Strassburg was located in still another area that belonged to France until 1871; after the city returned to French rule in 1918, it resumed the French spelling of its name: Strasbourg.) During the next 12 years, Schweitzer earned successive doctorates in theology, philosophy, and music and also fulfilled a German government requirement to spend a year in military training. His research for his doctoral dissertation in philosophy took him to Paris for extended periods of time, and there he took organ and piano lessons from prominent musicians.

Schweitzer had become increasingly interested in the music of Johann Sebastian Bach, an early-18th-century German composer who wrote many works for the organ. Schweitzer became a specialist in Bach: he gave concerts of the composer's work, founded the Paris Bach Society, and published a critical edition of Bach's organ compositions. For his doctorate in music, he wrote a biographical study of the composer that was published in

both French and German editions and later translated into English and other languages.

During his lifetime, Schweitzer was regarded as a leading authority on Bach. Both the critical edition of Bach's compositions and the biography were widely praised by music historians and are still considered important works today. In addition, Schweitzer wrote a book on organ construction and playing that inspired the restoration of many historic organs in Europe.

Meanwhile, Schweitzer had become associated as a preacher with St. Nicholas Church in Strassburg in 1899, shortly after receiving his doctorate in theology. He later served as deacon and curate of the church. In the early 1900s, he also served on the theological faculty of the university and wrote what is considered his most important book, a study of Christ that is known widely by the title of its English translation: *The Quest of the Historical Jesus* (1906; English translation, 1910).

While he was still a student, Schweitzer had resolved that when he reached the age of 30, he would devote the rest of his life to the service of humanity. In his late 20s, as he pursued his scholarly activities at the university and his duties at St. Nicholas Church, Schweitzer tried to determine what form that service would take. He devoted his leisure time to charitable work with prisoners and the homeless in Strassburg, but he believed that God intended him to do more.

Schweitzer's future path was determined one day in the fall of 1904 when he read a magazine article about medical missionaries in the Congo, a region in central Africa. He knew at once that this was the work he wanted to do, and in 1905 he entered the medical school at the University of Strassburg. During his seven years of study, Schweitzer continued to teach theology at the university; he paid for his medical training with his teacher's

Albert Schweitzer

BORN
January 14, 1875
Kaysersberg, Germany (now France)

DIED
September 4, 1965
Lambaréné, Gabon

EDUCATION
Ph.D., philosophy, music, and theology (1899); M.D. (1913), University of Strassburg (later Strasbourg)

OCCUPATION
Theologian; musicologist; organist; medical missionary

MAJOR ACCOMPLISHMENTS
Established hospital in Africa to serve the native population; author of numerous scholarly books, including major studies of Bach, Goethe, and Jesus, and a best-selling autobiography, *Out of My Life and Thought* (1933); acclaimed for his concerts and recordings of Bach's organ music

Schweitzer holds one his patients outside the hospital that he and his wife established at Lambaréné.

salary and profits from the sale of his Bach biography. During this period he also gave many organ recitals to raise money for the hospital he hoped to found.

Shortly after receiving his M.D. in the spring of 1913, Schweitzer left for Lambaréné, a Protestant mission in French Equatorial Africa (now Gabon) that was sponsored by the Paris Missionary Society. He was accompanied by his wife of one year, Hélène Breslau Schweitzer, who had trained as a nurse in order to help her husband in his new role. Upon his arrival in Lambaréné, Schweitzer established a hospital in the jungle that resembled a native village. It quickly drew many African patients, who were able to bring family members along to help care for them.

Sixteen months after its founding, the hospital was forced to close when World War I broke out. Lambaréné was in French-occupied territory, and the Schweitzers were citizens of Germany, with which France was at war. For several years, both Schweitzer and his wife were interned as enemy aliens. After being allowed to work briefly at the hospital, they were deported to France in 1917 as prisoners of war.

The Schweitzers did not return to Lambaréné for seven years. After their release from the French internment camp in the summer of 1918, they went back to Strassburg. When the war ended that fall, Schweitzer resumed his work at St. Nicholas Church and joined the staff of a city hospital. During the next few years, he also took advanced medical and dental courses at the university.

To raise funds for his eventual return to Africa, Schweitzer gave organ recitals and lectures in several European countries, including Sweden, where he appeared at the invitation of Archbishop Nathan Söderblom. During this period, the Schweitzers' only child, a daughter, was born.

In these years, Schweitzer wrote four books and did research for two others. The first, known widely by its English title, *On the Edge of the Primeval Forest*, discussed his work in Africa; the original German edition was published in Switzerland in 1921, and an English translation appeared in the United States a year later. This was followed by a two-volume series of philosophical reflections that were published in a German edition in Munich in 1923; they appeared in English translation in 1939 as *The Decay and Restoration of Civilization* and *Civilization and Ethics*. In the second of these works, Schweitzer described his personal philosophy, which he called "reverence for life."

Schweitzer defined "reverence for life" as follows: "It is good to maintain and further life; it is bad to damage and destroy life." This ethic, or moral teaching, was religious and universal, Schweitzer believed, and meant that all human beings "should sacrifice a portion of their own lives for others."

The fourth book that Schweitzer wrote during this period was a study of world religions. It was published in German and British editions in 1923, and it appeared in the United States 13 years later as *Christianity and the Religions of the World*. He also did research for studies of St. Paul and the German poet Goethe, both of which were published many years later.

When Schweitzer returned to Lambaréné in 1924 with his wife and daughter, he was dismayed to find his hospital in ruins. He immediately set about rebuilding it, again modeling it after a typical African village. There was no electricity except in the operating room, animals roamed about, and family members lived with their ailing relatives. Despite criticism from some outsiders, who accused Schweitzer of living and working in unsanitary conditions, the hospital thrived and treated hundreds of patients annually.

News of Schweitzer's hospital quickly spread, and by the late 1920s he was already celebrated throughout much of the world as a great humanitarian. In 1928 he received the first of many honors: the Goethe Memorial Prize from the city of Frankfurt. Schweitzer's fame grew even more following the appearance in 1933 of his autobiography, published in English as *Out of My Life and Thought*.

Schweitzer's hospital at Lambaréné eventually grew into a complex of 70 buildings staffed by volunteer medical personnel. Men and women attracted to Schweitzer's philosophy and to his humanitarian efforts came from around the world to donate their skills and efforts. In the United States, the Albert Schweitzer Fellowships of America, established in the late 1930s, enabled many Americans to work with Schweitzer at Lambaréné. Some of them later founded hospitals of their own in remote areas of the world.

For the rest of his life, Schweitzer made his home in Lambaréné, but traveled to Europe and other parts of the world on a regular basis to raise money by giving lectures and organ recitals. Funds for the hospital—and additional

fame for Schweitzer—also came from a series of organ recordings of the works of Bach that he made, beginning in the 1930s.

During World War II (1939–45), when France was again at war with Germany, the Schweitzers were allowed to continue their work at Lambaréné. This was not only because of Albert Schweitzer's international prominence but because he was now considered a French citizen: Alsace, his birthplace, had been restored to French rule after World War I ended in 1918. Medical and other supplies unavailable from wartorn Europe were sent to Lambaréné by individuals and charitable organizations in countries around the world, including the United States, Australia, and New Zealand.

In 1949, the same year that his study of Goethe was published in the United States, Schweitzer was invited to lecture at an international Goethe festival in Aspen, Colorado, held to celebrate the 200th anniversary of the poet's birth. During his visit Schweitzer became a celebrity in America and was mobbed by crowds of enthusiastic admirers whenever he appeared in public.

Back at Lambaréné, Schweitzer continued to receive tributes for his dedication to the welfare of humanity, including election to the French Academy in 1951. Two years later, while working at the hospital, he was told that he had won the biggest humanitarian award of all: the Nobel Peace Prize. The prize, designated for 1952, was announced in 1953. In its citation, the Nobel Committee praised Schweitzer for demonstrating that "a man's life and his dream can become one," and for turning the concept of brotherhood into a living reality.

Schweitzer used the $33,000 in prize money to build a separate facility for lepers at Lambaréné. By the early 1960s, the entire medical complex was able to care for about 500 patients at a time. It was staffed by three dozen

volunteer medical personnel from abroad and numerous native workers. In addition to offering treatment for various ailments, the Lambaréné settlement was also maintained as an animal refuge.

Schweitzer was active as both a manager and a physician at Lambaréné until the end of his life, although old age forced him to give up surgery in 1960. Now in his 80s, he also had to discontinue the Bach recitals that he had given for more than half a century.

In his last years, Schweitzer was an outspoken opponent of nuclear war and called for a ban on nuclear weapons. He published several books on international peace and his philosophy of reverence for life. He died at Lambaréné in September 1965 and was buried next to his wife, who had died eight years earlier.

FURTHER READING

Anderson, Erica. *The Schweitzer Album: A Portrait in Words and Pictures*. New York: Harper & Row, 1965.

Daniel, Anita. *The Story of Albert Schweitzer*. New York: Random House, 1957.

Langfeldt, Gabriel. *Albert Schweitzer: A Study of His Philosophy of Life*. New York: Braziller, 1960.

Marshall, George, and David Poling. *Schweitzer: A Biography*. New York: Doubleday, 1971.

Schweitzer, Albert. *Out of My Life and Thought*. 1933. Reprint, New York: Holt, 1990.

"Schweitzer, Albert." In *Current Biography Yearbook 1965*. New York: H. Wilson, 1966.

George C. Marshall

1953

George C. Marshall directed U.S. military operations during World War II. After the war, as secretary of state, he proposed a massive European aid program that became the Marshall Plan.

In the fall of 1897, a shy, skinny, and awkward 16-year-old entered the Virginia Military Institute (VMI), a college in Lexington, Virginia, that trained future army officers. The teenager, George C. Marshall, had decided on an army career because he could not think of anything else to do. His parents had reluctantly agreed to send him to VMI, despite the protests of George's older brother, Stuart, who was afraid that George would not do well there and would embarrass the family. George did not have much confidence, either, especially since the high school he had attended had not prepared him for college-level courses. However, his brother's ridicule spurred him on, and he determined to work as hard as he could to prove Stuart wrong. When the pressures of school-work seemed too strong, George took breaks by wandering off-campus to explore the Civil War battlefields near the school.

Four years after entering VMI, George C. Marshall graduated near the top of his class academically. He had also become an outstanding football player and was voted to the highest cadet rank by his classmates. Soon after graduation, Marshall was commissioned a second lieutenant in the U.S. Army. Everyone who knew him now expected Marshall to have an outstanding military career. No one, however, could have predicted in 1902 that Marshall's accomplishments as a peacemaker would be considered even greater than his performance as a celebrated army general.

George Catlett Marshall was born in Uniontown, Pennsylvania, on the last day of December, 1880. Most of his ancestors were from the American South, including his parents, who had moved north from Kentucky. Many members of the Marshall family had distinguished themselves, including a distant cousin, John Marshall, Chief Justice of the U.S. Supreme Court in the early 19th century. George seemed rather slow, however, and was an average student. When it became apparent that he could not get into West Point, the national military academy, the family sent him to VMI—over his brother's protests.

George Marshall later said that his brother's taunts made him determined to succeed. Entering the army following his excellent performance at VMI, Marshall spent several years with the 30th Infantry in the Philippines. (At that time, the Philippine Islands were a U.S.-held territory occupied by American troops.) He then returned to the United States to attend infantry-cavalry training school at Fort Leavenworth, in Kansas, and graduated with highest honors in 1907. Soon afterward he was promoted to the rank of first lieutenant and went on to attend the Army Staff

College, where he graduated at the top of his class in 1908.

Marshall's rise to prominence and high rank in the army was slow, however. Despite his hard work, he was at a disadvantage because he had not attended West Point, which traditionally produced the nation's military leaders. From 1908 to 1913, he served as an infantry instructor at several army posts around the country, then returned to the Philippines as an aide to the commanding general. During Marshall's three years of service there he impressed his superiors with his knowledge of military tactics and received a promotion to captain in 1916, shortly after his return to the United States.

When the United States entered World War I in April 1917, Marshall went overseas with American troops and served as an operations officer in France. During his outstanding service there, Marshall was assigned as an aide to General John J. Pershing, the head of U.S. forces engaged in the war. After the war ended in the fall of 1918, Marshall worked with Pershing in Washington, D.C., as the general tried to ensure that the country would be well prepared for any future wars. Together, Pershing and Marshall drafted a proposal that was passed by Congress as the National Defense Act of 1920. Although the act itself proved to be of little importance (it called for the establishment of a trained army of nearly half a million men, but Congress never appropriated the necessary funds), Marshall's experience in Washington was enormously valuable.

During the next few years, Marshall continued as Pershing's aide while receiving promotions to major and then lieutenant colonel. In the mid-1920s, he served with an infantry unit in China and later in the decade taught at the Army War College in Washington, D.C., and at an infantry school in Georgia. Through most of the 1930s, Marshall's career took him to half a

dozen military posts around the country as commander or instructor. By 1936 additional promotions had raised him to the rank of brigadier general.

At this point, Marshall seemed headed for retirement after a career of solid but not especially notable service. Military leaders in Washington, D.C., had their eye on him, however, and in the summer of 1938 he was recalled to the capital as an assistant chief in the War Plans Division of the Army General Staff. In September 1939, as World War II broke out in Europe, George Marshall was promoted to full general and army chief of staff—by the U.S. President himself, Franklin D. Roosevelt. Roosevelt had acted after conferring with General Pershing, and had passed over 34 officers of greater rank than Marshall to elevate him to this post.

As army chief of staff, Marshall immediately began working on military preparedness. This was a difficult job: The country's defense system was still very small because the United States was not yet fighting in World War II. Furthermore, many Americans opposed any U.S. involvement in the war, and they repeatedly blocked efforts by the national government to enlarge its military capability. Marshall realized, however, that sooner or later the United States would have to be drawn into the conflict, and he and his staff worked persistently to assemble an army capable of holding off enemy attack. By the fall of 1941, largely because of his efforts, a national military draft known as Selective Service had been established, and 1 million men were undergoing army training in the United States. Only weeks later, on December 8, 1941, the United States entered the war following the Japanese attack on Pearl Harbor the previous day.

As head of the nation's military forces during World War II, Marshall reorganized those forces into ground, air, and general service divisions that

PEACEMAKERS

George C. Marshall

BORN

December 31, 1880
Uniontown, Pennsylvania

DIED

October 16, 1959
Bethesda, Maryland

EDUCATION

B.S., Virginia Military Institute (1901)

OCCUPATION

Military officer; statesman

MAJOR ACCOMPLISHMENTS

First U.S. Army officer to achieve the rank of five-star general; as Secretary of State, created the European Recovery Program (the Marshall Plan); as Secretary of Defense, racially integrated the U.S. armed forces

A bombed-out railroad station in London during World War II. The Marshall Plan helped European nations rebuild their towns and cities as well as their economies after the war.

included 8.25 million men by the spring of 1945. Marshall's major job was to initiate and oversee military strategy during the war. In selecting officers to carry out the war effort, he screened candidates carefully and chose for top appointments only those who were most qualified to be leaders, including Dwight D. Eisenhower, the general who commanded European operations. He devised battle and supply lines throughout the world and oversaw the production of war materials, including tanks and planes.

Marshall's ability to inspire respect and cooperation was a major factor in his successful administration of military operations during the war. His abilities and contributions were officially honored by President Roosevelt in December 1944, eight months before the war ended, when he was given the title of General of the Army and the newly created rank of five-star general.

Throughout the war, Marshall was closely involved with U.S. foreign policy and attended important international conferences, including meetings in Casablanca, Teheran, and Yalta with President Roosevelt and other world leaders. In the final year of the war, Marshall's advice on the role of the United States in postwar international relations helped shape U.S. strategy in creating the United Nations. In August 1945, at war's end, he attended the Potsdam conference with President Harry S. Truman, Roosevelt's successor, British prime minister Winston Churchill, and Joseph Stalin, premier of the Soviet Union.

In November 1945, Marshall retired as chief of staff and was appointed ambassador to China by President Truman. His service was only brief, however, for in January 1947 he was called back to Washington, D.C., to become Secretary of State, with responsibility for U.S. foreign relations. This was not an easy time for Marshall to assume that post. The Soviet Union, which had joined the war against Germany in its final months, was no longer an ally of the United States. Along with other nations in Eastern Europe now ruled by Communist dictatorships, the Soviet Union had declared its opposition to all major Western nations, and a tense international political atmosphere now prevailed. This postwar period was known as the Cold War and lasted for more than four decades.

Despite the dangerous international situation, Marshall took on the job. One of his first acts as Secretary of State was to formulate the so-called Truman Doctrine, which declared U.S. support for democratic governments in Europe and U.S. opposition to the creation of new totalitarian regimes (dictatorships) by the Soviet Union and its allies. As part of the Truman Doctrine, announced in March 1947, the United States authorized $400 million in aid to Greece and Turkey.

That spring Marshall devoted his attention to wartorn Europe and its reconstruction. After considerable thought and study, he devised the European Recovery Program (ERP), which he announced in a speech at Harvard University's graduation exercises on June 5, 1947. The program was designed to strengthen and maintain democratic nations in Western Europe, including West Germany, by giving them massive economic aid. As a first step, Marshall asked leaders of these nations to submit proposals to the United States that outlined their plans for reconstruction.

Representatives of 16 European nations met in Paris in July 1947 to consider Marshall's proposal. There they established the Committee of European Economic Cooperation, which drafted a report outlining a recovery program. During the next three years, the U.S. Congress authorized more than $12 billion in aid under the Economic Recovery Program, which became popularly

known as the Marshall Plan. That aid enabled Europe—and particularly West Germany—to recover from the war in less than a decade.

Marshall faced a major Cold War crisis in 1948, when the Soviet Union blockaded the city of Berlin, which lay in Soviet-controlled East Germany. Berlin itself, like the entire country of Germany, had been divided into East and West sectors after the war. The Soviet Union already controlled East Berlin and was now blockading West Berlin in an attempt to seize the entire city. Marshall countered the blockade by organizing a major airlift of supplies, including food, medicine, and clothing, to the endangered city. The so-called Berlin Airlift was a major victory for U.S. foreign policy and a personal victory for George Marshall.

As Secretary of State, Marshall was credited with many other achievements. He established formal diplomatic relations between the United States and the newly created independent nations of Ceylon (now Sri Lanka), Israel, and Korea. He helped to create the Organization of American States, an alliance of nations in the western hemisphere, and he encouraged and supported negotiations that led to the creation of the North Atlantic Treaty Organization (NATO), a European multination security alliance.

Poor health forced Marshall to leave office when President Truman's first term ended in January 1949. In September 1950, however—three months after the United States went to war with North Korea—he agreed to Truman's request to rejoin the cabinet as Secretary of Defense. In this new post, Marshall streamlined the Defense Department bureaucracy to make it function more effectively. His major contribution as Defense Secretary, however, was in the field of civil rights: he ordered racial integration in the basic training programs of all branches of military service, removed racial quo-

tas in military schools, and abolished segregated military units serving in the Korean War.

Marshall retired as Secretary of Defense in September 1951, several months before his 71st birthday. Two years later he became the first professional soldier to win the Nobel Peace Prize, given to him for his efforts to create the ERP, or Marshall Plan. The Nobel Committee was criticized by many for giving the Peace Prize to a soldier, and Marshall answered those criticisms in his acceptance speech: "The cost of war in human lives is constantly spread before me, written neatly in many ledgers whose columns are gravestones. I am deeply moved to find some means or method of avoiding another calamity of war." Many years earlier, while still an active soldier, Marshall had expressed similar sentiments: "War is the most terrible tragedy of the human race," he said, "and it should not be prolonged an hour longer than is absolutely necessary."

Marshall was married twice, the first time in 1902. In 1930, three years after the death of his first wife, he married a widow with three young children and helped raise them. His stepson was killed while serving with the army in Italy during World War II. Marshall spent his retirement years with his wife at their home in Leesburg, Virginia. He died at the U.S. naval hospital in Bethesda, Maryland, after a brief illness in October 1959. He was buried with military honors at Arlington National Cemetery in Virginia.

FURTHER READING

Cray, Ed. *General of the Army: George C. Marshall, Soldier and Statesman*. New York: Norton, 1990.

"Marshall, George Catlett." In *Dictionary of American Biography*. Supplement 6. New York: Scribners, 1980.

Office of the UN High Commissioner for Refugees

1954

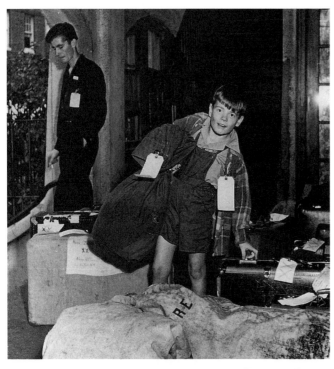

A refugee boy and his father prepare to leave Germany for a new home in the United States after World War II, with assistance from the UN Relief and Rehabilitation Administration.

Since the creation of modern nation-states in the 15th century, millions of refugees have crossed national borders seeking protection. Refugees are people who leave their native country because it is no longer safe to live there. Their reason for leaving their homelands is usually one or more of the following: political or religious persecution; natural disasters, including earthquakes and famine; or warfare.

Until the 20th century, aid to refugees was limited and usually came from church groups that helped members of their own denomination. The first large-scale refugee assistance occurred after World War I, when the League of Nations created the High Commission for Refugees. Under the direction of the Norwegian explorer, scientist, and humanitarian Fridtjof Nansen, the commission assisted millions of Russian, Armenian, Greek, and Bulgarian refugees who fled their homelands because of political or religious persecution.

In 1930 the League of Nations created a new organization as a successor to the High Commission. It was named the Nansen International Office for Refugees to honor the memory of Nansen, who had died earlier that year. During the 1930s, the Nansen International Office aided refugees from the Spanish Civil War (1936–39) as well as large numbers of Jews and others who were fleeing persecution by Nazis in Germany and countries being overrun by German troops.

When world war broke out in September 1939, the League of Nations and the organizations under its direction—including the Nansen International Office—became inactive. After the war ended in 1945, the United Nations was officially designated as the successor to the League of Nations. An agency called the United Nations Relief and Rehabilitation Administration (UNRRA) was created by the UN to assist some of the millions of European refugees who had been uprooted by war and persecution. UNRRA was later renamed the International Refugee Organization (IRO) and expanded its efforts to aid refugees in Asia and other parts of the world.

In 1951 the widespread refugee aid program of the IRO was reorganized and given a new name: the Office of the United Nations High Commissioner for Refugees (UNHCR). The UNHCR was given the task of working with governments and private voluntary organizations to give material assistance to refugees. It was also given responsibility for carrying out the provisions of the 1951 Convention Relating to the Status of Refugees. This international agreement, signed by UN member nations, pledged them to respect the political rights of refugees fleeing their homelands because of persecution. The first high commissioner in charge of UNHCR was G. J. van Heuven Goedhart of the Netherlands.

In its first year of operation, UNHCR assisted in the resettlement of 1.25 million refugees. Many of them were Russians and Armenians who had fled to Belgium and other Western European countries. During the next few years, UNHCR also sought to aid thousands of Europeans who had been stranded in China following its takeover by a Communist government in 1949. In addition, UNHCR assisted Austria as it tried to cope with thousands of refugees who kept pouring into that country from Eastern Europe, trying to escape Communist persecution.

To pay for these programs, UNHCR got a grant of $3.1 million from the Ford Foundation, a philanthropic (charitable) organization in the United States. Much of the money was used to aid resettlement of refugees in Europe by providing housing, vocational training, and loans to professional people, including doctors and lawyers, so that they could re-establish their practices.

UNHCR also raised money on its own. Beginning in 1954, the organization undertook a four-year fund-raising campaign with a goal of $16 million. This money was used to help resettle thousands who were still living in refugee camps across Europe that had been set up as temporary accommodations after the war. In 1954 UNHCR also began a five-year campaign to raise $12 million for the resettlement of a third of a million political refugees in Western Europe.

That fall, UNHCR was named the 1954 winner of the Nobel Peace Prize.

The citation praised the organization for its "untiring and sometimes thankless effort" to assist millions of refugees, and to do it in such a way that each individual felt that he or she had received personalized attention.

In accepting the award on behalf of his organization, High Commissioner van Heuven Goedhart expressed the admiration that UNHCR felt for those it cared for: refugees, he said, were courageous people who had given up their homelands rather than "abandon the human freedom which they valued more highly." True to its goals, UNHCR used the prize money to aid nearly 3,000 Romanian political refugees.

The Office of the United Nations High Commissioner for Refugees won a second Nobel Peace Prize in 1981. To read about the activities of UNHCR since 1954, see pages 23–33.

FURTHER READING

Holborn, L. *Refugees: A Problem of Our Time*. 2 vols. Metuchen, N.J.: Scarecrow Press, 1975.

"Office of the United Nations High Commissioner for Refugees." In *Nobel Prize Winners*. New York: H. W. Wilson, 1987.

Proudfoot, Malcolm J. *European Refugees, 1939–52*. Evanston, Ill.: Northwestern University Press, 1957.

Vernant, J. *The Refugee in the Post-War World*. New Haven: Yale University Press, 1953.

Office of the UN High Commissioner for Refugees

FOUNDER

Founded by the United Nations as a successor to the International Refugee Organization

FOUNDING

1951
Geneva, Switzerland

HEADQUARTERS

Geneva, Switzerland

PURPOSE

To aid refugees throughout the world by providing them with material and legal assistance and permanent settlement

MAJOR ACCOMPLISHMENTS, 1951–54

Aided nearly 2 million refugees, primarily European, in its first three years of operation; raised more than $19 million to fund these efforts

Lester Pearson

1957

B y the time he began working for the Canadian government at the age of 31, Lester Pearson had already tried six occupations. He had served as an army pilot, flight instructor, meatpacker, baseball player, history professor, and athletic coach. When friends suggested that he take a civil service exam, Pearson reluctantly agreed—and received the highest score. That performance resulted in his appointment to an important government post—and launched his career as one of the 20th century's most respected diplomats.

Lester Bowles Pearson was born in Toronto in 1897 to a Methodist minister and his wife. After attending local schools and college preparatory institutes in the Ontario cities of Peterborough and Hamilton, Pearson enrolled at the University of Toronto in 1913, at the age of 16. When World War I broke out a year later, he joined a hospital brigade sponsored by the university and served overseas for two years. After receiving flight training back in Canada, Pearson joined the Royal Flying Corps as an army flight lieutenant in 1917. He crashed on his first solo flight, however,

Canadian diplomat Lester Pearson served his country for nearly half a century. He was awarded the 1957 Nobel Peace Prize for helping to end the Suez Canal crisis a year earlier.

and for the remainder of the war served as a ground instructor.

Pearson was able to resume his studies part-time at the university during his last months in the army, and in 1919 he received a bachelor's degree with honors in history. Unsure of his future career, Pearson went to work at the Ontario branch of Armour & Company, a U.S. meatpacking firm. On weekends, in season, he played semiprofessional baseball for the Guelph Maple Leafs. He grew tired of these jobs after two years, however, and decided to do graduate work in history to prepare himself for a teaching career.

A fellowship from a private educational foundation enabled Pearson to enroll at Oxford University in England, where he earned a second bachelor's degree as well as a master's degree, both in history. Pearson returned to Canada in the fall of 1923 and joined the history department at the University of Toronto as a lecturer. He was also hired to coach the university's ice hockey and football teams. Pearson coached and taught for five years, and advanced to the rank of assistant professor. In 1928 he took the Canadian civil service exam, more or less on a dare, which resulted in his appointment as first secretary with the Department of External Affairs in Ottawa, the capital of Canada.

The government department that hired Pearson had responsibility for Canada's relationship with foreign nations. In his seven years as first secretary, Pearson traveled abroad to attend conferences on international law, naval preparedness, and disarmament, and also attended meetings of the League of Nations in Geneva, Switzerland. Canada, a country that belonged to the British Empire (now the British Commonwealth), also loaned Pearson to the British government in London for months at a time to serve on commissions concerned with government food purchasing.

In 1935 Pearson moved to London to assume an appointment as first secretary in the office of the high commissioner for Canada. Four years later, not long before the outbreak of World War II, he was promoted to the rank of counselor. Pearson remained in London until the spring of 1941, when he was recalled to Ottawa by the government to become assistant undersecretary of state for external affairs. A year later he was sent to Washington, D.C., to serve as counselor of the Canadian embassy.

During the next three years, as the war drew to a close, Pearson was active in international affairs. Promoted to the rank of minister plenipotentiary at the Canadian Embassy in 1944, he represented his country that year at the Dumbarton Oaks Conference, which drew up plans for the formal establishment of the United Nations. He was one of the founders of the United Nations Relief and Rehabilitation Administration (UNRRA) and represented Canada at UNRRA meetings. He was also a cofounder of the United Nations Food and Agriculture Organization (FAO) and helped draft its constitution.

Named Canadian ambassador to the United States early in 1945, Pearson attended the UN founding conference in San Francisco later that year and helped write the UN Charter. He was in line to become the first secretary-general of the United Nations but lost to the Norwegian statesman Trygve Lie because of pressure from the Soviet Union to appoint a European to the post. However, he continued as a member of the Canadian delegation to the United Nations and headed the General Assembly's Political and Security Committee, which paved the way for the establishment of the state of Israel in 1948.

Meanwhile, after serving as ambassador to the United States for little more than a year, Pearson was recalled to Ottawa from this post in 1946 to be-

Lester Pearson

BORN
April 23, 1897
Toronto, Canada

DIED
December 27, 1972
Ottawa, Canada

EDUCATION
B.A., University of Toronto (1919); B.A. (1923), M.A. (1925), Oxford University

OCCUPATION
Diplomat; statesman; politician

MAJOR ACCOMPLISHMENTS
Cofounded the United Nations Relief and Rehabilitation Administration (UNRRA) and the Food and Agriculture Organization (FAO) (both 1943); Canadian ambassador to the United States (1945–46); prime minister of Canada (1963–68); proposed the creation of the North Atlantic Treaty Organization (NATO); led UN efforts to end the Suez crisis of 1956; chairman, World Bank Commission on International Development (1968–72)

come undersecretary of state for external affairs, and two years later he was promoted to the department's top job, secretary of state. In 1948 he was also elected to a seat in the Canadian parliament, which he held for many years. As secretary of state for external affairs, Pearson represented Canada at major international conferences that dealt with such issues as German rearmament and the peace treaty ending the war with Japan.

One of Pearson's most important contributions to international relations was a proposal for the formation of a U.S.-Europe security association called the North Atlantic Treaty Organization (NATO). In 1949, at the Washington, D.C., conference that formally established NATO, Pearson signed the membership treaty on behalf of Canada. For the next eight years he also led the Canadian delegation to NATO meetings.

Between 1948 and 1956, Pearson was head of Canada's delegation to the United Nations, and he served as president of the UN General Assembly in 1952–53. In the early 1950s, he gained experience as a negotiator by mediating policy differences between Great Britain and the United States. In the fall of 1956, Pearson had another opportunity to put his mediating skills to good use following Egypt's seizure of the Suez Canal, an international waterway. Great Britain, France, and Israel responded by sending troops into the area, and a major war seemed likely. Working around the clock with representatives of all three governments, Pearson drafted a UN resolution that created an emergency international United Nations force to enter the area and eventually end the hostilities.

Lester Pearson's role in ending the Suez crisis earned him the 1957 Nobel Peace Prize. In the accompanying citation, the Nobel Committee noted that this had been the world's darkest hour since the war ended in 1945 and praised Pearson for doing "more than anyone else to save the world" during the crisis.

Pearson's career was not over, however. He continued to serve in the Canadian parliament, and in 1963 he was elected prime minister of his country. After serving for five years, he retired from politics at the age of 71 and became head of the World Bank Commission on International Development.

Pearson, who was married and had two children, received other awards during his lifetime, including two dozen honorary degrees and membership in the Order of the British Empire. Beginning in the mid-1950s, he also wrote seven books on international relations. Stricken with cancer in the last years of his life, Pearson died in Ottawa in December 1972.

FURTHER READING

Beal, John R. *Pearson of Canada.* New York: Duell, Sloan & Pearce, 1964.

Levitt, Joseph. *Pearson and Canada's Role in Nuclear Disarmament and Arms Control Negotiations, 1945–1957.* Montreal: McGill-Queen's University Press, 1993.

Pearson, Lester. *Peace in the Family of Man.* London: British Broadcasting Corporation, 1969.

Thordarson, Bruce. *Lester Pearson: Diplomat and Politician.* Oxford and New York: Oxford University Press, 1974.

Dominique-Georges Pire

1958

After World War II ended in 1945, the European continent was overrun with millions of refugees—men, women, and children who had fled their native countries because their homes had been destroyed or because their feared persecution. Much of the responsibility for looking after these refugees was assumed by the newly created United Nations Relief and Rehabilitation Administration (UNRRA).

UNRRA and its successor, the International Refugee Organization, resettled thousands of refugees in Western Europe and other countries between 1945 and 1951. Many refugees could not be resettled, however, and had to remain where they were because no other community wanted to take them in. These "hard-core" refugees were often elderly, chronically ill, or disabled. In 1949 a Roman Catholic priest in Belgium named Georges Pire assumed the responsibility for helping many of those who had no place to go. By 1958, thousands of refugees had been aided directly by Father Pire—and his efforts to heal the wounds of war earned him that year's Nobel Peace Prize.

Georges Henri Pire (pronounced *Peer*) was born in Dinant, Belgium, in 1910 to a local government official and his

Dominique-Georges Pire, a Roman Catholic priest, points out the site of a "European Village" that he helped build in Belgium to house refugees made homeless by World War II.

wife. Early in life, Georges Pire knew that he wanted to become a priest. After attending primary and secondary schools in Dinant, he entered La Sarte, a Dominican monastery in Huy, Belgium, at the age of 18. During his four years there, he received the equivalent of an undergraduate education. In 1932 he began graduate study in theology at the Collegio Angelico, a university in Rome run by the Dominican order. Pire was ordained to the priesthood in 1934, taking the religious name Dominique-Georges. Two years later he received his doctorate.

Pire then returned to Belgium, where he studied political and social science for a year at the University of Louvain. Settling at La Sarte, the monastery in Huy where he had studied as an undergraduate, he became a teacher of moral philosophy and sociology. Pire wanted to do more than teach, however, so he volunteered to become a chaplain to poor laborers in the local parish. He also founded an organization to help Belgian children living in poverty.

Soon after the outbreak of World War II, when German troops invaded and occupied Belgium in 1940, Pire joined the Resistance, a secret movement that aided the Allies (Great Britain, the United States, and other countries that were fighting Germany). Throughout the war he not only served as a chaplain to the Resistance; he also cofounded an intelligence service that provided secret information on the Germans to Allied countries, and he helped establish an escape network for Allied pilots who had been shot down. Pire's heroic service during World War II earned him the Belgian War Cross with Palms, the Medal of Resistance, and the Medal of National Reconnaissance from the Belgian government.

He later earned the French Legion of Honor and major awards from other European nations.

Following the war's end in 1945, Pire established several camps for French and Belgian refugee children. One evening in February 1949, he attended a public lecture given by Colonel Edward F. Squadrille, an American official with UNRRA. Squadrille described the sad situation of Europe's so-called displaced persons, or DPs, refugees who had fled to Central European countries from Communist governments in Eastern Europe. He gave his audience the names of 47 DPs living in the Tyrol region of Austria who were in the "hard-core" category—for various reasons, they could not be resettled elsewhere—and asked his listeners to send them letters offering friendship and assistance. Each of the audience members, including Pire, took one of the names and agreed to write.

But Pire was moved to do more. In April he traveled to Austria and visited camps that were housing more than 60,000 DPs. Believing that refugees needed to feel that others cared about them, he recorded the names of many and found people in Belgium who were willing to write to them, offering friendship and whatever assistance they could—small amounts of money as well as packages of food, clothing, and personal care items. Pire expanded his efforts, and by 1958 he had found 15,000 "sponsors by mail" in Western Europe for 15,000 refugees in Eastern Europe.

Pire's charity, which he named Aid to Displaced Persons, was financed entirely by private donations. With headquarters at Pire's monastery in Huy, the organization eventually formed branches in West Germany, Austria, Belgium, France, Luxembourg, Switzerland, Denmark, Italy, and the Netherlands.

In addition to the sponsorship program, Aid to Displaced Persons had a second component: refugee housing. Pire began by establishing homes for the aged in Huy and three other Belgian towns. He went on to construct what he called "European Villages" for refugees at locations throughout Europe. Pire believed that refugees desperately needed a sense of belonging, and he therefore built his villages within already existing towns and cities rather than separate from them.

Pire's first European Village, consisting of 20 houses, was built in 1956 in Aix-la-Chapelle, Germany, and soon became a thriving and self-supporting community of former DPs. Pire constructed additional villages in Germany, as well as Belgium and Austria, that housed nearly a thousand people by the late 1950s. Several of the villages were named after humanitarians whom Pire especially admired, including medical missionary Albert Schweitzer and explorer and scientist Fridtjof Nansen. A European Village in Germany was named after Anne Frank, the Dutch teenager who died in a German concentration camp during the war and who became famous after her diary was published in 1947.

In November 1958, the Nobel Committee announced that the recipient of that year's Peace Prize was the Reverend Dominique-Georges Pire, in recognition of his humanitarian work. The announcement took many by surprise: Pire had worked so anonymously over the years that few people knew who he was. When American newspapers asked the Belgian embassy in Washington, D.C., and Belgium's United Nations delegation in New York City for more information about Pire, they found that no one at either place had ever heard of him.

In accepting the prize, Pire expressed his belief that peace is created by an accumulation of individual efforts. "We must love our neighbors as ourselves," he said, and establish "little islands and oases of genuine kindness" that eventually "ring the world."

Pire used the prize money, totaling more than $41,000, to construct another European Village. During the next decade he intensified his efforts on behalf of world peace while continuing his work for refugees. In 1959 he established Heart Open to the World, an organization created to promote international friendship. A year later he founded the University of Peace, in Huy, to teach individuals how to work for peace in the world. In the nearly four decades of its existence, thousands of people have attended lectures and workshops at the university.

Pire also founded two more organizations in the remaining years of his life: World Friendships, an organization that aids refugee children in Africa and Asia, and Islands of Peace, an association of rural villages in India and Pakistan that have joined together to solve problems with the help of international aid.

In January 1969, at the age of 58, Pire became ill and entered a hospital in Louvain, Belgium, for treatment. He died there several days later, following an operation.

FURTHER READING

Pire, Dominique. *The Story of Father Dominique Pire, Winner of the Nobel Peace Prize*. New York: Dutton, 1961.

"Pire, (Dominique) Georges (Henri), Rev." In *Current Biography Yearbook 1959*. New York: H. Wilson, 1960.

Dominique-Georges Pire

BORN

February 10, 1910
Dinant, Belgium

DIED

January 30, 1969
Louvain, Belgium

EDUCATION

Doctorate in theology, Collegio Angelico, Rome (1936); postgraduate study, University of Louvain (1937)

OCCUPATION

Roman Catholic priest

MAJOR ACCOMPLISHMENTS

Founded Aid to Displaced Persons, an organization that offered assistance to and built housing for European refugees after World War II; founded the University of Peace to teach people practical ways to work for peace in the world; also founded World Friendships and Islands of Peace

Philip Noel-Baker

1959

Philip Noel-Baker's commitment to peace began when he was a child. Born Philip John Baker in London in 1889, he was raised in a Quaker household. His family belonged to the Society of Friends, a religious denomination that opposed war; its members were known as Friends, or Quakers. Philip Baker's parents were Canadians who had moved to London some years before. Philip's father had established a branch of the family engineering business in England, and he became a prominent industrialist as well as a member of Parliament.

The teachings of the Society of Friends, which centered on brotherhood, peace, and service to humanity, were emphasized by the Bakers in raising Philip and his six brothers and sisters. After graduating from a boarding school in Yorkshire, Philip was sent to Haverford College, a Quaker institution in the United States, before he enrolled at Cambridge University back in England.

Philip Baker graduated from Cambridge with an honors degree in history and economics in 1913, and a year later he received a master's degree from Cambridge. During his years at the university, he was president of the debating society as well as a track star. He competed for Great Britain in the 1912 Olympic Games in Stockholm; he also ran in the next Olympics, held in Antwerp in 1920; and in the 1924 Olympics, held in Paris, he served as captain of the British team.

In 1914 Baker became affiliated with Oxford University as the vice principal of an undergraduate college there. When World War I began in August of that year, Baker, like many other Quakers, chose to serve his country by performing humanitarian service rather than by joining the military. He immediately bought and equipped an ambulance and took it to France, where he became the head of a Friends' medical unit. After a year there, he went on to Italy as an officer with a British ambulance unit and served there until the war ended in 1918. Baker's distinguished war service earned him awards from the British, French, and Italian governments.

Following the war, Baker attended the Paris Peace Conference as an adviser to British delegates Robert Cecil (later Viscount Cecil of Chelwood) and Lord Parmoor, who helped draft the League of Nations Covenant. After the conference, he moved to League headquarters in Geneva, Switzerland, where he worked as an aide to the organization's first secretary-general, Sir Eric Drummond. He returned to England in 1922 to become a fellow of King's College, Cambridge, and two years later he became a professor of international

Philip Noel-Baker is congratulated by his son after hearing that he has won the Nobel Peace Prize for his efforts to secure world disarmament.

PEACEMAKERS

Philip Noel-Baker

BORN
November 1, 1889
London, England

DIED
October 8, 1982
London, England

EDUCATION
B.A. (1913), M.A. (1914), Cambridge University

OCCUPATION
Diplomat

MAJOR ACCOMPLISHMENTS
Member of Parliament (1929–31, 1936–70, 1977–82); chairman, British Labour party (1946–47); participated in the founding of the United Nations and its agencies; as an authority on international law and disarmament, wrote numerous articles and books for both scholars and the general public, including *The Arms Race: A Program for World Disarmament* (1958)

relations at the University of London, where he remained until 1929.

Since his college days, Baker had been a supporter of the Labour party, and during the 1920s he became active in Labour party politics. In 1929 he was elected as a Labourite to a seat in Parliament, which he held for two years. During this time he served as parliamentary secretary to Secretary of State Arthur Henderson, a leading supporter of world disarmament. Baker was also a longtime supporter of disarmament and had written two books about it in the late 1920s. He accompanied Henderson to the Tenth Assembly of the League of Nations, held in 1929–30 in Geneva, where he worked closely with Fridtjof Nansen and other delegates on an international arbitration agreement that was signed by more than 40 nations.

It was about this time that Philip Baker became known as Philip Noel-Baker, joining his wife's maiden name with his own. In 1915, while on leave from service with his ambulance unit, Baker had married Irene Noel of Greece, a daughter of English parents; five years later they had a son, their only child.

When the Labour party was defeated in the 1931 elections, Noel-Baker lost his seat in Parliament. He continued his association with Arthur Henderson, however, and in 1932–33 served in Geneva as an aide to Henderson, who was presiding over the League-sponsored World Disarmament Conference. By this time Noel-Baker had become widely recognized as a scholar in the field of international law, and in 1933 he was invited by Yale University in the United States to become a visiting lecturer for the academic year 1933–34. In 1934, at the conclusion of his lectureship, Yale awarded Noel-Baker its Howland Memorial

Prize for distinguished contributions to the study of government.

Noel-Baker was re-elected to Parliament in 1936 and this time kept his seat for more than three decades. During World War II he served as parliamentary secretary to the Ministry of War Transport in the coalition government led by Prime Minister Winston Churchill. (In a coalition government, power is shared by several political parties.) After the war ended in 1945, and the Labour party came to power, Noel-Baker became minister of state in the new government led by Prime Minister Clement Atlee.

As minister of state, Noel-Baker represented Great Britain in the establishment of the United Nations in 1945. He was closely involved with the founding of UNRRA, the United Nations Relief and Rehabilitation Administration, an organization that assumed major responsibility for relief and refugee assistance in the aftermath of World War II. He also helped to organize the UN Food and Agriculture Organization, and became a British delegate to the UN Economic and Social Council, where he supported measures to ease unemployment and poverty throughout the world.

In addition to his UN responsibilities, Noel-Baker remained active in Parliament. In 1946 he was appointed to the British cabinet as secretary of state for air power and also was elected chairman of the Labour party. From 1947 to 1950, Noel-Baker served as minister of commonwealth relations and participated in negotiations that led to the independence of India, which had been under the control of Great Britain for nearly 200 years.

In the years following his work with Arthur Henderson, Noel-Baker had continued to be a strong supporter of disarmament, and this became his major focus in Parliament during the 1950s. In *The Arms Race: A Program for World Disarmament*, published in 1958, Noel-Baker outlined the history of world disarmament efforts and offered his own analysis and suggestions. The book was viewed as a major statement on disarmament, and it focused worldwide attention on its author, who had devoted much of his adult life to the cause of peace.

The following year, in recognition of that long commitment, Philip Noel-Baker was awarded the Nobel Peace Prize for 1959. In his acceptance address, he warned against the growing threat of nuclear weapons and called on the United Nations to make world disarmament a reality. Disarmament, Noel-Baker said, was "the safest and most practicable system of defense."

Noel-Baker continued to be a vigorous spokesman for peace for the rest of his life. After retiring from Parliament at the age of 80, he became president of the British Vietnam Committee, a group that opposed the Vietnam War until it ended in 1975. Noel-Baker died in London in October 1982, a month before his 93rd birthday.

FURTHER READING

"Noel-Baker, Philip J(ohn)." In *Current Biography Yearbook 1946*. New York: H. W. Wilson, 1947.

Noel-Baker, Philip. *Disarmament*. 1926. Reprint, New York: Garland, 1972.

————. *The First World Disarmament Conference, 1932–1933, and Why It Failed*. New York: Pergamon, 1979.

Albert Luthuli

1960

T he exact date and year of Albert Luthuli's birth are not known, and probably never will be, but Luthuli's name will always be a part of African—and world—history. In the mid-20th century, Albert Luthuli led a mass movement to liberate native Africans from oppressive rule in South Africa. His rejection of violence, and his insistence on brotherhood and human equality, won him widespread sympathy and respect—and the 1960 Nobel Peace Prize.

Albert John Luthuli was born in Rhodesia, a British colony in East Africa, sometime around the year 1898. He grew up in Groutville, a mission station near the city of Durban in the province of Natal, South Africa. Luthuli's family was part of the native African aristocracy: his parents came from two distinguished Zulu tribes, and an uncle was a Zulu tribal chieftain. Luthuli's father worked as an interpreter at

Albert Luthuli, a prominent tribal chieftain in South Africa, receives the Nobel Peace Prize for his fight to achieve racial equality in his country. He was the first African to win the prize.

As part of the defiance campaign begun in 1952 by the African National Congress, black South Africans ride in a "Europeans only" railroad car. ANC leader Albert Luthuli helped launch the defiance campaign to protest South Africa's rigid apartheid laws

the Congregationalist mission in Groutville, which had been founded by American missionaries.

Luthuli attended area mission schools, where he was deeply impressed by the Christian religious training that he received. From an early age, Luthuli was taught to believe in the dignity and equality of all people, regardless of race or religion. After completing his secondary education, during which he became fluent in English, Luthuli received a teaching certificate. Beginning in 1921, he taught at Adam's Mission Station College, near Groutville, for 15 years.

In 1936 Luthuli was elected chieftain of the Abasemakholweni tribe of the Zulu nation, the same tribe that his uncle had led earlier. Centered in Natal province, the 5,000-member tribe was headed by Luthuli for 17

years. In addition to presiding over the tribal council, Luthuli oversaw the production of sugar cane, the tribe's main source of income, and also enforced laws and settled disputes. During this time, he was also active in several Christian religious organizations, including the Christian Council of South Africa, which he represented at the International Missionary Council conference held in India in 1938.

During the early 1940s, Luthuli became increasingly drawn to the liberation and independence movement that was growing among native peoples throughout Africa. Most African countries at that time were still under the rule of various European nations, and South Africa was one of several territories on the continent that belonged to Great Britain. Under white colonial rule in Africa, the majority black population had few political rights and was considered inferior.

In 1946 Luthuli joined the African National Congress (ANC), a movement founded in 1912 by blacks to end European domination in Africa. Soon after joining the ANC, Luthuli was elected president of the organization's division in Natal.

Luthuli's association with the ANC drew him into political activity as the South African government adopted harsh restrictive policies against the nonwhite population in the postwar years. In 1948, these policies became legalized into a system of segregation, or racial separation, known as apartheid (pronounced *uh-PAR-tide*). Under apartheid, the lives of nonwhite peoples in South Africa—who numbered more than 80 percent of the population—were rigorously controlled by the white governing minority.

Nonwhite resistance to apartheid grew during the next few years, and the ANC became the leader of that resistance. In 1952 Albert Luthuli helped launch the ANC's so-called Defiance Campaign, in which thousands of Africans staged sit-in demonstrations to protest segregation in various public facilities, including libraries, railroad stations, and post offices.

Because of his role in the ongoing Defiance Campaign, Luthuli was told by the South African government in October 1952 that he would be removed as tribal chief unless he quit the ANC. (Although chiefs were democratically elected by tribe members, the government reserved the right to remove them from office if they opposed official policy.) When Luthuli refused to resign from the ANC, the government not only ended his rule as chieftain but confined him to Groutville for 12 months. The government's move

backfired, however: the tribe responded by refusing to elect a replacement chief, and the incident, which attracted wide publicity, made Luthuli a national hero. Soon after his removal as chieftain, he was elected president of the entire ANC.

The government responded by placing Luthuli under house arrest at his farm in Groutville for two years. After his release in 1955, Luthuli continued to lead the ANC in peaceful protests against apartheid. He believed that the ANC's chief weapon against the system should be economic in nature, since the South African economy depended heavily on cheap native labor. He therefore encouraged and supported work stoppages as well as boycotts of certain goods and services. After a year of such protests, Luthuli was arrested in December 1956 on a charge of high treason and kept in custody until the charge was dropped a year later. Less than 18 months after his release, in May 1959, Luthuli was again placed under house arrest, this time for five years.

Luthuli's farm home was a simple five-room cottage where he lived with his family. (He was married in 1927 and had seven children.) The small tin and concrete house, which he built himself, was filled with books on philosophy, religion, and politics. Luthuli farmed during the day and read in the evenings.

In March 1960, Luthuli was taken to Pretoria, the South African capital, to appear as a defense witness in the trial of other ANC members accused of treason. While the trial was going on, a mass protest was launched by the ANC against the so-called pass system, which required all nonwhite Africans to carry an identity card at all times. On March 21, during a peaceful demonstration in

Albert Luthuli

BORN
About 1898
Rhodesia (now Zimbabwe)

DIED
July 21, 1967
Groutville, South Africa

EDUCATION
Attended missionary schools in South Africa, where he earned a teaching certificate

OCCUPATION
Teacher; political leader

MAJOR ACCOMPLISHMENTS
As president of the African National Congress (ANC), led campaign of passive resistance against South Africa's apartheid system

the town of Sharpeville against the pass system, government troops charged the demonstrators, killing 72 and wounding nearly 200 others.

Word of the Sharpeville Massacre quickly spread throughout a shocked world. Luthuli protested by publicly burning his own pass, and he called for a national day of mourning. The government responded by fining Luthuli $280 and imprisoning him briefly. In poor health—he suffered from high blood pressure and the after-effects of severe beatings by white toughs—he was soon released and sent back to permanent exile in Groutville.

Despite all that he had endured, Luthuli continued to believe in peaceful protest—passive resistance—and he counseled his followers to follow the Christian path of nonviolence. He was cutting sugar cane on his farm on the afternoon of October 23, 1961, when word reached him that, hours earlier, he had been belatedly named the recipient of the 1960 Nobel Peace Prize—the first black winner in the history of the award.

In its announcement, the Nobel Committee said that Luthuli had been honored for his use of nonviolent methods in fighting racial discrimination. Their choice was praised throughout the rest of the world but condemned in South Africa, and the government even stalled for weeks before issuing Luthuli and his wife a 10-day passport to attend the award ceremony.

When the Luthulis returned to South Africa from Oslo they were greeted by cheering crowds, but Luthuli was forbidden by the government from speaking to them. He returned to exile in Groutville and lived there quietly, under government order not to make public appearances. For some years he had been writing his autobiography,

and in 1962 he managed to send the manuscript out of the country. It was published that year in England and the United States as *Let My People Go* and was widely acclaimed. In South Africa, however, the book was banned. It was now a crime, punishable by fine and imprisonment, to print or even utter any words that Luthuli had ever written or spoken.

Luthuli's health declined in the remaining years of his life, and he suffered from deafness and a gradual loss of eyesight. On July 21, 1967, he was struck and killed by a train while attempting to cross a railroad bridge that passed over his farm.

Luthuli died before the liberation of South Africa's nonwhite population could be achieved. At the time of his death, younger black South Africans had become impatient with his philosophy of nonviolence, and he was dismissed by many activists as old-fashioned because of his religious outlook. Luthuli had faith until the end of his life, however, that the day would come when blacks throughout Africa would be able to lead purposeful lives in a peaceful, nonsegregated society.

Luthuli's own country took steps in that direction after years of continued protests against racial discrimination. In 1993 the hated apartheid laws were abolished in South Africa, and one year later, a black man, Nelson Mandela, head of the African National Congress, was elected president of the nation. Albert Luthuli's efforts had mattered after all.

FURTHER READING

Luthuli, Albert. *Let My People Go.* New York: McGraw-Hill, 1962.

Gordimer, Nadine. "Chief Luthuli." *Atlantic Monthly,* April 1959.

Dag Hammarskjöld

1961

In October 1961, the Nobel Peace Prize Committee announced two awards, one for 1960 and one for the current year. The Peace Prize for 1960 went to Albert Luthuli, the first African to receive the award. The recipient of the 1961 prize was also a "first": Dag Hammarskjöld, who had died violently a month earlier, became the first posthumous winner of the Nobel Peace Prize.

Dag Hjalmar Agne Carl Hammarskjöld (pronounced *HAM-mer-shuld*) was born in Jonkoping, Sweden, in 1905. He was descended from a long line of statesmen and military leaders that dated back to the early 1600s. His father was a distinguished legal scholar and politician who later served as Sweden's prime minister.

Hammarskjöld received bachelor's and master's degrees in social science from the University of Uppsala, and then earned a law degree at the university in 1930. He went on to work for a Swedish government committee on unemployment and also taught economics at the University

United Nations Secretary-General Dag Hammarskjöld inspects UN peacekeeping forces in Egypt in 1958. Hammarskjöld died three years later while on a UN mission to the Congo and received the Nobel Peace Prize posthumously.

of Stockholm while he continued doctoral studies in political economy at the University of Uppsala. After receiving his doctorate in 1934, he served as secretary of the Bank of Sweden for a year.

Hammarskjöld was now well known in Swedish government circles as an expert in finance and economics, and in 1936 he became undersecretary of the national department of finance. During his nine years in that post, he also served as an adviser on economic affairs to the Swedish government. Beginning in 1941, Hammarskjöld was also chairman of the board of governors of the Bank of Sweden and a member of the Board of Foreign Exchange, and held both positions until 1948. In addition, he served as a financial specialist at the Swedish Foreign Office in 1946 and 1947. This job drew him into negotiations with other countries, including the United States, over trade agreements, tariffs, and exports, and his skill and expertise attracted international notice.

Hammarskjöld represented Sweden at the 1947 Paris Conference that drew up the European Recovery Program, or Marshall Plan. The following year he was named Sweden's delegate to the Organization for European Economic Cooperation (OEEC), a predecessor of today's European Union. In 1949 he became Sweden's assistant foreign minister and two years later was promoted to deputy foreign minister with cabinet rank. In these posts he played an active role in Sweden's international economic relations.

In the fall of 1952 Hammarskjöld accompanied the Swedish delegation to the United Nations General Assembly

meeting in New York City as its vice chairman, and the following February he became head of the delegation. Two months later, he was the unexpected choice of the General Assembly to serve as the UN's second secretary-general, succeeding Trygve Lie of Norway.

As secretary-general, the chief presiding officer of the General Assembly, Hammarskjöld headed an administrative office called the Secretariat. Soon after taking office, he made changes in the organization of the Secretariat that enabled it to operate more efficiently. He then began to enlarge the role of the secretary-general by taking a more active role in international diplomacy on behalf of the United Nations. Hammarskjöld believed that the UN Charter gave him the authority to consult personally with heads of state whenever an international dispute appeared likely, and during the next few years he assumed the role of chief UN negotiator.

Hammarskjöld also believed that the United Nations should be active in what he called "preventive diplomacy." In other words, he wanted the UN to do more than just be a forum where individual nations brought their problems to be solved. He tried to make the United Nations into an organization that worked actively on behalf of world peace rather than waiting to act until crises arose.

Hammarskjöld's quiet diplomacy undoubtedly kept many arguments between nations from growing into full-blown disputes, but he was also ready to negotiate when crises erupted. His peacemaking skills were demonstrated several times during his eight years as secretary-general. In 1954, he flew to

Beijing and persuaded the Chinese government to release 11 U.S. prisoners who had been held since the end of the Korean War a year earlier. In September 1956, when Egypt nationalized the Suez Canal, an international waterway, and war appeared likely, Hammarskjöld quickly assembled a UN peacekeeping force, headed by Ralph Bunche, that restored order to the region. Two years later, when Lebanon and Jordan complained that their security was being threatened by neighboring Arab states in the Middle East, Hammarskjöld set up UN observation posts in both countries that discouraged further threats.

The greatest challenge to Hammarskjöld's peacemaking skills arose in 1960, when the Congo (later Zaïre), an African colony of Belgium for more than half a century, became independent. Civil war broke out when the province of Katanga seceded from the country, and Belgian troops re-entered the country to restore order. The troops were not welcomed by the Congolese, who appealed to the United Nations for help. The UN Security Council responded by unanimously calling for the withdrawal of the Belgians, but this request was ignored. The crisis grew more complicated when the Congolese president, Patrice Lumumba, threatened to ask the Soviet Union for military aid.

As the situation dragged on over many months, Hammarskjöld worked to negotiate a truce and to reunite Katanga with the central government. Finally, in the late summer of 1961, he decided to meet personally with Moise Tshombe, the president of Katanga. Hammarskjöld and a party of UN advisers were en route to Katanga on September 17, 1961, when their plane crashed over Northern Rhodesia. Everyone on board was killed.

In October, the Nobel Peace Prize Committee announced that the 1961 award would be made posthumously to Dag Hammarskjöld. Two months later, at ceremonies in Oslo, the Swedish ambassador to Norway accepted the award on behalf of the Hammarskjöld family. At the same ceremonies, South African Zulu chieftain Albert Luthuli received the 1960 Peace Prize. Many observers thought that this linking of Hammarskjöld and Luthuli was highly appropriate. As a *New York Times* editorial commented: "The Swedish diplomat and the African tribesman are united in life and death by their humility and their love of humanity."

At his death, Hammarskjöld was praised for his years of selfless government service. There was much more to his life, however. He excelled in sports, including gymnastics, skiing, and mountain climbing, and for many years served as president of the Swedish Alpinist Club. He was also well read in world literature and philosophy, and for relaxation he enjoyed translating many classic works into Swedish. From 1953 until his death, he was a member of the Swedish Academy, which awards the Nobel Prize for Literature; Hammarskjöld is credited by many with convincing the committee to give the 1958 prize to Boris Pasternak, the Russian author of *Dr. Zhivago*.

Three years after his death, Hammarskjöld's admirers were offered a glimpse of his inner life with the publication of his personal diary. Translated into many languages, it appeared in English as *Markings*. The diary is a series of philosophical and religious meditations on the meaning of life, and it is now considered a modern classic.

In 1962, Hammarskjöld's Nobel Peace Prize money was used to create the Dag Hammarskjöld Foundation, a living memorial to Hammarskjöld and his longtime interest in the developing nations, the so-called Third World. Contributions were also received from donors in many countries. The purpose of the foundation is "the promotion of social, political, economic, and cultural progress within the nations whose development Dag Hammarskjöld had so closely at heart, by providing training for citizens of those countries to hold responsible positions." Headquartered in Uppsala, the foundation sponsors conferences and seminars on Third World issues and publishes books, monographs, and a semiannual journal on international development.

FURTHER READING

Foote, Wilder, ed. *Servant of Peace: A Selection of the Speeches and Statements of Dag Hammarskjöld.* New York: Harper & Row, 1962.

Hammarskjöld, Dag. *Markings.* New York: Knopf, 1964.

Levine, I. E. *Champion of World Peace: Dag Hammarskjöld.* New York: Julian Messner, 1962.

Sheldon, Richard. *Dag Hammarskjöld.* New York: Chelsea House, 1987.

Urquhart, Brian. *Hammarskjöld.* New York: Knopf, 1972.

Dag Hammarskjöld

BORN
July 29, 1905
Jonkoping, Sweden

DIED
September 17, 1961
Northern Rhodesia

EDUCATION
B.A. (1925), M.A. (1928), Ph.D. (1934), L.L.B., 1930, University of Uppsala

OCCUPATION
Economist; diplomat

MAJOR ACCOMPLISHMENTS
As secretary-general of the United Nations (1953–61), mediated disputes throughout the world; his personal diary, *Markings* (1964), became an international best-seller

Linus Pauling

1962

I
n 1954 a distinguished American scientist named Linus Pauling received the highest award in his field—the Nobel Prize for Chemistry. Pauling was cited for his longtime investigation of the forces that hold molecules together in matter. He had developed what he called the resonance theory to explain molecular bonding, and his studies had led to his discovery of the atomic structure of protein molecules. That finding eventually paved the way for new discoveries, by Pauling and other scientists, about the chemistry of the human body and its diseases.

By 1954, Pauling's interest in human chemistry had led him to begin investigating the effects on the body of radioactive fallout, particles and gases that are the by-products of exploding nuclear weapons. He became convinced that increasing amounts of fallout in the world—the consequence of atomic bomb blasts and the testing of other nuclear

Linus Pauling demonstrates against nuclear weapons testing in Washington, D.C., in 1961, during a visit by British prime minister Harold Macmillan to President John F. Kennedy.

weapons, beginning in the mid-1940s—had become a major cause of certain types of disease as well as mental retardation and physical deformity.

Pauling was alarmed by his findings, and he became a vigorous crusader against nuclear weapons testing, as well as a strong advocate of disarmament. In 1962, 8 years after winning the Nobel Prize for Chemistry, Pauling's efforts to end the threat of nuclear war earned him the Nobel Peace Prize. He became the first person to win separate Nobel Prizes in both a scientific and a nonscientific field. (Only one other person besides Pauling has won more than one Nobel Prize in any field: Marie Curie, who shared the Physics Prize in 1903 and won the Chemistry Prize in 1911.)

Linus Carl Pauling's early life did not indicate that he was headed for international distinction. Born in 1901 in Portland, Oregon, to a pharmacist and his wife, Pauling did well enough in his studies when he found the course work interesting, but in high school he did not bother to take many of the required courses, and as a result he was not allowed to graduate. Lacking a diploma, Pauling was admitted to Oregon State College anyway because of his aptitude for science and math.

Following graduation from Oregon State in 1922 with a bachelor's degree in chemistry and physics, Pauling attended graduate school at the California Institute of Technology in Pasadena. There he focused on physical chemistry and also continued to develop his interest in atomic physics. Pauling received a doctorate with highest honors in 1925 and was awarded a Guggenheim Fellowship, which enabled him to do postgraduate study in atomic physics at institutions in Munich, Zurich, and Copenhagen for several years.

Pauling returned to Caltech in the fall of 1927 and joined the faculty as an assistant professor of chemistry. He ad-vanced quickly in rank and four years later had become a full professor. Beginning in the late 1920s, Pauling undertook extensive research on chemical bonding and developed his resonance theory. During the 1930s he continued this work at Caltech. The importance of Pauling's research was recognized as early as 1931, when the American Chemical Society awarded him its prestigious Langmuir Prize. Eight years later he published a book about his scientific investigations that is still considered an important study: *The Nature of the Chemical Bond and the Structure of Molecules and Crystals* (1939).

In 1937 Pauling became chairman of the division of chemistry and chemical engineering at Caltech. About this time he began research on the structure of proteins, substances that occur naturally in living matter. From 1942 to 1945, as World War II was fought in Europe and Asia, Pauling aided the U.S. government defense effort by doing research on explosives. He also served as a government consultant on medical research. At Caltech, Pauling and several colleagues spent the war years developing a gelatin product as a substitute for blood plasma, a feat they finally accomplished in 1945, not long before the war ended. Pauling's wartime contributions to national defense earned him the Presidential Medal for Merit in 1948.

In the postwar years of the late 1940s, Pauling joined with other scientists in continuing the study of proteins. At the same time he did research on a related topic: the biochemical effects of the polio virus on human nerve cells. (Until a preventive vaccine became widely available in the mid-1950s, polio killed or permanently crippled thousands of people, primarily children, every year.)

In 1951 Pauling announced a major achievement in his protein structure research: the discovery, with fellow scientist Robert B. Corey, of the atomic

Linus Pauling

BORN
February 28, 1901
Portland, Oregon

DIED
August 19, 1994
Big Sur, California

EDUCATION
B.S., Oregon State College (1922); Ph.D., California Institute of Technology (1926)

OCCUPATION
Scientist; peace activist

MAJOR ACCOMPLISHMENTS
Led U.S. movement to ban nuclear weapons testing; drafted a proposal that served as the basis for the 1963 nuclear test ban treaty signed by the United States, Great Britain, and the Soviet Union; first person to win separate Nobel Prizes in both scientific and nonscientific fields

An atomic bomb test in Nevada. Linus Pauling's concern about the health hazards of fallout—the radioactive debris created by atomic explosions—motivated his crusade for a ban on nuclear weapons testing.

structure of several types of protein molecules. This was the first time in history that the "architecture" of a protein molecule had been drawn. Pauling and Corey's achievement paved the way for later biochemical research by thousands of scientists throughout the world, and that research in turn led to programs for the prevention and control of many diseases. Three years after announcing this groundbreaking discovery, Linus Pauling received the 1954 Nobel Prize for Chemistry for nearly three decades of research on chemical bonding and molecular structure.

Since the development of atomic weapons during World War II, Pauling had become increasingly disturbed by the potential harm of radioactive fallout. Pauling's studies in atomic physics had convinced him that radioactivity could cause permanent damage to the structures of all living things. In the mid-1950s, Pauling became increasing-

ly outspoken in his opposition to nuclear weapons testing by the United States, the Soviet Union, and other countries, and he began calling publicly for multilateral disarmament. Pauling's support of disarmament drew wide criticism, however, and he was even investigated by U.S. authorities on suspicion of trying to overthrow the government.

Despite this opposition, Pauling continued his campaign. He soon became a familiar figure to millions of Americans, who read about him in newspapers and magazines and saw him interviewed on television. By 1958 he had become the unofficial head of the antinuclear movement in the United States. At the beginning of that year he presented to the United Nations a petition, signed by more than 11,000 scientists, calling for an end to nuclear weapons testing. The petition was somewhat successful: by the end of the year, both the United States and the Soviet Union had called for a temporary halt to atmospheric weapons testing (that is, testing done in the open air, above the ground).

In February 1958, Pauling participated in a widely broadcast television debate on disarmament with Edward Teller, a physicist who had helped build the hydrogen bomb and believed that fallout from nuclear testing was not harmful. The text of the debate was published later that year as *Fallout and Disarmament: A Debate* (S. F. Fearon, editor). Also in 1958, Pauling filed a lawsuit against the U.S. Department of Defense and the U.S. Atomic Energy Commission that sought to ban further nuclear testing. The suit was not judged in Pauling's favor, but it generated a lot of publicity for the antinuclear movement. Finally, in that same year, Pauling presented his case for disarmament in his widely read book *No More War!* and followed this up with a series of lectures and articles on the subject during the next few years.

Pauling's efforts to ban nuclear weapons earned him the Nobel Peace Prize for 1962. The award was not announced, however, until October 10, 1963—the same day that a partial nuclear test ban agreed to by the United States, Great Britain, and the Soviet Union went into effect. In fact, Pauling had drafted a proposal that served as the basis of the test ban treaty. In presenting him with the award, the Nobel Peace Prize Committee praised Pauling for opposing not only nuclear weapons testing but all warfare as a means of resolving international conflicts.

Although Pauling remained committed to world peace and disarmament, he devoted most of the remainder of his life to scientific research. He left Caltech in 1964 to become a professor at the Center for the Study of Democratic Institutions, a research organization in Santa Barbara, California. Three years later he also became a professor of chemistry at the University of California at San Diego. In 1969 he left UC San Diego to become a chemistry professor at Stanford University, in Palo Alto, California, and resigned from the Center for the Study of Democratic Institutions.

In the mid-1960s, Pauling had begun doing research on the use of vitamins, especially vitamin C, to cure a variety of illnesses. He gave the name "orthomolecular medicine" to this form of healing. Pauling's first book on the subject, *Vitamin C and the Common Cold*, was published in 1970 and became a best-seller. Pauling retired from the chemistry department at Stanford three years later to establish the Linus Pauling Institute of Science and Medicine in Palo Alto. There he did extensive research on vitamin therapy and published another best-selling book called *Cancer and Vitamin C* (1979).

Although the general public praised Pauling for his work on vitamin therapy, the scientific establishment was generally critical. The opposition of his colleagues did not stop Pauling, however. In the 1970s and 1980s he became as widely identified with vitamin therapy as he had been several decades earlier with antinuclear protests. In 1986 he published another best-seller on orthomolecular medicine, *How to Live Longer and Feel Better*.

In the last decades of his life, Pauling divided his time between a house in Palo Alto and a cabin in Big Sur, California. He shared both residences with his wife until her death in 1981. (Pauling was married in 1922 and had four children.)

In addition to two Nobel Prizes, Pauling received dozens of other major awards, including France's Pasteur Medal, the National Medal of Science, the International Lenin Prize, and the Priestley Medal from the American Chemical Society, as well as honorary degrees from more than 50 leading universities around the world. During his lifetime he published more than a thousand articles and books. Linus Pauling died in Big Sur in August 1994 at the age of 93.

FURTHER READING

Goertzel, Ted G. *Linus Pauling: A Life in Science and Politics*. New York: Basic Books, 1995.

Hager, Thomas. *Force of Nature: The Life of Linus Pauling*. New York: Simon & Schuster, 1995.

————. *Linus Pauling and the Chemistry of Life*. New York: Oxford University Press, 1998.

Marinacci, Barbara, ed. *Linus Pauling in His Own Words*. New York: Simon & Schuster, 1995.

Pauling, Linus. *No More War!* 1958. Reprint, Westport, Conn.: Greenwood Press, 1975.

White, Florence Meiman. *Linus Pauling: Scientist and Crusader*. New York: Walker, 1980.

International Committee of the Red Cross and League of Red Cross Societies

1963

T he International Committee of the Red Cross, which received the Nobel Peace Prize in 1917 and 1944, won for a third time in 1963. This time it shared the award with the League of Red Cross Societies, an association of national Red Cross and Red Crescent societies in countries throughout the world that had been formed in 1919. (Red Crescent was the name given to Red Cross societies in Muslim countries beginning in 1906.)

Following the end of World War II in 1945, the main task of the International Committee of the Red Cross (ICRC) was to help resettle millions of military and civilian war prisoners in both Europe and Asia. When this effort ended in 1948, the ICRC turned its attention to broadening the 1929 Geneva Convention, which had specified guidelines for humane treatment of military war prisoners. The revised agreement, known as the 1949 Geneva Convention, extended these earlier guidelines to cover civilian war prisoners.

In the 1950s and early 1960s, numerous conflicts throughout the world required the services of both the ICRC and the League of Red Cross Societies (LRCS). During the Korean War (1950–53), the ICRC aided prisoners of war and civilians in South Korea. Following the armistice that ended the war in the summer of 1953, the ICRC helped repatriate (return to their native countries) North Korean and Chinese prisoners.

The ICRC provided food and medical aid to the wounded during the Suez Crisis of 1956 (a conflict that arose over Egypt's nationalization of the Suez Canal, an international

In Austria, a Red Cross nurse distributes aid packages to Hungarian refugees in 1957. They were forced to flee their country after the Soviet Union crushed Hungary's attempts to overthrow Communist rule.

waterway). Both the ICRC and the LRCS provided aid in Budapest, Hungary, during the 1956 Hungarian Revolution and later helped resettle thousands of Hungarian refugees who fled to Austria.

During the long revolt of Algeria, a North African colony, against French rule, beginning in the late 1950s, the ICRC aided thousands of refugees and monitored conditions in prisoner-of-war camps.

In the civil war that erupted after Belgium granted independence to the Congo (now Zaire) in 1960, the ICRC once again provided medical relief, aided war prisoners, and helped resettle refugees. The LRCS brought more than 100 volunteer doctors and nurses from around the world to care for the wounded during the conflict.

For these and many other services, the International Committee of the Red Cross and the League of Red Cross Societies were named cowinners of the 1963 Nobel Peace Prize. Since then, both the ICRC and the LRCS have continued to provide humanitarian assistance in both peacetime and war throughout the world. Major recipients of their aid have included survivors of such major natural disasters as the 1970 cyclone in East Pakistan (Bangladesh), the 1974 hurricane in Honduras, and the 1988 earthquake in Armenia. The ICRC and the LRCS have also helped thousands of victims of various ongoing conflicts in the Middle East.

From 1919 until the mid-1980s, the ICRC, the LRCS, and the many national Red Cross societies were known collectively as the International Red Cross. In 1986 that name was changed to the International Movement of Red Cross and Red Crescent Societies. Today there are national Red Cross societies in more than 100 countries around the world. These national Red Cross societies not only provide disaster relief; they also sponsor health and safety programs and maintain blood banks.

The official certificate presented by the Norwegian parliament names the International Committee of the Red Cross as the winner of the 1963 Nobel Peace Prize.

Although some national Red Cross societies receive government aid, most of their work—as well as most of the work of the ICRC and the LRCS—is supported by voluntary contributions.

FURTHER READING

Durand, André. *From Sarajevo to Hiroshima: History of the International Committee of the Red Cross*. Geneva: Henri Dunant Institute, 1984.

Epstein, Beryl, and Sam Epstein. *The Story of the International Red Cross*. New York: Nelson, 1963.

Gumpert, Martin. *Dunant: The Story of the Red Cross*. Oxford: Oxford University Press, 1938.

Joyce, James A. *Red Cross International and the Strategy of Peace*. New York: Oceana, 1959.

Willemin, Georges, and Roger Heacock. *The International Committee of the Red Cross*. Groningen: Martinus Nijhoff, 1984.

International Committee of the Red Cross and League of Red Cross Societies

FOUNDERS
Henri Dunant and the Geneva Public Welfare Society

FOUNDING
October 1863
Geneva, Switzerland

HEADQUARTERS
Geneva, Switzerland

PURPOSE
Founded to assist the sick and wounded during wartime; after World War I, expanded its efforts to caring for victims of natural disasters and to other humanitarian relief

MAJOR ACCOMPLISHMENTS, 1945–63
Helped resettle millions of military and civilian war prisoners following World War II; led efforts to create the 1949 Geneva Convention; provided relief to victims of conflict in Korea, the Middle East, Hungary, and Africa

Martin Luther King, Jr.

1964

O ne Sunday afternoon during the winter of 1949, a curious young African-American divinity student at a seminary just outside Philadelphia traveled into the city to hear a lecture about Mohandas Gandhi (1869–1948), a Hindu religious leader in India. Gandhi had led the longtime movement for India's independence from Great Britain, and he had done so by preaching a philosophy of nonviolent defiance, which he called *satyagraha* (pronounced *sat-tee-ah-GRAH-ha*).

Gandhi believed that the power of love was greater than the power of hate, and that love could be used to change people's ideas and actions. For years he had led peaceful, nonviolent demonstrations against the British, and in 1947 his tactics finally paid off: Great Britain freed India from colonial rule. Gandhi is revered as one of the greatest peacemakers in history—yet he never received a Nobel Peace Prize.

The young divinity student, whose name was Martin Luther King, Jr., was deeply impressed by the concept of satyagraha, or peaceful defiance, and he never forgot it. Six years later, Gandhi's philosophy inspired King to launch his nonviolent crusade against racial segregation in America—a

Martin Luther King, Jr., with his wife, Coretta Scott King, at a news conference in Montgomery, Alabama, in 1956, during the Montgomery bus boycott.

crusade that eventually earned *him* the Nobel Peace Prize.

Martin Luther King, Jr., was born in Atlanta, Georgia, in 1929. His father, Martin Luther King, Sr., was pastor of the Ebenezer Baptist Church, a prominent black church in Atlanta. Martin's grandfather on his mother's side was a former pastor of the same church. Growing up in the city in the 1930s and 1940s, Martin and his brother and sister were always aware that they lived in a segregated society: blacks were considered inferior to whites, and the two races were kept apart in both private and public facilities. In general, the facilities available to blacks, including schools and housing, were inferior to those for whites, and discrimination against black people was widespread.

Nevertheless, the King children were brought up by their parents to respect people of all races, and to value themselves as well. Young Martin grew up in a warm and loving family, and he enjoyed both schoolwork and sports. After graduating from high school at the age of 15, he entered Morehouse College, an institution for black men in Atlanta that his father and maternal grandfather had also attended.

Both parents assumed that Martin would enter the ministry, too, but at first he opposed the idea. He later said that "the emotionalism," the "shouting and stomping" that he saw in his father's church had turned him against religion for a brief period when he was in his early teens. However, Martin changed his mind when he heard the dignified preaching of another Baptist minister, Morehouse College president Benjamin Mays, in the college chapel. Mays believed that black churches should lead a movement for social change and an end to discrimination, and his sermons on that subject convinced Martin Luther King, Jr., to become a clergyman, too.

In February 1948, King was ordained a Baptist minister and became an assistant pastor at Ebenezer. He graduated from Morehouse in June and the following September entered Crozer Seminary in Chester, Pennsylvania, to study theology. King's three years at Crozer, where nearly all the students were white, were crucial to his future development: he excelled in his courses, was one of the most socially popular students on campus—and discovered a philosophy that would guide him for the rest of his life.

After graduating at the head of his class in 1951 with a bachelor's degree in divinity, King entered Boston University on a scholarship to do graduate work in religion. Again he excelled both academically and socially, and his professors encouraged him to become a teacher. King remained committed to the ministry, however, as he worked toward his doctorate. In 1953 he married Coretta Scott, a native of Alabama who was studying voice at the New England Conservatory of Music in Boston. A year later, in the fall of 1954, the couple returned to the South when King was hired as the pastor of the Dexter Avenue Baptist Church in Montgomery, Alabama.

Like all cities in the South at that time, Montgomery was racially segregated—but change was coming. Only a few months earlier, the U.S. Supreme Court had declared, in *Brown* v. *Board of Education*, that segregation in public schools was unconstitutional. The Supreme Court decision meant that public schools would have to be integrated. Many white people in the South were angered by the decision and vowed to maintain segregation by any means possible, including violence.

King urged his congregation at the Dexter Avenue Baptist Church to take an active role in opposing segregation. He encouraged them to join the National Association for the Advancement of Colored People (NAACP), a

Martin Luther King, Jr.

BORN

January 15, 1929
Atlanta, Georgia

DIED

April 4, 1968
Memphis, Tennessee

EDUCATION

B.A., Morehouse College (1948); B.D., Crozer Theological Seminary (1951); Ph.D., Boston University (1955)

OCCUPATION

Clergyman; civil rights leader

MAJOR ACCOMPLISHMENTS

Led successful effort to integrate public transportation in Montgomery, Alabama; founded Southern Christian Leadership Conference to work for nonviolent social change; influenced passage of major civil rights legislation in the United States

King in his cell at the Birmingham city jail in 1963. During his confinement, he wrote "Letter from a Birmingham Jail," which defended the civil rights movement as a justifiable disobedience of unjust laws.

to fight Alabama state laws that legalized segregation in public transportation. In addition to filing a lawsuit, the NAACP urged blacks to boycott the city buses, and they persuaded King to support the action. An organization called the Montgomery Improvement Association (MIA) was formed to direct the boycott, and King was elected its president.

As the head of MIA, King preached his philosophy of nonviolent resistance in black churches throughout Montgomery. He urged his listeners to use the power of love to overcome segregation. King and his family received death threats from supporters of segregation and their house was bombed, but he persisted in leading the successful boycott—which paralyzed the bus system—and supporting the lawsuit.

King's actions made him known throughout the United States, and he was widely praised for his courage. The lawsuit eventually reached the U.S. Supreme Court, which in November 1956 declared that Alabama's state and local laws requiring segregation on public buses were unconstitutional. One month later—a year after the boycott began—buses in Montgomery were running again, this time fully integrated.

The success of the bus boycott made King into a leading spokesman for civil rights in the United States. In the spring of 1957, he carried his message of nonviolent resistance to Washington, D.C. There he joined with several other prominent blacks to lead a public demonstration in support of civil rights legislation then being considered by the U.S. Congress. The demonstration, called the Prayer Pilgrimage for Freedom, was held at the Lincoln Memorial on May 17 and attracted a crowd of 25,000, blacks as

leading civil rights organization, and to register to vote. In 1955, the year he finally received his Ph.D. from Boston University, King himself became a social activist when he agreed to lead a boycott of Montgomery's discriminatory bus system.

The boycott began on December 1, 1955, when a black woman named Rosa Parks refused to give up her seat on a city bus to a white man, as required by law. She was arrested, jailed overnight, and required to pay a $10 fine upon her release. The NAACP decided to make Parks's arrest a test case well as whites. King was one of several black speakers who appeared at the gathering, but his speech received the most praise. Afterwards the leading black newspaper in the United States declared that King was "the number-one leader" of the nation's black population.

King and other black leaders were disappointed when the proposed legislation was considerably weakened by Congress and then passed as the Civil Rights Act of 1957. This disappointment, however, only strengthened King's resolve. That summer he decided to create a new organization to carry the message of nonviolent resistance throughout the country, and he named it the Southern Christian Leadership Conference (SCLC).

King and the SCLC became the driving force behind the U.S. civil rights movement. From SCLC headquarters in Atlanta, King directed a nationwide effort with a single goal: the participation of all blacks as full citizens of the United States. The SCLC conducted voter registration drives, launched peaceful sit-ins to integrate eating facilities, and organized what it called Freedom Rides, in which interracial groups toured the South by bus, integrating waiting rooms, bathrooms, and other public facilities.

King participated personally in many of these activities, leading supporters in peaceful marches that were often met with violence. He was arrested several times and his life was frequently threatened; nevertheless he persisted. When he was jailed following a demonstration in Birmingham, Alabama, in April 1963, King wrote a response to opponents of the civil rights movement. Called "Letter from a Birmingham Jail," it argued that everyone had "a moral responsibility to disobey unjust laws." King's letter attracted

worldwide attention and made him an international hero.

Later that year, on August 28, 1963, King spoke at the March for Jobs and Freedom in Washington, D.C., a gathering of 250,000 blacks and whites that he had helped organize to show support for desegregation. Standing in front of the Lincoln Memorial, King declared, "I have a dream today . . . of a time when sons of former slaves and sons of former slave-owners will be able to sit down together at the table of brotherhood." In the following months, King met with President Lyndon B. Johnson and encouraged him to support strong civil rights legislation. King's dream came closer to reality in July 1964, when the President signed the Civil Rights Act, making segregation a federal crime.

That fall, Martin Luther King, Jr., was named the winner of the 1964 Nobel Peace Prize for his nonviolent defiance of segregation. He was 35 years old—the youngest person ever to receive the award. In his acceptance speech, he asked men and women throughout the world to practice brotherhood and to reject "revenge, aggression, and retaliation."

Back in the United States, King continued to lead the SCLC in its peaceful protest against segregation. In January 1965, he launched a voter registration drive in Selma, Alabama. His efforts there, which attracted nationwide attention, led to the passage of the Voting Rights Act, another major piece of civil rights legislation, which President Johnson signed in early August. This was to be the last major achievement of King's career.

A few days after the signing of the Voting Rights Act, a major race riot erupted in Watts, a black community in Los Angeles. King flew there immediately and walked through the heavily

Hindu religious leader Mohandas Gandhi (center) was guided by a philosophy of nonviolent protest during his long struggle for India's independence. King adopted Gandhi's philosophy, and it became the guiding principle of his movement.

damaged area, pleading for an end to violence. He discovered, however, that his nonviolent philosophy was not welcomed, and he returned to Atlanta. In 1966 King launched another protest movement, this time aimed at housing discrimination in Chicago. His efforts were unsuccessful here, too: hostile white mobs threatened him with violence as he tried to lead peaceful protest marches through the city streets.

In early 1967, when King publicly proclaimed his opposition to the Vietnam War, he lost the support of many SCLC members. The United States had become deeply involved in the war under the leadership of President Johnson—the same President who was a strong supporter of civil rights legislation. Many of King's followers believed that he was harming the black cause by criticizing the President's foreign policy. Meanwhile, more and more blacks were turning to violence to protest discriminatory conditions in cities across the country. Hundreds were killed, thousands were injured, and entire neighborhoods were burned to the ground in a series of race riots that erupted during the summer of 1967.

Deeply disturbed by violence both at home and abroad, King was nevertheless determined to use peaceful resistance to achieve his ultimate goal of racial equality. While serving as cochairman of a leading antiwar organization, Clergy and Laymen Concerned About Vietnam, he launched still another effort, called the Poor People's Campaign, to call national attention to economic injustice, and began planning for a march in Washington, D.C. To gain publicity for the march, planned for April 1968, King traveled to Memphis, Tennessee, at the end of March to lead a demonstration of striking garbage men. Several days

later he was shot to death by a white sniper as he stood on the balcony of his motel room.

Ironically, both King and the man he most admired, Mohandas Gandhi—men who devoted their lives to the peaceful pursuit of justice—ended their lives in violence: both were killed by assassins. Like Gandhi, King was mourned as a martyr throughout the world, and many public tributes were paid to him. In 1983, 15 years after his death, the U.S. Congress set aside the third Monday in January as Martin Luther King Day, an annual holiday. Three years later, a bust of King was installed in the Great Rotunda of the Capitol Building in Washington, D.C.—making him the first black person to be so honored. King's work has been continued by the Martin Luther King, Jr. Center for Nonviolent Social Change, an organization founded in Atlanta by his followers.

FURTHER READING

Gandhi, Mohandas K. *An Autobiography, or The Story of My Experiments with Truth.* 1927–29. Reprint. London: Penguin Books, 1982.

Jakoubek, Robert. *Martin Luther King, Jr.* New York: Chelsea House, 1989.

King, Martin Luther, Jr. *Stride Toward Freedom: The Montgomery Story.* New York: Harper & Row, 1958.

———. *A Testament of Hope: The Essential Writings of Martin Luther King, Jr.* Edited by James Melvin Washington. San Francisco: Harper, 1986.

———. *Why We Can't Wait.* New York: Harper & Row, 1963.

McKissack, Patricia. *Martin Luther King, Jr.: A Man to Remember.* Chicago: Childrens Press, 1984.

Oates, Stephen B. *Let the Trumpet Sound.* New York: Harper, 1982.

United Nations Children's Fund (UNICEF)

1965

The United Nations Children's Fund was established in London in December 1946 by a unanimous resolution of the newly created United Nations General Assembly. The full name of the organization was the United Nations International Children's Emergency Fund, or UNICEF. In 1953, seven years after its founding, the words "International" and "Emergency" were dropped from its official name, but the organization continues to be known by the familiar acronym UNICEF (pronounced *YOON-ih-seff*).

UNICEF was created initially as a short-term solution to an emergency situation: After World War II ended in 1945, some 20 million children were living in squalid conditions in Europe. Many were confined to overcrowded refugee camps; others were homeless orphans who roamed the streets of major cities, seeking food and shelter. The UN General Assembly gave UNICEF responsibility for helping these children, and the UN secretary-general appointed an American named Maurice Pate to direct its efforts. Pate was well qualified to do the job, for he had directed major U.S.-sponsored relief efforts in Europe after World War I ended in 1918.

Using funds contributed voluntarily by both private foundations and governments of UN member nations, Pate

American relief expert Maurice Pate was the first executive director of UNICEF after its founding in 1946. He led UNICEF for 18 years, working to meet the needs of children everywhere.

Children in Indonesia are tested for tuberculosis by a UNICEF health care worker.

set up an intensive relief network. In addition to financial aid, the United States and several other nations with large dairy industries also provided UNICEF with enormous quantities of powdered milk. In its first three years of operation, UNICEF spent $112 million to distribute clothing, vaccinate children against tuberculosis, establish facilities to process and distribute milk, and provide a daily meal to millions of European children.

By 1950, the emergency situation in Europe had passed and economic conditions were returning to normal, thanks to the European Recovery Plan (Marshall Plan) devised by George C.

Marshall. With its remaining funds, UNICEF turned its attention to developing health and nutrition programs for children in developing nations, primarily in Africa and Southeast Asia. In December 1953, the General Assembly recognized the value of UNICEF's work—and the continuing need for it—by making it a permanent agency of the United Nations.

During the 1950s, UNICEF combated many diseases that affected children in developing countries, including yaws, leprosy, and malaria. UNICEF workers improved sanitation, provided health education to parents and other caretakers, and developed nutrition programs. In some of these areas, UNICEF worked cooperatively with representatives of other UN agencies, in particular the World Health Organization (WHO) and the Food and Agriculture Organization (FAO). One of UNICEF's major accomplishments was the development of soybean milk as a protein substitute in countries that lacked sufficient dairy products.

In 1958, UNICEF began offering various social services to children and their families. It set up counseling, youth, and day-care centers and sponsored classes on child rearing and homemaking. Three years later, UNICEF further enlarged its concerns by providing aid in the field of education at the request of individual countries. This help included teacher training, curriculum development, and technical assistance.

UNICEF was awarded the 1965 Nobel Peace Prize for its role in furthering international cooperation. Sadly, Maurice Pate died before the award was made. However, his successor as executive director, Henry Labouisse, paid tribute to Pate in his acceptance speech. UNICEF used the prize money to create the Maurice Pate Memorial Award, which is given annually "to strengthen the training or experience of people serving in child welfare-related fields in countries with which UNICEF is cooperating."

As the only agency of the United Nations devoted exclusively to the welfare of children, UNICEF has continued its assistance programs throughout the world. It has also launched major new efforts: In 1976, which UNICEF proclaimed the International Year of the Child, it began an international campaign to help governments provide wide-ranging health care to women and children. UNICEF representatives also helped draft the UN Convention on the Rights of the Child, which was adopted unanimously by the General Assembly in November 1989. In the early 1990s UNICEF joined with the World Health Organization (WHO), another UN agency, in creating a worldwide immunization program against childhood diseases.

UNICEF spends millions of dollars each year on its various programs in health, social services, and education. Most of this money continues to come from voluntary contributions made by UN-member nations; the remainder is provided by private charitable organizations and by profits from the sale of UNICEF greeting cards.

UNICEF is administered by an executive board of representatives from 30 member nations. These representatives meet regularly at UNICEF headquarters—part of the United Nations complex in New York City—to oversee the running of the organization. UNICEF also has more than two dozen regional offices throughout the world. Since its founding half a century ago, UNICEF has contributed to the well-being of an estimated half billion children.

FURTHER READING

Black, Maggie. *The Children and the Nations: Growing Up Together in the Postwar World.* Sydney: Macmillan of Australia, 1987.

Heilbroner, R. L. *Mankind's Children: The Story of UNICEF.* New York: Public Affairs Committee, 1959.

Spiegelman, Judith M. *We Are the Children: A Celebration of UNICEF's First Forty Years.* Boston: Atlantic Monthly Press, 1986.

Yates, Elizabeth. *Rainbow Around the World: A Story of UNICEF.* Indianapolis: Bobbs-Merrill, 1954.

United Nations Children's Fund (UNICEF)

FOUNDER
United Nations General Assembly

FOUNDING
December 1946
London, England

HEADQUARTERS
New York, New York

PURPOSE
Initially founded to aid refugee and homeless children in Europe following World War II; in 1950 redirected its attention and resources to child welfare in developing countries

MAJOR ACCOMPLISHMENTS
Aided millions of children in Europe following World War II; since 1950 has offered health and nutrition programs as well as various social services and educational assistance to an estimated half billion children in developing countries throughout the world

René Cassin

1968

René Cassin displays the telegram informing him that he has won the Nobel Prize.

René Cassin won the Nobel Peace Prize when he was more than 80 years old—an accomplishment that might not have been possible except for an odd coincidence. As a young Frenchman fighting for his country in World War I, Cassin was severely wounded in the stomach by enemy shrapnel. He was taken to a field hospital, but the staff there were overwhelmed with casualties. Like many other victims, he was therefore left to himself, to get by as best he could until medical help was available—or to die.

And then something of a miracle occurred. Cassin's mother appeared by his stretcher. When her son had gone off to war, she had volunteered her services to the French army as a nurse. By coincidence, she had been assigned to the very hospital where her wounded son was taken. When Madame Cassin discovered him, she recognized at once the severity of his condition and insisted that he receive immediate medical attention.

Thanks to his mother's efforts, René Cassin survived to become a distinguished legal scholar and peacemaker. In fact, though he suffered abdominal pain for the rest of his life as a consequence of his war injuries, Cassin lived to be nearly 90 years old.

The future Nobel Peace Prize winner was born René-Samuel Cassin (pronounced *Kah-SAN*) in 1887 to a prosperous Jewish family in Bayonne, France. His father was a merchant, and both parents encouraged their son's education. René was sent to a secondary school in the city of Nice to prepare him for entry to the University of Aix-en-Provence. He graduated from the university in 1908 with degrees in both humanities and law. He then enrolled at the University of Paris and earned a doctorate in social science in 1914.

Cassin practiced law before being drafted into the French army following the outbreak of World War I in August 1914. He was commissioned as an officer in the infantry and served with distinction until his near-fatal injury two years later.

After his recovery, Cassin became a professor of international law, first at the University of Lille and then at the University of Paris, where he remained on the faculty until 1960. During the 1920s he served as a French delegate to the League of Nations. He also attended numerous disarmament conferences in Geneva, Switzerland, the headquarters of the League, during the 1920s and 1930s.

One of Cassin's primary interests during this period was seeing to it that both military and civilian French citizens who had been disabled, widowed, or orphaned by war received government help. To work toward that goal he was active in two organizations: he founded the Federal Union of Associations of Disabled and Aged War Veterans and served as its president, and he served as vice president of the High Council for Wards of the Nation. Cassin did not confine his efforts to France: he organized conferences of war veterans in several other European countries to publicize their plight.

World War II broke out in September 1939, and once again Germany and France were enemies on the battlefield. In June 1940, when the German army invaded France, Cassin left Paris and joined French General Charles de Gaulle's Free French government-in-exile in London. For the next four years, Cassin served in several key positions in the exile government: first as secretary of the Council of Defense, which directed the military activities of the exile government, and then as commissioner of justice and public education.

When France was liberated from German occupation in June 1944, Cassin and other Free French leaders returned to their native country. Cassin was appointed vice president of the Council of State, the administrative high court of France. He also served as a member of the Constitutional Council, a government body that decides whether or not French laws are constitutional. In 1945 Cassin assumed another post as president of the council of the National School of Administration in France.

When the United Nations was created as the successor organization to the League of Nations following the end of World War II in 1945, Cassin was chosen by the French government to represent his country as a delegate to the Commission on Human Rights. The commission had been established by the United Nations Charter in response to the many atrocities committed during the war, especially the killing of millions of Jews, Gypsies, and other minority populations in German-run concentration camps. The commission was given the task of drafting a Universal Declaration of Human Rights.

Eleanor Roosevelt, the widow of U.S. President Franklin D. Roosevelt, was chosen as chairwoman of the Commission on Human Rights, and René Cassin served as vice-chairman. For several years, Roosevelt and Cassin worked together with other commission members on the draft of the Declaration of Human Rights. The task was difficult and sometimes seemed impossible, as the drafters tried to take into account the differing philosophies, religious beliefs, and political systems of peoples throughout the world. Finally, a version submitted to the UN General Assembly by Cassin was adopted on December 10, 1948. Two years later, the United Nations officially proclaimed December 10 as Human Rights Day.

The UN Declaration of Human Rights proclaims the following principles: all people are entitled to the right to life, liberty, and personal security; freedom of conscience, religion, and assembly; equality before the law; free education; and the right to work, equal compensation for equal work, and reasonable working hours. Many new nations that have been formed since 1948 have incorporated provisions of the Declaration of Human Rights into their constitutions.

In 1966 the Declaration of Human Rights was drafted as a treaty and adopted by the UN General Assembly. Cassin was now chairman of the Commission on Human Rights, and he had added two covenants, or agreements, to the original text: one specified civil and political rights, the other economic, social, and cultural rights.

While serving with the Commission on Human Rights, Cassin was also a cofounder of a UN agency, the United Nations Educational, Scientific, and Cultural Organization (UNESCO), created in 1945. He served as the French delegate to UNESCO until

René Cassin

BORN
October 5, 1887
Bayonne, France

DIED
February 20, 1976
Paris, France

EDUCATION
Baccalaureate and diploma in law, University of Aix-en-Provence (1908); Ph.D., University of Paris (1914)

OCCUPATION
Attorney; legal scholar

MAJOR ACCOMPLISHMENTS
As vice-chairman of the UN Commission on Human Rights, drafted the UN Declaration of Human Rights (1948); led humanitarian efforts to aid disabled veterans, orphans, and other victims of World War I; aided Free French during World War II; cofounder, UNESCO; member, Court of Arbitration, The Hague; president, European Court of Rights; helped draft the human rights provisions of the Helsinki Declaration (1975)

Eleanor Roosevelt displays a copy of the Universal Declaration of Human Rights, adopted by the United Nations on December 10, 1948. Roosevelt, who devoted much of her life to humanitarian concerns, was the chairwoman of the committee that drafted the declaration.

1952. During the 1950s, Cassin was also a member of the Court of Arbitration at The Hague, and from 1965 to 1968 he served as president of the European Court of Rights.

René Cassin was awarded the 1968 Nobel Peace Prize on the 20th anniversary of the adoption of the UN Declaration of Human Rights. The citation by the Nobel Prize Committee praised Cassin for his perseverance in overcoming enormous difficulties to draw up a meaningful agreement acceptable to people of diverse backgrounds. In accepting the award, Cassin called the Declaration of Human Rights "the first document of an ethical sort that organized humanity has ever adopted." The adoption of the declaration, Cassin said, meant that for the first time in history, humankind had subjected itself to the rule of international law.

In addition to his work for the United Nations, the Court of Arbitration, and the European Court of Rights, Cassin also served as president of the International Institute of Human Rights in Strasbourg, France.

In 1972, the International Institute and the American Jewish Committee joined together to sponsor a conference that drafted the human rights provisions of the Helsinki Declaration, an international agreement signed by 35 countries in 1975. Cassin was a strong supporter of Jewish rights throughout his life and served as president of the Jewish Alliance in France.

Cassin received numerous other honors in addition to the Nobel Peace Prize, including the Croix de Guerre, the Grand Cross of the Legion of Honor, the Goethe Prize, and the United Nations Human Rights Prize. He was married twice but had no children: after the death of his first wife, he married again in 1975 while recuperating from a heart attack in a Paris hospital. He died in Paris the following year, at the age of 88.

FURTHER READING

Abrams, Irwin. "René Cassin." In *The Nobel Peace Prize and the Laureates*. Boston: G. K. Hall, 1988.

Andrus, Beth, and Sonia A. Rosen, eds. *The Universal Declaration of Human Rights, 1948–1988: Human Rights, the United Nations, and Amnesty International*. New York: AIUSA Legal Support Network, 1988.

Cassin, René. "How the Charter on Human Rights Was Born." *UNESCO Courier*, January 1968.

Green, James F. *The United Nations and Human Rights*. Washington, D.C.: The Brookings Institution, 1956.

The United Nations and Human Rights. New York: United Nations Department of Public Information, 1984.

International Labor Organization

1969

T he International Labor Organization was created by the Treaty of Versailles, which was signed in Paris, France, in April 1919 to mark the formal ending of World War I. The roots of the organization, however, reach back to the 19th century.

In the 1860s, workers in Europe began joining together into unions to demand improved working conditions from their employers. They also called for the establishment of some kind of worldwide organization that would oversee these improvements and make certain that they were carried out. During the 1890s, a series of international labor conferences was held in Europe. These conferences prepared the way for the founding, in 1900, of the International Association for Labor Legislation (IALL). The IALL had no real authority, but it acted as a clearinghouse for information and published reports on labor legislation around the world.

In the years prior to World War I, labor unions grew in membership in both Europe and the United States. After the Armistice ended the war in November 1918,

At an industrial training center in Peru sponsored by the International Labor Organization, students learn about the parts of an automobile engine. The ILO created such centers throughout the world as part of its mission to train workers in various skills.

David Morse (left), longtime director-general of the ILO, meets with U.S. President John F. Kennedy at the White House in 1963.

representatives of various unions demanded a voice in preparing the peace treaty. Their demands led to the creation of the International Labor Legislation Commission (ILLC) at the Paris Peace Conference, held in early 1919. The 15 members of the ILLC included French labor leader Léon Jouhaux as well as representatives from other European countries and the United States.

As its contribution to the peacemaking process at the conference, the ILLC sought to establish peaceful relations among the different social classes in every nation by working for social justice based on fair working conditions. To that end, the ILLC sponsored the creation of the International Labor Organization (ILO) as part of the Treaty of Versailles. The ILO became an agency of the League of Nations, which was also created by the Treaty. Both the League of Nations and the ILO established headquarters in Geneva, Switzerland.

Several months after its founding, the ILO sponsored the first International Labor Conference, held in

Washington, D.C. The conferences have been held nearly every year since then, usually in Geneva. They are attended by representatives from ILO member countries, which today number more than 140. Each member country is allowed to send four delegates: two from the national government, one worker, and one employer.

At each conference, members continue to develop the International Labor Code, a guideline for the establishment of fair working conditions. The code has two levels: *Conventions* are rules agreed to by the entire conference and must be put into practice by all member nations. *Recommendations* are suggested but not required changes in a country's labor practices. A committee of experts within the ILO makes certain that member nations comply with conventions, and it reports its findings to the annual International Labor Conference.

The first conventions, adopted in 1919, are considered a kind of bill of rights for workers throughout the world. They call for a reasonable wage, the establishment of an 8-hour day/48-hour week, equal pay for men and women doing the same work, and a ban on child labor. Conventions adopted by later conferences have called for an end to forced labor and discrimination in employment, and for the establishment of minimum-wage scales and health and safety standards. Since 1919, the International Labor Code has grown to include some 300 conventions and recommendations.

Besides adding new conventions and recommendations to the International Labor Code, the annual International Labor Conference elects the executive council of the ILO: 28 government representatives, 14 workers' representatives, and 14 employers' representatives. The executive council, called the Governing Body, is led by an elected director general and meets three times a year in Geneva. Its chief duties include planning the annual International Labor Conference and overseeing the International Labor Office in Geneva. In addition to being an information clearinghouse, the International Labor Office sponsors numerous publications, including the annual *Year Book of Labor Statistics*. It also oversees hundreds of ILO-sponsored technical experts who work in countries all over the world.

When World War II ended in 1945, the League of Nations was dissolved and replaced by the United Nations. At that time, the ILO became the first specialized agency of the UN. In the postwar years, the ILO adopted a new goal: furthering understanding between rich and poor nations. As part of that goal, the ILO created the International Institute for Labor Studies in Geneva in 1960. The institute brings together government administrators, union officials, and management and industrial experts from all over the world to study and do research in social and labor policy. In 1965, the ILO founded a related organization in Turin,

Italy: the International Center for Advanced Technical and Vocational Training, which has been attended by residents of more than 100 countries.

The International Labor Organization was awarded the 1969 Nobel Peace Prize for its 50 years of work for social justice as a basis for world peace. In making the presentation, the Nobel Committee praised the ILO for living up to the ideal expressed in its unofficial motto, a Latin phrase that is included in the cornerstone of the ILO's main building in Geneva: *Si vis pacem, cole justitiam*—If you desire peace, cultivate justice.

The ILO continues to further the well-being of workingmen and women throughout the world. Through its World Employment Program, the ILO helps developing countries use human resources efficiently. The ILO's International Program for the Improvement of Working Conditions and Environment promotes occupational health and safety. Other ILO programs address such continuing issues as labor-management relations, rural development, urban unemployment, international migration, and work issues of special concern to women.

FURTHER READING

Alcock, Anthony. *History of the International Labor Organization*. New York: Octagon, 1971.

Galenson, Walter. *The International Labor Organization: An American View*. Madison: University of Wisconsin Press, 1981.

Johnston, G. A. *The International Labour Organisation: Its Work for Social and Economic Progress*. London: Europa, 1970.

Shotwell, James T., ed. *The Origins of the International Labor Organization*. 2 vols. New York: Columbia University Press, 1934.

The Story of Fifty Years. Geneva: International Labor Organization, 1969.

International Labor Organization

FOUNDER

Created by the Treaty of Versailles

FOUNDING

April 1919
Paris, France

HEADQUARTERS

Geneva, Switzerland

PURPOSE

To improve working conditions, raise labor standards, and promote economic and social stability throughout the world

MAJOR ACCOMPLISHMENTS

Developed the International Labor Code, which sets standards for working conditions in countries throughout the world; sponsors various programs at its headquarters in Geneva and in urban and rural areas throughout the world to strengthen the workforce and to foster productive relationships between labor and management

Norman E. Borlaug

1970

From earliest childhood, Norman E. Borlaug assumed that he was going to be a farmer when he grew up. He was born in 1914 on a farm near Cresco, Iowa, that his Norwegian-immigrant parents had established some years earlier. Cresco was the center of an area known as Little Norway because so many Norwegians had settled there, and nearly all of them were farmers.

Norman's grandfather had other ideas, however. Recognizing that his grandson was very bright, he encouraged the teenage Norman to attend college. Somewhat reluctantly, Norman agreed. After graduating in 1932 from the local high school—he captained the football team in his senior year—he enrolled at the University of Minnesota.

Times were hard: the United States, like much of the world, was in the midst of a major economic depression. The family had limited financial resources, and Norman Borlaug was forced to work his way through the university by laboring at a series of odd jobs. He was also a member of Minnesota's wrestling and football teams. Majoring in forestry, he took a year off to work as a field assistant with the U.S. Forest Service and received his undergraduate degree in 1937. In September of that year, Borlaug married; the couple later had two children.

In the fall, Borlaug began graduate study at the University of Minnesota in plant pathology—the study of plant diseases—but had to alternate between study and work for the Forest Service in Idaho and Massachusetts. He was an instructor at the university during his last year of graduate school and received his doctorate in 1941. Borlaug was immediately recruited by E. I. du Pont de Nemours, a Delaware-based chemical company, and worked there for three years as a scientist studying the effects of recently developed weed- and pest-killing chemicals on plants.

In 1944 Borlaug was hired for an agricultural project in Mexico by the Rockefeller Foundation, a philanthropic organization in New York that provided technical aid to developing countries. As a member of a four-person team of agricultural scientists, Borlaug was supposed to help farmers increase their small crop yields. As it turned out, Borlaug found his life's work when he went to Mexico.

In the late 1940s and 1950s, Borlaug developed new varieties of wheat that were suitable to Mexico's climate and growing conditions. These varieties proved extremely productive in Mexico, and they have since been grown in other countries throughout the world. Borlaug's success in creating new varieties of wheat won him international acclaim as the father of the so-called Green Revolution, a worldwide increase in crop yields in developing countries in the mid-20th century. These increased crop yields meant the difference between life and death by famine for millions, as the world's population exploded during this period.

Borlaug remained headquartered in Mexico as a Rockefeller Foundation employee, directing the Wheat Research and Production Program under the auspices of the International Center for Maize and Wheat Improvement in Mexico City. While continuing to develop new wheat varieties, he traveled frequently to countries in Asia and Africa as an agricultural adviser. He was back in Mexico, working at an experimental farm plot some 50 miles from the family's home in Mexico City, on October 21, 1970, when his wife came running into the fields to tell him he had been awarded that year's Nobel Peace Prize. She had taken the call from the Nobel Committee and had driven quickly into the countryside to find her husband. Borlaug reportedly looked pleased but kept on hoeing. "I still have a day's work to do here," he said. "After that we'll celebrate."

In its presentation of the award to Borlaug on December 10, 1970, the Nobel Committee praised him for improving the lives of millions through his leadership of the Green Revolution. Borlaug became the first agricultural expert and the 15th American to win the Peace Prize.

Borlaug retired in 1979 as director of the Wheat Research and Production Program, but he continues to be a consultant to the International Maize and Wheat Improvement Center. In 1983 he was named a life fellow of the Rockefeller Foundation. A year later he became Distinguished Professor of International Agriculture at Texas A&M University, a post he still holds.

Borlaug has received many other awards besides the Nobel Peace Prize, including honorary doctorates from several universities and decorations

During a visit by U.S. President Richard Nixon to Mexico in the early 1970s, Norman Borlaug (left) shows the President the strains of high-yield wheat that he developed.

from governments throughout the world. In 1977 he was named a recipient of the United States Medal of Freedom, the country's highest civilian award. Grateful citizens in Ciudad Obregón, the wheat capital of Mexico, named a street in his honor. Although he has devoted most of his professional life to fieldwork, Borlaug has published several books and more than seventy articles. He is also a frequent speaker at international agricultural conferences. Borlaug says that he is pleased with the results of the Green Revolution, but he remains cautious about the continuing threat of overpopulation and has called repeatedly for population control throughout the world.

FURTHER READING

Bickel, Lennard. *Facing Starvation: Norman Borlaug and the Fight Against Hunger*. Pleasantville, N.Y.: Reader's Digest Press, 1974.

"Borlaug, Norman E(rnest)." In *Current Biography Yearbook 1971*. New York: H. W. Wilson, 1972.

Freeman, Orville. *World Without Hunger*. New York: Praeger, 1968.

PEACEMAKERS

Norman E. Borlaug

BORN
March 25, 1914
Cresco, Iowa

EDUCATION
B.S. (1937), Ph.D. (194)1, University of Minnesota

OCCUPATION
Agricultural scientist

MAJOR ACCOMPLISHMENTS
Developed high-yield varieties of wheat to increase the food supply in developing nations, earning him the title "Father of the Green Revolution"

Willy Brandt

1971

For more than four decades after World War II ended in 1945, the Western democracies and the Soviet Union were unofficially at war. No formal declaration of war was ever made, and no battles were fought. The conflict was real, however, and it expressed itself in ongoing tension as each side developed even greater stockpiles of nuclear weapons. This so-called Cold War finally came to an end in 1989, but its conclusion was in part the result of efforts by one man, Willy Brandt, nearly two decades earlier.

Many Nobel Peace Prize recipients have been born poor and suffered childhoods filled with hardship, but none had a worse beginning than the 1971 winner. He was born Herbert Ernst Karl Frahm in December 1913 in Lübeck, Germany, to an unmarried young shop clerk named Martha Frahm. At that time, illegitimate birth was considered a disgrace of the worst sort, and young Herbert had to endure the taunts of other children. He grew up never knowing who his father

Willy Brandt, mayor of West Berlin, on a visit to the United States in 1958 to confer with government officials. Brandt guided the city through the darkest days of the Cold War.

was. He discovered his identity many years later but never revealed it.

Herbert Frahm was raised by his mother and her family in near-poverty. He apparently had only two advantages, but they were crucial to his development: First, he was highly intelligent and did well in school. Second, he formed a close attachment to his grandfather, a laborer. Although Grandfather Frahm had little formal education, he was well informed about liberal politics and a devoted member of the Social Democratic party. Herbert's grandfather passed along his interest in politics to his young grandson. Herbert, however, dreamed of becoming a sea captain.

In secondary school—the prestigious Lübeck Johanneum, which he attended on scholarship—Herbert Frahm was encouraged by his history teacher to become a political writer. He began contributing articles to the Social Democratic party newspaper, *Volksbote*, under the pseudonym "Willy Brandt." The paper's editor, Julius Leber, was impressed by the boy and arranged for him to formally join the party when he was not yet 17, more than a year younger than the minimum age normally required.

Herbert Frahm was beginning to think for himself, however, and he became disturbed by the growth of another political group, the National Socialist (Nazi) party. Despite its name, the Nazi party was rigidly conservative, and its leader, Adolf Hitler, wished to establish himself as the ruling dictator of Germany. Herbert Frahm was disappointed when the Social Democratic party did not oppose the growing danger of Hitler and his Nazis, and he joined the more radical Socialist Workers party in 1931. A year later, he graduated from the Johanneum and was hired as a clerk by a Lübeck shipping company, but he continued to write newspaper articles under the name "Willy Brandt."

When Hitler finally seized control of the German government early in 1933, Herbert Frahm went into hiding, for he was now considered a political enemy of the state. In April, friends arranged for him to leave the country secretly and settle in Oslo, Norway, where he established the headquarters-in-exile of the Socialist Workers party. At this time he began using "Willy Brandt" as his real name, and he was known publicly by that name for the remainder of his life.

In Oslo, Willy Brandt was aided by the Norwegian Labor party, which helped him get a job as chairman of a refugee organization in the city. He also wrote articles for the party newspaper, *Arbeiterbladet*. In 1934 Brandt applied for and won a scholarship to the University of Oslo, where he studied history and philosophy for several years.

Brandt lived in Norway until 1940. In the late 1930s, he traveled secretly to Germany and to other European countries to encourage underground opposition to the Nazis and to fascism, as their political philosophy was called. In 1937, he also spent time in Spain, writing about the Spanish Civil War (1936–39) for several Scandinavian newspapers.

When Germany invaded Norway in the spring of 1940, six months after the start of World War II, Brandt was briefly interned, or held prisoner, by the new government. Later that year he made his way to neutral Sweden and settled there with his Norwegian wife and their infant daughter. For the next seven years, Brandt lived in Sweden, earning his living as a journalist. During that time he also wrote five books on contemporary European politics.

Brandt traveled to Germany in October 1946, a year after the war ended, as a Norwegian newspaper correspondent covering the Nuremberg Trials. These were trials of Nazi leaders accused of war crimes, and they were publicized all over the world. Brandt

Willy Brandt

BORN
December 18, 1913
Lübeck, Germany

DIED
October 8, 1992
Unkel, Germany

EDUCATION
Secondary school diploma; attended University of Oslo

OCCUPATION
Journalist; politician

MAJOR ACCOMPLISHMENTS
As mayor of West Berlin and later chancellor of West Germany, led efforts to end the Cold War between Western nations and the Soviet Union

The Berlin Wall was erected by East Germany in 1961 to prevent contact between the two halves of the city. The wall was a symbol of Communist oppression for nearly 30 years.

believed that all Germans had to acknowledge responsibility for the atrocities committed by Hitler and his followers, and he said so publicly.

In late 1947, Brandt finally moved back to Germany after leaders of the revived Social Democratic party invited him to work for the party at its Berlin headquarters. As part of the peace agreement that ended the war, Germany was now divided into two countries: East Germany, which had a Communist government and strong ties to the Soviet Union, and West Germany, which had established a democratic form of government with the encouragement of the United States and other Western European countries. The city of Berlin, the historic capital of the country, was divided into separate—Communist and non-Communist—sections, too.

Brandt had divorced his first wife several years earlier, and after moving to Berlin he married another Norwegian woman; they eventually had three sons. Brandt quickly emerged as a leader of the Social Democratic party in West Berlin through his close associ-

ation with a prominent politician named Ernst Reuter. Brandt attracted attention through his many speeches that denounced the Communists and the Soviet Union, especially the Soviet takeover of Czechoslovakia in the spring of 1948.

Beginning in June of that year, the famous Berlin Blockade occurred: the Soviet Union sealed off West Berlin for nearly a year from the rest of the world, and residents were on the verge of starvation. Months of suffering were relieved only by the so-called Berlin Airlift, which was organized by the United States and brought food, clothing, and medical supplies to the needy residents. During this time of hardship, Brandt helped Ernst Reuter, now the mayor, to rally the spirits of the population.

Brandt was elected as Berlin's representative to the Bundestag, the lower house of the West German parliament, not long after the blockade ended in 1949. The following year he was also elected to the local Berlin governing council and later served as its chairman. In both the Bundestag and on the local governing council, Brandt was an acknowledged leader. In the fall of 1956 he won national acclaim when he single-handedly calmed an angry mob of tens of thousands of West Berliners who were protesting the recent Soviet invasion of Hungary. His heroism in that situation helped him to be elected as mayor of West Berlin in 1957.

As the mayor of half a divided city, surrounded and threatened by a Soviet-controlled nation, Willy Brandt was in the middle of the Cold War. Despite the difficulties, he managed to keep West Berlin independent and free. He remained firmly allied to the Western democracies, including the United States, France, and England, and resisted attempts by the Soviet Union to incorporate West Berlin into East Germany.

A major crisis occurred in August 1961, when the East German government erected a wall between East and West Berlin and patrolled it with armed guards. This physical division meant that East Germans and West Germans were forbidden to cross back and forth between the two parts of the city. Anyone attempting to enter or leave East Berlin was shot on sight by East German guards. Brandt openly denounced the Berlin Wall, as it was called, and he became an international symbol of courage for his defiance.

Brandt had become increasingly powerful in the Social Democratic party, and in 1963 he was elected party chairman. He made several unsuccessful attempts during the next few years to win election as West Germany's chancellor (prime minister). Brandt's childhood still haunted him: one of his political opponents, Chancellor Konrad Adenauer, always referred to him as "Herbert Frahm" in his speeches to call attention to Brandt's illegitimate birth.

In 1966 Brandt became West German foreign minister in a coalition government. (A coalition government is one in which several political parties share power.) Three years later he was finally elected chancellor. Brandt distinguished himself by working to secure stable relations among Central and Eastern European nations. As an opponent of militarism, he publicly encouraged troop reductions on all sides in Europe. In late 1970 he was acclaimed for negotiating treaties that normalized West Germany's relations with Poland and the Soviet Union, and for securing an agreement that allowed West Berliners to visit relatives in East Berlin and travel across East Germany.

Brandt's success in easing international tension earned him the Nobel Peace Prize for 1971. He was frustrated, however, because the Berlin Wall was still standing. During the next few years, while still serving as chancellor, he worked for West German participation in the European Common Market and promoted West Germany's admission to the United Nations, which occurred in 1973.

Brandt retired as chancellor in 1974 after one of his personal aides was arrested as an East German spy. He remained chairman of the Social Democratic party, however, until 1987. During this time he also served as chairman of an international socialist organization that called attention to the plight of Third World nations and urged economic support for them. In 1985 he received another award for his peacemaking efforts: the Einstein Peace Prize, established to honor physicist Albert Einstein's commitment to world peace.

Brandt lived to see a long-held dream come true: in 1989 the Cold War officially ended as the Soviet Union made peace overtures to Western nations. The Berlin Wall came down, and East and West Germany moved toward reunification. Brandt died in October 1992 at the age of 78 after a long struggle with intestinal cancer. He was survived by his four children and by his third wife, whom he had married in 1983.

FURTHER READING

Binder, David. *The Other German: Willy Brandt's Life and Times*. New York: New Republic Book Co., 1975.

Brandt, Willy. *Arms and Hunger*. New York: Pantheon, 1986.

———. *In Exile: Essays, Reflections, Letters, 1933–1947*. Philadephia: University of Pennsylvania Press, 1971.

———. *My Life in Politics*. New York: Viking, 1992.

———, as told to Leo Lania. *My Road to Berlin*. New York: Doubleday, 1970.

Prittie, Terence. *Willy Brandt: Portrait of a Statesman*. New York: Schocken, 1974.

Henry Kissinger
Le Duc Tho

1973

I n New York City more than 50 years ago, while
World War II raged in Europe and Asia, a young
German immigrant named Henry Kissinger
dreamed of a better life for himself. He had graduated as a straight-A student from a city high school in
1941, but he could not afford to attend a university full time.
So after graduation he had gotten a job in a shaving-brush
factory in order to support himself. Every evening, after a
long day of work at the factory, he attended night school at
City College, which offered free classes to New York residents at that time. Kissinger was studying accounting, and
he longed for the day when he could leave his job at the factory and become a professional accountant.

For nearly a decade Henry Kissinger's life had not been
easy, although it had begun well. He was born in Fürth, Ger-

North Vietnamese negotiator Le Duc Tho and U.S. Secretary of
State Henry Kissinger shake hands after reaching a cease-fire
agreement in January 1973 between their two nations.

many, in 1923 to Jewish parents who had another son several years later. His father was a teacher in a local high school, and the Kissinger family led a fairly comfortable existence until 1933, when Henry was 10 years old. In that year, Adolf Hitler and his National Socialist (Nazi) party gained control of the German government. Hitler immediately began a program of discrimination against Jews. Henry's father lost his job, and life became increasingly difficult for the family. Many Jews were imprisoned by the Nazis, and the Kissingers feared that they, too, would be sent to jail.

The Kissinger family managed to escape from Germany, and they immigrated to the United States in 1938. They settled in New York City, where Mr. Kissinger found work as a clerk and bookkeeper, while his wife became a cook for wealthy families. Henry and his brother attended local schools and learned to speak English.

In 1943 Henry Kissinger's dream of becoming an accountant was halted abruptly when he was drafted into the U.S. Army. This setback, however, proved to be a blessing in disguise. After serving in combat in Europe, Kissinger became a German interpreter for his commanding general and also interrogated German prisoners captured by the U.S. Army. Army officials were impressed by Kissinger's ability, and when the war ended in 1945, he became an official with the military government that now ruled Germany. He also taught history at a school for U.S. soldiers in Germany before returning to the United States in 1946.

Kissinger had become interested in government and politics during his army service, and he decided to go back to college to study those subjects. He won a New York State Scholarship, which enabled him to attend Harvard University. He enrolled there in the fall of 1946 and four years later received a bachelor's degree with highest honors. Kissinger remained at Harvard to do graduate work in government, receiving an M.A. in 1952 and a Ph.D. two years later.

While Kissinger was a graduate student, he also worked as a consultant to the U.S. Army. In 1954, after receiving his doctoral degree, Kissinger began working for the Council on Foreign Relations, a private foundation that studied foreign policy issues. He was assigned to direct a research program on how the United States should respond to the threat of nuclear war.

At that time the U.S. government was in the midst of the so-called Cold War with the Communist-run Soviet Union, and tensions between the two countries threatened to erupt in nuclear warfare. The U.S. government, under President Dwight D. Eisenhower, had an official policy of "massive retaliation," which meant that if the country was attacked by nuclear weapons, it would respond with a strong nuclear counterattack. Many people believed, however, that such a policy was too aggressive and might actually invite war. Although Kissinger was strongly anti-Communist, he believed that the United States had a better chance of maintaining peace in the world if it took a less aggressive attitude toward the Soviet Union. At the Council on Foreign Relations, he devised a less aggressive defense policy, which he called "flexible response." Under this proposed policy, the United States would explore other alternatives before engaging in all-out nuclear war following an enemy attack. Kissinger discussed this policy in an important book, *Nuclear Weapons and Foreign Policy* (1957), which was widely read. In 1961, "flexible response" was adopted by President John F. Kennedy as a key part of U.S. foreign policy.

Meanwhile, in 1956 Kissinger had become the director of a study of East-West relations sponsored by the Rockefeller Brothers Fund, another private

Henry Kissinger

BORN
May 27, 1923
Fürth, Germany

EDUCATION
A.B. (1950), M.A. (1952), Ph.D. (1954), Harvard University

OCCUPATION
University professor; government official

MAJOR ACCOMPLISHMENTS
Initiated Strategic Arms Limitation Talks (SALT, 1969); masterminded President Richard M. Nixon's historic trip to China (1972); U.S. Secretary of State (1973–77); negotiated cease-fire in Vietnam War (1973)

In 1968, Vietnamese women attempt to move back into the city of Cholon, devastated by fighting during the Vietnam War.

policy consultant to several private foundations, and he participated in several international gatherings on world affairs, including the Pugwash conferences (meetings of nuclear scientists who were committed to ending the threat of nuclear war). In addition, he wrote numerous articles and several more books on foreign policy in the nuclear age.

In 1968 Kissinger was sent by President Lyndon B. Johnson to Hanoi, North Vietnam, to establish peace talks to end the Vietnam War. (The United States had been drawn into the war between North and South Vietnam several years earlier, and several million U.S. troops were helping South Vietnamese troops fight against the Communist North Vietnamese.) While Kissinger was attempting to set up peace talks, U.S. Presidential elections were held and Richard M. Nixon was elected President. Nixon immediately asked Kissinger to become his foreign policy adviser, and Kissinger began working for the new President in January 1969.

Kissinger proved to be an important figure in the Nixon administration as he worked to establish peaceful relations between the United States and other nations. During his first year as Nixon's adviser, Kissinger played a major role in establishing the Strategic Arms Limitation Talks (SALT), a series of negotiations that began in November 1969 between the United States and the Soviet Union. He proposed other peacemaking strategies that Nixon adopted: the U.S. decision never to engage in chemical or biological warfare; a reduction in U.S. defense missiles; and the return of Okinawa, a U.S. territory, to Japan.

foundation. The result of his study was another book about U.S. foreign policy, *The Necessity of Choice* (1961). In it he argued that the U.S. government had to continually explore ways to avoid all-out war with the Soviet Union, even though it seemed unlikely that real peace between the two nations would ever be achieved.

Kissinger joined the faculty of the Center for International Affairs at Harvard University in 1957 and was its associate director from 1958 to 1960. In 1962 he became a professor of government at Harvard, where his course on foreign policy was one of the most popular offered by the university. From 1959 to 1969 Kissinger was also director of Harvard's Defense Studies Program.

During his years at Harvard, Kissinger served as a consultant to various defense-related organizations in the U.S. government. He was also a foreign

One of Kissinger's most notable accomplishments was arranging for the historic trip of Nixon to Communist-ruled China—the first visit of a U.S. President to that nation. China and the United States had been enemies since 1949, when the Communists came to power there, but Nixon's visit in 1972 restored diplomatic relations between the two countries and eased years of tension.

Meanwhile, Kissinger had continued to seek an end to the ongoing Vietnam War as Nixon's representative to a series of meetings in Paris with representatives of the North Vietnamese government. While these meetings were going on, Nixon was elected to a second Presidential term in 1972, and Kissinger became his Secretary of State in January 1973. That same month, Kissinger reached a cease-fire agreement with Le Duc Tho, the chief North Vietnamese negotiator. Under the agreement, the United States withdrew its troops from South Vietnam, and in exchange the North Vietnamese government agreed to return American prisoners-of-war.

For these peacemaking efforts, Kissinger and Le Duc Tho were named the joint winners of the 1973 Nobel Peace Prize. Many people opposed the choice of these two men as winners of the award, however: Le Duc Tho had spent most of his life engaged in warfare, and Kissinger represented a government that was blamed by many for prolonging the Vietnam War.

Worried about his personal safety, the U.S. government advised Kissinger not to go to Oslo to receive the award. When the U.S. ambassador to Norway accepted the award on Kissinger's be-half, there were major protest demonstrations in the city.

Kissinger continued to serve as Secretary of State, and when Nixon resigned in 1974, Kissinger remained in office under President Gerald Ford until 1977. During those years he made major efforts to end tensions between Israel and neighboring Arab states in the Middle East. Those efforts led to separate cease-fire agreements between Israel and the Arab states of Egypt and Syria.

Since leaving office in 1977, Kissinger has served as a private consultant to government and industry, and he continues to write books and articles on foreign policy. Kissinger has been married twice, and he has two children from his first marriage.

Little is known about the early life of Le Duc Tho (pronounced *Lay-dook-toe*), who was awarded the 1973 Nobel Peace Prize with Henry Kissinger. He was born Phan Dinh Khai to a middle-class family in a small village of northern Vietnam in 1911. At that time Vietnam, a country in Indochina, was a colony ruled by the French government.

As a child, Phan Dinh Khai attended French-run schools. There his opposition to French rule grew. By the time he was a teenager, he had become a member of the local Communist party, which met secretly to plot the overthrow of the government. While working as a postal clerk he organized antigovernment protests. He was finally arrested and spent several years in jail. Sometime during this period he assumed the name Le Duc Tho. Upon his release in 1936, he served as regional information specialist for the Communist party until he was arrested again three years later.

PEACEMAKERS

Le Duc Tho

BORN
October 11, 1911
Nam Ha Province, Indochina

DIED
October 13, 1990
Hanoi, Vietnam

EDUCATION
Attended local French-run elementary and secondary schools

OCCUPATION
Postal worker; political leader

MAJOR ACCOMPLISHMENT
With Henry Kissinger of the United States, negotiated a cease-fire that ended U.S. participation in the Vietnam War (1973)

In 1944 Le Duc Tho was released again from jail, and he quickly rose in the Communist party leadership. He began to organize uprisings against the French in 1945 and became a senior party official in the southern part of Vietnam. Years of warfare between the French and Communist-led natives ended with the defeat of French forces in Indochina in 1954. As part of the peace agreement, Vietnam was divided into two separate nations, North and South. North Vietnam became a Communist state, and South Vietnam tried to establish a democratic government.

In 1955 Le Duc Tho returned to North Vietnam from the south and settled in its capital, Hanoi. He became a member of the ruling council, called the Politburo, and served there until 1986. During that time he became one of the country's most powerful political figures. In 1957 Le Duc Tho was sent to Saigon, the South Vietnamese capital, to advise military forces of the so-called National Liberation Front, which was trying to establish Communist rule in South Vietnam. During the next 15 years he played a major role in devising military strategy as conflict between the two Vietnams grew into full-scale war.

By the late 1960s, several million U.S. troops were fighting in Vietnam and many were being killed. There was heavy pressure on the U.S. government to end American involvement in the war, and in 1969 President Nixon asked Henry Kissinger to seek a cease-fire with North Vietnam. Le Duc Tho was chosen by the North Vietnamese government to be its major representative at a series of talks with Kissinger in Paris.

Finally, after four years of negotiations, a cease-fire was signed in January 1973. Le Duc Tho was named a cowinner of the Nobel Peace Prize that fall for his role in establishing the cease-fire. However, he declined the award, saying that "peace has not yet been established."

In fact, the fighting had continued between the two Vietnams even after U.S. troops withdrew in the spring of 1973. Finally, in 1975, Saigon fell to the Communists and North Vietnam announced its victory in the war. During the next decade, Le Duc Tho continued to serve in the Politburo as the two countries were united under a single Communist government. He resigned from the Politburo in 1986, following a major reorganization in party leadership.

Le Duc Tho was reportedly married twice, but nothing more is known of his personal life. He died of throat cancer in 1990 at the age of 79.

FURTHER READING

Isaacson, Walter. *Kissinger: A Biography.* New York: Simon & Schuster, 1992.

"Kissinger, Henry A[lfred]." In *Current Biography Yearbook 1972.* New York: H. W. Wilson, 1973.

Kissinger, Henry. *Nuclear Weapons and Foreign Policy.* 1957. Abridged edition. New York: Norton, 1969.

———. *White House Years.* Boston: Little, Brown, 1979.

———. *Years of Upheaval.* Boston: Little, Brown, 1982.

"Le Duc Tho." In *Current Biography Yearbook 1975.* New York: H. W. Wilson, 1976.

Pace, Eric. "Le Duc Tho, Top Hanoi Aide, Dies at 79." *New York Times,* October 14, 1990, p. 32.

Seán MacBride

Eisaku Sato

1974

Seán MacBride, cowinner of the 1974 Nobel Peace Prize, is celebrated as one of Ireland's leading statesmen, but his mother is as well known as her son in their native country. MacBride's mother was Maud Gonne (pronounced *Gunn*), an actress who was celebrated for her beauty in 19th-century Dublin, Ireland's capital city. She is called "the Joan of Arc of Ireland" because she was a leading supporter of the movement for Irish independence from Great Britain. The great Irish poet William Butler Yeats—who later won the Nobel Prize for Literature (1923)—was in love with Maud Gonne, and she inspired many of his most famous poems. But Maud Gonne chose to marry another Irishman, an army officer named John MacBride. In 1904 their only child, Seán, was born in Paris, where the couple had gone to avoid prosecution by British authorities for revolutionary activities.

Major John MacBride had founded the Irish Brigade, which fought against the British in the Boer War

In his youth, Seán McBride fought with the Irish Republican Army. Many years later, after a career as a politician, he served as a skilled negotiator on behalf of many humanitarian causes. This streaky news photo was taken in 1972 in the Soviet Union.

Seán MacBride

BORN

January 26, 1904
Paris, France

DIED

January 15, 1988
Dublin, Ireland

EDUCATION

Attended private church-run schools in Paris and Ireland; diploma in law, University of Dublin (1937)

OCCUPATION

Attorney; statesman

MAJOR ACCOMPLISHMENTS

Foreign minister, Republic of Ireland (1948–51); secretary-general, International Commission of Jurists (1963–70); president, International Peace Bureau (1972–85)

(1899–1902). He and his wife separated shortly after Seán's birth, and MacBride returned to Ireland in 1905, where he resumed a leading role in the Irish independence movement. He was executed by the British in 1916 for participating in an uprising known as the Easter Rebellion.

Meanwhile, young Seán had grown up in Paris and attended a church-run school there. However, he was filled with Irish patriotic fervor, thanks to his mother, and after Major MacBride's execution the two set off for Ireland. His mother was arrested in London but escaped to Dublin with the aid of her son. Twelve-year-old Seán MacBride soon joined the Irish Republican Army (IRA), the revolutionary organization fighting for independence.

For his antigovernment activities, Seán MacBride was imprisoned by the British on three separate occasions over the next 14 years. Between prison terms, and while working for the revolutionary movement full time, he attended a secondary school in County Wexford and went on to earn a law degree from Dublin's National University.

Political independence had been partially achieved in 1922 through the partition (separation) of Ireland. The southern part of Ireland, which included Dublin, was given its freedom from British rule and became the Irish Free State. The remaining part, Northern Ireland, continued to be governed by Great Britain. The IRA opposed the partition and continued to fight for complete independence and reunion.

In 1936 Seán MacBride became the IRA's commander-in-chief, but he left the organization a year later because he opposed the organization's use of violence to achieve its political goals. He was admitted to the bar shortly after resigning, and he soon

became the most successful trial lawyer in Dublin. In 1939 the IRA was outlawed by the national government, but it continued to operate as a secret revolutionary organization.

During the years of World War II (1939–45), MacBride became active in the national politics of his country, which had been renamed Eire in 1937, through his association with Eamon De Valera, a former IRA comrade who was now prime minister. In 1946 MacBride formed a new political party, the Republican, whose Gaelic name was the Clann na Poblachta. One of its goals was the peaceful reunification of Ireland and the complete withdrawal of British forces. However, its major purpose was to work for economic reform in Ireland, a traditionally poor country.

Running on the Republican ticket, MacBride was elected to the Dail, the lower house of the Eire parliament, in 1947 and held that seat for 11 years. One of MacBride's major accomplishments during this period was helping to pass the Republic of Ireland Act, which resulted in the official declaration of Eire as a republic in 1948.

In 1948–51 MacBride also served as Ireland's foreign minister and as vice president of the newly formed Organization for European Economic Cooperation (OEEC), a predecessor of the European Economic Community (EEC). In 1951 he was, in addition, president of the Council of Foreign Ministers of the Council of Europe. In the 1950s MacBride also served as an assistant secretary-general of the United Nations.

In 1961 MacBride helped organize Amnesty International, a human rights organization with headquarters in London. He became one of the organization's leading staff attorneys and also served for a time as its chairman. From 1963 to 1970 MacBride was secretary-general of the International Commission of Jurists, another human rights group. In 1972 he became head of the International Peace Bureau in Geneva, Switzerland.

MacBride's many activities on behalf of human rights earned him a share of the 1974 Nobel Peace Prize. Three years later he also received the International Lenin Prize, and thus became the second person to receive both peace awards. (The first was Linus Pauling.)

MacBride continued to serve as head of the International Peace Bureau until 1985, when he became president emeritus. His wife of 50 years, with whom he had two children, died in 1976. Seán MacBride died in Dublin in January 1988, less than two weeks before his 84th birthday.

Eisaku Sato, who shared the 1974 Nobel Peace Prize with Seán MacBride, was the first Asian to win the award. Sato, who was born in the village of Tabuse, Japan, in 1901, was descended from a famous samurai (Japanese warrior), Nobuaki Sato, who had been a provincial governor in the early 19th century.

After attending area schools, Sato entered Tokyo Imperial University, where he received a law degree in 1924. After graduation he entered the civil service, joining the Ministry of Railways. He became an expert on transportation during his 24 years of service, and traveled to the United States and Europe on behalf of the Japanese government in the mid-1930s. By the end of World War II he had become head of the national railway system, and in 1947–48 he served as vice minister of transportation.

Sato left the civil service in 1948 to enter politics. He became active in the Democratic-Liberal party and was elected to a seat in the Diet, the Japanese parliament. He quickly rose in the party ranks to become a close associate of Prime Minister Shigeru Yoshida, and during the early 1950s he held several party and cabinet posts. In 1954 the Yoshida government collapsed when several of the prime minister's associates, including Sato, were accused (although never convicted) of accepting bribes from a shipbuilding association.

After staying out of politics for several years, Sato became Japan's finance minister in 1958 in the cabinet of his brother, Prime Minister Nobusuke Kishi. He remained in that post for two years. During the early 1960s, Sato held various other cabinet posts while he worked for his longtime goal: becoming prime minister.

In the fall of 1962 Sato made a lengthy tour of Europe and the United States, meeting with major political leaders, including U.S. President John F. Kennedy. He headed several government agencies in succession and served as chairman of the organizing committee for the 1964 Olympic Games, held in Tokyo. Later that year he was finally elected prime minister by the Japanese Diet.

During the postwar years, Japan had recovered from near-destruction to become a major political power in Asia, largely because of economic aid from the United States. Sato had already forged close ties with the U.S., and upon becoming prime minister he pledged to continue that harmonious relationship while maintaining Japan's independence. As a staunch pacifist, Sato also promised to pursue peaceful relations with other Asian nations.

Sato immediately began efforts to carry out those pledges. During the 1960s he re-established diplomatic relations with South Korea, which had

Eisaku Sato

BORN
March 27, 1901
Tabuse, Japan

DIED
June 2, 1975
Tokyo, Japan

EDUCATION
Diploma in law, Tokyo Imperial University (1924)

OCCUPATION
Attorney; government official

MAJOR ACCOMPLISHMENTS
Prime minister of Japan (1965–72); established peace as the cornerstone of Japan's foreign policy; restored Japanese control of Okinawa (1972)

Japanese prime minister Eisaku Sato pledged his government to a policy of peace and called for world disarmament. Here, Sato (left) speaks at a banquet held by the World Affairs Council of Northern California. At the right is California governor Edmund Brown, and standing behind Sato is his interpreter.

been Japan's enemy during World War II. He also toured 10 other Asian nations, seeking closer trade and cultural ties. In addition, Sato's pacifism led him to try to improve relations between the Soviet Union and Communist China during this period.

One of Sato's greatest accomplishments was achieved in 1972, when his negotiations with U.S. envoy Henry Kissinger led to the return of the island of Okinawa to Japanese control. Shortly afterward, Sato's prime ministership ended when he was replaced as party leader.

Eisaku Sato shared the 1974 Nobel Peace Prize for his efforts to maintain peace as the basis of Japan's foreign policy. In particular, he was cited for efforts that led Japan to become the only major power to renounce nuclear arms. In his acceptance speech in Oslo, Sato called for world disarmament and for international regulation of the peaceful uses of atomic energy.

Sato's selection as a Peace Prize winner was controversial. Many of his critics expressed doubt that he was a true pacifist, especially since he had endorsed U.S. bombing of North Vietnam during the Vietnam War.

Sato, who was married and had two sons, lived less than six months after receiving the Nobel Peace Prize. In May 1975 he was stricken with a cerebral hemorrhage while dining at a restaurant. He never regained consciousness and died in a Tokyo hospital two weeks later, at the age of 74.

FURTHER READING

Blair, William G. "Seán MacBride of Ireland Is Dead at 83." *New York Times*, January 16, 1988, p. 10.

Krebs, Albin. "Eisaku Sato, Ex-Premier of Japan, Dies at 74." *New York Times*, June 3, 1975, p. 36.

"MacBride, Seán." In *Current Biography Yearbook 1949*. New York: H. W. Wilson, 1950.

"Sato, Eisaku." In *Current Biography Yearbook 1965*. New York: H. W. Wilson, 1966.

Andrei Sakharov

1975

A ndrei Sakharov (pronounced *SOCK-ah-roff*), who was born in Moscow in 1921 and won the Nobel Peace Prize 54 years later, was the first Russian to receive the award. However, he was not the first person in his family to be concerned with social issues and the quest for peace. Sakharov came from a well-educated, politically liberal, and highly cultured background. As he later remarked, he grew up in "an atmosphere of decency, mutual help, and tact," and this atmosphere had a profound effect on determining the course of his life. One of his grandfathers, who conducted a lifelong campaign to end capital punishment (the death penalty) in Russia, had an especially strong influence on Sakharov.

Sakharov's father was a noted physics professor at Moscow University who had written many books on the subject, and when Andrei completed secondary school in Moscow he, too, decided to study physics at the university. He was such a brilliant student that he was exempted from military service during World War II so that he could complete his undergraduate degree. After graduating in 1942 he worked as an engineer in a military plant until the war ended in 1945.

Russian physicist and human rights activist Andrei Sakharov (center) leads a demonstration in Moscow protesting the exclusion of candidates, including himself, for government posts in a general election.

Sakharov then returned to the university, where he completed graduate studies in 1948. For the next decade Sakharov worked at a top-secret laboratory in Turkmenistan, a remote republic in the Soviet Union. There he helped develop nuclear weapons, including the hydrogen bomb, and also worked on projects to find peaceful uses for atomic energy.

Sakharov's abilities brought him many honors, including election to membership in the Soviet Academy of Sciences when he was only 32 years old. Sakharov was never a member of the Communist party, which governed the Soviet Union, but for many years he believed that he had a patriotic duty to develop nuclear weapons in order to help protect his country. By the late 1950s, however, Sakharov had begun to question the wisdom of his work. In 1957 he wrote a letter to the Soviet premier, Nikita Khrushchev, asking that planned test explosions of the hydrogen bomb be canceled because the radiation released by the testing would eventually harm thousands of people.

When the testing went on as scheduled, Sakharov began sending more protests to government leaders, and these continued after his return to Moscow to work in a defense laboratory there. He complained not only about nuclear weapons development but also questioned government policy in other areas. He criticized Soviet science and education for being backward and also pointed out other negative aspects of Soviet life, including social injustice, censorship, and widespread poverty.

One of Sakharov's major targets was Lysenkoism, a theory named after a Soviet biologist who had first advanced it in the 1930s. According to Lysenkoism, environmental influences on a living organism could be inherited genetically by future generations. This theory had already been disproved in the West, but many Soviet biologists— agricultural specialists in particular— were continuing to use it as the basis of their research. As a result, much of Soviet biological and medical science was hopelessly backward. Sakharov and other prominent Soviet scientists publicly criticized Lysenkoism in the early 1960s and eventually broke its hold on Soviet science.

The government of the Soviet Union tolerated Sakharov's criticisms for a number of years. By the late 1960s, however, Soviet leaders had begun cracking down on dissidents not only in Russia but in other Communist countries allied with the Soviet Union. In the summer of 1968, as Soviet troops prepared to invade Czechoslovakia to restore a Communist government there, Sakharov composed a manifesto that he circulated among other members of Moscow's intellectual community.

The 10,000-word document, entitled "Progress, Coexistence, and Intellectual Freedom," examined the numerous dangers that threatened the contemporary world—"war, hunger, environmental pollution, stultifying mass culture, and demagogic myths." Sakharov then went on to argue that the only hope of saving the world from these dangers lay in cooperation between East and West—between the Soviet Union and other Communist nations of the East, and the United States and its allies in the West. Finally, the document called upon the Soviet Union to end its decades-long policy of suppressing free speech and to initiate widespread public debate.

Sakharov and his daring document became internationally known after a copy of it was secretly removed from Russia and printed in the *New York Times* in July 1968.

Virtually overnight, Sakharov became a hero throughout the non-Communist world for his boldness in standing up to the repressive Soviet regime. The Soviet government responded by ending his defense work, removing him from his top-security laboratory, and cutting his salary substantially. However, it still allowed him to keep many of his state benefits, including a private car and driver, his Moscow apartment, and a country house. Sakharov was also given access to a non-defense laboratory and allowed to remain a member of the Academy of Sciences.

Sakharov refused to give up, however. In the mid-1960s he had shifted his professional field of interest from nuclear physics to theoretical studies of matter and the origins of the universe, and he continued to write and publish articles about his findings. He also continued his dissident activities by meeting frequently with other protesters in Moscow, by staging vigils outside courtrooms and prisons where political prisoners were tried and detained, and by writing open letters to the government that were highly critical of Soviet policy and were publicized abroad.

In November 1970, Sakharov and two fellow dissidents announced the formation of the Committee for Human Rights. Its goal was the actual adoption by the Soviet Union of all the terms specified in the United Nations Universal Declaration of Human

Rights. Sakharov's antigovernment activities further intensified after his marriage the following year to a fellow dissident, Yelena G. Bonner, a physician. (His first wife, with whom he had three children, had died in the late 1960s.)

Four years later Sakharov was named the winner of the 1975 Nobel Peace Prize for what the Nobel Committee called his "fearless personal commitment in upholding the fundamental principles for peace between men." The Soviet government refused to let Sakharov travel to Oslo to receive the award but allowed Yelena Bonner to accept it on her husband's behalf.

The Soviets continued to tolerate Sakharov's dissidence until December 1979, when he began a series of public protests against the invasion of Afghanistan by Russian troops. He called upon other countries around the world to show their disapproval by boycotting the upcoming Olympic Games, scheduled for the summer of 1980 in Moscow. This time the government moved to silence Sakharov. In January he was arrested, informed that he had been stripped of all state honors, and taken to Gorky, an isolated settlement 250 miles east of Moscow. There he was kept in detention and isolated from the world for nearly seven years.

During Sakharov's exile he became an international symbol of protest and courage. Despite constant surveillance by security police, Sakharov managed to write an account of his experience, together with another lengthy criticism of the Soviet regime. Called "A Time of Anxiety," the document was smuggled out of the country and eventually published in the *New York Times*. Back in Moscow, Yelena Bonner kept alive

the hopes of the dissidents until she, too, was sent to Gorky in 1984.

The political climate in the Soviet Union began to change a year later, when Mikhail Gorbachev became the country's leader. Gorbachev indicated that he wanted to make changes in the Soviet Union so that it would be less repressive and more open to public debate and to change. As one gesture in this direction, he freed Sakharov and his wife from exile in December 1986.

Back in Moscow, Sakharov resumed his scientific research. At the same time he assumed an active role in encouraging the liberalization of the Soviet system under Gorbachev. He was elected to the newly formed Congress of Peoples' Deputies, where he continued to call for the democratization of the Soviet Union.

Sakharov had suffered for many years from a heart ailment, which had worsened during his years in exile, and he died suddenly in December 1989 of a heart attack. At his death he was mourned throughout the world as the "conscience" of the Soviet Union and hailed for his tireless campaign on behalf of human rights.

FURTHER READING

Bonner, Yelena. *Alone Together*. Translated by Alexander Cook. New York: Knopf, 1986.

LeVert, Suzanne. *The Sakharov File*. New York: Julian Messner, 1986.

Lozansky, Edward D., ed. *Andrei Sakharov and Peace*. New York: Avon, 1985.

Sakharov, Andrei. *Memoirs*. Translated by Richard Lourie. New York: Knopf, 1990.

Andrei Sakharov

BORN
May 21, 1921
Moscow, Russia

DIED
December 14, 1989
Moscow, Russia

EDUCATION
B.A. (1942), Ph.D. (1948), Moscow University

OCCUPATION
Nuclear physicist

MAJOR ACCOMPLISHMENTS
Helped modernize Russian scientific studies (1960s); author of the manifesto "Progress, Coexistence, and Intellectual Freedom" (1968), which urged cooperation between East and West; founded Committee for Human Rights (1970)

Mairead Corrigan

Betty Williams

1976

One day in August 1976 in a working-class neighborhood of Belfast, Northern Ireland, a getaway car driven by a member of the Irish Republican Army (IRA) went out of control and crashed into an iron railing, killing three young children and seriously injuring their mother. This tragedy was the consequence of yet another confrontation between the IRA and British troops who were trying to restore order to a city and country wracked by civil war. One of the witnesses to the tragedy was a passerby named Betty Williams. She was so horrified that she determined to devote what time she could to restoring peace to her troubled city. She immediately set out to collect signatures on a petition calling for an end to hostilities between the IRA and the British-controlled government of Northern Ireland.

The incident also touched another woman deeply: Mairead (pronounced *MAH-raid*) Corrigan, the sister of the injured woman, Anne Maguire, and the aunt of the three

Betty Williams, cofounder with Mairead Corrigan of Peace People. They established the organization to end the long conflict in Northern Ireland between Protestants and Catholics.

dead children. A grieving Corrigan appeared on television the next day and condemned the IRA for the violence that had led to the death of her relatives. Two nights later she saw Betty Williams read her petition on another television newscast, and she immediately called Mrs. Williams and invited her to the funeral. Together the two organized a protest march of some 10,000 women from Andersontown, where the deaths had occurred, to the grave sites. Thus a peace movement was launched that resulted a year later in the awarding of the Nobel Peace Prize to Corrigan and Williams.

The origins of "the troubles"—the name that the Irish have given to their long civil war in the north—reach back into history, perhaps as far as the first invasions of Ireland by the English in the 12th century. Through the centuries the Irish resisted rule by Great Britain, and by the late 1800s a strong movement for independence had gained momentum, led by an organization called the Irish Republican Army. Bloody uprisings in the early 1900s led Great Britain to divide the country into northern and southern Ireland in 1921, each with its own parliament. The division, or partition, also separated the island of Ireland along religious lines: nearly all residents in the southern part are Roman Catholic, while two-thirds of the residents of the north are Protestant.

When the 1921 division occurred, southern Ireland became an independent country, the Irish Free State, though its status as a dominion of Great Britain continued its ties to that country. Sixteen years later the Irish Free State changed its name to Eire; in 1948 it severed all ties with Great Britain and became an independent republic.

Since the 1921 division, Northern Ireland has been part of the United Kingdom, which also includes England, Scotland, and Wales. However, the Republic of Ireland has continued to insist that Northern Ireland is part of the republic and that the country should be reunited.

After the division, the Irish Republican Army continued to call for complete independence, and it remained active in both the north and the south. The IRA's advocacy of violence and terrorism to achieve its ends caused it to be outlawed in 1939 by governments in both parts of the island. The IRA then became an underground terrorist organization, dedicated to ending British rule in Northern Ireland.

The IRA and its supporters have traditionally been Catholic and have claimed that they are working to improve working and living conditions for the mostly poor minority Catholic population in Northern Ireland. The IRA's campaign against British domination intensified in 1968 and thereafter with demonstrations, bombings, and sniper shootings; it has continued, with brief cease-fires, for nearly three decades.

In response to IRA terrorism, militant Protestant groups formed in the north and began conducting a terrorist campaign of their own. By the summer of 1976, when tragedy united Betty Williams and Mairead Corrigan in a quest for peace, violence in Northern Ireland caused by confrontations between Catholics, Protestants, and British troops had killed hundreds of people, injured thousands, and destroyed millions of dollars' worth of property.

After their meeting at the funeral, Mairead Corrigan and Betty Williams discovered that they had much in common. They were both Roman Catholics from working-class backgrounds, they had been born only a year apart in Belfast, and they had become office workers before completing secondary school.

Mairead Corrigan was born in 1944 to a window cleaner and his wife;

Mairead Corrigan

BORN
January 27, 1944
Belfast, Northern Ireland

EDUCATION
Business school

OCCUPATION
Secretary

MAJOR ACCOMPLISHMENT
Cofounder, Peace People (1976), an organization dedicated to ending violence in Northern Ireland

Mairead Corrigan continues to work with Peace People in its efforts to bring an end to religious strife in Northern Ireland.

she was the second of seven children. She left school at the age of 14 because her father could not afford to pay for further schooling. She supported herself as a babysitter while attending business classes and eventually was hired by the Guinness brewing company, where she rose to become private secretary to a director of the firm.

Corrigan's memories of growing up in Belfast include fears of both the IRA and the British, and she claims that she was never interested in Irish reunification. However, although she never felt anti-Catholic discrimination personally, she believes that many Catholics in the north are treated as second-class citizens.

Betty Williams has similar feelings. She was the elder of two daughters born to a Catholic butcher named Smyth and his Protestant wife, a waitress, in 1943. After her mother was paralyzed by a stroke when Betty was 13, she had to run the household herself and care for her younger sister. Betty Williams remembers being

brought up in a spirit of tolerance by both her father and her maternal grandfather, a Polish Jew who had lost most of his family in Europe during World War II.

Like Mairead Corrigan, Betty Smyth Williams attended Catholic schools and had few opportunities to meet Protestant children. As a teenager she took classes at a secretarial school in Belfast and was employed at various office jobs. She married Ralph Williams, an engineer in the merchant marine and a Protestant, when she was 18, and for several years she traveled with her husband before they returned to Belfast.

Betty Williams acknowledges that for a while she felt some sympathy for the IRA in the ongoing civil war but gradually came to realize that violence by either side could not be approved. In 1972 she decided to join Witness for Peace, an organization founded by a Protestant clergyman to bring Catholics and Protestants closer together and to demonstrate for an end to violence.

Williams found herself drawn personally into the conflict a year later, when she witnessed the sniper shooting of a British soldier on a Belfast street. When she rushed over to comfort the dying man, local women screamed at her that she had no business offering compassion to "the enemy."

Although Mairead Corrigan was busy with a full-time job in the late 1960s and 1970s, she spent much of her free time doing volunteer work in the poorest sections of Belfast. She helped set up a nursery school and organized recreational facilities, and her work brought her in contact with both

Catholic and Protestant religious leaders. In 1972 Corrigan joined a local Protestant minister and attended a meeting of the World Council of Churches in Thailand. A year later she traveled to Russia for a Catholic organization to make a film on religion in that country. Throughout the early 1970s, Corrigan witnessed confrontations between the IRA and British troops, and she frequently visited jailed IRA members to persuade them to renounce violence.

In the aftermath of the tragic incident in August 1976 that brought Mairead Corrigan and Betty Williams together, both women decided to create an organization devoted to bringing lasting peace to Ireland. With the help of Ciaran McKeown, a journalist, they founded Peace People. McKeown suggested the organization's name and planned its strategy, composed a statement of its purpose called "Declaration of Peace," and also wrote a pamphlet that Peace People distributed called *The Price of Peace*.

In late August 1976, Peace People organized its first public event, a march from Catholic to Protestant sectors in Belfast to dramatize the cause of peace. Some 35,000 people participated, and other marches throughout Northern Ireland followed. Peace People and its two women founders became celebrated all over the world for their heroism, and by mid-autumn they were mentioned as obvious choices for that year's Nobel Peace Prize. However, Peace People had been founded after the Nobel Committee's deadline, and when the committee decided that there were no other deserving candidates for that year's award, it postponed the naming

of a winner. A group of Norwegian civic leaders and journalists then established what they called the "Norwegian People's Peace Prize" and raised $340,000 in private donations for Peace People. Williams and Corrigan traveled to Oslo in late November to accept the prize.

In the following months, Williams and Corrigan carried the nonviolent message of Peace People to other cities in the United Kingdom and to countries throughout the world, where they made speeches and led more marches and demonstrations. They were frequently threatened with death by terrorists on both sides of the conflict, and on several occasions they were set upon and beaten. Despite this, they carried on and were encouraged by reports that violent acts related to the conflict had been reduced by more than half by the late summer of 1977.

In the fall of 1977, Mairead Corrigan and Betty Williams were named the winners of the 1976 Nobel Peace Prize at the same time that the 1977 award to Amnesty International was announced. The citation from the Nobel Committee praised the women for their courage and for giving "fresh hope to people who believed that all hope was gone." In accepting the award, both women expressed regret that Ciaran McKeown, the cofounder of Peace People, had not been named as a corecipient, and they later shared part of the $140,000 cash award with him.

After winning the Peace Prize, Corrigan and Williams continued the work they had begun with Peace People. They established programs to help survivors of terrorist attacks, assist victims of violence in claiming com-

Betty Williams

BORN
May 22, 1943
Belfast, Northern Ireland

EDUCATION
Secretarial school

OCCUPATION
Office worker

MAJOR ACCOMPLISHMENT
Cofounder, Peace People (1976), an organization dedicated to ending violence in Northern Ireland

pensation from the government, build community centers in poor neighborhoods, and restore damaged businesses and schools. They also sponsored a campaign in which terrorists were persuaded to surrender their weapons. Peace People raised more than $5 million to support these programs from donors throughout the world in the first few years after its founding.

Corrigan and Williams received other awards as well for their work with Peace People. These included the Carl von Ossietzky Prize from the Federal Republic of Germany and honorary doctorates from Yale University.

Corrigan, Williams, and McKeown resigned from the staff of Peace People in April 1978 in order to let others assume leadership roles in the organization. McKeown returned to his career as a journalist, but Corrigan has continued to participate in Peace People activities as director of an allied organization, Peace People's Commitment to Active Non-Violence. One of her major efforts is the establishment of volunteer work camps that bring Catholic and Protestant youths together.

After the death of Corrigan's sister Anne Maguire, who had lost three of her children in the 1976 incident, Corrigan married her brother-in-law Jack Maguire in 1981. She lives in Belfast with her husband, their two sons, and three stepchildren, and is known as Mairead Corrigan-Maguire.

After continuing to work with Peace People for several years, Betty Williams broke off contact with the organization. However, she has continued to be active in various political causes and describes herself as "working for peace." She divorced her first husband in 1982 and married an American named T. J. Perkins. Today Betty Williams Perkins lives in Florida with her second husband and her two children from her first marriage.

FURTHER READING

Boyd, A. "Everywhere but Ireland: Success of the Peace People." *Nation*, April 16, 1977, pp. 453–56.

"Corrigan, Mairead." In *Current Biography Yearbook 1978*. New York: H. W. Wilson, 1979.

Deutsch, Richard. *Mairead Corrigan and Betty Williams*. New York: Barron's, 1977.

"Williams, Betty [Smyth]." In *Current Biography Yearbook 1979*. New York: H. W. Wilson, 1980.

Amnesty International

1977

I n November 1960, a lawyer in London named Peter Benenson read a newspaper story that made him angry. The story described the plight of two students in Portugal who had committed the "crime" of drinking a toast to freedom in their dictator-led country. They had been arrested and sentenced to seven years in prison.

Benenson, who had given legal assistance to political prisoners in Cyprus, Hungary, South Africa, and Spain during the 1950s, was outraged. To protest the action, he organized a mass letter-writing campaign directed at Portugal's dictator, Antonio Salazar. That campaign grew into a year-long effort—organized by Benenson and two associates, Eric Baker and Louis Blom-Cooper—to publicize the plight of men and women throughout the world who had been imprisoned for their political or religious beliefs. The effort was called Appeal for Amnesty, and it was launched on May 28, 1961, through an article written by Benenson in the *Observer,* a London newspaper. (An amnesty is an official government pardon of a prisoner or prisoners.)

Benenson's article attracted worldwide attention, and inquiries began pouring into his London office from people who wanted to know what they could do to help. This overwhelming response led Benenson and his associates to turn their yearlong appeal into a permanent organization dedicated to defending political and religious prisoners throughout the world. In July 1961 they met in Luxembourg with representatives from Great Britain, the United States, Ireland, Belgium, France, and Switzerland and founded Amnesty International. Peter Benenson was elected its first director-general.

AMNESTY INTERNATIONAL

The logo of Amnesty International features a lighted candle of hope emerging from a circlet of barbed wire. The organization, founded in 1961, defends political and religious prisoners.

A demonstration by Amnesty International volunteers protests the abusive treatment of political prisoners in Paraguay.

The new organization, staffed by volunteer attorneys, began work immediately. One of its first cases was that of Josef Beran, the archbishop of Prague, who had been imprisoned for giving a sermon that criticized the Communist-run Czechoslovakian government. Irish political leader Seán MacBride, who had helped found Amnesty International and now worked as one of its staff attorneys, was sent to Prague to secure Beran's release. MacBride eventually persuaded Czech authorities to free Beran as well as four other imprisoned bishops.

Amnesty International did not publicize its success, however, nor has it publicized the thousands of releases it has secured since then. Since its founding, the organization has operated under the principle that governments are more likely to free political prisoners if they can do so quietly. (Governments are usually reluctant to admit publicly that they jail citizens on political or religious grounds.)

During the 1960s, Amnesty International succeeded in freeing thousands of political prisoners in Africa, Europe, and Asia as hundreds of chapters of the organization were established worldwide. In the early 1970s, Amnesty International launched a campaign to end torture and ensure humane treatment of political and religious prisoners. Campaign workers collected more than a million signatures on a petition calling for the outlawing of torture and submitted the petition to the UN General Assembly in 1973. Four years later, Amnesty International proclaimed 1977 "Prisoners of Conscience Year" to focus attention on the many women and men throughout the world imprisoned for their personal beliefs, language, or ethnic origin.

In the fall of 1977, Amnesty International was named the winner of that year's Nobel Peace Prize for its services on behalf of human rights. In making the award, the Nobel Committee cited the organization for contributing to world peace by defending human dignity and opposing torture, violence, and degradation.

Not long after the award ceremonies, Amnesty International sponsored a conference in Stockholm, Sweden, on capital punishment (the death penalty). At its conclusion, a statement was issued that denounced government-ordered executions. Two years later, Amnesty International published a summary report of the conference entitled *The Death Penalty,* which was circulated throughout the world and which called for an end to capital punishment.

In the years since winning the Nobel Peace Prize, Amnesty International has continued to champion human rights and to oppose government denial of those rights. In addition to helping free thousands of political prisoners, it has sponsored major campaigns to call attention to the activities of repressive political regimes, including torture, and to end international arms traffic by these regimes. Amnesty International also sponsors so-called adoption groups, individuals who band together to work for the release of a political prisoner. Thousands of these adoption groups are currently active throughout the world.

Headquartered in London, Amnesty International has thousands of members throughout the world who pay dues that contribute to the support of the organization. Amnesty International is also funded by private grants, and much of its work is accomplished by legal experts who volunteer their services.

FURTHER READING

Andrus, Beth, and Sonia A. Rosen, eds. *The Universal Declaration of Human Rights, 1948–1988: Human Rights, the United Nations, and Amnesty International.* New York: AIUSA Legal Support Network, 1988.

Bronson, Marsha. *Amnesty International.* Morristown, N.J.: New Discovery Books/Silver Burdett, 1994.

Power, Jonathan. *Amnesty International: The Human Rights Story.* New York: McGraw-Hill, 1981.

PEACEMAKERS

Amnesty International

FOUNDERS
Peter Benenson, Eric Baker, and Louis Blom-Cooper

DATE AND PLACE OF FOUNDING
1961
Luxembourg

HEADQUARTERS
London, England

PURPOSE
Human rights organization that defends prisoners jailed for their political or religious beliefs

MAJOR ACCOMPLISHMENTS
Has secured the release of thousands of prisoners around the world who were jailed for their personal beliefs

Menachem Begin

Anwar Sadat

1978

From the time he was a small child growing up in a Jewish family in Poland, Menachem Begin (pronounced *BAY-gin*) was aware of anti-Semitism—prejudice against Jews. That prejudice took a violent turn in 1920, during the Russo-Polish War, when Menachem was only seven years old. At that time he and his family witnessed scenes of extreme brutality against Jews in their hometown of Brest Litovsk, where Menachem Begin was born in 1913. His father, one of the leaders of the Jewish communal organization in the town, said over and over again that the only way for Jews to survive was to return to Israel, the land of their ancestors in the Middle East.

For centuries Jews had dreamed of re-creating the ancient nation of Israel, which had fallen to the Romans in the 2nd century A.D. After the fall, the Jewish people migrated to Europe and eventually to other parts of the world. However, a small Jewish community remained in the area, which was renamed Palestine. It was controlled by the Romans until the 7th century A.D. and then by a series of Arab rulers until the second decade of the 20th century.

For nearly 2,000 years, as Jews faced persecution throughout the world, they dreamed of returning one day to their homeland. In the late 19th century, the political movement known as Zionism was founded in Europe to focus those dreams. Leaders of the Zionist movement encouraged Jews to immigrate to Palestine, and they called repeatedly for the formal establishment of a new Jewish state of Israel there.

By the early 1900s hundreds of Jews had migrated to Palestine, but they were considered outsiders: the region had been ruled for 400 years by the Ottoman Empire, whose religion was Islam. Then, in 1917, the Zionist cause received a boost: in that year, the control of Palestine passed to Great Britain, and the British government pledged to create a homeland there for Jews.

Menachem Begin took his father's words seriously and determined that one day he would "return to Israel." His first step in that direction was to join a local Zionist scouting organization when he was only 10 years old; the group prepared children for life on a *kibbutz*, or farm settlement in Palestine.

During the 1920s, as negotiations continued on the establishment of a politically independent Jewish state in Palestine, Begin attended a Hebrew primary school and a Polish secondary school in Brest Litovsk. In 1929, while still in secondary school, he joined Betar, a militant youth organization with Zionist connections that demanded the immediate creation of the new Israel. Begin entered the University of Warsaw in 1931 to study law and a year later became the head of a division within Betar. He worked part time as a tutor to pay his expenses and helped found a Jewish student defense group on the campus.

Begin received his law degree in 1935, and in early 1936 he moved to Czechoslovakia to head the Betar organization there. He returned to Poland in 1938 and early the following year became the head of Polish Betar. The Betar leadership was becoming increasingly impatient with the British government for not moving more quickly to keep its promise of creating a Jewish state. That promise had been postponed because there was considerable opposition from Arabs in Palestine, and that opposition had been expressed in frequent violent clashes with Jewish settlers.

In the spring of 1939, the British government enacted a series of measures to restrict Jewish immigration to Palestine in order to prevent more violence. These restrictions were announced in the midst of intense persecution of Jews in Germany, many of whom had tried without success to enter Palestine. Begin responded to the new restrictions by leading a mass protest by Betar members outside the British embassy in Warsaw. He was arrested by Polish police and spent several months in prison. In late August, as German troops began their invasion of Poland—the beginning of World War II—Begin escaped and fled to Vilnius, Lithuania, with his wife, whom he had married earlier that year, and a group of Betar members.

After several months in Vilnius, Begin hoped to lead the group on to Palestine, but he was prevented from doing so when the Soviet Union annexed Lithuania in July 1940. The new Communist government did not trust Begin or the Betar organization, and

Begin was arrested. He was sentenced to eight years of hard labor and sent to a work camp in the Siberian Arctic. However, when Germany attacked the Soviet Union in 1941, Begin and other Polish prisoners were released to serve in a newly formed Polish army. Later that year, Begin's unit was sent to Amman, a city in the Middle Eastern country of Transjordan. In May 1942 he entered Palestine, where he became head of the Betar organization in the city of Jerusalem.

By 1943 Begin had been discharged from the Polish army, and in December of that year he became commander of the Irgun, a paramilitary Zionist force. The Irgun had engaged in sabotage against British rule prior to the outbreak of World War II, but after the war began in 1939 they had cooperated with British authorities to oppose their common enemy, Germany.

By the early 1940s, millions of Jews were being imprisoned and killed by the Germans in countries they now occupied throughout Europe. When the Irgun learned of this, it began to take a hard-line stand against the British in Palestine, demanding that they end restrictions on Jewish immigration and immediately create an independent Jewish state. When these demands were not met, the Irgun declared war on the British administration in Palestine in early 1944, which earned them condemnation by both the Jewish leadership in Palestine and the World Zionist Organization.

The British responded by cracking down on the Irgun, and Begin had to conceal his identity when it became known that the British had offered up to $50,000 for his capture, dead or alive. For several years he directed the Irgun's operations while living under a variety of disguises in the cities of Tel Aviv and Jerusalem. He commanded a guerrilla force of some 2,000 members, and during a three-year period (1944–47) was responsible for a series

Menachem Begin

BORN

August 16, 1913
Brest Litovsk, Poland (now Brest, Belarus)

DIED

March 9, 1992
Tel Aviv, Israel

EDUCATION

Master of Jurisprudence, University of Warsaw (1935)

OCCUPATION

Political leader

MAJOR ACCOMPLISHMENT

Cosigned the Camp David Accords, a two-part peace agreement between Israel and Egypt (1978)

Israeli prime minister Menachem Begin, who had been a terrorist in his youth, made history in 1978 when he met with Egyptian president Anwar Sadat to draw up a peace agreement.

of attacks, including the bombing of the King David Hotel in Jerusalem, which killed many civilians as well as soldiers.

Begin was later criticized for these activities and branded a terrorist even by many of his fellow Jews, but he claimed that the actions of the Irgun were necessary to call attention to the plight of the Jewish people. Some 6 million Jews had been killed by the Germans before the war ended in 1945—including Begin's parents and brother.

In 1946 control of Palestine passed from Great Britain to the United Nations, and in December 1947 the UN decided to partition (divide) Palestine into separate sections for Jews and Arabs. Following this decision the Irgun ended its secret operations. It was reorganized as a regular military unit and joined forces with Haganah, the long-established militia maintained by the Jewish community in Palestine.

In May 1948 the Jewish state of Israel declared its independence. However, the celebrations were overshadowed by an act of violence that had occurred a month earlier, when Haganah and Irgun forces, which included Begin, attacked an Arab village in Palestine and killed 250 civilians. This was another cloud over Begin's head, and like the bombing of the King David Hotel, it would haunt him for the rest of his life.

Begin was opposed to the more moderate political leader David Ben-Gurion, Israel's first prime minister and the leader of the Labor party. In the summer of 1948 Begin and his associates formed a new political party, the Herut (Freedom), and he became its chairman. In 1949 he was elected to a seat in the Knesset, the Israeli parliament.

In 1952 Ben-Gurion announced that he wanted to negotiate with the West German government for war reparations (payments for damages or property loss). Begin was strongly opposed to any dealings whatsoever with Germany, and he staged a major protest demonstration in Jerusalem. The demonstration turned into a riot, and Ben-Gurion had to call out the army to restore order. As a consequence, Begin was suspended from his seat in parliament for 15 months.

Despite this setback, Begin continued to increase his political power as he worked to enlarge the membership of Herut. Under his direction it grew to include not only middle-class members but also many from the working class, and it became the second largest party in Israel, after the Labor party. By the mid-1960s, Begin had become chairman of a coalition (temporary merging) of Herut and the Liberal party, and he was recognized as the leader of the opposition to the Labor party.

In June 1967 the so-called Six-Day War occurred between Egypt and Israel, during which Israel seized Arab-held territories along its borders. The war ended with a UN-negotiated cease-fire, but the territories remained in Israel's possession. Many Israelis were in favor of releasing the territories, but Begin and other political conservatives believed that for reasons of security Israel had to hold onto two of them: the Gaza Strip and the West Bank of the Jordan River. Begin emerged as the leader of this coalition of conservatives, which became known as Likud (Unity).

Likud became a strong force in Israeli politics and helped elect Yitzhak Rabin as premier in 1974. Three years later Likud gained full control of the government and Begin became prime minister. Upon taking office in June 1977 he immediately announced that the main goal of his government was peace, and he called for talks with the Arab governments of Egypt, Jordan, and Syria—countries that had been opposed to Israel since its founding. He also expressed an interest in creating stronger ties with the United States and France.

In November 1977, Egyptian president Anwar Sadat, a Moslem, made an unexpected gesture of peace to the state of Israel: he offered to visit Jerusalem. Begin welcomed him openly, and a long series of negotiations began on establishing peaceful relations between Egypt and Israel. By the summer of 1978, however, these negotiations seemed to be failing, and U.S. President Jimmy Carter tried to save them by inviting both men to a conference at Camp David, in rural Maryland.

In August 1978 Begin and Sadat met at Camp David over a 13-day period and drew up two agreements, "A Framework for Peace in the Middle East" and "A Framework for the Conclusion of a Peace Treaty Between Egypt and Israel." Under these agreements, called the Camp David Accords, Israel promised to give back most of the Sinai Peninsula, a large mass of Egyptian-owned territory that it had occupied since the Six-Day War.

For their efforts to make peace, Begin and Sadat were awarded the 1978 Nobel Peace Prize. In presenting the award, the Nobel Committee noted that the Camp David Accords offered "a genuine opportunity for peace in an area over which the shadow of war has hovered so long."

Begin continued to serve as Israel's prime minister for five more years, but during this period further conflict occurred between Israel and neighboring Arab countries. In 1982 major warfare followed Israel's invasion of Lebanon. Begin claimed that he had to send troops into Lebanon to fight Palestinian guerrillas (guerillas are soldiers not attached to an official army) who were menacing Israel along its border. As the war continued, Israel was widely criticized for its actions, including the intensive bombing of Beirut, the Lebanese capital, and Begin's popularity declined.

Begin suffered another blow in the fall of 1982 when his wife died while

he was on a trip abroad. Begin began to lose interest in politics during the following months, and he finally resigned as prime minister in September 1983. Thereafter Begin lived with one of his daughters in Jerusalem and was rarely seen in public. In March 1992 he died in a Tel Aviv hospital at the age of 78, a week after suffering a heart attack.

Anwar Sadat, who shared the 1978 Nobel Peace Prize with Menachem Begin, also had a military background. Sadat was born in 1918 in the Egyptian village of Mît Abu el-Kôm, on the Nile delta. His father was a clerk in a military hospital, and the family were all devout Moslems. Although they had little money, Sadat's parents insisted that their son receive the best education possible. After attending a local Moslem primary school, Sadat was sent to secondary school in Cairo, the Egyptian capital.

As he was growing up, Sadat knew that Egypt was not free and independent but under the control of the British government. Sadat dreamed of becoming an army officer, fighting British troops who occupied his country, and winning Egypt's independence. Even after Great Britain gave up much of its governing authority to Egyptian control in 1936, it still maintained

Signing the Camp David Accords in August 1978 (from left): Anwar Sadat; U.S. President Jimmy Carter, who mediated the agreement; and Menachem Begin.

Anwar Sadat, a longtime Egyptian army officer, became president of Egypt in 1970 and held that office until his assassination in 1981.

military bases in Egypt and had considerable power there. That same year, Sadat was admitted to the Abbassia Military Academy. There he became friendly with a fellow student named Gamal Abdel Nasser, who was to play an important role in Sadat's life.

After graduating from the academy in 1938, Sadat and Nasser were commissioned as army officers and sent to a garrison in northern Egypt. There they joined 10 other officers in forming a secret revolutionary group dedicated to Egyptian liberation. That group became the nucleus of the Free Officers Committee that overthrew King Farouk of Egypt 14 years later.

Meanwhile, during World War II, which began in 1939, Sadat made several attempts to collaborate with the Germans in an effort to weaken Britain's control of Egypt. Despite constant bungling and failure, Sadat persisted, and in the fall of 1942 he was arrested after trying unsuccessfully to work with a German spy. Sadat was court-martialed for the incident, dismissed from the army, and imprisoned.

Sadat escaped in November 1944 and adopted a variety of disguises as he plotted and carried out further revolutionary activities. He was imprisoned again in 1946, after a series of terrorist attacks on pro-British Egyptian officials, and remained behind bars for three years. After his release in 1949, he worked as a newspaper reporter. In 1950, through the intervention of influential friends, he was able to get his army commission restored.

After several years of plotting, the Free Officers Committee, led by Nasser, seized control of Egyptian military headquarters on the night of July 22, 1952, and demanded the abdication of King Farouk. Sadat missed most of the action because he had been out of town prior to the incident, but Nasser gave him the job of announcing the seizure early the following morning. Sadat also oversaw the departure of King Farouk from the country.

During the next few years, another of the conspirators, General Mohammed Naguib, acted as the head of Egypt, which proclaimed itself a republic in 1953. Nevertheless, Nasser remained a powerful force behind the scenes. During this time Sadat served on the government's Revolutionary Command Council but had little authority. In 1954 Naguib resigned and Nasser became prime minister; two years later he was elected president.

After Nasser came to power, he kept Sadat in a series of minor government jobs, presumably because the Egyptian leader did not want Sadat to gain too much authority. Sadat managed to stay in the public eye, however, by being active in the National Union, then the only political organization in Egypt, and he eventually became an official with the group. That led to Sadat's election in 1961 as president of the National Assembly, and he remained in that post for seven years.

By the late 1960s Sadat was one of the few men left around him that the now-ailing Nasser trusted, and in 1969 Sadat became Nasser's vice president. In September 1970 Nasser suffered a fatal heart attack, and Sadat automatically succeeded him as temporary president. The following month he was nominated for the office by the National Assembly and later won a nationwide election. During his campaign he pledged to recover Egyptian land lost in the Six-Day War between Israel and Egypt in 1967, even if this meant attacking Israel.

Sadat had not played a major role in the Six-Day War or in the truce that followed. In 1968 Nasser had begun what he called a "war of attrition" against Israel, meaning that he would try to wear down that country by any means necessary until it gave up Egyptian territory. One month before his death, Nasser had agreed to a 90-day cease-fire, which Sadat privately opposed. However, as president, Sadat extended the cease-fire for another 90 days when it expired in November 1970. As a consequence, Israel agreed to resume peace talks with Egypt.

Sadat emerged as a popular leader and was praised for several actions in his first years in office, including reducing the powers of the secret police and expelling Russian military advisers. However, by 1973 negotiations with Israel had stalled, and Sadat was increasingly accused of being ineffective. At this point he decided to act on his campaign promise to attack Israel.

On October 6, 1973, Sadat launched his invasion, joined by the army of Syria, one of Egypt's Arab neighbors. The date of the attack happened to be Yom Kippur, the holiest day in the Jewish religious calendar, and the Israelis were enraged. They immediately struck back so strongly that they drove out the Syrians and went on to invade Egypt. By October 24, they were within 45 miles of Cairo. Faced with this threat, Sadat agreed to a cease-fire. The U.S. government sent Secretary of State Henry Kissinger to negotiate a peace settlement. Kissinger succeeded in persuading Israel to return a small portion of Egyptian territory, but months went by without any noticeable progress toward peace.

Sadat's political support sharply declined as a series of setbacks occurred during 1977. When he announced a decision to raise food prices, major riots followed. He was repeatedly unsuccessful in his attempts to convene a peace conference in Geneva, Switzerland (a neutral country), on the Middle East. Finally, the election of the militant Menachem Begin as prime minister of Israel threatened a possible Israeli takeover of Egypt.

In November 1977 Sadat decided to make a bold move. Without notifying anyone, including the Egyptian parliament, of his decision, he announced that he was willing to speak personally with the leaders of Israel in an effort to establish peace. A week later Sadat made his offer more specific: he expressed his willingness to travel to Jerusalem for the meeting if Begin would invite him. Begin quickly responded and on November 19 Sadat went to Jerusalem.

There Sadat addressed a meeting of the Israeli parliament and listed a series of demands, which included returning Arab lands seized in 1967 to Egypt and agreeing to the establishment of a homeland for thousands of

Anwar Sadat

BORN
December 25, 1918
Mît Abu el-Kôm, Egypt

DIED
October 6, 1981
Cairo, Egypt

EDUCATION
Royal Military Academy (Cairo)

OCCUPATION
Military officer; political leader

MAJOR ACCOMPLISHMENT
Cosigned the Camp David Accords, a two-part peace agreement between Israel and Egypt (1978)

stateless Palestinians in the Middle East. In return, Sadat offered both official diplomatic recognition of Israel by Egypt and permanent peace.

A series of negotiations between Egypt and Israel followed Sadat's address. By the summer of 1978, however, little progress had been made. At this point U.S. President Jimmy Carter invited Sadat and Begin to meet at his Presidential retreat in rural Maryland to try to iron out their differences. The 13-day conference at Camp David resulted in the production of two historic documents, "A Framework for Peace in the Middle East" and "A Framework for the Conclusion of a Peace Treaty with Israel." Sadat and Begin, once deadly enemies, signed both documents, the Camp David Accords, on September 17.

Later that fall, Sadat and Begin were declared cowinners of the 1978 Nobel Peace Prize. The Nobel Committee made it clear that in awarding the prize to these "courageous" men, it was not only honoring them but also trying to encourage the completion of the peace process. Popular opinion blamed Begin for delaying the process and cited Sadat as being more deserving of the Peace Prize. Nevertheless, Begin personally attended the ceremonies in Oslo while Sadat sent a representative to accept his award.

Sadat continued in office for three difficult years as peace negotiations continued. Many Egyptians expressed their opposition—often violently—to his peace overtures to Israel, and by the early fall of 1981 Sadat had begun a severe crackdown on his political opponents. On October 6, 1981, as Sadat witnessed a military parade in Cairo commemorating the 1973 war against Israel, he was assassinated by a group of men posing as military officers who threw hand grenades and fired rifles into the reviewing stand.

Sadat was married twice. By his first wife, a woman from his native village, he had three daughters. After divorcing her, he married a woman of Egyptian and English ancestry with whom he had a son and three daughters.

To read more about the ongoing conflict between Israel and its Middle East neighbors, see the profile of the 1994 Nobel Peace Prize winners on pages 276–82.

FURTHER READING

Friedlander, Melvin A. *Sadat and Begin: The Domestic Politics of Peacemaking.* Boulder, Col.: Westview, 1983.

Gervasi, Frank. *The Life and Times of Menachem Begin.* New York: Putnam, 1979.

Hirst, David, and Irene Beeson. *Sadat.* London: Faber and Faber, 1981.

Rosen, Deborah N. *Anwar el-Sadat: Middle East Peacemaker.* Chicago: Childrens Press, 1986.

Sadat, Anwar. *In Search of Identity: An Autobiography.* New York: Harper & Row, 1978.

Temko, Ned. *To Win or to Die: A Personal Portrait of Menachem Begin.* New York: Morrow, 1987.

Mother Teresa of Calcutta (Agnes Gonxha Bojaxhiu)

1979

O ne day in 1946, a Roman Catholic nun was traveling by train from her convent in Calcutta, India, to a religious retreat in the small city of Darjeeling. Sitting in the train, she reflected on the sight she had left behind in Calcutta: on her way to the railway station from the convent she had been driven past thousands of beggars, poor and homeless people of all ages dressed in rags and suffering from disease and malnutrition.

The nun had long been aware of the misery that lay outside her convent walls, for she had seen it often during her 18 years in India. But on this particular day the experience overwhelmed her. She later recalled that as she sat on the train, she received a message from God to leave the convent and devote the rest of her life to helping the poor.

The nun, whose religious name was Mother Teresa, was born Agnes Gonxha Bojaxhiu in 1910 in Skopje, a city in the Ottoman Empire that later became part of Yugoslavia and is now part of the independent nation of Macedonia.

Mother Teresa of Calcutta wears the blue-and-white sari that she designed as a habit for members of the Missionaries of Charity, the religious order that she founded in 1950.

Mother Teresa visits with poor children aided by the Missionaries of Charity in the Philippines.

She was the youngest of three children of parents who had come from Albania and settled in Skopje. Her father was a building contractor and food importer who was involved in the Albanian nationalist movement, and he died when Agnes was less than a year old.

Agnes Bojaxhiu attended public schools in Skopje and was active in Roman Catholic youth organizations from an early age. By the time she was 12, she knew that she wanted to become a foreign missionary, to spread her religious beliefs in other countries. Three years later, at the age of 15, she learned of the work of Catholic missionaries in India and decided that someday she would work there, too.

After graduating from secondary school, Agnes Bojaxhiu joined the Sisters of Loretto, a Roman Catholic order of Irish nuns who ran a large mission in Calcutta. After training as a teacher in Dublin, Ireland, she went to India in 1929.

The young nun adopted Teresa as her religious name in honor of a 19th-century French nun who had spent her short life joyfully performing menial tasks. She became known as Mother Teresa in the late 1930s, after taking her final vows. She taught at St. Mary's High School in Calcutta for nearly 19 years and also served for part of that time as principal of the school while living at the Sisters of Loretto convent.

After Mother Teresa experienced her call from God on the train that day in 1946, she applied for permission from the bishop of Calcutta to work outside the convent. Two years later that permission was finally granted, and Mother Teresa left St. Mary's High School to begin her life of helping the poor.

Mother Teresa became a citizen of India and adopted a new habit: a white sari similar to those worn by India's poor, which was trimmed in blue and fastened at the shoulder with a crucifix. She completed an intensive three-month nursing course in Patna, India, and then opened a school in the Calcutta slums. In 1950 she founded a new religious order for women, the Missionaries of Charity, and many of its first members were former students from St. Mary's High School. By the mid-1950s, more than two dozen had joined the order.

The rules of the order were very strict: members could own only one change of clothing, had to eat the same diet as the poor people they served, and were required to work 16 hours a day. In addition to her school, Mother Teresa established a home for dying people who had been abandoned on the streets of Calcutta. Donations helped her to expand her efforts, and by the early 1960s she had founded an orphanage, a leper colony, a home for the elderly, a workshop to teach skills to the unemployed, and shelters for homeless mothers and children. She also set up clinics to provide inoculations and medical treatment.

Beginning in the mid-1960s, as Mother Teresa's work attracted more volunteers, the Missionaries of Charity established similar centers for the poor in South America, Africa, Europe, the Caribbean, and North America. In 1969 the government of India honored her for her work, and two years later she received the Pope John XXIII Peace Prize from the Roman Catholic Church.

In the fall of 1979 Mother Teresa was named the winner of that year's Nobel Peace Prize for her devotion to the poor. In the words of the Nobel Committee, Mother Teresa contributed to international peace by "bridging the gulf that exists between the rich nations and the poor nations" and "by her confirmation of the inviolability of human dignity."

In accepting the award, Mother Teresa emphasized her belief that love had to be the basis for the establishment of peace in the world. She used the prize money to build more centers to serve the poor, including homes for lepers.

After winning the Nobel Peace Prize, Mother Teresa continued her work in both India and other parts of the world. She made frequent speeches to publicize the need for greater concern for the poor among wealthy nations, including an address to the United Nations General Assembly in 1985, on the occasion of its 40th anniversary. She and her order also established and staffed hospices (hospitals for the dying) in large cities, including New York, for patients with the fatal disease AIDS.

In the last years of her life, Mother Teresa's health declined, and in the spring of 1997 she had to retire as head of the Missionaries of Charity. She died of a heart attack at her convent in Calcutta and was honored with a state funeral in her adopted country.

FURTHER READING

Clucas, Joan Graff. *Mother Teresa*. New York: Chelsea House, 1988.

Doig, Desmond. *Mother Teresa: Her People and Her Work*. New York: Harper & Row, 1976.

Le Joly, Edward. *Mother Teresa of Calcutta: A Biography*. New York: Harper & Row, 1985.

Teresa, Mother. *Life in the Spirit: Reflections, Meditations, Prayers*. New York: Harper & Row, 1983.

———. *My Life for the Poor*. New York: Harper & Row, 1985.

Mother Teresa of Calcutta (Agnes Gonxha Bojaxhiu)

BORN
August 27, 1910
Skopje, Ottoman Empire (later Yugoslavia; now Macedonia)

DIED
September 5, 1997
Calcutta, India

EDUCATION
Secondary school

OCCUPATION
Roman Catholic nun; missionary

MAJOR ACCOMPLISHMENTS
Founded the Missionaries of Charity, a Roman Catholic religious order for women, to help the poor of Calcutta (1950); later expanded her work to cities throughout the world

Adolfo Pérez Esquivel

1980

Sculptor and human rights advocate Adolfo Pérez Esquivel remembers that as a poor child growing up in his native Argentina he developed a strong passion for both art and God. His artistic talent was obvious, and young Adolfo knew that some-day art would become his vocation. He was also strongly drawn to religion and read as much as he could about it. He not only read about his own religion, Roman Catholicism, but also enjoyed works by people of other faiths, including the autobiography of the Hindu pacifist Mohandas Gandhi. His interest in religious teachings and his personal faith grew even stronger as he devoted his life to sculpture, and by the time he was in his mid-30s he decided that his religious beliefs compelled him to try to ease the suffering of his fellow Argentinians.

The future Nobel Peace Prize-winner was born Adolfo Esquivel in Buenos Aires to a poor Spanish fisherman and

Argentinian sculptor Adolfo Pérez Esquivel became the leader of a nonviolent protest movement in South America after learning of human rights abuses there.

his wife who had emigrated to Argentina. His father became a traveling salesman for a coffee company. After his mother's death, which occurred when he was still a small child, Adolfo was taken in by nuns and priests at a nearby Roman Catholic boarding school.

In addition to showing a talent for drawing, Adolfo was an excellent reader and excelled in many school subjects. He won a scholarship to a private secondary school in Buenos Aires, and after graduation was awarded another scholarship to study at the National School of Fine Arts of Buenos Aires and La Plata.

Adolfo Esquivel received his diploma in 1956, the same year that he married Amanda Pérez, a pianist and composer. He then combined his wife's last name with his own. Pérez Esquivel began a successful career as a sculptor and professor of art at several institutions in Buenos Aires, including the Manuel Belgrano National School of Fine Arts. In his work he tried to express such eternal concepts as motherhood in a form that drew upon South America's Pre-Columbian heritage (the culture that existed before the arrival of Europeans in the early 16th century). His sculptures were widely exhibited in Argentina and won a number of awards, and some of them were acquired by South America's leading museums.

By the mid-1960s, however, Pérez Esquivel could not ignore the political situation in Argentina. His country had been governed harshly by a series of military dictatorships for more than a decade, and there were frequent clashes between government troops and citizens protesting not only the denial of civil rights but the terrible economic conditions in which most of the population lived. Some opponents of the government had organized into terrorist units and committed violent acts that were met with equally violent responses from the military.

Other countries in Latin America were experiencing similar problems, and a grass-roots movement of priests, nuns, and church members had developed to help the poor in these nations. In 1968, Pérez Esquivel attended a conference in Montevideo, Uruguay, where church leaders joined with representatives of labor, student, and community groups to discuss the political, social, and economic problems that affected Latin America. The conference tried to identify ways to make positive changes in these countries through nonviolent means. As a consequence, it laid the groundwork for an organization called Servicio de Paz y Justicia en América Latina, or Service for Peace and Justice in Latin America, which was formally founded in 1971 at a second conference in Costa Rica.

In addition to his membership in this organization, Pérez Esquivel joined a group in Argentina dedicated to the principle of "militant nonviolence," which based its beliefs on the teachings of Mohandas Gandhi. This group became the Argentine branch of Service for Peace and Justice, and Pérez Esquivel organized one of its first projects: creating workshops in weaving, carpentry, and ironworking in poor inner-city neighborhoods to teach residents self-supporting skills. These were modeled after similar workshops that Gandhi had established in India earlier in the century.

Pérez Esquivel's involvement with Service for Peace and Justice included the founding of its monthly magazine, *Paz y Justicia*, and taking part in peaceful demonstrations to protest terrorism. In 1974 he became director-general of the organization, which now had chapters throughout Latin America, and established its official headquarters in Buenos Aires.

Pérez Esquivel resigned his teaching position to assume his new role, which involved constant traveling through Central and South America

Adolfo Pérez Esquivel

BORN
November 26, 1931
Buenos Aires, Argentina

EDUCATION
Diploma, National School of Fine Arts of Buenos Aires and La Plata (1956)

OCCUPATION
Sculptor; human rights advocate

MAJOR ACCOMPLISHMENTS
Cofounded (1971) the human rights organization Service for Peace and Justice and served as its director-general (1974–86); president, International League for the Rights and Liberation of Peoples (1987)

to establish contact among the various far-flung chapters. He helped launch various campaigns sponsored by the organization, including support for Ecuadorian Indians seeking to reclaim their land from the government, and his activities led to his arrest on several occasions in the mid-1970s. He also traveled to Europe and the United States, seeking support for his organization.

In Pérez Esquivel's home country of Argentina, the political situation had grown even worse as a new military government, which had assumed power in 1976, cracked down on its opponents with extreme brutality. Tens of thousands of Argentinians were jailed and tortured by government troops, and many were murdered. Equally repressive military governments in Chile, Bolivia, Paraguay, Brazil, and Uruguay were treating their citizens in a similar brutal fashion.

In response to this violence, Pérez Esquivel led a campaign to publicize the United Nations Universal Declaration of Human Rights, a list of fundamental liberties that governments of UN member nations—including the countries of South America—had pledged themselves to observe. Pérez Esquivel called for the enforcement of the Declaration of Human Rights throughout Latin America, and he founded an organization to press for that enforcement in Argentina: the Ecumenical Movement for Human Rights.

Pérez Esquivel made many public speeches that denounced the violence of the Argentine government, and finally, in early April 1977, he was arrested and jailed. Although he was never formally charged with any crime, he was told that he was being held as a "subversive." As soon as news of his arrest became known, human rights advocates organized an international campaign to secure his release.

Pérez Esquivel was imprisoned for nearly 15 months, and during that time he was frequently tortured. He was finally released from prison in late June 1978 but kept under house arrest for nine more months. After recovering from his injuries, he resumed his work on behalf of Service for Peace and Justice in early 1980.

By this time, the government had eased its campaign against its opponents, but some 10,000 to 20,000 Argentine citizens were unaccounted for. They were known as the *desaparecidos*, or "disappeared ones," and Pérez Esquivel took up their cause. He joined a large group of women who gathered every week at the Plaza de Mayo, a central area in Buenos Aires, to appeal publicly for more information on their missing relatives.

For several years, Pérez Esquivel had been nominated as a candidate for the Nobel Peace Prize by previous winners, including Mairead Corrigan and Betty Williams. Finally, in October 1980, he was named the winner of that year's prize. The award was clearly intended to draw international support for his efforts to aid political prisoners in Argentina. The Argentine govern-

ment was angered by the Nobel Committee's choice and issued a statement claiming that Pérez Esquivel had contributed to terrorism in the nation. However, elsewhere in the world Pérez Esquivel was hailed as a courageous peacemaker for his efforts on behalf of human rights.

After winning the Nobel Peace Prize, Pérez Esquivel continued his efforts to help the women of the Plaza de Mayo. Their demonstrations finally ended in 1984, after the government acknowledged that some 9,000 citizens had been illegally imprisoned and executed. A number of military officers were arrested and tried for these crimes, and some received prison terms.

Adolfo Pérez Esquivel retired as the head of Service for Peace and Justice in 1986 and was named honorary president, a title he still holds. Since 1987 he has been president of the International League for the Rights and Liberation of Peoples, a worldwide human rights organization. He lives in Buenos Aires with his wife, with whom he has three grown sons.

FURTHER READING

"Pérez Esquivel, Adolfo." In *Current Biography Yearbook 1981*. New York: H. W. Wilson, 1982.

Pérez Esquivel, Adolfo. *Christ in a Poncho: Testimonials of the Nonviolent Struggles in Latin America*. Translated by Robert R. Barr. Maryknoll, N.Y.: Orbis, 1983.

Office of the UN High Commissioner for Refugees

1981

I n its first three years of operation (1951–54), the Office of the UN High Commissioner for Refugees (UNHCR) aided nearly 2 million refugees, primarily European, and was awarded the 1954 Nobel Peace Prize for these efforts. The UNHCR continued to carry out its mission of assisting refugees after receiving this honor. By the end of 1955, it had resettled three-fourths of all refugees in Europe—more than half a million people who had been homeless since the end of World War II a decade earlier. However, there were still an estimated 2.2 million refugees worldwide who needed the services of the organization.

Less than a year later, another major refugee problem appeared in Europe following the outbreak of revolution in Hungary. More than 160,000 Hungarian refugees had fled to neighboring Austria by the end of 1956. Within a few short months, the UNHCR had helped resettle two-thirds of them, and it aided the remainder during the following year.

The United Nations declared 1959 World Refugee Year, and the UNHCR responded by making a major effort to resettle refugees who still remained in European camps. It

Hungarian refugees gather at a Red Cross center in Austria in early 1957, in the aftermath of the Hungarian revolution that had occurred the previous year. Thousands of refugees who fled from Hungary into neighboring countries were resettled with help from the Office of the UN High Commissioner for Refugees.

Nearly 7 million Pakistani refugees poured into India in 1971, fleeing political turmoil in their nation. Many of them were aided by the Office of the UN High Commissioner for Refugees.

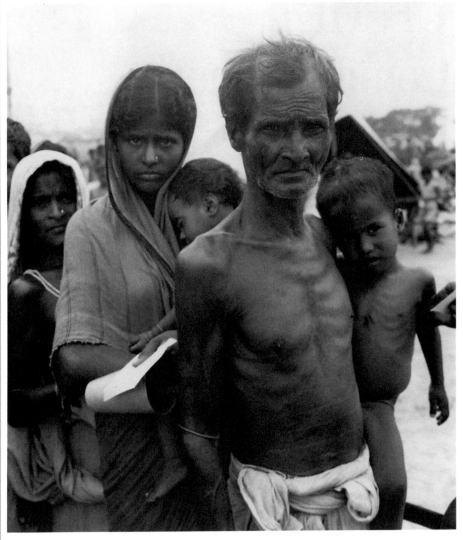

undertook another major fund-raising campaign and raised millions of dollars in contributions from public and private sources throughout the world. In 1961 the UNHCR formally separated its activities into two programs, one for refugees displaced by World War II and another for postwar refugees.

The postwar-refugee program faced its first major challenge in Africa shortly after its creation, when warfare created influxes of refugees to Togo and the Congo. The UNHCR provided aid to approximately 150,000 of these refugees, and as a result, many of them were able to remain in their new countries.

Another challenge for the postwar-refugee program occurred in 1962 in North Africa. Algeria had begun its war for independence from France in 1958, and by early 1962 250,000 Algerian refugees had fled to Tunisia and Morocco. That spring the UNHCR joined with the League of Red Cross Societies to provide food, clothing, medical care, and schooling to these refugees, and by the end of 1962 they were able to return to their homes in Algeria.

By 1963 the UNHCR was able to turn its entire attention from Europe to Africa and Asia. During the next few years, the organization aided thousands of refugees in Mozambique, Senegal, and Ethiopia. In the early 1970s, the UNHCR aided some 10 million refugees who had fled to India from East Pakistan during that country's civil war. (As a consequence of the war, East Pakistan became independent of West Pakistan and was renamed Bangladesh.)

Also in the early 1970s, the UNHCR established an ongoing program to resettle disabled refugees. In the mid-1970s the UNHCR helped close to half a million refugees in various African nations return to their homes in Guinea-Bissau, Mozambique, and Angola after these countries gained their independence from Portugal.

A major refugee problem occurred in Southeast Asia following the end of the Vietnam War in 1975, and it received much of the UNHCR's attention during the next decade. Several hundred thousand so-called Boat People fled Vietnam by sea, seeking refuge in Malaysia, Hong Kong, Indonesia, and Thailand. Many died before reaching their destinations, but many more crowded into these already overpopulated countries and filled hundreds of temporary camps.

While attempting to offer aid to these refugees, the UNHCR established the Orderly Departures Program with the government of Vietnam in May 1979. Under this program, Vietnamese were provided with both exit visas and, if they qualified, entry visas for admittance to another country. Many did not qualify, however, and the exodus of Boat People continued.

While the UNHCR was devoting its full attention to the refugee problem in Southeast Asia, it was awarded a second Nobel Peace Prize in 1981. The prize was given not only for the UNHCR's many accomplishments but also to call attention to the continuing plight of refugees all over the world.

In the years following receipt of its second Peace Prize, the UNHCR has continued to assist refugees around the world. During the early 1980s it remained focused on refugees in Southeast Asia, and by 1986 more than 100,000 Vietnamese had been resettled under the Orderly Departures Program. In the mid-1980s the UNHCR turned its attention again to Africa to aid thousands of Ethiopians who had fled to Somalia and Sudan following a famine in their country. Most were able to return to Ethiopia after receiving emergency assistance as well as livestock, tools, and seeds.

In the last decade the UNHCR has helped millions of refugees fleeing turmoil in Central America, Africa, and Asia, despite the fact that it has had fewer resources in recent years. As it looks ahead to the 21st century, the Office of the UN High Commissioner for Refugees intends to aid people throughout the world who need its services. However, the UNHCR—faced with having to run its programs on tighter budgets—hopes that political solutions can be found to many future crises *before* they produce large refugee populations.

FURTHER READING

Holborn, L. *Refugees: A Problem of Our Time*. 2 vols. Metuchen, N.J.: Scarecrow Press, 1975.

"Office of the United Nations High Commissioner for Refugees." In *Nobel Prize Winners*. New York: H. W. Wilson, 1987.

Office of the UN High Commissioner for Refugees

FOUNDERS

Founded by the United Nations as a successor to the International Refugee Organization

DATE AND PLACE OF FOUNDING

1951
Geneva, Switzerland

HEADQUARTERS

Geneva, Switzerland

PURPOSE

To aid refugees throughout the world by providing them with material and legal assistance and permanent settlement

MAJOR ACCOMPLISHMENTS, 1954–1981

Resettled nearly half a million European refugees remaining from World War II; aided 160,000 refugees fleeing Hungarian Revolution (1956–57); sponsored major relief programs in North Africa (1962), Central Africa (mid-1960s and mid-1970s), India (early 1970s), and Southeast Asia (1975 onward) that aided more than 12 million refugees

Alfonso García Robles
Alva Myrdal

1982

When he was a boy, the future Mexican diplomat Alfonso García Robles wanted very much to become a priest, a goal that his parents encouraged. As a teenager, however, García Robles became convinced that he could help people more by joining his country's foreign service and becoming a diplomat. His decision to study law and international relations at the National University of Mexico—instead of enrolling at a seminary to be trained as a priest—was justified many years later when he won the 1982 Nobel Peace Prize.

Alfonso García Robles was born into a prosperous family in Zamora, the capital of the Mexican state of Michoacán, in 1911. After attending local private schools, he enrolled at the National University in Mexico City and graduated in 1933. For five years, beginning in early 1934, he did graduate work in international law abroad, first at the University of Paris and then at the International Law Academy at The Hague, the Netherlands. In 1939, while still in Europe, he joined the Mexican foreign service and was sent to the Mexican embassy in Stockholm for two years.

García Robles returned to Mexico City in 1941 to become head of the government's Department of International Organizations. Over the next few years he rose to a higher post, director-general of political affairs and the diplomatic service. In 1945 he traveled to San Francisco as part of the Mexican delegation to the conference that founded the United Nations. A year later he was given a leave of absence to serve as director of the UN Secretariat's Division of Political Affairs, and he remained in this post for 11 years.

García Robles returned to Mexico City in 1957 to become head of the Department for Europe, Asia, and Africa within the Ministry of Foreign Affairs. In his five years of service there he represented Mexico at several important conferences on international law. García Robles's next assignment was in Brazil, where he served as Mexico's ambassador from 1962 to 1964.

Shortly after García Robles's appointment to his Brazilian post, the so-called Cuban Missile Crisis occurred following the discovery by the U.S. government that the Soviet Union had installed nuclear missiles in Cuba, off the coast of Florida. After tense negotiations, the U.S. government persuaded Soviet authorities to remove the missiles, and warfare was avoided. However, the incident alarmed other governments in the western hemisphere, and García Robles called upon Latin American nations to sign a treaty establishing the region as a nuclear-free zone—in other words,

As Mexico's ambassador to the United Nations, Alfonso García Robles addresses the General Assembly in 1975. He won the Peace Prize seven years later for his efforts to halt the spread of nuclear weapons.

Alfonso García Robles

BORN
March 20, 1911
Zamora, Mexico

EDUCATION
L.L.B., National University of Mexico (1933); graduate study in law, University of Paris and International Law Academy, The Hague (1934–39)

OCCUPATION
Diplomat

MAJOR ACCOMPLISHMENTS
Held major diplomatic posts in the Mexican government and with the United Nations; established and coauthored the Treaty for the Prohibition of Nuclear Weapons in Latin America (the Treaty of Tlatelolco, 1967); coauthored the Nuclear Nonproliferation Treaty of 1968; chairman, UN Disarmament Committee (1985)

pledging themselves to forbid any nuclear weapons within their borders.

In April 1963 the heads of Bolivia, Brazil, Chile, Ecuador, and Mexico signed a declaration that endorsed this proposal, and in November of the same year the United Nations General Assembly adopted a resolution supporting such a treaty. However, by 1964, when García Robles returned to Mexico City to become undersecretary for foreign affairs, he was dismayed that nothing further had been done to create the treaty. That November he called a conference of Latin American diplomats in Mexico City for the purpose of drawing up the nuclear-free-zone agreement.

Following the conference, a series of negotiations among Latin American government leaders occurred for more than two years. Finally, in February 1967, a final draft of the treaty—which García Robles coauthored—was approved. Called the Treaty for the Prohibition of Nuclear Weapons in Latin America, or the Treaty of Tlatelolco—it was signed on February 14 by representatives of 14 Latin American nations at Tlatelolco Plaza, the site of the Foreign Affairs Ministry in Mexico City. Later, 10 more Latin American nations signed the treaty. In addition, the United States, Great Britain, the Soviet Union, the People's Republic of China, France, and the Netherlands signed separate agreements to the treaty, called protocols, in which they pledged that they would never introduce weapons into Latin America or use them in the region.

In the latter part of 1967, García Robles led the Mexican delegation to the United Nations disarmament conference in Geneva, Switzerland. There

Alva Myrdal, who shared the 1982 Nobel Prize with García Robles for her nuclear disarmament work, was also an expert on social welfare issues, including those involving child welfare, training for the disabled, and the status of women in the work force.

he met and worked closely with Alva Myrdal, the Swedish sociologist who would share the Nobel Peace Prize with him 15 years later. As an outgrowth of the conference, the Nuclear Nonproliferation Treaty of 1968 was created. This treaty, which García Robles coauthored, called upon countries throughout the world to stop the spread of nuclear weapons. It was eventually signed by more than a hundred nations.

After serving as Mexico's ambassador to the United Nations for five years, beginning in 1970, García Robles was appointed foreign minister of his country in 1975. A year later, he asked to be appointed as Mexico's permanent representative to the UN Disarmament Committee in Geneva. In that capacity, García Robles continued to work for international disarmament for more than a decade.

García Robles made a major contribution to the cause of world peace in 1982, when he introduced a motion in the UN General Assembly calling for the United Nations to launch an international disarmament crusade. The motion was not adopted, but García Robles's call received widespread support as millions of people demonstrated against nuclear weapons later that year in the United States and in many European countries.

Alfonso García Robles's longtime support for nuclear disarmament earned him a share of the 1982 Nobel Peace Prize. After winning the award he continued his crusade, and in 1985 he was elected chairman of the UN Disarmament Committee.

García Robles has been married since 1950 to a former diplomat from Peru whom he met while leading a UN mission to the Middle East; the couple has two sons. In addition to fulfilling his formal duties, García Robles has written more than 300 articles on foreign affairs and is the author of nearly two dozen books, many of them on disarmament.

Alva Myrdal, cowinner of the 1982 Nobel Peace Prize for her own crusade on behalf of disarmament, was already quite familiar with the awards established by her fellow Swede Alfred Nobel: eight years earlier, her husband, Gunnar Myrdal, had shared the 1974 Nobel Prize in Economic Science.

Alva Myrdal was born Alva Reimer in Uppsala, Sweden, in 1902. Her father was a building contractor who served as a member of the city council and was especially interested in social welfare issues, including adult education for workers. Alva Reimer Myrdal later said that her father and her teacher in primary school, Swedish Quaker leader Per Sundberg, had the greatest influence on her while she was

Alva Myrdal

growing up. (The Quakers, or Friends, are members of the religious sect called the Society of Friends, founded in the 18th century by the Englishman George Fox. Quakers are pacifists: they are opposed to warfare for any reason.)

Both of Alva Reimer's parents encouraged their bright daughter to enroll at the University of Stockholm after she completed secondary school, although women at that time were not expected to pursue higher education. She received a scholarship to study social science at the university and received her undergraduate degree in 1924. Later that year she married Gunnar Myrdal, a lawyer who later became a renowned economist.

Following her graduation and marriage, Alva Myrdal became active in the Workers' Educational Association, an organization devoted to the promotion of adult education. She shared her interest in social welfare issues with her husband, and the two of them decided to pursue further studies in that field. From 1925 to 1928 they attended graduate classes in economics and social science at the universities of London, Leipzig, and Stockholm. In 1929–30 they traveled in the United States on a fellowship from the Rockefeller Foundation, and then studied in Switzerland before returning to Sweden in 1932.

During the 1930s, both Alva and Gunnar Myrdal became recognized authorities in socioeconomics, a field of study that includes both sociology and economics. Alva Myrdal also did graduate work in philosophy, psychology, and philosophy, and received a combined master's degree from the University of Uppsala in 1934. That year she and her husband published their first

important study, "Crisis in the Population Problem," which led to the passage of social welfare legislation in Sweden and several other Scandinavian countries.

As a recognized expert on population studies, Alva Myrdal went on to write other articles on the subject, both alone and in collaboration with her husband. By the end of the 1930s, Alva Myrdal's primary academic field had become sociology, while her husband was now a professor of economics and public finance at the University of Stockholm.

Alva Myrdal was especially interested in child welfare, and she published many articles on the subject. One of her major accomplishments was the founding of a training college in Stockholm for nursery and kindergarten teachers in 1936. She became its director and served in that capacity for 12 years. She also served as the head of several government commissions on education, including one on training for the disabled.

Another major concern of Alva Myrdal's throughout her life was equality for women in the workforce, from the least skilled to the most highly trained professionals. As a member of the Labor party (also known as the Social Democratic party), she was active in party affairs and edited a monthly publication aimed at women. In addition, she served on government committees concerned with women workers' issues and addressed these issues as a representative to international labor conferences during the 1940s. Her concerns for the status of business and professional women led her to an active leadership role in several national organizations concerned with their welfare.

BORN
January 31, 1902
Uppsala, Sweden

DIED
February 1, 1986
Stockholm, Sweden

EDUCATION
B.A., University of Stockholm (1924); M.A., University of Uppsala (1934)

OCCUPATION
Sociologist

MAJOR ACCOMPLISHMENTS
Became one of Sweden's leading experts on social welfare issues affecting women and children; director, United Nations Department of Social Affairs (1950–55); Swedish ambassador to India (1955–61); member of Swedish Parliament (1962–73); head of Sweden's delegation to the UN disarmament conference in Geneva (1962–66); author (and coauthor with her husband, Gunnar Myrdal) of numerous articles and books on social and economic issues, including disarmament

In the years immediately following the end of World War II in 1945, Alva Myrdal devoted much of her time to aiding European refugees and helping many of them resettle in Sweden. She also served as Sweden's delegate to UNESCO, the United Nations Educational, Scientific, and Cultural Organization, and in 1950 she was named director of the UN's Department of Social Affairs. In this role she supervised international projects relating to human rights, the status of women, population growth, and other areas.

In 1955 Alva Myrdal left her United Nations post to become Sweden's ambassador to India, where she served for six years and became widely admired. When she returned to Stockholm in 1961, the Swedish foreign minister asked her to become his special assistant on disarmament. This was a new field for Alva Myrdal, but with characteristic energy she studied the subject intensely and it quickly became the major focus of her interest. Following her election to the Swedish parliament in 1962, she became head of her country's delegation to the ongoing UN disarmament conference in Geneva. Although her term of office officially ended in 1966, she continued to attend the conference until 1973, when she retired from government service. One milestone that occurred during that period encouraged Alva Myrdal to continue her work: in 1968, Sweden renounced the manufacture, import, and use of nuclear weapons.

Now working independently, Alva Myrdal became a one-woman crusade on behalf of disarmament. She gave many speeches, wrote numerous arti-cles, and published an influential book, *The Game of Disarmament: How the United States and Russia Run the Arms Race* (1977). In that book she attacked both countries for wasting enormous amounts of money on weapons instead of spending that money on health care, housing, and education.

Alva Myrdal's crusade won her the Albert Einstein Peace Prize in 1980. Two years later, she shared the 1982 Nobel Peace Prize with Alfonso García Robles. Alva Myrdal was forced to give up her campaign for peace in 1984, when her chronic heart disease grew worse. She spent most of the next two years in a Stockholm hospital and died in February 1986 at the age of 84.

Alva and Gunnar Myrdal had a son and two daughters; one of their daughters, Sissela Myrdal Bok, became a noted philosopher. Gunnar Myrdal survived his wife by little more than a year and died in May 1987.

FURTHER READING

Bok, Sissela. *Alva Myrdal: A Daughter's Memoir*. Reading, Mass.: Addison-Wesley, 1991.

García Robles, Alfonso. *The Denuclearization of Latin America*. Translated by Marjorie Urquidi. New York: Carnegie Endowment for International Peace, 1967.

"García Robles, Alfonso." In *Nobel Prize Winners*. New York: H. W. Wilson, 1987.

Myrdal, Alva. *The Game of Disarmament: How the United States and Russia Run the Arms Race*. New York: Pantheon, 1977.

"Myrdal, Mrs. Alva." In *Current Biography Yearbook 1950*. New York: H. W. Wilson, 1951.

Lech Walesa

1983

In 1967 a young Pole named Lech Walesa (pronounced *Lek Va-WENZ-a*) could hardly have imagined that one day he would win the Nobel Peace Prize—or that he would be elected president of his country. Walesa had recently completed several years of military service, required of all male Polish citizens. Before entering the army, he had worked briefly as an electrician, the trade that his vocational school in Lipno, Poland, had prepared him for. Now he was back in Gdansk, a port city on the Baltic Sea, to resume his work in the shipyard there. Despite the hardships imposed by the Communist government, Walesa was confident that he could earn a reasonably good living. Eventually, he wanted to marry and raise a family: that was his dream.

Walesa was born in 1943 in Popowo, Poland, during the occupation of that country by German troops in World War II. He was one of eight children. His father, a carpenter, was sent to a German forced-labor camp sometime after Lech's

Polish labor leader Lech Walesa speaks to his fellow workers in the Gdansk shipyards in 1980, the year he founded Solidarity.

Pope John Paul II, a native of Poland, greets crowds during a visit to Warsaw in 1979.

birth, and the injuries that he received there caused his death in 1946.

From earliest childhood, Lech Walesa was a devout Roman Catholic, the religion of his family and much of Poland. He attended local Catholic schools before receiving his vocational training. Walesa later recalled that he was never a very good student, but he was always a popular leader in school. His army service and his early years as an electrician passed uneventfully, and in 1969 Walesa married; he eventually became the father of eight children.

Walesa's life began to change in December 1970, when the government announced a sharp rise in food prices. Many citizens staged protest demonstrations in cities throughout Poland. In Gdansk a group of shipyard workers, led by Walesa and others, called a strike, demanding improvements in their working conditions as well as a lowering of food prices. As they joined other Poles in protest, police shot at them, trying to force them back to the shipyard. Before order was finally restored, 55 workers had been killed.

Walesa avoided injury, and he returned to his job after the government agreed to several of the workers' demands. However, as economic conditions in the country grew worse, Walesa and other shipyard workers formed a labor union—illegal at the time in Poland—to press for change. When prices were raised again in 1976, Walesa joined new protest demonstrations in Gdansk and was fired. For the next few years, he supported his family by doing odd jobs while he became involved with the growing Polish labor movement. He also joined an anti-Communist discussion group, edited an antigovernment newspaper, and founded a trade union. In 1979 he joined with other labor leaders to present a series of demands to the government, which included recognition of trade unions and the right of workers to strike. Although he was followed by the secret police and arrested several times, Walesa continued these activities.

In the summer of 1980 a new wave of riots occurred in Poland following the government's announcement that it was raising meat prices. Walesa and other union members at the Gdansk shipyard went on strike. They refused to continue working until fired striking employees, including Walesa, had been rehired. The government was forced to negotiate with the strikers, and Walesa served as their spokesman.

After several weeks, the peaceful negotiations ended with the signing of the Gdansk Agreement, a major victory for Walesa. Under the terms of the agreement, workers throughout Poland got the right to form unions and to strike. They also received wage increases and other benefits, and secured other concessions, including the release of political prisoners who had opposed the Communist regime. In return, all union members had to agree to respect the sovereignty of the Communist party.

When the government had not complied with the agreement by early October, Walesa and his followers staged a one-day warning strike. Two weeks later, a court in Warsaw, the Polish capital, legally recognized the various labor unions in the country as a single organization, called Solidarity. Walesa became chairman of Solidarity's national commission, and in this role he continued to put pressure on the government to fulfill the other terms of the Gdansk Agreement. A series of small strikes occurred in the following months as the demands remained unmet, and in March 1981 another brief nationwide strike was called by most of Poland's 13 million industrial workers, more than two-thirds of whom were members of Solidarity.

Solidarity held its first national congress in September 1981 and re-elected Walesa as party chairman. As

Lech Walesa

BORN
September 29, 1943
Popowo, Poland

EDUCATION
Vocational school

OCCUPATION
Electrician; labor leader

MAJOR ACCOMPLISHMENTS
Founded Solidarity, a nationwide labor alliance in Poland (1980); president of Poland (1990–)

one of their goals, delegates called for free elections in Poland. Three months later a group of Solidarity leaders in Gdansk challenged the Communist government to hold a national referendum (vote) on whether or not it should continue to lead the country. Walesa disagreed with this demand, for he feared that the government would respond with violence. He believed that change had to be achieved slowly, and through nonviolent negotiation, not confrontation.

Walesa's fears were confirmed on December 13, 1981, when the government responded to the demand by proclaiming martial law. Union leaders, including Walesa, were arrested and Solidarity was banned as army units took control of cities and towns throughout the country. In December 1982 Walesa was released from solitary confinement. He was given back his old job in the Gdansk shipyard but found that his movement had been destroyed.

In the fall of 1983, as Walesa and other Poles remained tightly in the grip of martial law, the Nobel Peace Prize Committee named Lech Walesa as the winner of that year's award. In announcing the award, the committee praised Walesa as "an inspiration and a shining example to all those who, under difficult conditions, fight for freedom and humanity." Because Walesa was afraid that he would not be allowed to re-enter Poland if he attended the award ceremony in Oslo, he sent his wife instead.

Walesa continued to work in Gdansk but did not end his criticism of the government as he slowly rebuilt Solidarity in secret. In January 1986 he was arrested after charging that voter fraud had occurred in parliamentary elections the previous year, but was re-leased a month later when he withdrew the charges. In 1988 Solidarity was once again given legal status in Poland, and Walesa was encouraged by signs that the Communist government was slowly crumbling as calls for democratic reform swept across the country. In the mid-1980s Walesa also wrote his autobiography, which was smuggled out of Poland and published in English translation as *A Path of Hope* (1987).

Finally, a breakthrough came in the spring of 1989 when the government and opposing factions came to an agreement on major political and economic reforms, including free elections. In June candidates endorsed by Solidarity won a majority of seats in the Polish parliament, and a year later Lech Walesa became president of the new Polish republic.

Walesa has won numerous awards for his work on behalf of a free Poland, including the Presidential Medal of Freedom from the United States and membership in the French Legion of Honor. He remains a loyal member of the Roman Catholic Church and credits its teachings with helping him to develop his philosophy of nonviolent protest.

FURTHER READING

Eringer, Robert. *Strike for Freedom! The Story of Lech Walesa and Polish Solidarity.* New York: Dodd, Mead, 1982.

Stefoff, Rebecca. *Lech Walesa: The Road to Democracy.* New York: Ballantine, 1992.

Vnenchak, Dennis. *Lech Walesa and Poland.* New York: Franklin Watts, 1994.

Walesa, Lech. *The Struggle and the Triumph: An Autobiography.* Translated by Franklin Philip and Helen Mahut. New York: Arcade, 1992.

Desmond Tutu

1984

Whon he was a teenager in the mid-
1940s, Desmond Tutu had an experience that he would never forget. He
was standing with his mother on a
street corner in the city of Johan-
nesburg, South Africa, when a priest wearing a long black
cassock and a large black hat walked by. Noticing Tutu's
mother, the priest did what any polite man would have done
in the presence of a woman: he raised and lowered his hat as
a symbol of respect.

What made the experience remarkable to Desmond
Tutu was that the priest was white, whereas Tutu's mother
was black. In South Africa, white men did not show respect
to black women. In that country, which was ruled by a minority white population that had occupied it since the 19th
century, blacks were considered inferior and unimportant.

Who was this extraordinary white man who acted kind-
ly toward his mother? Desmond Tutu soon found out. The

Desmond Tutu rose from poverty to become an archbishop and
head of the Anglican Church in southern Africa, and to lead a
campaign of nonviolent resistance to apartheid.

Trevor Huddleston receives an honorary doctor of divinity degree from Whittier College, a Quaker institution in southern California, in May 1994, a month before his 81st birthday. Huddleston, an Anglican priest who ministered to South Africa's black community for many years and actively opposed apartheid, inspired Desmond Tutu to enter the priesthood.

man's name was Trevor Huddleston, and he was an Anglican (Church of England) priest in Sophiatown, Johannesburg's black slum neighborhood. Huddleston believed strongly in the equality of all human beings, a central teaching of Christianity, and he taught that belief to his parishioners. In the following decade, Huddleston was to become a leading voice for racial equality in South Africa, and as he did so he gave Desmond Tutu's life special meaning. Largely because of Huddleston's influence, Desmond Tutu also became an Anglican priest.

Desmond Tutu was born in the fall of 1931 in the gold-mining town of Klerksdorp, South Africa. His father, a member of the Bantu tribe, was a schoolteacher; his mother, who belonged to the Tswana tribe, worked for white families as a servant.

Although the family was originally Methodist, they joined the Anglican Church during Desmond's childhood. When he was 12, the family moved to Johannesburg, and his mother found work as a cook at an Anglican mission-

ary school for the blind. Desmond was impressed by the concern that the missionaries showed for their students, but it was Trevor Huddleston's act of kindness to his mother that drew him closer to the Anglican faith. He became friendly with the priest, who encouraged him to pursue his education. Their friendship deepened after Tutu became seriously ill with tuberculosis: during his 20 months in the hospital, Huddleston visited him almost daily.

During his high school years, Tutu earned money by selling peanuts at railroad stations and caddying at a white golf course. Although he was religious, he did not yet plan to become a priest. He knew that he wanted to help other people, and for many years he had dreamed of becoming a doctor. However, his family could not afford the medical school tuition after he graduated from high school, and he decided to become a teacher. He enrolled at a training school for black teachers in Pretoria, South Africa, and after receiving his diploma, he went on to the University of Johannesburg, where he earned a bachelor's degree in 1954.

Tutu taught at black high schools in Johannesburg and in the town of Krugersdorp for several years. His plans to make teaching his career ended abruptly in 1957, however, when the government introduced a new, inferior curriculum for all black students. Tutu and several colleagues resigned in protest, and he now had to choose another career.

The priesthood seemed the logical choice, and Tutu enrolled at an Anglican theological college in Johannesburg. He received his diploma in 1960 and was ordained a year later. Tutu served black churches in the South African towns of Benoni and Alberton before being sent to London for further training in 1962. There he earned undergraduate and graduate degrees in divinity at a theological school while working in several Anglican parishes.

The Anglican Church sent Tutu back to Africa in 1967, where he taught at both a theological seminary and at what is now the National University in Lesotho, a Bantu tribal enclave within South Africa. He returned to England in 1972 to become associate director of a scholarship fund for theology students in Africa and Asia. In this position he traveled widely on both continents for the next three years. In 1975 Tutu was named the Anglican dean of Johannesburg (a dean is the administrative head of a cathedral), and a year later he became bishop of Lesotho.

In the nearly two decades of Tutu's rise from divinity student to bishop in the Anglican Church, significant changes had occurred in his country. For one thing, there was now a powerful movement among blacks calling for equality and an end to apartheid (pronounced *uh-PAR-tide*), the system of forced separation of the races that was introduced by the South African government in the late 1940s. That movement was growing despite the government's 1960 ban on the African National Congress. That organization, which had been led by Albert Luthuli, was dedicated to securing the peaceful independence of African nations. In 1961 the Union of South Africa had broken its long political ties with Great Britain, following repeated British criticism of South Africa's treatment of blacks. It was now the independent Republic of South Africa.

As black protests grew, the government cracked down even harder, and Tutu found himself drawn into the conflict in the 1970s. From the outset, Tutu tried to persuade blacks to reject violence as they sought to make the government change its policies.

Shortly before becoming the bishop of Lesotho in 1976, Tutu became aware of a growing antigovernment movement among angry young black youths in Soweto, a black township in Johannesburg. Working with a local activist, Tutu tried to channel their anger into peaceful demonstrations. At the same time, he wrote a letter to the South African prime minister, warning him that a tense situation had developed in Soweto. The prime minister ignored the letter, and a month later, in June 1976, riots broke out. The government responded by sending in troops, who shot to death at least 600 blacks. The prime minister blamed Tutu for the riots, and the priest now came under suspicion from the government for radical activities.

Tutu continued to advocate nonviolent opposition to the government's racist policies. In 1978 he became general secretary of the South African Council of Churches, an interdenominational group associated with the World Council of Churches. The South African Council of Churches represented 13 million Christians in the country, more than 80 percent of them black. In his post as general secretary, which he held for seven years, Tutu called repeatedly for the South African government to end apartheid. He used council funds to provide legal assistance to blacks who were arrested for protesting against the government and to help their families. He also became an outspoken opponent of the government's so-called homelands policy, under which blacks were removed against their will from cities and resettled in barren rural areas. In addition, he expressed his support for the outlawed African National Congress.

Desmond Tutu

BORN

October 7, 1931
Klerksdorp, South Africa

EDUCATION

Diploma, Bantu Normal College, Pretoria; B.A., University of Johannesburg (1954); L.Th., St. Peter's Theological College, Johannesburg (1960); B.D., M.Th., King's College, London (1966)

OCCUPATION

Anglican clergyman

MAJOR ACCOMPLISHMENTS

Bishop of Lesotho (1976–78); general secretary, South African Council of Churches (1978–85); Bishop of Johannesburg (1985–86); Archbishop of Cape Town and Metropolitan of Southern Africa (1986–); president, All Africa Conference of Churches (1987–)

The government had at first been merely annoyed by Tutu's public opposition, but it became outraged in the early 1980s when Tutu began asking other nations to put economic pressure on South Africa to end its racist practices. He suggested that such pressure be delivered in a variety of ways, most notably by restricting trade with South Africa and by refusing to invest in businesses within the country. In response, the government ordered a formal investigation of the financial affairs of the South African Council of Churches. The report issued early in 1984 denounced Tutu and his activities.

Later that year Tutu traveled to New York City to study for a year at the General Theological Seminary. He was in New York when he learned that he had been named the winner of the 1984 Nobel Peace Prize. In a statement that accompanied its announcement, the Nobel Peace Prize Committee declared that the award was "a renewed recognition of the courage and heroism shown by black South Africans in their use of peaceful methods in the struggle against apartheid." The committee praised not only Tutu and the South African Council of Churches but also other individuals and groups in South Africa who were working for human rights.

In November 1984, one month before receiving the Nobel Peace Prize in Oslo, Desmond Tutu was named the Anglican bishop of Johannesburg—the first black to hold that post. Not long afterward he was elevated to archbishop. Rather than move to the bishop's official residence in the white section of Johannesburg, Tutu chose to live in Soweto as a gesture of his ties to the black community, and he continued his call for the peaceful achievement of black equality in South Africa.

In 1986 Tutu became archbishop of Cape Town, South Africa's largest city. Along with this appointment, he received the title Metropolitan of Southern Africa, which made him the head of the Anglican Church in several African countries. In 1987 he became head of the All Africa Conference of Churches.

Tutu's dream of achieving racial equality in South Africa moved closer to reality in 1994, when free elections open to all races were held for the first time in his country and ANC leader Nelson Mandela became president. In 1995 Tutu headed a government commission investigating human rights abuses. His report contributed to the drafting of a new constitution for South Africa, which went into effect in December 1996.

Desmond Tutu has received many other awards for his work on behalf of human rights and is the author of numerous articles and reviews; he has also written four books. He has been married since 1955 and has four grown children.

FURTHER READING

Du Boulay, Shirley. *Tutu: Voice of the Voiceless*. Grand Rapids, Mich.: Eerdmans, 1988.

Honor, Deborah Duncan, ed. *Trevor Huddleston: Essays on His Life and Work*. Oxford: Oxford University Press, 1988.

Huddleston, Trevor. *Naught for Your Comfort*. New York: Doubleday, 1956.

Tutu, Desmond. *Crying in the Wilderness: The Struggle for Justice in South Africa*. Grand Rapids, Mich.: Eerdmans, 1990.

———. *Hope and Suffering: Sermons and Speeches*. Grand Rapids, Mich.: Eerdmans, 1984.

———. *The Rainbow People of God: The Making of a Peaceful Revolution*. New York: Doubleday, 1994.

Wepman, Dennis. *Desmond Tutu*. New York: Franklin Watts, 1989.

International Physicians for the Prevention of Nuclear War

1985

Dr. Bernard Lown of the United States and Dr. Yevgeny Chazov of Russia cofounded International Physicians for the Prevention of Nuclear War in 1980.

The organization called International Physicians for the Prevention of Nuclear War was officially founded in 1980, but its origins go back to 1961. In that year, Dr. Bernard Lown, a heart specialist at Harvard University's School of Public Health, heard a speech by Philip Noel-Baker, a British diplomat and longtime advocate of disarmament. In his speech Noel-Baker warned against the medical perils of nuclear warfare, especially the long-term effects of radiation from atomic explosions.

Inspired by Noel-Baker's speech, Lown joined with several other U.S. doctors to form Physicians for Social Responsibility (PSR), and he served as the organization's first president. For nearly two decades, PSR publicized the terrible after-effects of nuclear explosions in an effort to help end the international arms race.

One of Lown's longtime friends was Yevgeny Chazov, also a heart specialist and director of a heart research center in Moscow. In 1979 Lown suggested to Chazov that they organize an international movement of physicians similar to PSR. A year later, Lown and Chazov met in Geneva, Switzerland, with four other physicians—two Russians and two Americans—and founded International Physicians for the Prevention of Nuclear War (IPPNW).

IPPNW quickly grew, and by the mid-1980s had 135,000 members in 41 countries. From the outset, IPPNW made education a major focus and sponsored major initiatives to inform the public of the dangers of nuclear war. One of the group's earliest educational efforts occurred in 1982, when it organized a televised discussion by American and Russian physicians on the medical aspects of nuclear war. The program was broadcast live throughout the Soviet Union and later aired on videotape in the United States and Europe.

That same year, IPPNW published a collection of essays, *Last Aid: The Medical Dimensions of Nuclear War,* by medical specialists from the United States, Great Britain, the Soviet Union, and Japan. The book was circulated throughout the world and has been used frequently as a university and medical school textbook.

In the first years after its founding, IPPNW sponsored a study of children's reactions to the threat of nuclear war. It also created the Soviet-American Physicians Campaign, an exchange program in which teams of doctors tour each other's countries and hold public forums to discuss the dangers of nuclear warfare. Many of IPPNW's educational efforts are carried out by chapter affiliates throughout the world, and IPPNW provides them with publications, research data, and access to a large reference library.

International Physicians for the Prevention of Nuclear War

FOUNDERS

Bernard Lown and Yevgeny Chazov

DATE AND PLACE OF FOUNDING

1980
Geneva, Switzerland

HEADQUARTERS

Cambridge, Massachusetts, and London, England

PURPOSE

Founded to express the opposition of the worldwide medical community to nuclear weapons and warfare, and to educate the public on their harmful medical effects; in recent years, has widened its focus to include opposition to all forms of warfare, and has also publicized war's harmful psychological and environmental effects

MAJOR ACCOMPLISHMENTS

Has alerted millions throughout the world to the harmful effects of warfare by sponsoring major public education programs and scientific research projects

A policeman attempts to treat burn victims on the outskirts of Hiroshima, Japan, on August 6, 1945, several hours after an atomic bomb was dropped on the center of the city.

In addition to being an educational organization, IPPNW sponsors major scientific research on not only the medical but also the psychological and biospheric (environmental) effects of nuclear war. In both its research and educational efforts, it has worked closely with both the United Nations and the World Health Organization.

IPPNW's efforts to publicize the consequences of nuclear war earned it the 1985 Nobel Peace Prize. Both Lown and Chazov, who were then co-presidents of the organization, attended the award ceremonies in Oslo and accepted the Peace Prize on behalf of IPPNW.

Today IPPNW maintains international offices in London, England, and Cambridge, Massachusetts. It has 200,000 members, who belong to local chapters in 81 countries. In the United States, Physicians for Social Responsibility is the IPPNW chapter. Chapter representatives from around the world meet every two years at an international conference sponsored by IPPNW. More frequent regional meetings are also held.

Although IPPNW was initially founded to focus only on nuclear war, in recent years it has publicly proclaimed the dangers arising from any form of warfare. In particular, it has focused both its research and its educational efforts on the negative effects of militarism (a government's emphasis on military power) on Third World (underdeveloped) countries. IPPNW publishes research studies, brochures, and books on the dangers of warfare, many of which are available to the general public.

FURTHER READING

"International Physicians for the Prevention of Nuclear War." In *Nobel Prize Winners*. New York: H. W. Wilson, 1987.

Makhijani, Arjun, *et al.*, eds. *Nuclear Wastelands: A Global Guidebook to Nuclear Weapons Production and Its Health and Environmental Effects*. Report of the Special Commission of International Physicians for the Prevention of Nuclear War and the Institute for Energy and Environmental Research. Cambridge: MIT Press, 1995.

Elie Wiesel

1986

Elie Wiesel (pronounced *Vee-ZEL*) wanted to be a writer from the time he was a small boy. At the age of 12, he wrote a series of commentaries on the Bible. When he was 19 and a university student, he began working as a journalist. By this time, Wiesel knew that someday he wanted to write books, and he knew what their subject would be: the systematic killing of 6 million Jews by the leaders of the German government during World War II (1939–45).

Elie Wiesel was born in 1928 in what is now Romania to a Jewish couple. His father owned a grocery store and was active in the Jewish community in the town of Sighet. The Wiesels were very religious, and Elie and his three sisters were taught the traditions of Judaism as well as the tales and folklore of the Hasidim, a sect within the Jewish faith.

Wiesel attended local schools and led a fairly normal life until the spring of 1944, when German troops overran the area and ordered the deportation of Sighet's 15,000 Jews to concentration camps. Even before the official beginning of World War II in September 1939, the German government,

Elie Wiesel, a survivor of Nazi concentration camps during World War II, has devoted his life to public discussion of the Nazis' mass murder of the Jews, an event he named the Holocaust.

U.S. congressmen investigating Nazi atrocities during World War II are shown a pile of corpses at the Buchenwald concentration camp in 1945.

under the direction of Adolf Hitler, had begun persecuting Jews. By the early 1940s, the Germans had set up an extensive system of camps where they sent Jews as well as disabled people, Gypsies, homosexuals, political opponents, and others whom Hitler called "undesirables." These camps were not only in Germany but in several other European countries that German troops now occupied. Once at the camps, inmates were forced to work until they died of disease or starvation; those unable to work were put to death in gas chambers.

Elie Wiesel and the other members of his family were taken to a concen-

tration camp in Poland called Auschwitz. His mother and younger sister were killed almost immediately; Elie, along with his father, was separated from his two older sisters. He did not learn that they survived until after the war ended. After a year of hard labor at Auschwitz, Wiesel and his father were sent in early 1945 to Buchenwald, a concentration camp in Germany, where the father starved to death.

After Buchenwald was liberated by American troops in April 1945, the teenage Wiesel traveled with hundreds of other orphans to a resettlement camp in France. There he was looked after by a Jewish children's aid organization for several years and learned to read and speak French. In 1948 he moved to Paris and enrolled at the university to study literature and philosophy. He supported himself not only as a part-time journalist but also by working as a choir director, Hebrew teacher, and translator.

While Wiesel was still attending the university, his newspaper work took him briefly to the new state of Israel, the Jewish homeland, and to Tel Aviv, one of its major cities. After leaving the university without receiving a degree, Wiesel traveled to India in 1952 as a correspondent for a Tel Aviv newspaper and acquired a working knowledge of English. Other assignments followed, and a few years later he was sent to New York City to report on the United Nations. One day in 1956 Wiesel was struck by a taxi in the city and had to spend a year in a wheelchair. When he was unable to have his French travel documents extended, U.S. immigration officials allowed Wiesel to become a permanent resident. He later became a U.S. citizen.

Ever since his release from Buchenwald, Wiesel had been convinced that his life was spared for a reason: "to give testimony, to bear witness" to the terrible events that he and other Jews had endured and that so many had not survived. But Wiesel had vowed in 1945 that he would remain silent on the subject for 10 years, in order to be certain that he knew what he wanted to say.

Wiesel's opportunity to end his silence came a year ahead of schedule. In 1954 he interviewed the French Roman Catholic novelist François Mauriac, who had won the 1952 Nobel Prize for Literature. Mauriac said that Christians had to acknowledge some responsibility for the mass killings of Jews, and he urged Wiesel to write about his concentration camp experiences. Wiesel immediately began to write the story in Yiddish, a language formed from German and Hebrew. Two years later Wiesel completed an 800-page manuscript, which was published in Argentina. When he could not find a publisher for the lengthy book in France, he condensed the manuscript to 127 pages, translated it into French, and published it in 1958 as *La Nuit*. It was dedicated to the memory of his parents and sister. Two years later it was published in English translation as *Night*.

Wiesel is credited with being the first person to use the word "Holocaust" to describe the extermination of the Jews during World War II. But after writing about the events of the Holocaust in *Night*, he turned his attention to the theme of the Holocaust survivor—himself. In a series of short, semi-autobiographical novels written in French, he examined different ways in which those who survived the camps came to terms with the guilt they felt. These books appeared in English translation as *Dawn* (1961), *The Accident* (1962), *The Town Beyond the Wall* (1964), *The Gates of the Forest* (1966), and *A Beggar in Jerusalem* (1970), which became a best-seller.

During the 1960s, Wiesel was moved by accounts of anti-Semitism (persecution of Jews) in the Soviet Union. He made several visits to the country to observe Jewish life there and wrote a book about his experience (*The Jews of Silence*, 1966). Wiesel became one of the earliest champions of Soviet Jewry and on several occasions called upon the Soviet Union to allow Jews to emigrate to Israel. He also criticized Jews in Western democratic nations for

Elie Wiesel

BORN
September 30, 1928
Sighet, Transylvania (now Romania)

EDUCATION
Attended the University of Paris (1948–52)

OCCUPATION
Writer

MAJOR ACCOMPLISHMENTS
Through numerous writings, beginning with the book *La Nuit* (*Night*, 1958), has drawn international attention to the Holocaust

their indifference to their fellows in Russia. Anti-Semitism in the Soviet Union inspired Wiesel's first play, translated as *Zalmen; or, The Madness of God* (1968).

Wiesel returned to his hometown of Sighet, Romania, in the fall of 1964 and realized during his brief visit that the Holocaust had destroyed all memories of his birthplace. He later wrote about the experience in a book published in English as *Legends of Our Time* (1968), a collection of essays and short stories. During the next decade Wiesel published two additional collections, *One Generation After* (1970) and *A Jew Today* (1978), in which he discussed suffering in South Africa, Vietnam, Biafra, and Bangladesh—strife-torn places that he has visited—from a sympathetic Jewish perspective. He also published several collections of Hasidic tales; another novel, called *The Oath* (1973); and another play about Jewish suffering, *The Trial of God* (1979). In addition, during the late 1970s and early 1980s he wrote several studies of the Bible and biblical figures.

By 1980 Wiesel had found his message as a writer: All Jews, he believes, have to bear witness to all human suffering, not just their own. Remaining silent and indifferent, he feels, is the greatest sin of all. Wiesel has become best known, however, for drawing public attention to the Holocaust, which was not widely discussed until the 1970s. To some extent, he is troubled by this attention, for he worries that the terrible events have become trivialized. Sometimes, he says, few words are better than more words—something he realized in 1945 when he imposed the vow of silence upon himself.

For many years, Wiesel's eloquent advocacy of brotherhood and his sympathy for human suffering led him to be mentioned frequently as a candidate for the Nobel Peace Prize. In the fall of 1986 he was finally named as the winner of that year's award. The Nobel Committee called him "a messenger to mankind" bringing news of "peace, atonement, and human dignity." Wiesel accepted the award on behalf of all Holocaust survivors and their children, and he expressed the belief that it would enable him to "speak louder" and "reach more people" with his message.

Wiesel has continued to write books, essays, and short stories since winning the Nobel Peace Prize, and has also received other awards for both his humanitarianism and his literary accomplishments. He is a popular lecturer and has spoken frequently on the Holocaust and on biblical topics. During the early 1970s he taught Judaic studies at the City University of New York, and since 1976 he has been a professor of humanities at Boston University. Wiesel is married to a fellow Holocaust survivor and is the father of a son and a stepdaughter.

FURTHER READING

Schuman, Michael. *Elie Wiesel: Voice from the Holocaust*. Springfield, N.J.: Enslow, 1994.

Wiesel, Elie. *All Rivers Run to the Sea: Memoirs*. New York: Knopf, 1995.

———. *From the Kingdom of Memory: Reminiscences*. New York: Schocken, 1995.

———. *Night*. 1958. Translated by Stella Rodway. New York: Hill & Wang, 1960.

Oscar Arias Sánchez

1987

Once a medical student, Oscar Arias Sánchez changed his career plans to politics after meeting with U.S. Presidential candidate John F. Kennedy in 1960.

I n the fall of 1960, a 20-year-old youth from Costa Rica named Oscar Arias Sánchez enrolled at Boston University to study medicine. In choosing the medical profession as a career, Arias was going against family tradition, for he was descended from a long line of businessmen and politicians.

Only weeks after Arias began his studies in Boston, he watched a series of debates between John F. Kennedy and Richard Nixon, who were running against each other in the upcoming U.S. Presidential election. The debates claimed Arias's entire attention, and he was especially impressed by Kennedy. Not only was the future President full of youthful vigor, but he seemed to represent a fresh, open approach to politics as he encouraged all Americans to take an active role in their government.

Arias admired Kennedy so much that he even traveled to the candidate's home on nearby Cape Cod to meet him. That experience changed Arias's life. Vowing to make Kennedy his role model, he abandoned medicine and returned to his homeland to study political science—taking what he hoped were the first steps toward becoming president of Costa Rica.

Oscar Arias Sánchez was born in Heredia, near the Costa Rican capital of San José, in 1940. His family owned one of the largest coffee plantations in the country. In addition to being businessmen, male family members had also served in the executive and legislative branches of the national government for several generations.

Arias attended local schools, where he excelled in soccer, and he completed the equivalent of junior college before going to the United States to study medicine in 1960. Returning to Costa Rica after only a few months in Boston, he enrolled at the national university in San José. During his years of study there, he became an active member of the Partido de Liberación Nacional (National Liberation party), or PLN, one of Costa Rica's major political parties.

Arias attracted the attention of national PLN leaders when an essay he had written contrasting freedom with totalitarianism was published in a local magazine. As a consequence, he was hired to work part time at party headquarters, and in 1965–66 he was an aide to presidential candidate Daniel Oduber during his unsuccessful campaign.

After receiving his degree in political science in 1966, Arias won a grant from the British government to do graduate study at the University of Essex. There he earned a doctorate with a dissertation on Costa Rican politics that was later published locally. From 1969 to 1972 Arias was a professor of political science at his alma mater, the University of

As president of Costa Rica, Arias (far right) and the heads of four other Central American nations sign a joint peace agreement on August 7, 1987.

Costa Rica. During his years there he wrote a second book, on Costa Rican pressure groups, that earned him a national award.

While he was still on the faculty of the University of Costa Rica, Arias served as an economic adviser to President José Figueres. In 1972 Arias left the university to join Figueres's cabinet as minister of national planning. He continued in that post when Daniel Oduber succeeded Figueres as president in 1974, and he remained in the cabinet until 1977.

As minister of national planning, Arias established programs to encourage economic growth, technological development, and full employment. Under his leadership, a large park was constructed in the center of San José. In the fall of 1976 he sponsored a widely publicized conference in San José at which various prominent people discussed the future of Costa Rica.

During the 1970s, Arias also held various positions in the PLN and eventually was elected to the party's top post, secretary-general. In those years he frequently traveled abroad as Costa Rica's representative to various international conferences on economic and social issues, including development in Third World (underdeveloped) countries.

Arias left the cabinet in July 1977 to campaign for a seat in the national legislature, and in February 1978 he was elected to represent his hometown, Heredia. During his three years in the legislature, he led attempts to bring about constitutional and election reform. He resigned in May 1981 to campaign for PLN presidential candidate Luis Alberto Monge, who was elected in February 1982.

Arias continued as secretary-general of the PLN until January 1984, when he resigned to pursue his party's nomination for president. Under national law, Monge could not run for a second term, and national elections were scheduled for February 1986. Arias received the nomination, and after an intensive campaign, he achieved the goal he had set for himself in 1960: he was elected president of Costa Rica. Like his hero John F. Kennedy, he was also the youngest president in his country's history.

During the campaign, Arias proclaimed himself a "peace candidate," and after he took office he was true to his word. Several of Costa Rica's Central American neighbors—El Salvador, Nicaragua, and Guatemala—were involved in civil wars. Arias was determined that Costa Rica, a neutral nation, would not be drawn into these conflicts.

Shortly after taking office in May 1986, Arias met with the presidents of Guatemala, El Salvador, Honduras, and Nicaragua to discuss a previously proposed peace accord for the region. The accord called for demilitarization and the holding of democratic elections in all Central American countries. At the conclusion of the talks, the participants acknowledged that further details of the accord needed to be worked out. However, they issued a declaration calling for continued open discussions to encourage democracy in Central America and to promote regional economic development. They also called for the future creation of a Central American parliament.

At a follow-up meeting a year later with the heads of Honduras, Guatemala, and El Salvador, Arias proposed a new regional peace plan for Central America. It called for immediate cease-fires in ongoing wars and for the suspension of military aid from outside sources, including the United States. Cease-fires would then be followed by peace negotiations, free elections, and national guarantees of human rights.

After considerable debate in the United States and other Latin American countries, a version of Arias's regional peace plan was signed in Guatemala City on August 7, 1987, by Arias and the presidents of Guatemala, El Salvador, Honduras, and Nicaragua. The agreement, which was to take effect three months later, was widely hailed for bringing the possibility of lasting peace to a long-troubled region.

In October 1987 Oscar Arias Sánchez was named the winner of that year's Nobel Peace Prize for his efforts to end conflict in Central America. A month later, his peace plan took effect, and many of its terms were met by participating countries in the years that followed. Although Central America is still far from conflict-free, the peacemaking efforts of Arias were a historic milestone in efforts toward that goal.

During the remainder of his presidential term, Arias tried with limited success to solve major economic problems in his country. After leaving office in the spring of 1990, he founded the Arias Foundation for Peace to continue working for an end to conflict in Central America. Arias is married to a biochemist and has two children. In addition to the Nobel Peace Prize, he has won many other awards and received honorary doctorates from Harvard and other universities.

FURTHER READING

"Arias Sánchez, Oscar." In *Current Biography Yearbook 1987*. New York: H. W. Wilson, 1988.

Oscar Arias Sánchez

BORN
September 13, 1940
Heredia, Costa Rica

EDUCATION
Undergraduate degree, University of Costa Rica (1966); doctoral degree in political science, University of Essex (1969)

OCCUPATION
Politician

MAJOR ACCOMPLISHMENTS
President of Costa Rica (1986–90); initiated a peace plan to end ongoing conflict in Central American nations (1987)

United Nations Peacekeeping Forces

1988

The United Nations Peacekeeping Forces were created by the United Nations Security Council in 1948. The forces are an "army of peace" that has brought calm to troubled regions throughout the world.

The first assignment for UN Peacekeeping Forces was in the Middle East, in June 1948. Nearly 300 peacemakers—specially trained soldiers from 16 countries, including the United States—were sent to Beirut, Lebanon, and the Sinai Peninsula as the UN Truce Supervision Organization. They went there to support a UN truce mission that had established temporary peace between Arabs and Israelis soon after the establishment of the new state of Israel.

Less than a year later, another unit of Peacekeeping Forces called the UN Military Observer Group in India and Pakistan was sent to the border between those two countries in January 1949. This unit numbered about three dozen "soldiers of peace" from 10 countries. Their job was to enforce a cease-fire that had temporarily ended the ongoing war between India and Pakistan.

During the next four decades UN Peacekeeping Forces were sent to other major world trouble spots, including Cyprus, Syria's Golan Heights, southern Lebanon, Afghanistan, and the Iran-Iraq border. During these years, some 10,000 individuals representing more than 36 countries

The United Nations Iran-Iraq Military Observer Group (UNIIMOG), a unit of United Nations Peacekeeping Forces, arrives in Baghdad in August 1988 to monitor a cease-fire during the Iran-Iraq War.

A UN armored personnel carrier patrols the streets of war-torn Sarajevo during a visit in 1994 by UN Secretary-General Boutros Boutros-Ghali.

United Nations Peacekeeping Forces

FOUNDER

United Nations Security Council

DATE AND PLACE OF FOUNDING

1948
New York, New York

HEADQUARTERS

New York, New York

PURPOSE

To maintain cease-fires between warring factions and reduce tensions through negotiation

MAJOR ACCOMPLISHMENTS

Since their creation, have brought peace to troubled regions throughout the world

served in Peacekeeping Forces throughout the world. Their job was not easy: members of the forces risked their lives—and often lost them—to keep the spirit of peace alive and to prevent hostile opponents from engaging in all-out war.

In 1988, the 40th-anniversary year of their founding, the United Nations Peacekeeping Forces were announced as the winners of that year's Nobel Peace Prize. In the words of the Nobel Committee, "the Peacekeeping Forces through their efforts have made important contributions toward the realization of one of the fundamental tenets of the United Nations." The committee called the forces representatives of "the manifest will of the community of nations to achieve peace through negotiations" and praised them for making "a decisive contribution toward the initiation of actual peace negotiations."

UN Secretary-General Javier Pérez de Cuellar accepted the award on behalf of the forces. The prize money, about $388,000 in U.S. dollars, was used to pay some of the expenses of the Peacekeeping Forces, which in recent years had been in debt. The 1988 award was the fourth Nobel Peace Prize won by an organization associated with the United Nations. (UN agencies also won the award in 1954, 1965, and 1981.)

Since winning the Nobel Peace Prize, the UN Peacekeeping Forces have continued to serve around the world in ever-increasing numbers. In the 1990s, units of Peacekeeping Forces numbering in the thousands have been sent to Angola, Bosnia, Haiti, Somalia, and other regions in an effort to end conflict. As local wars continue to flare up throughout the world, it seems likely that the "army of peace" will continue its mission for some time to come.

FURTHER READING

Patterson, Charles. *The Oxford 50th Anniversary Book of the United Nations.* New York: Oxford University Press, 1995.

Rule, Sheila. "U.N. Peacekeeping Forces Named Winner of the Nobel Peace Prize." *New York Times,* September 30, 1988, pp. 1, 10.

The Dalai Lama (Tenzin Gyatso)

1989

I n 1937 Buddhist monks in the mountainous Asian country of Tibet came to the end of a long search. In the small village of Taktser they found a two-year-old boy to take the place of their late religious leader, the 13th Dalai Lama. (A lama is a Buddhist monk; "dalai" [pronounced *DAL-la*y] means "ocean," a symbol of vast wisdom.)

The monks were members of Gelugpa, the most prominent Buddhist sect in Tibet. According to tradition, every Dalai Lama is a reincarnation—a reborn version—of the previous holder of the title. When the monks discovered two-year-old Lhamo Thondup in Taktser, they found many resemblances between the child and the 13th Dalai Lama, who had died in 1933. This led them to conclude that Lhamo Thondup was his successor.

Lhamo Thondup, born to a Tibetan peasant family, became the Dalai Lama, the spiritual and political leader of Tibet, when he was just two years old.

At that time the region around Taktser was controlled by a Chinese governor, who demanded a large sum of money before he would allow the monks to take the child and his family to the holy city of Lhasa, the Buddhist religious center in Tibet. After long negotiations the money was paid, and in February 1940 the 14th Dalai Lama was duly installed on Lhasa's Lion Throne, the traditional chair of generations of Dalai Lamas. He was now addressed as "Gyalwa Rinpoche" ("the virtuous and precious one"), and the shortened version of his new official name was Tenzin Gyatso.

The 14th Dalai Lama had been born in Taktser in July 1935 to a simple peasant couple. He was one of five children. At the Potala Palace, the thousand-room building in Lhasa where he was taken to live in 1940, he was privately tutored by other monks. He was exceptionally bright and studied not only the Buddhist religion but also English, math, and world geography. He eventually earned the equivalent of a doctoral degree in philosophy. Guided by his teachers, the 14th Dalai Lama ruled as both the spiritual and political leader of Tibet.

For centuries Tibet had been under Buddhist rule, although regions of the country were periodically taken over by secular invaders from neighboring China. In the 20th century, Tibet had been almost entirely free of Chinese domination since 1912, when the 13th Dalai Lama had evicted most of the Chinese who had settled in the country.

The new Dalai Lama knew only peace until 1950, when troops from the recently established Communist government of China invaded his country. After a series of negotiations between senior monks and Chinese authorities, Tibet was declared a province of China but was allowed to keep its religious and political system intact.

During the 1950s, as more and more Chinese moved into Tibet, the Dalai Lama tried to maintain Tibet's peace and dignity. He traveled to Beijing, China's capital, several times to meet with the Chinese premier, Mao Zedong, and he visited many parts of China. As a man of peace, the Dalai Lama worked hard to keep all-out warfare from breaking out between the two countries. However, in many regions of Tibet a series of small wars were continuing between local Tibetans and Chinese troops. The Dalai Lama felt helpless to change the situation because, like all Buddhists, he opposed violence in any form. Therefore, he refused to take either side, although he was pressed by both the Tibetans and the Chinese to do so.

In early 1959 the growing militancy of the Chinese occupying Tibet led to a rebellion by Tibetans, and thousands of them were killed by Chinese troops. Because the Dalai Lama represented Tibet itself, Tibetan leaders feared that his death at the hands of the Chinese would symbolize the end of Tibet, too. Therefore, they helped him flee south, along with his mother and sister, to India. There he was granted asylum and eventually settled in the Indian town of Dharamsala, in the Himalayas near the border with Pakistan.

In the following decade, China imposed a strict Communist government on Tibet and declared that the Dalai Lama was no longer the country's legitimate ruler. The Chinese waged war against Tibetan Buddhists, killing monks and nuns and destroying monasteries and priceless artwork. In the mid-1960s, China renamed the country and it became known as the Tibet Autonomous Region.

As the head of Tibet's government-in-exile, the Dalai Lama offered strong but peaceful protests against the actions of the Chinese and worked to arouse world opinion against the destruction of his homeland. He succeeded in getting the United Nations

The Dalai Lama (Tenzin Gyatso)

BORN
July 6, 1935
Taktser, Tibet

EDUCATION
Privately tutored

OCCUPATION
Buddhist religious leader

MAJOR ACCOMPLISHMENTS
Has been a lifelong advocate of peace as the leader of Tibetan Buddhists

The Dalai Lama's home in exile in Dharamsala, India.

General Assembly to pass several resolutions calling for the respect of human rights in Tibet. To further publicize his cause, he wrote an autobiography, *My Land and My People* (1962), which became an international best-seller.

For a number of years, the Dalai Lama was unable to travel outside India because the Indian government did not wish to risk offending the Chinese. During his confinement in Dharamsala he helped the immigrant community of some 80,000 Tibetans who had, like himself, fled to northern India. He worked hard to preserve Tibetan culture and religion, and he often led Buddhist religious ceremonies. He also studied Western cultures and current events, and kept up his knowledge of these areas through contacts with Western journalists who traveled to India to interview him.

The ban on the Dalai Lama's travel was lifted in 1967, when he was allowed to visit Japan. Six years later he made a six-week tour of Europe. In the 1970s the national Chinese government in Beijing began easing the harshness of its rule. The government allowed monasteries to reopen in Tibet, and in 1979 it invited the Dalai Lama to return.

The Dalai Lama was wary of the offer, however, and neither accepted nor rejected it. Instead he immediately resumed his travels abroad. He attended an international Buddhist peace conference in Mongolia and visited Moscow, and he also made his first trip to the United States. There he visited Buddhist congregations, gave talks on college campuses, and met with government officials. He returned to the United States for additional visits in the early 1980s. Over and over again, he stressed the need for an end to violence between nations and a commitment to world peace.

By now the Dalai Lama was hailed internationally as a man of courage, and he realized that in exile he could do more to help Tibet than he could if he returned home to live under a Communist regime. Since the late 1950s, he had received a series of awards for his courageous stand and been named an honorary citizen of half a dozen countries, including the United States. In 1989 he was awarded that year's Nobel Peace Prize for his lifelong opposition to violence.

Today the Dalai Lama continues to live in Dharamsala, where he is still regarded by Tibetan Buddhists as their spiritual leader. In addition to his autobiography, he has written a number of books on Buddhism and its pacifist teachings, including *A Human Approach to World Peace* (1984).

FURTHER READING

Dalai Lama. *My Land and My People*. New York: Potala, 1983.

———. *Freedom in Exile: The Autobiography of the Dalai Lama*. New York: HarperCollins, 1990.

Freise, Kai. *Tenzin Gyatso, the Dalai Lama*. New York: Chelsea House, 1989.

Levenson, Claude B. *The Dalai Lama: A Biography*. London: Unwin Hyman, 1988.

Mikhail Gorbachev

1990

Soviet premier Mikhail Gorbachev addresses the UN General Assembly on December 7, 1988. His efforts to improve relations with Western nations led to the end of the Cold War.

The Russian political leader Mikhail Gorbachev may not have seemed a likely international peacemaker in his early years, but his friends remember that his political skills marked him as a leader even in childhood. Eventually he would use those skills to put his country on the road to peace—and win the Nobel Peace Prize for his efforts.

Gorbachev was born in the small town of Privolnoye in 1931 to a Russian peasant couple. His first experience of war occurred in 1942, when German troops occupied his town and the surrounding countryside during World War II. Despite this disruption, Gorbachev continued his studies in local schools. Following graduation, he enrolled at Moscow Sate University and earned a law degree some years later, in 1955.

Although Gorbachev was not an especially good student, he persisted in studying law because he believed it would help him find a career in government. In the early 1950s he joined the ruling Communist party—the only political party then allowed in the Soviet Union—and became active in its youth division, the Young Communist League (Komsomol), in his home district of Stavropol. There he rose in the organization's leadership, and by the early 1960s he had secured a government appointment as head of agriculture for Stavropol. To help him in his new post, he took courses on the economics of farming at the Stavropol Agricultural Institute and earned a degree in the field in 1967.

Gorbachev excelled in his government post as he reorganized the local state-run farms to make them more productive. During the late 1960s he was also appointed to a series of leadership positions with increasing responsibility in the Communist party. By 1970 he had risen to a prominent party post in the national legislative body, the Supreme Soviet. A year later Gorbachev became a member of the powerful Soviet Central Committee, the country's primary governing body. In this capacity he traveled as a delegate to party congresses throughout the Soviet Union. He also made trips to several Western European countries, which expanded his knowledge of these areas. Gorbachev is a friendly man, and his pleasing personality helped ease many tensions that had long existed between Communist and non-Communist nations in Europe—tensions that were known as the Cold War.

Gorbachev's administrative talents and his ability to get along with people were looked upon favorably by top party leaders, and several of them helped to advance his career. In 1978 he climbed further upward when he was named

Premier Gorbachev and U.S. President Ronald Reagan at the signing of the Intermediate Nuclear Forces Treaty (INF) on December 8, 1987, in Washington, D.C. This was the first international agreement to reduce nuclear weapons stockpiles.

corruption in government. As Andropov's right-hand man, Gorbachev helped him carry out these reforms.

It was apparent that Andropov was grooming Gorbachev to be his successor, but after Andropov's unexpected death in early 1984, Gorbachev was passed over for the top post in favor of Konstantin Chernenko. However, Chernenko was old and sick, and as he became increasingly unable to carry out his duties, Gorbachev quietly assumed more and more of them. When Chernenko himself died in March 1985, Gorbachev was finally elected general secretary by the Central Committee.

Upon taking office, Gorbachev announced that economic development was one of his major goals. As for the role of the Soviet Union in international affairs, Gorbachev vowed to maintain his country's strong defense system, but he said that he would continue to follow its traditional policy of "peaceful coexistence" with non-Communist nations.

Gorbachev strengthened his power by forcing the resignation of older Politburo members and replacing them with younger associates who were sympathetic to his goals. He then embarked on a series of political, social, and economic reforms designed to liberalize the country. He used two Russian words to characterize his new goals: *glasnost*, meaning "openness," and *perestroika*, or "restructuring."

During the next few years Gorbachev carried out these reforms by freeing thousands of political prisoners, including physicist and peace activist Andrei Sakharov, encouraging greater freedom of expression, and allowing many Russians to leave the country. He also led a full-scale attack on governmental corruption. In addition, he called for a realistic look at recent

national agriculture secretary, a post that took him to Moscow, the Soviet capital. In this position Gorbachev was less successful than he had been as Stavropol's agriculture secretary, but he still continued to be popular with party officials. By the fall of 1980 he had become a full voting member of the Politburo, the Communist Party's policymaking body.

In the early 1980s the Soviet Union went through an unsettled period as a succession of its heads of state died after short terms in office. In 1982 Gorbachev advanced still further to the top post of general secretary when he became the chief assistant to Yuri Andropov, the new holder of that position. Andropov surprised many Russians by introducing numerous reforms, including a widespread fight against

Russian history and criticized previous efforts to hide the failures of the Communist government. Gorbachev encouraged greater independence among member republics of the Soviet Union by easing Moscow's control of their governments.

To improve relations between the Soviet Union and Western nations, especially the United States, Gorbachev held a series of talks with President Ronald Reagan. These led to the signing of a nuclear-arms-elimination treaty in 1987 (the Intermediate Nuclear Forces Treaty, or INF). Two years later, Gorbachev ended the Soviet Union's long occupation of Afghanistan. By this time, Communist governments throughout Eastern Europe were beginning to fall, and Gorbachev encouraged this process by acknowledging it as inevitable and refusing to try to stop it.

In 1990 a newly created national legislative body in the Soviet Union voted to end the Communist party's 70-year control of the government, and members then elected Gorbachev executive president of the Soviet Union. Later that year, Gorbachev was awarded the 1990 Nobel Peace Prize for his efforts to ease tension between Eastern and Western nations.

However, despite the international acclaim that Gorbachev had earned for his efforts to liberalize his country, his popularity declined rapidly in the Soviet Union following his receipt of the Nobel award. The Soviet economy was in danger of failing completely, and the easing of central control had led to the eruption of tensions between different ethnic minorities in many of the Soviet republics.

By the end of 1991, Gorbachev had dissolved the Communist party and replaced the old Soviet Union with a looser confederation of its member republics, called the Commonwealth of Independent States (CIS). In December of that year, believing that he could no longer rule the country effectively, Gorbachev resigned the presidency.

In recent years Gorbachev has served as president of the International Foundation for Socio-Economic and Political Studies, a research organization he founded in Moscow to help rebuild his country. He remains active in Russian public life as the CIS still struggles to overcome the disastrous effects of Communist rule.

Gorbachev is married to a former university professor of political science and has one daughter. He is the author of half a dozen books on contemporary politics and the peacemaking process, and has also written several volumes of memoirs.

FURTHER READING

Butson, Thomas. *Mikhail Gorbachev.* New York: Chelsea House, 1986.

Gorbachev, Mikhail. *The Coming Century of Peace.* Mamaroneck, N.Y.: Richardson & Steirman/Eagle Publishing Corp., 1985.

———. *Speeches and Writings.* 2 vols. New York: Pergamon, 1986–87.

———. *A Time for Peace.* Mamaroneck, N.Y.: Richardson & Steirman/Eagle Publishing Corp., 1986.

Kaiser, Robert G. *Why Gorbachev Happened: His Triumphs and His Failure.* New York: Simon & Schuster, 1991.

Morrison, Donald, and the Editors of *Time. Mikhail Gorbachev: An Intimate Biography.* New York: Time, Inc., 1988.

Sheehy, Gail. *The Man Who Changed the World: The Lives of Mikhail S. Gorbachev.* New York: Harper, 1990.

Smith, Hedrick. *The New Russians.* New York: Random House, 1990.

Mikhail Gorbachev

BORN
March 2, 1931
Privolnoye, Russia

EDUCATION
Law degree, Moscow State University (1955); diploma, Stavropol Agricultural Institute (1967)

OCCUPATION
Political leader

MAJOR ACCOMPLISHMENTS
General secretary, Communist Party of the Soviet (1985–90); president of the Soviet Union (1990–91); led reform movement to liberalize the government and end 70 years of Communist rule

Aung San Suu Kyi

1991

Until 1988, few people outside of her native Burma had heard of Aung San Suu Kyi (pronounced *Ong Sahn Soo Chee*) In fact, she was not that well known in her own country either. However, her father, Aung San, was—and still is—one of the most revered figures in Burma's history. His face is as well known there as George Washington's is in the United States—and for the same reason: he is considered the father of his country.

Aung San Suu Kyi was the youngest of Aung San's three children and his only daughter. He had died when she was two years old, and she had spent most of her life abroad. During that time Burma had gone steadily downhill because of years of misrule by dictators. When Suu Kyi returned to Burma in the spring of 1988, she discovered that a pro-democracy movement was in progress, and that it had been inspired by the deep love the Burmese still felt for her father. It thus seemed natural for Suu Kyi to assume the leadership of the movement. Less than four years later, Suu Kyi's struggle for democracy was known throughout the world, and she received the 1991 Nobel Peace Prize.

Aung San Suu Kyi was born in Rangoon, Burma, in 1945, at the end of World War II. Her father, an army general, was the leader of a nationalist movement to secure Burma's independence from Great Britain, which had controlled the Southeast Asian nation for more than half a century. Although British rule had formally ended in 1937, the country did not become completely independent until 1948. However, Aung San did not live to see independence come to Burma: he was assassinated in 1947 by political opponents.

Suu Kyi lived with her widowed mother in Rangoon for the next 13 years and attended school there. Her life changed dramatically in 1960, however, when her mother was appointed Burma's ambassador to India. She spent the next four years in New Delhi, living in the luxurious ambassador's residence. During those years, a military dictator named Ne Win seized control of the Burmese government. He was to rule the country for nearly three decades.

Despite the temptation to lead a leisurely life filled with horseback riding, ballet lessons, and partygoing, Suu Kyi excelled in her studies at the private school she attended in New Delhi. At that school she learned for the first time about Mohandas Gandhi, India's legendary nationalist leader who preached a philosophy of nonviolent resistance to all forms of wrongdoing. Twenty-five years later, Gandhi would have a strong influence on Suu Kyi's life.

In 1964 Suu Kyi traveled to England to enroll at Oxford University, where she studied politics, philosophy, and economics. She was eager to learn about Western culture, but she maintained her Buddhist religion and her devotion to Burmese culture. After graduating in 1968, she taught for a while in England and then worked as a researcher at the United Nations headquarters in New York City.

In 1972 Suu Kyi married Michael Aris, a scholar of Tibetan civilization whom she had met at Oxford. For a year after the marriage, she and her husband lived in Bhutan, an independent kingdom in the Himalayas. While he served as a tutor for the royal family, Suu Kyi worked in the country's foreign ministry. The couple then returned to Oxford, where Michael Aris resumed his university career and Suu Kyi gave birth to their first son. A second son was born four years later.

For 12 years—from 1973 to 1985—Suu Kyi lived the comfortable life of an Oxford professor's wife. While she was caring for her family, however, she never forgot Burma. She grew increasingly interested in her father's life, and she wrote a brief biography of him that was published in England in 1984.

Suu Kyi's emerging independence and her desire to learn more about her father led her to travel to Japan in 1985, where she spent the year as a visiting scholar at the Center for Southeast Asian Studies at the University of Kyoto. By the end of her stay in Japan, she felt a complete identification with her father and his dream for a democratic Burma. Her feelings were intensified by the knowledge that Burma, under the dictator Ne Win, had declined socially, politically, and economically.

Once the richest country in Southeast Asia, Burma was now one of the three poorest nations in the world. In addition to physical hardships, the Burmese also had to live under a political system that prohibited free elections and severely limited such basic civil rights as freedom of speech and

freedom of the press. By 1986, Suu Kyi became convinced that one day she would return to Burma and fight for the democratic cause—the cause that her father had died for.

After her studies in Kyoto, Suu Kyi was reunited in 1986 with her family in India, where her husband was doing research. She spent a year there writing a book on Burma and India under colonial rule. In 1987, when the family returned to England, Suu Kyi enrolled as a doctoral student in Burmese literature at the University of London.

In April 1988 Suu Kyi was called to Rangoon to care for her dying mother. When she arrived, she discovered that a series of confrontations were taking place between armed soldiers and small groups of university students protesting various government policies.

Aung San Suu Kyi addresses a group of supporters in Rangoon in July 1989, shortly before she was placed under house arrest by the Burmese government.

Pro-democracy demonstrators march in Rangoon in August 1988. Featured on many of their banners were portraits of Aung San, a Burmese national hero and the father of Aung San Suu Kyi.

During the next few months, the clashes increased and grew more violent, and by June several hundred student demonstrators had been killed. In July Ne Win resigned and was replaced by an even harsher military ruler, General Saw Maung.

By early August the protest movement had gained momentum as tens of thousands of people from all walks of life marched in Rangoon and other Burmese cities. Many of them carried large placards bearing the photo of General Aung San, Burma's hero. Soldiers began firing into the crowds of demonstrators, and in one five-day period, August 8–13, some 3,000 people were killed. As Suu Kyi tended her mother at the family estate on Inya Lake, on the outskirts of Rangoon, she listened to radio reports of these events, and she decided that she could no longer remain a bystander. On August 26 Suu Kyi made her first public appearance on behalf of the demonstrators as she spoke to a crowd of half a million at a Buddhist shrine in downtown Rangoon. Up until then, the demonstrators had been united only by their opposition to the government. They had not yet focused on what they wanted to achieve, and they did not have a single leader. In her speech, Suu Kyi gave the demonstrators a focus: she told her audience that they must work for the restoration of basic human rights in Burma—and the most important of them all was the right to hold free elections.

Aung San Suu Kyi not only had her father's name; she also looked very much like him. Her effect on the crowd was electric, and she realized that she would have to remain in Rangoon after her mother's death to head the struggle for human rights. In September she founded a political party, the National League for Democracy, to work for those rights. On behalf of the party, she began traveling throughout Burma, encouraging the people to seek freedom—but to do so without using violence. She preached nonviolent civil disobedience—the philosophy of Gandhi that she had learned about in a New Delhi classroom 25 years earlier.

Armed soldiers often tried to break up Suu Kyi's pro-democracy rallies. She was frequently threatened and her followers were often arrested. She never backed down, however, and continued to speak out. She traveled to the most remote areas of Burma, often using cattle-drawn carts or primitive rafts for transportation.

Finally, in July 1989, the government retaliated by placing Suu Kyi under house arrest. Her contact with her family was severely restricted, her telephone line was cut, and her only contact with the outside world was a small shortwave radio on which she could hear international news broadcasts.

Despite appeals throughout the world from human rights organizations to free Suu Kyi, she was still under house arrest in the fall of 1991, when the Nobel Peace Prize committee announced that she was the recipient of that year's award for leading "a democratic opposition which employs nonviolent means to resist a regime characterized by brutality." Because she could not leave her house, much less the country, her older son, now 18 years old, accepted the Peace Prize in Oslo in December for his mother.

Suu Kyi remained under house arrest for six years. During that time Saw Maung renamed the country Myanmar and its capital Yangon. In response to continuing protests he did grant small reforms, and even allowed a free national election to be held. When he lost, however, he declared the election invalid.

While she was in captivity, Suu Kyi tried to lead as normal a life as possible. She observed Buddhist rituals and practices, read, sewed, and followed international events on her shortwave radio. Finally, without fanfare, Suu Kyi was notified in July 1995 that she was no longer under house arrest. The news of her release traveled quickly around the world and made the front pages of every major newspaper.

Following her release, Suu Kyi immediately set out to revive the National League for Democracy. Her house on Inya Lake became the headquarters of the party. Today Suu Kyi continues to call for democratic rule in her nation, and she hopes someday to achieve what her father gave his life for half a century ago.

FURTHER READING

Aung San Suu Kyi. *Freedom from Fear and Other Writings*. New York: Viking, 1991.

"Aung San Suu Kyi." In *Current Biography Yearbook 1992*. New York: H. W. Wilson, 1993.

Dreifus, Claudia. "The Passion of Suu Kyi." *New York Times Magazine*, January 7, 1996, pp. 32ff.

Parenteau, John. *Prisoner for Peace: Aung San Suu Kyi and Burma's Struggle for Democracy*. Greensboro, N.C.: Morgan Reynolds, 1994.

Shenon, Philip. "Head of Democratic Opposition Is Released by Burma Military." *New York Times*, July 11, 1995, pp. 1, 8.

Aung San Suu Kyi

BORN

June 19, 1945
Rangoon, Burma (now Yangon, Myanmar)

EDUCATION

B.A., Oxford University (1968); doctoral study, University of London (1987–88)

OCCUPATION

Scholar; human rights activist

MAJOR ACCOMPLISHMENT

Founder, National League for Democracy, a nationwide movement to restore democratic government to Myanmar (Burma)

Rigoberta Menchú

1992

Sometime in 1959—no one remembers exactly when—a sixth child, a girl named Rigoberta Menchú, was born to Vicente Menchú and his wife, poor peasants who lived in the village of Chimel in northern Guatemala. In the next few years, the Menchús had three more children.

As soon as they were able, these children and the children of other Guatemalan peasant families—Mayan Indians—worked from October until February beside their parents on coffee and cotton plantations along the southern coast. Their 18-hour days of labor began at 3:00 A.M. and ended at dusk. Working conditions were terrible, and they earned very little. For the remaining months of the year they helped their parents farm small plots of land to raise beans and corn for food.

Millions of Mayan Indian Guatemalans—as many as 8 million, or 80 percent of the population—lived, and still live today, like the Menchús. Most of them are illiterate, have never attended school, and are plagued by malnutrition, disease, and cruel treatment by the ruling class of wealthy landowners—the remaining 20 percent of the population in Guatemala that is descended from European settlers, primarily Spanish.

In the 1960s, relations between the Mayan Indians and the landowners grew worse as the government allowed landowners to seize more and more Mayan land. Rigoberta Menchú grew up in the midst of increasing clashes between the Mayans and the landowners, which turned into a civil war. As a small child she worked with her family on the coffee and cotton plantations. By the time she was eight, two of her brothers had died—one from starvation and the other from pesticides sprayed on the crops. In 1971, when she was 12, her family sent her to Guatemala City to work as a maid in the home of a wealthy family, but she was treated badly and returned to Chimel after several months.

Upon her return, Rigoberta discovered that her father had been imprisoned for protesting the seizure of Mayan land near the village. When Vicente Menchú was released a year later, he resumed his efforts to organize opposition to the takeover of Mayan Indian land. This time he was joined by Rigoberta, who traveled throughout the countryside with him and listened admiringly to his speeches. One day Vicente told his daughter that after his death she would have to carry on his work, and she took his words seriously.

The Menchús were Christians who also held to the traditional beliefs of the Mayan religion, and their faith sustained both father and daughter. As she grew older, Rigoberta became more active in her father's cause, and she

Rigoberta Menchú

BORN
1959
Chimel, Guatemala

EDUCATION
Self-educated

OCCUPATION
Human rights activist

MAJOR ACCOMPLISHMENTS
As an active member of the Committee of Peasant Unity (CUC), worked for fair treatment of Guatemala's Mayan Indian population; author of a best-selling autobiography, *I, Rigoberta Menchú*; founder, Vicente Menchú Foundation, a human rights organization

Rigoberta Menchú accepted the 1992 Nobel Peace Prize on behalf of the Indian peoples of Central and South America. The Nobel committee cited her "work for social justice and ethno-cultural reconciliation" in awarding her its prize.

personally encouraged fellow peasants in their fight to keep their land.

In the late 1970s Vicente Menchú founded a political organization whose name in English is the Committee of Peasant Unity; it is more widely known as the CUC, the initials of its Spanish name. The CUC was created to advance the cause of the Mayan Indians, and Rigoberta and her brothers became active members. Rigoberta, who then spoke only a Mayan dialect and could not read or write, realized that to fight for her rights she needed to know Spanish, the language of those who ruled Guatemala. She taught herself to read, write, and speak the language,

and she also learned other Indian dialects.

The Menchú family's political activities were being watched closely by government authorities, and in September 1979 they began to clamp down. That month one of Rigoberta's brothers was captured and burned alive by government troops. Four months later, in January 1980, Vicente was killed during a demonstration in Guatemala City. In April Rigoberta became an orphan: her mother was kidnapped, tortured, and left to die on a hillside near their village.

By now, Rigoberta Menchú had become one of the CUC's most active members. She began organizing labor strikes at Guatemalan plantations to protest working conditions. The CUC grew to include not only members of Guatemala's Mayan population but also many non-Indians who were sympathetic to the Mayan cause, including university professors, students, and Roman Catholic nuns and priests.

By the summer of 1981, Rigoberta Menchú's activities had put her life in danger as the government sought her capture. She managed to escape to neighboring Mexico, where thousands of other Guatemalan refugees had settled. There she was aided by members of a Roman Catholic organization called the Guatemalan Church in Exile. Through them she met other people who were sympathetic to the plight of the Mayan peasants.

In 1982 Menchú traveled to Europe, where she met an anthropologist and journalist named Elisabeth Burgos-Debray. She told the woman her life story, and it was published as her autobiography a year later. The book quickly became a best-seller and has been translated into more than a dozen languages. The English version, called *I, Rigoberta Menchú*, was first published in 1984 and is widely read on college campuses in the United States.

Living in exile in Mexico City, Menchú devoted herself to drawing international attention to the political and social problems of Guatemala, which has the most violations against human rights of any country in the western hemisphere. She also followed the ongoing civil war in Guatemala between government troops and peasant rebels fighting for equality. In 1987 Menchú cofounded the National Committee for Reconciliation, a group that continues to appeal to the Guatemalan government to negotiate with CUC and other rebel groups and end the long civil war.

Menchú's struggles to bring justice to the Mayan Indians of Guatemala earned her the 1992 Nobel Peace Prize. The news of her award was greeted with joy by Menchú and her supporters around the world, but there was criticism as well. Guatemalan officials criticized the Nobel Committee's choice, and prominent members of Guatemela's upper class publicly ridiculed her. In other countries, conservative political commentators accused her of being a Communist revolutionary interested only in encouraging violence, not in establishing peace.

Menchú used the $1.2 million prize money to establish a foundation in memory of her father. The Vicente Menchú Foundation works to promote human rights and education among indigenous (native) populations not only in Guatemala but throughout North and South America.

Rigoberta Menchú's long-held dream of peace in Guatemala was finally realized in 1996. On September 19, the Guatemalan government and rebel groups signed the first agreement toward ending the country's 36-year-long civil war. On December 29, the final agreements, which included the framework for establishing a more open, democratic society in Guatemala, were signed. Menchú was a prominent guest at both events, ending her long exile from her home country.

Menchú continues her work with the foundation she established. She also travels frequently, making speeches on behalf of human rights.

FURTHER READING

Menchú, Rigoberta. *I, Rigoberta Menchú: An Indian Woman in Guatemala*. Translated by Ann Wright. London: Verso, 1984.

"Menchú, Rigoberta." In *Current Biography Yearbook 1993*. New York: H. W. Wilson, 1994.

F. W. de Klerk

Nelson Mandela

1993

From the time of his birth in 1936, there was little doubt that F. W. de Klerk, cowinner of the 1993 Nobel Peace Prize, would one day become active in the political life of his native South Africa. After all, he had been born into a prominent Afrikaner family whose male members had long played a prominent role in national affairs. Afrikaners are descendants of Dutch, German, and French settlers who began arriving in South Africa in the 17th century. They have their own language, Afrikaans, and most of them belong to the Dutch Reformed Church. The de Klerks, however, belonged to the Reformed Church of South Africa, a more liberal denomination.

The white population has always been a small minority in South Africa—today it numbers only 14 percent—but it controlled the country's government until very recently. More than half of the whites are Afrikaners, and they have long dominated South African politics. De Klerk's own family included members of parliament and a prime minister; his

Nelson Mandela (center), head of the African National Congress, and South African prime minister F. W. de Klerk receive the 1993 Nobel Peace Prize from Francis Sejersted, chairman of the Norwegian Nobel Committee, in Oslo.

F. W. de Klerk

BORN

March 18, 1936
Johannesburg, South Africa

EDUCATION

J.D., Potchefstroom University
(1958)

OCCUPATION

Attorney; political leader

MAJOR ACCOMPLISHMENTS

As president of South Africa
(1989–94), introduced reforms that
gave nonwhite residents civil rights
in South Africa; participated in negotiations with African National
Congress leader Nelson Mandela
that led to national elections open
to all citizens of the country (1994)

father, an educator who served in several national cabinets, was acting president of South Africa in the 1970s.

Frederik Willem de Klerk was born
in Johannesburg. From childhood he
was known by his initials, F. W., to distinguish him from his maternal grandfather, after whom he had been named.
Following graduation from high school,
de Klerk attended Potchefstroom University, a church-run institution, where
he edited the college newspaper and
was active in the student branch of the
National party. He received a law degree with honors in 1958 and married
shortly afterward; he and his wife eventually had three children.

Upon graduation, de Klerk still
had only limited English-language
skills, since most of his education had
been in Afrikaans. In the summer of
1958 he traveled to England, and when
he returned to South Africa he joined
a firm of English-speaking lawyers to
continue improving his English.

In 1961 de Klerk opened his own
practice in Vereeniging, a mining town
near Johannesburg, and remained there
for 11 years. During that time he was
active in National party affairs. In 1972
he was asked to return to Potchefstroom University as a law professor,
but before he could do so he was picked
by the National party to run for a parliamentary seat from Vereeniging.

De Klerk won the election and
moved to Cape Town, the national capital. During the next few years he was
groomed by National Party leaders for
higher office. Beginning in 1978 he
held a series of cabinet posts under a
succession of prime ministers, and by
December 1986 he had become the
leader of the lower house of parliament.

De Klerk's rise in politics coincided
with the growth of a movement for
constitutional reform in South Africa.
This movement concerned the controversial issue of apartheid (pronounced
uh-PAR-tide), a policy of racial separation introduced in the country in the

late 1940s. Under apartheid, the majority nonwhites were allowed to have
only limited contact with whites, and
they were denied political power.

There were different categories of
nonwhites, including people of mixed
races (called "coloreds") and various
Asian nationalities, but those who suffered the most under apartheid were
native blacks, who made up 75 percent
of South Africa's total population.
They received inferior or no schooling,
were required to live in certain areas in
poor housing, and had few job opportunities except as servants or laborers.

For many years South Africa had
been criticized throughout the world
for its policy of apartheid, and many
countries had put increasing economic
pressure on South Africa to end the
practice. In the early 1980s, Prime
Minister P. W. Botha responded to
growing international criticism of the
South African government by announcing a limited program of constitutional reforms that went into effect
in 1984.

Under these reforms, some nonwhites—"coloreds" and Asians—were
allowed to participate in South Africa's
government. Also under Botha's reforms, the presidency of South Africa
was changed from a largely ceremonial
position into a powerful political role,
more important than that of the prime
minister. However, none of these reforms improved the condition of
blacks, and pressure grew even greater
to end apartheid entirely.

Apartheid had been created by
leaders of F. W. de Klerk's own National party, and de Klerk himself had supported efforts to keep racial separation
in place in South Africa. However, he
was a practical man, and by the mid-
1980s he realized that the combined
pressure from the black majority, international human rights organizations,
and economic restrictions would eventually lead to the end of white domination in his country. As a politician who

was skilled in negotiation and compromise, he assumed a major role in making the transition from apartheid to equality as smooth as possible.

During the late 1980s, as he continued to hold his parliament seat, de Klerk worked closely with Botha while also serving as minister of education. He was also the head of the National Party in the Transvaal, South Africa's largest state. In 1989 Botha suffered a stroke and de Klerk became party leader and acting president. In September of that year he was elected to the presidency.

De Klerk took office in the midst of major public protests against apartheid, led by both blacks and white sympathizers. In the past, police and government troops had cracked down on similar demonstrations, and deaths and injuries had resulted. De Klerk announced that peaceful demonstrations would now be allowed. To ease tensions, he met with leading antiapartheid activists, including Archbishop Desmond Tutu.

During the next few months, de Klerk took steps toward further reform. In February 1990 he lifted the 30-year ban on the African National Congress (ANC), a political organization that had sought political rights for blacks throughout Africa. He also freed ANC leader Nelson Mandela, South Africa's highest-ranking black political figure, who had been in prison for more than 25 years.

In August 1990, after a series of joint meetings, de Klerk and Mandela signed an agreement called the Pretoria Minute. Under this agreement, the government released several thousand political prisoners, and the ANC agreed to halt its campaign of armed struggle against the government. The Pretoria Minute also called for continuing negotiations on the creation of a new constitution for South Africa.

A constitutional convention finally began in December 1991, and dis-

cussions were led in the following months by de Klerk and Mandela. In September 1992 the two men signed another agreement, this time providing for the election of a new legislature that would draft a new constitution. In June 1993 another important agreement was reached between de Klerk and Mandela: the new elections—the first in the history of South Africa open to citizens of all races—were scheduled for April 27, 1994.

De Klerk and Mandela shared the 1993 Nobel Peace Prize for their cooperation in bringing open elections to South Africa. In April 1994, four months after the prizes were awarded in Oslo, Mandela was elected South Africa's president. De Klerk became deputy president.

When Nelson Mandela became South Africa's first black president, he fulfilled a long-held dream: he was at last in a position to lead his country's nonwhite population to full equality. Yet he realized that the "long walk to freedom" he had begun so many years earlier would have to continue before justice was finally achieved.

Mandela was born Rolihlahla Dalibhunga Mandela in 1918 in the village of Mvezo, on South Africa's southeastern coast. He acquired the first name "Nelson" later, in school. His father, the local tribal chief, died when Mandela was nine. He was then placed under the guardianship of the tribal regent, who taught him that true leadership could be achieved only through consensus—obtaining the full agreement of all followers.

Despite his tribal upbringing, Mandela was more heavily influenced by Western values, which he learned in school. After attending local institutions run by British Methodists, he studied at an area college. He moved to Johannesburg in 1941 and was hired as a clerk in the office of a liberal white lawyer. A year later he earned a bachelor's degree through a correspondence

Nelson Mandela

BORN
July 18, 1918
Mvezo, South Africa

EDUCATION
B.A., University of South Africa (1942); diploma in law, University of Witwatersrand (1946)

OCCUPATION
Attorney; political leader

MAJOR ACCOMPLISHMENTS
Led efforts by the African National Congress (ANC) to promote racial justice in South Africa; negotiated with South African president F. W. de Klerk for the establishment of national elections open to all citizens; president of South Africa (1994–); author of an autobiography, *Long Walk to Freedom* (1994)

Black South Africans line up to vote for the first time in elections held on April 26, 1994. Nelson Mandela won the presidential election on that date, six months after receiving the Nobel Peace Prize.

course from the University of South Africa, and in 1943 he began studying law part time at the University of Witwatersrand.

Through work, school, and friendships, Mandela became interested in politics, and in 1944 he joined the African National Congress, the black political organization then led by Albert Luthuli. Mandela helped create the ANC's Youth League, which grew into the dominant force in the organization. The Youth League was more radical than its parent organization, and it worked to overthrow the white-run government in order to achieve full democracy in the country.

Fearing the increased demands of blacks for power in South Africa, the government began establishing the system of racial separation called apartheid in the late 1940s. In 1952, with the restrictive laws now in place, the ANC leaders wrote a letter to the prime minister demanding that the laws be repealed. When the letter was ignored, Mandela and other ANC members launched the Campaign for the Defiance of Unjust Laws. They participated

in a series of illegal but nonviolent actions: entering "whites only" areas such as toilets and restaurants, and taking part in strikes against employers.

For these activities, Mandela and other ANC members were accused of being Communists—the Communist party was banned in South Africa—and were prohibited from attending political gatherings on several occasions during the next few years. Meanwhile, Mandela had established the first black-run law practice in South Africa, and he did not resume his political activities until 1955. A year later, he and more than 200 other black resistance leaders were accused of plotting to overthrow the government and were charged with treason. They remained free on bail until 1959, when their trial finally began. When it ended two years later, they were acquitted.

However, a year earlier the ANC had been banned by the government. When Mandela continued his association with the organization after his trial ended, a warrant was issued for his arrest. Mandela abandoned his law practice and went into hiding, working at a series of menial jobs.

Up until this point Mandela had been committed to nonviolent opposition to apartheid, but the government's own use of violence to end demonstrations convinced him that the ANC had to begin a militant struggle of its own. He helped create an armed wing of the ANC called Spear of the Nation, which planned to overthrow the government through acts of sabotage. After a year of living underground and eluding capture, Mandela was finally arrested in the summer of 1962. He was charged with several minor violations of apartheid laws, convicted, and sentenced to five years in prison.

In the summer of 1963, government authorities raided ANC headquarters at a farm in Rivonia and discovered documents outlining the proposed campaign of Spear of the Nation. Mandela was retried on charges of treason, and he and other ANC leaders were sentenced to life in prison in June 1964. The so-called Rivonia Trial and its outcome attracted international attention, and many prominent individuals and human rights organizations pleaded unsuccessfully with the South African government to release the prisoners.

Mandela was jailed for more than 25 years. For most of that time he was confined to maximum-security prisons, his activities were severely restricted, and he was not allowed to have visitors. The outside world did not forget him, however, and an international campaign was organized by human rights activists to secure his release.

By the late 1980s, as the South African government became liberalized under President P. W. Botha, there were signs that Mandela would eventually be freed. It is now known that several high government officials met with him in prison to discuss the terms of his release. Finally, on February 2, 1990, several months after Botha left office, his successor F. W. de Klerk lifted the ban on the ANC. Nine days later, Mandela was freed.

Mandela's release was headline news around the world. After resting for several months, the 72-year-old Mandela embarked on a trip around the world. He visited major cities and met with world leaders, including U.S. President George Bush. When he returned to South Africa, he began the series of meetings with de Klerk that led to the historic agreement to hold free elections on April 27, 1994—and to Mandela's receipt with de Klerk of the 1993 Nobel Peace Prize.

Mandela ran for president of South Africa in April 1994 and was easily elected, winning two-thirds of the vote. After taking office in May, he began work on a national program to bring full equality to all South African citizens. Under his leadership, a postapartheid constitution became law in December 1996.

Mandela has been widely praised for reaching out to all ethnic groups in South Africa, whites and nonwhites alike, and including representatives of each group in his cabinet. Through these efforts, he has gained the confidence of many South Africans who had once strongly opposed granting political rights to nonwhites.

Mandela has been married several times and has five children. He has received other honors, including a joint honorary degree in 1990 from 38 black American universities and colleges. His autobiography, *Long Walk to Freedom*, was published in 1994.

FURTHER READING

Clark, Steve. *Nelson Mandela Speaks: Forging a Democratic Nonracial South Africa.* New York: Pathfinder, 1993.

"de Klerk, F(rederik). W(illem)." In *Current Biography Yearbook 1990.* New York: H. W. Wilson, 1991.

Mandela, Nelson. *Long Walk to Freedom: The Autobiography of Nelson Mandela.* Boston: Little, Brown, 1994.

————. *No Easy Walk to Freedom.* London: Heinemann, 1973.

"Mandela, Nelson." In *Current Biography Yearbook 1995.* New York: H. W. Wilson, 1996.

Ottaway, David. *Chained Together: Mandela, de Klerk, and the Struggle to Remake South Africa.* New York: Times Books, 1993.

Yasir Arafat
Shimon Peres
Yitzhak Rabin

1994

I n 1994, for the first time in the history of the Nobel Peace Prize, the award was shared by three winners, all of them politicians: Yasir Arafat, Shimon Peres, and Yitzhak Rabin. All three men had been enemies of one another at various times in the past. In 1994, however, they were honored by the Nobel Peace Prize Committee for their cooperation in trying to bring lasting peace to the Middle East.

Yitzhak Rabin (pronounced *Rah-BEAN*) was the oldest of the three. He was born in 1922 to a Jewish family in the historic city of Jerusalem, at that time part of Palestine. Palestine's population was mostly Arab, and the predominant religion was Islam.

Historically, Palestine was the site of the ancient Jewish nation of Israel, which had fallen to Roman invaders in the 2nd century A.D. Rome governed the area until the 7th century A.D., when it came under the control of Arab rulers.

After the fall, most Jews had migrated to Europe and eventually to other parts of the world, but a small Jewish population remained in Palestine. For centuries, Jews dreamed of

As Israel's prime minister, Yitzhak Rabin worked to improve his nation's relations with neighboring countries in the Middle East.

returning to their homeland, and by the late 19th century an international movement called Zionism had developed to focus those dreams. Encouraged by Zionist leaders, Jewish settlers began moving back to Palestine to join the small Jewish population there. These new settlers included Yitzhak's Rabin's parents, who emigrated from Russia in the early 20th century. By the time of his birth, several thousand Jews had established settlements, many of them farms, in Palestine.

In 1917 control of Palestine passed from the Ottoman Empire (Turkey) to Great Britain. The British promised to establish a Jewish state within the territory. However, this idea was not popular with the majority Arab (Islamic) population, and a series of violent conflicts began. Those conflicts continued through Rabin's childhood as Great Britain delayed plans to create the new Israel.

Both of Rabin's parents were intellectuals and active Zionists. Rabin and his younger sister were raised to be strong supporters of the new Israel. Like many other children of Jewish settlers, they were sent to agricultural schools to prepare them for lives as farmers, since Palestine was largely rural.

After graduating from an agricultural secondary school in 1940, Rabin planned on further study in the United States. However, World War II had begun a year earlier, and Great Britain was now at war with Germany. Rabin had to abandon not only his plans to go to America but also his intention to become a farmer. Although he had no interest in becoming a soldier, he felt compelled to join a Jewish underground army called Haganah. He was assigned to a commando wing of Haganah called Palmach, which worked with the British government to fight Germans who had infiltrated Palestine and the nearby countries of Lebanon and Syria.

After the war ended in 1945, Rabin abandoned his plans to study abroad. Instead, he concentrated his energies on helping to found the new Jewish state by continuing to serve with Palmach, which was now fighting the British. Some years earlier, Great Britain had begun restricting Jewish immigration to Palestine because of continued hostilities between Jews and Arabs, a policy that Palmach opposed.

When Rabin participated in a Palmach-sponsored raid on a camp where would-be Jewish immigrants were being held to be deported to their countries of origin, he became a wanted man. After a series of other raids with Palmach, Rabin was arrested by the British in the summer of 1946 and sent to prison. That November, not long after his release, Great Britain turned its control of Palestine over to the United Nations.

In December 1947, the UN voted to partition Palestine into two states, one Jewish and the other Palestinian Arab. Israel declared itself an independent state in May 1948, and angry Arabs responded by invading Israeli territory. In the months of warfare that followed, Rabin commanded a Palmach brigade. He later participated in negotiations that led to an armistice, or temporary halt to the fighting, in 1949.

By this time Palmach had been merged with the Israeli Defense Forces (IDF), the country's new military unit. Rabin became an officer in the IDF and served for the next 20 years. He received regular promotions, and by 1964 he had become chief of staff, the top position in the IDF. During these years small-scale warfare had continued between Israelis and Arabs, and Rabin was accused by many of aggravating the hostilities rather than trying to end them.

In early June 1967 the so-called Six-Day War occurred between Israel and its Arab neighbors—Egypt, Jordan, Iraq, and Syria. Israel won the brief

Yasir Arafat

BORN
August 24, 1929
Cairo, Egypt

EDUCATION
B.Eng., University of Fuad (now Cairo University) (1956)

OCCUPATION
Politician

MAJOR ACCOMPLISHMENTS
Founder (mid-1950s) and chairman of Fatah; co-founder and chairman (1969–) Palestine Liberation Organization (PLO); head of the Palestine National Council (1993–)

Israeli political leader Shimon Peres at a press conference in New York City in May 1991. Peres, who had served as Israel's prime minister in the mid-1980s, returned to that post in 1995 following the assassination of Yitzhak Rabin.

war, and in doing so it took possession of large expanses of Arab territory: the Sinai Peninsula and the Gaza Strip from Egypt, the West Bank of the Jordan River from Jordan, and the Golan Heights from Syria.

Although defense minister Moshe Dayan played a major role in Israel's victory, most Israelis considered Rabin the real hero, and he began to be talked about for a government post. His immediate desire was to become Israel's ambassador to the United States, his country's strongest supporter. Rabin received the appointment in 1968, and during the next five years he succeeded in getting the United States to continue supplying Israel with military assistance and other forms of aid.

When Rabin returned to Israel in 1973, he ran for a seat in Israel's parliament, the Knesset, as a member of the Labor party. The elections, scheduled for late October, had to be postponed when Egypt and Syria—who were still demanding that seized Arab lands be returned—made a surprise attack on Is-

rael on October 6. This date was Yom Kippur, the holiest day in the Jewish religious calendar, and the conflict became known as the Yom Kippur War. Israeli troops succeeded in driving back the invaders within two weeks, and United Nations Peacekeeping Forces were sent to the area to restore order.

When the postponed elections were finally held in December, Rabin and other Labor party candidates were victorious. In April 1974 Golda Meir resigned as prime minister and Rabin succeeded her. At 52, he became the youngest person, as well as the first native-born Israeli (*sabra*) to hold the post of prime minister.

Rabin served for three years, during which time he led efforts to strengthen defense forces and improve the economy. He also participated in a series of peace talks with Egypt that were mediated by U.S. Secretary of State Henry Kissinger. However, a political scandal involving family finances forced Rabin to leave his post as prime minister in 1977. For the next seven years he remained in parliament under a series of more conservative prime ministers. One of them was Menachem Begin, who signed a peace agreement, called the Camp David Accords, with President Anwar Sadat of Egypt in 1978.

When no party had a clear majority following national elections in 1984, a coalition (shared) government was formed. Following the terms of an agreement reached by party leaders, two Israeli politicians, Shimon Peres (pronounced *SHEE-moan PAIR-ez*) and the more conservative Yitzhak Shamir, served successive two-year terms as prime minister, while Rabin served as defense minister for the entire four years.

Peres was born in 1923 in a small Polish village that is now part of Belarus. (Its exact location is unknown.) His parents were enthusiastic Zionists, and in the early 1930s the family emigrated to Palestine. There Peres became an active member of Zionist youth organizations and, like Rabin, he was sent to an agricultural school to prepare for a future career as a farmer.

After graduating from the agricultural school in 1941, Peres received further training at a *kibbutz,* or farming settlement, instead of joining the military. He then founded a new kibbutz in the Jordan Valley of Palestine and worked there as one of its leaders. Peres had continued his strong involvement in Zionist organizations, and those connections led to his appointment in 1947 as director of manpower for Haganah, the Jewish Palestinian defense organization. Following the establishment of the state of Israel in May 1948 and the creation of the Israeli Defense Forces, Peres became a member of the IDF and served as head of the naval department in the defense ministry.

In 1949 Israel's first prime minister, David Ben-Gurion, sent Peres to Washington, D.C., as the head of a mission to secure U.S. military aid. Peres remained there for several years and won praise for his skill in negotiating continued aid for his country. During this time he also continued his formal education by attending classes at several American institutions, including Harvard University.

Peres returned to Israel early in 1952 and continued working in the defense ministry, where he was soon appointed director-general. In his seven years in that post, Peres masterminded the development of Israel's weapons industry and nuclear research. He also created close ties between his country and France, which became the main supplier to Israel of weapons that it could not produce.

Peres's formal political career began in 1959, when he won a seat in the Israeli parliament. Prime Minister Ben-Gurion chose Peres to join his cabinet as deputy minister of defense, and Peres held that office for seven

years. In 1962, on a return visit to the United States, he persuaded President John F. Kennedy to sell major defensive weapons systems to Israel. By 1967, the United States had replaced France as Israel's leading supplier of arms.

After leaving his post as deputy defense minister in 1965, Peres continued to serve in parliament. In 1969 he rejoined the cabinet, this time under the new prime minister, Golda Meir, and during the next four years held a series of positions relating to immigration, economic development, transportation, and communications.

Peres had now emerged as the leader of the Labor party, but in 1974, following Golda Meir's resignation as prime minister, he lost the party leadership to Yitzhak Rabin. When Rabin became prime minister that year, he appointed Peres to the post of defense minister as a gesture of reconciliation.

Nevertheless, bad feeling persisted between Peres and Rabin even as Peres worked to strengthen Israel's defense forces. Following Rabin's forced resignation in 1977, Peres left his cabinet position to become chairman of the Labor party. During the next seven years, Peres continued to serve in parliament, along with Rabin, while he worked to strengthen the party.

Peres and Rabin returned to power in 1984, when Peres became prime minister and Rabin defense minister. As prime minister, Peres guided Israel through a severe economic crisis and improved the country's diplomatic relations with other nations. Putting their hard feelings aside, Peres and Rabin joined to negotiate a withdrawal of Israeli troops from Lebanon, where the troops had served since 1982 to prevent attacks against Israel from that country. However, Peres was unable to make progress in resolving the Arab-Israeli conflict.

At the end of his two-year term in 1986, Peres became both vice prime minister and foreign minister under his

Shimon Peres

BORN
August 16, 1923
Poland (now Belarus)

EDUCATION
Diploma, Ben Shemen Agricultural School, Tel Aviv; attended New York University, New School of Social Research (New York), and Harvard University (1949–52)

OCCUPATION
Politician

MAJOR ACCOMPLISHMENTS
Chairman of the Israeli Labor party (1977–); member, Israeli parliament; holder of a series of cabinet posts, including head of defense and foreign ministries; prime minister of Israel (1984–86,1995–)

Yasir Arafat, head of the Palestine Liberation Organization, arrives in the United States on September 12, 1993, for his historic meeting in Washington, D.C., with Israeli leaders Yitzhak Rabin and Shimon Peres. The next day, Arafat, Rabin, and Peres signed the "Declaration of Principles on Interim Self-Government Arrangements," an important step toward establishing peace in the Middle East.

successor, Yitzhak Shamir, while continuing as party chairman. Rabin, who continued as defense minister, faced a major challenge in late 1987, when Palestinian Arabs in the Israeli-occupied territories began a major uprising, called an *intifada*. The uprising was violent, and Rabin responded with violent counterattacks.

For years the Palestinians had been demanding the creation of their own state, which had never occurred in spite of the 1947 UN declaration. Their demands were represented by a group called the Palestine Liberation Organization (PLO), led by a Palestinian political leader named Yasir Arafat.

Arafat had been born in Cairo, Egypt, in 1929 to a successful Arab merchant. Arafat's mother died when he was four years old, and he went to live with an uncle in her home city of Jerusalem, then the capital of Palestine. The daily conflict between native Arabs and immigrant Jews made a strong impression on Arafat, and when he returned to Cairo in his early teens he was a strong supporter of Arab rights. By the time Israel declared its

independence in 1948, Arafat had already become involved in smuggling arms into Palestine to help the Arabs while he continued his studies at the University of Fuad (now Cairo University).

Arafat claims that he tried to fight in the Arab-Israeli conflict that followed Israel's independence, but he was turned down by Palestinian soldiers—the very soldiers to whom he had provided weapons. His anger at this refusal was intensified by the peace settlement in 1949, which put aside the issue of Palestinian statehood and left close to a million Palestinians without a homeland.

While continuing his studies in engineering at the university, Arafat participated in a student military training program and became president of the Palestinian Students' League. After graduating in 1956, he worked for a while in Egypt and then immigrated to Kuwait, where he established a successful engineering company.

In college Arafat had often discussed forming a political group to evict Israel from Palestine, and sometime in the late 1950s he and several colleagues founded such a group: the Palestinian National Liberation Movement. The first letters of this name in Arabic spell *HATAF*, the Arabic word for "death," and the organization soon became known by its initials in reverse: Fatah.

Fatah encouraged an armed struggle against Israel through the publication of an underground magazine, *Filistinuna (Our Palestine)*. At the same time Fatah distanced itself from the leadership of Arab nations, which at that time were stressing Arab unity rather than independent action against Israel.

By the early 1960s Arafat had given up his business to run Fatah, and beginning in 1965 he launched the first of a series of raids into Israeli territory. As these raids increased, Fatah's reputation as a major force grew among Palestinians and their sympathizers.

Arab-Israeli relations grew even worse following Israel's victory in the Six-Day War of 1967 and its capture of Arab land. Following the war, Arafat and Fatah began operating in the Israeli-occupied territories. In one major battle with Israeli troops in Jordan in the spring of 1968, Fatah inflicted heavy casualties on the Israelis, and this victory brought Arafat and his organization international attention.

In 1964 Fatah had joined with other Palestinian liberation groups in forming the Palestine Liberation Organization (PLO), an umbrella group. Five years later, following a string of military successes by Fatah, Arafat became chairman of the PLO. Under his leadership it grew into a powerful organization as it masterminded repeated guerrilla attacks against Israel.

The PLO launched its attacks from several adjoining Arab nations, but by the early 1970s it was using Lebanon as its headquarters. In addition to direct attacks on Israel, the PLO became involved in terrorist operations in other countries to call attention to the Palestinian cause, most notably at the 1972 Olympic Games in Munich, where PLO fighters assassinated Israeli athletes.

Although much of the world viewed Arafat as a criminal, he now had the grudging respect of most Arab leaders, who acknowledged his right to speak as the sole representative of the Palestinian cause. The United Nations allowed the PLO observer status at its sessions, and the General Assembly passed a resolution supporting the right of Palestinians to self-determination.

The PLO's activities were disrupted somewhat following the breakout of a bloody civil war in Lebanon in the mid-1970s, but the organization continued to launch damaging raids against Israel. Finally, in June 1982, Israel fought back by invading Lebanon

to crush PLO operations there. Arafat and the PLO were forced to flee in a humiliating defeat. When they tried to return later that year, they were pushed out again, not only by Israelis but also by Arabs opposed to Arafat.

Arafat and the PLO were forced to take refuge in Tunis, the capital of Tunisia, where they established new headquarters. During the 1980s, in an effort to reestablish his ties with leaders of the Arab world, Arafat held a series of talks with King Hussein of Jordan, a moderate Arab who had forced the PLO out of his country some years earlier. Arafat hoped that he could join with Jordan in negotiating a peace settlement with Israel, but Jordan seemed unwilling to involve itself with Arafat.

With the outbreak of the *intifada* uprising among Palestinians in December 1987, Arafat and the PLO gained new attention and respect in the Arab world. Many people, most of them young Palestinians, participating in the uprising were members of Fatah, and they looked to Arafat as their leader. Arafat responded by giving the *intifada* his full support. He now believed that the Palestinians were in a strong position to negotiate a peaceful settlement with the Israel government.

Israel and its leaders had consistently opposed the PLO's demands for a Palestinian state, claiming that such a state would threaten Israel's security. By the spring of 1988, however, as the *intifada* continued, Defense Minister Rabin had come to realize that the Palestinians' demands would not simply vanish.

While continuing to oppose the creation of an independent Palestine, Rabin made two moves toward peace: He suggested that Israel might give Jordan authority over some of the territory that it still occupied. (The Sinai Peninsula had been returned to Egypt in 1982.) He also indicated that he was willing to negotiate with the

Yitzhak Rabin

BORN
March 1, 1922
Jerusalem, Palestine (now Israel)

DIED
November 4, 1995
Tel Aviv, Israel

EDUCATION
Diploma, Kadoorie Agricultural High School

OCCUPATION
Politician

MAJOR ACCOMPLISHMENTS
Chief of staff, Israeli Defense Forces (1964–68); Israeli ambassador to the U.S. (1968–73); defense minister (1984–90); prime minister of Israel (1974–77, 1992–95)

PLO if it would acknowledge Israel's right to exist as a nation.

Rabin's stand put him in conflict with the more conservative Prime Minister Shamir, who remained firmly opposed to any compromises with the PLO. Shamir's stand prevailed, although Rabin continued as defense minister until 1990. That year Shamir formed a new government, and Rabin was ousted in Shamir's attempts to maintain a strongly conservative government that took a hard line against the PLO.

Meanwhile, in November 1988, the Palestine National Council, the PLO's parliament-in-exile, had adopted a resolution proclaiming the existence of an independent Palestinian state on the West Bank and the Gaza Strip. The resolution also acknowledged the existence of Israel as a permanent state.

The next month, in a speech to a special session of the UN General Assembly in Geneva, Switzerland, Arafat declared that the PLO was renouncing terrorism and that it supported the rights of "all parties" in the Middle East, including Palestine, Israel, and their neighbors, to live in "peace and security."

There were positive responses throughout the world to Arafat's declaration, and in the following months more than 70 countries formally recognized Palestine as an independent state. Israel and its major allies were still skeptical of Arafat's intentions, although the United States expressed an interest in supporting diplomatic negotiations between Israelis and the PLO.

A major shift in Israel's position occurred in 1992, when Shamir left office as prime minister. He was succeeded by Yitzhak Rabin, who had taken back control of the Labor party from Shimon Peres. With the support of Peres, now foreign minister, Rabin im-

mediately began to work toward a negotiated peace settlement.

After a series of secret talks between Israeli and PLO representatives in Norway in the summer of 1993—talks in which Peres played an active role—a breakthrough followed: Israel agreed to work toward Palestinian self-rule in the occupied territories. Rabin took a further step toward peace by writing a letter to Arafat stating Israel's willingness to recognize the PLO as the sole representative of the Palestinian people. He also indicated that he was willing to begin peace negotiations with the PLO. A "Declaration of Principles on Interim Self-Government Arrangements" was drawn up by PLO and Israeli representatives, and on September 13, 1993, this historic document was signed in Washington, D.C., by Rabin and Arafat.

Peace negotiations were in progress a year later when Rabin, Arafat, and Peres were announced as the winners of the 1994 Nobel Peace Prize for their joint efforts to create peace in the Middle East. Not long after that announcement, in late October 1994, Israel signed a peace treaty with Jordan, and in the following months the two countries began to establish not only diplomatic relations but also a series of cooperative programs involving such areas as tourism, economic development, and environmental protection.

In September 1995 Rabin signed another historic agreement that expanded Palestinian self-rule in the West Bank. It also authorized the withdrawal of Israeli troops from many West Bank settlements.

Although Israel's peace overtures were praised throughout the world, they were not supported by all Israelis. A large number of conservatives in Israel were strongly opposed to making peace with the PLO, and they bitterly criti-

cized Rabin, calling him a traitor. On November 4, 1995, Rabin was assassinated by an Israeli right-wing extremist as he left a peace rally in Tel Aviv. He was survived by his wife of nearly 50 years and two grown children.

Shimon Peres succeeded Rabin as prime minister and inherited the ongoing task of establishing peace between Israel and its Arab neighbors. In addition to the Nobel Peace Prize, Peres has received many other awards, including the French Legion of Honor. He is married and has two grown sons.

Yasir Arafat continues to lead the PLO and its Palestine National Council as they work toward the creation of an independent Palestine. He lives in the Gaza Strip with his wife, a Palestinian Christian whom he married in 1991.

FURTHER READING

"Arafat, Yasir." In *Current Biography Yearbook 1994.* New York: H. W. Wilson, 1995.

Golan, Matti. *The Road to Peace: A Biography of Shimon Peres.* New York: Warner, 1989.

Hart, Alan. *Arafat: A Political Biography.* Bloomington: Indiana University Press, 1989.

Kiernan, Thomas. *Arafat: The Man and the Myth.* New York: Norton, 1976.

Peres, Shimon. *Battling for Peace: A Memoir.* New York: Random House, 1995.

"Peres, Shimon." In *Current Biography Yearbook 1995.* New York: H. W. Wilson, 1996.

Rabin, Yitzhak. *The Rabin Memoirs.* Boston: Little, Brown, 1979.

"Rabin, Yitzhak." In *Current Biography Yearbook 1995.* New York: H. W. Wilson, 1996.

Slater, Robert. *Rabin of Israel.* New York: St. Martin's, 1993.

Joseph Rotblat

1995

T he village of Pugwash, Nova Scotia, has only 800 inhabitants, but thanks to the peacemaking efforts of a physicist named Joseph Rotblat and several of his associates, Pugwash is now famous throughout the world. The rise to fame of the tiny town began in 1955, when a wealthy American industrialist named Cyrus Eaton made a gesture for peace.

Eaton had been born poor in Pugwash in the late 19th century. He had gone to the United States to make his fortune, and while becoming a multimillionaire he also became a humanitarian. By 1955 Cyrus Eaton's main humanitarian interest had become the achievement of world peace, and he was determined to do all that he could to make it a reality.

In that year, two world-famous men, German-born physicist Albert Einstein and British philosopher-mathematician Bertrand Russell, along with Rotblat and several other scientists, called for a conference on science and world peace. When Eaton read about their proposal, he invited them to hold the conference at his Pugwash estate, which he had built after making his fortune. The invitation was accepted, and the first gathering, organized by Rotblat, was held there in 1957. The conferences became an annual affair, attended not only by scientists but also by prominent thinkers in other fields. For his role in establishing and

Internationally prominent scientists gather in Pugwash, Nova Scotia, in 1957 to attend the first annual Pugwash Conference on Science and World Affairs. Organized by physicist Joseph Rotblat, the conferences have given birth to major peacemaking efforts, including the creation of nuclear arms limitations treaties.

Josef Rotblat (right) congratulates philosopher and peace activist Bertrand Russell, a cofounder of the Pugwash Conference, at a celebration on his 90th birthday in 1962.

running the Pugwash Conferences on Science and World Affairs for nearly forty years, Rotblat received the 1995 Nobel Peace Prize.

Joseph Rotblat's quest for world peace predates the first Pugwash conference. In fact, it goes back a decade, to December 1944. For several years Rotblat had been working in Los Alamos, New Mexico, on a top-secret effort to build the first atomic bomb. World War II was raging in Europe and the Far East, and the United States and Great Britain wanted to beat Germany in developing the bomb.

Germany had invaded Rotblat's homeland of Poland in 1939, and he was only too happy to help defeat the Germans. However, in December 1944 he learned that the war would be over before Germany could develop its own bomb, and he worried that the U.S.-made bomb would be used on other targets. He concluded that the bomb was dangerous and wrong, and he abruptly resigned from the project. His crusade against atomic weapons had begun.

Joseph Rotblat was born in Warsaw, Poland, in 1908 to a prosperous Jewish businessman and his wife. He attended the Free University of Poland after graduating from secondary school and earned a master's degree there in 1932. He continued his studies in physics at the University of Warsaw and received a doctorate in 1938.

In 1939, as war threatened to erupt in Europe, Rotblat won a fellowship to study at the University of Liverpool in England with the celebrated physicist James Chadwick. As he was preparing to leave Poland, an important event in the history of science occurred: two German chemists devised a way to split the uranium atom, a process called nuclear fission that caused the release of an enormous amount of energy.

After hearing of this event, physicists in major European universities immediately began trying to cause a chain reaction of such explosions, in order to release a continuous powerful stream of what became known as atomic, or nuclear, energy. There were several possible uses for such energy, but as war drew closer, the creation of a powerful bomb powered by nuclear fission seemed the most important goal.

Because he had limited funds, Rotblat had to leave his wife behind when he went to Liverpool in the summer of 1939. By the time he was able to send for her in early September, Germany had invaded Poland. His wife disappeared, and Rotblat never saw her again. She is believed to have died in a concentration camp.

Rotblat tried to ease his sorrow by devoting all his attention to his work. With Chadwick he investigated the possibility of creating an atomic bomb. By 1941 Rotblat and several other scientists had independently proved that the necessary chain reactions could be produced and that such a bomb was possible. Learning of this possibility, the British and U.S. governments set up a joint research effort, called the Manhattan Project, in Los Alamos, New Mexico, to work on the development of the A-bomb, as it was called.

Rotblat went to Los Alamos to join the Manhattan Project, but his conscience increasingly bothered him: he was troubled by the many lives that would be destroyed by an A-bomb explosion. Finally, in December 1944, he resigned before the project was completed, for he was convinced that such a weapon should never be used.

Rotblat returned to Liverpool to work in his laboratory. Less than a year later, the United States dropped atomic bombs on the Japanese cities of Hiroshima and Nagasaki, ending World War II—and officially beginning the nuclear age. Rotblat was distressed by the news of the explosions, but by now he had shifted the focus of his work from weapons to medicine. He began to investigate the relationship between radioactive fallout—particles and gases released by the explosion of nuclear weapons—and human disease, specifically cancer. His research earned him a second doctoral degree, from the University of Liverpool, in the late 1940s.

By now Rotblat was a British citizen. He moved to London, where he continued working on his cancer and radioactivity studies at St. Bartholomew's Hospital. He was now convinced that fallout from nuclear explosions was deadly and posed a great threat to humankind. He was therefore dismayed as the United States, the Soviet Union, and other nations began a nuclear arms race and tested increasingly powerful weapons that released enormous quantities of radioactive matter.

In the early 1950s Rotblat joined a growing number of thoughtful and highly educated men and women in the sciences and other fields who were expressing alarm over the nuclear arms race. In 1954 Rotblat met Bertrand Russell, a leading opponent of nuclear weapons. Russell suggested that an international conference be held to discuss the issue. That suggestion resulted in the 1955 public proclamation signed by Rotblat, Russell, and Einstein. Two years later the first Pugwash Conference on Science and World Affairs was held in Nova Scotia.

Twenty-two internationally known scientists from countries throughout the world came to Pugwash in 1957. After several days of discussions, they issued a report listing the dangers of nuclear testing, calling for arms control, and asking scientists to accept social responsibility for their actions.

With Rotblat serving as secretary-general of the conferences, they became an annual affair. At each meeting, the latest research on the dangers of nuclear weapons was presented and nuclear-related activities of countries throughout the world were reviewed. The conferences attracted the attention of world leaders and played a major role in the growing movement for a ban on all nuclear weapons.

Slowly but surely, the Pugwash conferences brought about change: An international treaty banning aboveground testing of nuclear weapons was signed in 1963. Peace talks to end hostilities between the United States and North Vietnam were begun in the late 1960s, thanks to pressure from Pugwash. A treaty limiting nuclear missile systems was signed in 1972 by the United States and the Soviet Union—the first of a series of agreements to limit nuclear arms that were made between the two nations during the next two decades.

Rotblat's office at St. Bartholomew's was the Pugwash headquarters for many years. He organized each conference and kept careful records of the proceedings. In 1988 he was elected president of Pugwash. He retired from St. Bartholomew's in 1976 and continues to live in London.

In October 1995, a month before his 87th birthday, Joseph Rotblat was named the winner of that year's Nobel Peace Prize. According to the Peace Prize Committee, the award was made not only to honor Rotblat's work with Pugwash but also to protest continuing nuclear arms testing in the world—specifically, recent explosions set off by France and China, the only countries that still have nuclear weapons testing programs. Rothblat donated half of the $1 million award to the Pugwash conferences.

FURTHER READING

Landau, Susan. "Joseph Rotblat: From Fission Research to a Prize for Peace." *Scientific American*, January 1996, pp. 38–39.

Marshall, Eliot. "Physicist Wins Nobel Peace Prize." *Science*, October 20, 1995, p. 372.

Stevenson, Richard W. "Nobel Prize Goes to A-Bomb Scientist Who Turned Critic." *New York Times*, October 14, 1995, p. 3.

Joseph Rotblat

BORN
November 4, 1908
Warsaw, Poland

EDUCATION
B.S. and M.S., Free University of Poland (1932); D.Sci., University of Warsaw (1938); Ph.D., University of Liverpool (1949)

OCCUPATION
Physicist; antinuclear activist

MAJOR ACCOMPLISHMENTS
Cofounded the Pugwash Conferences on Science and World Affairs (1957–), an annual gathering of prominent scientists opposed to nuclear weapons; secretary-general of Pugwash (1957– 73); president (1988–)

Carlos Felipe Ximenes Belo

José Ramos-Horta

1996

José Ramos-Horta (left) and Bishop Carlos Felipe Ximenes Belo display their 1996 Nobel Peace Prize certificates and medals at the award ceremony. The two men shared the prize for their longtime efforts to bring peace to their native East Timor.

The Southeast Asian nation of Indonesia is a collection of many small islands in the Indian and Pacific oceans. For centuries the various islands of Indonesia were ruled as colonies, some by the Portuguese and some by the Dutch. After World War II ended in 1945, these islands gradually secured their independence from European rule and became provinces of the new nation of Indonesia.

By 1975, only the island of Timor was not entirely under Indonesian rule. The western half of the island, a former Dutch colony, had been turned over to Indonesia by the Dutch in 1949, but the eastern half was still a Portuguese colony. Finally, in early 1975, Portugal abandoned the colony and civil war erupted. The Roman Catholic majority population wanted independence, but many of the minority Muslim population wanted to become part of Indonesia, a largely Muslim nation. As warfare continued, Indonesian troops marched into East Timor, as the region was now called, and annexed it as a province of Indonesia.

Many East Timorese resisted this takeover, and they fought against the Indonesian soldiers who continued to occupy their land. In response, Indonesia tried to put down all opposition to its rule by invoking harsh and violent measures against the people. The fighting has continued for more than 20 years, and an estimated one-third of East Timor's population has been killed.

Until the late 1980s, few people outside East Timor were aware of what was happening there. One man who changed that was a Roman Catholic priest named Carlos Felipe Ximenes Belo. In 1988 Belo, the newly appointed bishop of East Timor, decided that it was time for him to make the world take notice of atrocities in his native country.

For many years, Belo had distanced himself from the harsh government as much as he could, quietly ministering to the needs of East Timor's large Roman Catholic population and trying to give them hope. He knew only too well what was happening: over and over again, he heard stories about attacks against the East Timorese—family members killed at random, crops and livestock seized, villages burned, all in an effort to stamp out resistance to Indonesian rule.

Belo had been born in Portuguese Timor in 1948, and he loved the land and its people. His parents were rice farmers in a small village about 100 miles east of Dili, then the capital of the colony, and as a child he drove water buffalo in the rice fields. But Belo did not want to be a farmer: he was studious by nature, and his mother encouraged his interest in books and religion. At the age of 20, he traveled to

Lisbon, Portugal, to enter a Roman Catholic seminary there, and eventually he decided to become a priest. After many years of study, in Lisbon as well as at seminaries in Rome and the Portuguese colony of Macao, Belo was ordained in 1981.

Belo returned to East Timor that year to become the head of a seminary near the town of Baucau, where thousands of Indonesian troops were quartered to keep order. Belo had, of course, known of the Indonesian takeover of his homeland while he was abroad, but he had not realized the full extent of the horror that the new government had inflicted on his people. Traveling around the countryside, he discovered that many villages had no male residents; they had been forcibly removed and made to fight against the independence movement.

But Belo kept silent, believing that it was his duty to nurture the spiritual life of the people, not to join in political movements, even though other priests on the island were openly sympathetic to those fighting for independence. During the 1980s, Belo was given increasing authority within the Roman Catholic Church in East Timor, in large part because of his non-involvement in politics, and in 1988 he was named bishop of East Timor, the highest church post on the island.

As a bishop, Belo decided that he could be silent no more; he had to speak out. He approached military authorities on the island about their treatment of his people, but he was rebuffed and told to mind his own business. If he did not, he was warned, he would be killed. Ignoring their warnings, he began condemning human rights abuses in statements read during church services. In early 1989 he sent a letter to the United Nations secretary-general, Javier Pérez de Cuellar, describing the injustices occurring in East Timor and asking that the UN sponsor

a referendum (vote) in East Timor on independence. But there was no response; the annexation of East Timor had happened years earlier, and the leading Western nations had no desire to antagonize Indonesia.

On November 12, 1991, the plight of Belo's people was made terribly clear to him. That morning, several thousand young East Timorese began marching to a cemetery near the bishop's residence in Dili. They were peacefully protesting the recent government killing of a member of the independence movement. Suddenly government troops began shooting, and scores of wounded protesters ran into Belo's garden seeking refuge. Without hesitation, he took in several hundred, many of them teenagers, and saw that they received medical attention. He then went to the cemetery and was horrified to find bullet-riddled bodies of protesters lying everywhere, even in the small chapel on the cemetery grounds. At that moment, Belo promised himself that such disregard for human life had to stop.

Secretly cooperating with followers of José Ramos-Horta and other East Timorese political activists, he helped smuggle two witnesses of the massacre to Geneva, Switzerland, where they testified before the UN Human Rights Commission about the systematic extermination of their people and culture. In the face of death threats and assassination attempts, Belo began calling more openly upon the Indonesian government to end its persecution of the East Timorese. He became a hero to the people, and as a consequence membership in the Roman Catholic Church in East Timor more than doubled over the next few years.

Gradually the story of what was happening in East Timor was picked up by journalists in the West, and governments and organizations began responding. Indonesia was criticized pub-

Carlos Felipe Ximenes Belo

BORN
1948
Wailacalma, Portuguese Timor (now East Timor)

EDUCATION
Attended local schools; studied for the priesthood at Roman Catholic seminaries in Lisbon, Macao, and Rome (1968–81)

OCCUPATION
Roman Catholic priest

MAJOR ACCOMPLISHMENTS
Bishop of East Timor (1988–); led efforts to end mistreatment of the East Timor population by the Indonesian government

José Ramos-Horta

BORN

December 26, 1949
Dili, Portuguese Timor (now
East Timor)

EDUCATION

Attended local schools and
universities in Europe and the
United States

OCCUPATION

Journalist and political activist

**MAJOR
ACCOMPLISHMENTS**

Led campaign to gain independence for East Timor and to draw
international attention to mistreatment of the East Timor
population by the Indonesian
government

licly by high officials of several nations
for its failure to preserve human rights.
The prisoner-welfare organization
Amnesty International issued a report
that documented torture on the island.
In the United States, a major weapons
supplier to Indonesia, Congress passed
legislation barring the sale of small
arms and crowd-control equipment to
that nation, which had been using
them against the East Timorese.

The Indonesian government finally responded to international pressure
by setting up a commission to study
human-rights abuses in East Timor.
One of the first cases it investigated
was the 1995 killing of six unarmed
civilians by soldiers near Dili. Two of
the soldiers were court-martialed and
given brief jail terms—a relatively light
punishment but notable because this
was the first time that government
troops had been held accountable for
their treatment of the East Timorese.
In the meantime, further appeals from
Belo to the United Nations were being
heeded. The UN began sponsoring a
series of negotiations with Portuguese
and Indonesian officials to discuss op-
tions for peace in East Timor.

As Belo continued to press for an
end to human-rights abuses, political
activist José Ramos-Horta remained
firmly committed to gaining independence for East Timor. Ramos-Horta
had been an outspoken supporter of
the independence movement since
1975, when Indonesian troops had
begun taking over his country.

Ramos-Horta was born in Portuguese Timor in 1949. His father was
a Portuguese political activist who had
been deported to the island; his mother
was Timorese. Ramos-Horta attended
local schools and then studied for extended periods in Europe. As an ado-
lescent he had supported independence
for the Portuguese colony, and by 1975
he had become a leader of the Revolutionary Front for an Independent East

Timor, an organization known as
Fretilin for short.

Soon after the Indonesian annexation, Ramos-Horta and other Fretilin
leaders went into self-imposed exile
abroad, where they continued to press
for independence. Ramos-Horta lived
for a while in New York City, where he
attended graduate school and worked
as a journalist. He later moved to Australia, where he has continued his journalistic career and also remained active
in Fretilin, which supports uprisings
and guerrilla warfare among the East
Timorese.

For their work in drawing attention to the plight of East Timor, Carlos
Belo and José Ramos-Horta were
named joint winners of the 1996
Nobel Peace Prize. Both men continue
their work to resolve the crisis in East
Timor. Belo remains committed to
ending violence and establishing respect for human rights, while Ramos-
Horta insists that only independence
will satisfy the East Timorese.

FURTHER READING

"East Timor Activists Win Nobel Prize."
Christian Century, October 30, 1996, pp.
1031-32.

Raffaele, Paul. "Champion of a Forgotten
People [Belo]." *Reader's Digest*, February
1997, pp. 185-94.

Tomasky, Michael. "The Low-Profile Laureate [Ramos-Horta]." *New York*, November 25, 1996, pp. 20-21.

Jody Williams and the International Campaign to Ban Landmines

1997

O f all the weapons devised by mankind, land mines, invented in the mid-19th century, are among the most deadly. Without warning, these explosive devices, shallowly buried in the earth, can be set off by a mere footstep, killing or maiming anyone nearby. Land mines have been used in warfare throughout the world, and they are unique among weaponry: years after a conflict, when once-warring nations are again at peace, land mines planted long ago to kill the enemy live on undetected below ground, ready to explode without warning if anyone walks over them.

Humanitarian aid worker Jody Williams learned first-hand about the terrible legacy of land mines in the early 1980s, during a mission to wartorn El Salvador on behalf of a Los Angeles–based aid group. Williams's job was to obtain artificial limbs for children who had lost arms and legs from exploding land mines.

Williams was deeply troubled by the sight of so many horribly wounded children, and by the knowledge that even more young victims had not survived at all: small children are usually killed outright by land-mine explosions. Nor was there any foreseeable end to the catastrophe: land mines kept on being planted in El Salvador and other warring nations in Central America, causing destruction, crippling, and death.

And Central America was just one of many regions with land-mine victims. In the Southeast Asian nation of Cambodia, for example, land mines had killed thousands and left an estimated 40,000 people missing limbs. There were similar statistics from other wartorn nations in Asia, Africa, and the Middle East.

During the 1980s, Williams continued to work with land-mine victims as an employee of other humanitarian aid organizations, and her frustration grew. From a study by the International Red Cross, she learned that some 100 million land mines were buried throughout the world. Each year they claimed an estimated 26,000 victims, nearly all of them civilians.

After nearly a decade of helping land-mine survivors, Williams decided that the only way to end such pointless suffering was to find and destroy every single land mine in the world and to ban their future use.

Such goals seemed hopeless. Digging up land mines is a dangerous and painstaking task—how could *100 million* of them be found and destroyed? And it hardly seemed likely that military leaders would allow their nations to give up

Jody Williams

BORN

October 9, 1950
Rutland, Vermont

EDUCATION

B.A., University of Vermont
(1972); M.A., Johns Hopkins
School of Advanced International
Studies (1984)

OCCUPATION

Humanitarian aid worker and
human rights advocate

**MAJOR
ACCOMPLISHMENTS**

As founding coordinator (1991) of
the International Campaign
to Ban Landmines (ICBL), led
worldwide effort to destroy all land
mines, and ban their production
and use

As coordinator of the International Campaign to Ban Landmines, Jody Williams has created worldwide awareness of the dangers of land mine use. The organization's efforts led to the signing of the first international treaty to ban land mine production and use in 1997.

the use of a weapon that had been so effective in waging war. But Jody Williams was determined to achieve her goals.

Williams was no stranger to achievement—or to a commitment to ease human suffering. Born in a small town in Vermont in 1950, Williams felt herself drawn at an early age to helping the defenseless. For years she looked after a handicapped younger brother and defended him against schoolyard taunts.

At the University of Vermont, Williams majored in psychology; she then studied to become a Spanish teacher. During this period she lived for a while in Mexico, where the extremes of poverty and wealth disturbed her.

Inspired to "save the world" by pursuing a career in international relations, Williams moved to Washington, D.C., in the late 1970s and enrolled at the Johns Hopkins School of Advanced International Studies to earn a master's degree. By the time she graduated, however, Williams knew that she did not want to join a large governmental organization. She wanted a job that brought her into immedi-

ate contact with people who needed help, and she began working for Medical Aid to El Salvador, a Los Angeles–based group founded by actor Ed Asner to help victims of that nation's long civil war.

After her work in El Salvador, Williams was associated with other relief organizations in Central America, where she continued to help land-mine victims. In 1991 she joined the Washington, D.C.–based Vietnam Veterans of America Foundation, another humanitarian association. The head of the foundation, Robert Muller, was a disabled Vietnam War veteran; like Williams, he had spent much of his professional career aiding land-mine victims.

In the fall of 1991, Williams and other foundation representatives met with officials of Medico International, a German medical aid group, to discuss their mutual efforts on behalf of land-mine victims. By this time, both Williams and Muller had decided that fitting artificial limbs was not enough. The only solution, impossible though it seemed, was to eliminate and ban all land mines.

At Muller's direction, Williams banded together with friends and associates from other humanitarian relief organizations to form the International Campaign to Ban Landmines, or ICBL. Their goals were twofold: to secure a total worldwide ban on land mines and to establishment an international fund to pay for the clearing of all land mines still present in the earth.

As the coordinator of ICBL, Williams encouraged nations throughout the world to create local, affiliated organizations to achieve these goals. During the next six years, ICBL grew into an alliance of more than 1,000 human rights, civic action, and veterans' groups worldwide, and it attracted the support of many well-known figures, including Diana, Princess of Wales.

ICBL's success was astonishing: Thanks to their efforts, the European Parliament passed a resolution in 1995 banning land mines in European Union member nations. A year later at the so-called G7 conference, a gathering of leaders of the world's major nations, the group called for an international ban. By 1997, more than 50 countries had prohibited the export of land mines, 15 countries had destroyed their stockpiles, 30 countries had banned the use of land mines, and 20 countries had banned their production. In addition, many countries had begun detecting and destroying land mines in their soil, using the resources of the ICBL land-mine clearance fund. ICBL had also persuaded major weapons manufacturers, such as Bofors in Sweden, to stop producing land mines.

On October 10, 1997, Jody Williams and the International Committee to Ban Landmines were declared the winners of that year's Nobel Peace Prize. In granting the award, the Nobel Committee praised Williams and ICBL for their outstanding accomplishments on behalf of peace in such a brief period.

At the time the award was announced, an international treaty to ban land mines was being drafted, again thanks to the efforts of ICBL. Only weeks later, on December 3, 1997, Jody Williams watched as leaders of 120 nations met in Ottawa, Canada, to sign the treaty—the first-ever comprehensive agreement banning global production and use of land mines. Williams rejoiced, but her happiness was tempered by the knowledge that the United States had not signed the treaty: President Bill Clinton refused because he claimed that land mines were still needed to protect U.S. troops in various parts of the world, especially on the border between North and South Korea.

Getting the U.S. to sign the treaty is a challenge that Williams willingly accepts. She vows to continue her crusade against these deadly weapons until every nation has signed the treaty—and the last land mine on earth has been destroyed.

FURTHER READING

DePalma, Anthony. "As U.S. Looks On, 120 Nations Sign Treaty Banning Land Mines." *New York Times*, December 4, 1997, pp. A1, A14.

Goldberg, Carey. "Peace Prize Goes to Land-Mine Opponents." *New York Times*, October 11, 1997, pp. A1, A6.

International Campaign to Ban Land-mines

FOUNDERS
Jody Williams, together with representatives of the Vietnam Veterans of America Foundation, Washington, D.C., and Medico International, Frankfurt, Germany

FOUNDING
1991
Washington, D.C.

HEADQUARTERS
Washington, D.C.

PURPOSE
To destroy all land mines in existence and to secure a worldwide ban on their production and use

MAJOR ACCOMPLISHMENTS
Elimination of many land mines in countries throughout the world and a ban on their production; led efforts to create the first international treaty banning land mines, signed by 120 nations in Ottawa, Canada, in 1997

Appendix 1
A Century of Nobel Peace Prize Winners

YEAR	WINNERS	BIRTH/DEATH	COUNTRY
1901	Jean Henri Dunant	1828–1910	Switzerland
	Frédéric Passy	1822–1912	France
1902	Élie Ducommun	1833–1906	Switzerland
	Albert Gobat	1843–1914	Switzerland
1903	William R. Cremer	1828–1908	Great Britain
1904	Institute of International Law	1873–	Switzerland
1905	Bertha von Suttner	1843–1914	Austria
1906	Theodore Roosevelt	1858–1919	United States
1907	Ernesto Moneta	1833–1918	Italy
	Louis Renault	1843–1918	France
1908	Klas Arnoldson	1844–1916	Sweden
	Fredrik Bajer	1837–1922	Denmark
1909	Auguste Beernaert	1829–1912	Belgium
	Paul d'Estournelles de Constant	1852–1924	France
1910	International Peace Bureau	1891–	Switzerland
1911	Tobias Asser	1838–1913	Netherlands
	Alfred Fried	1864–1921	Austria
1912	Elihu Root	1845–1937	United States
1913	Henri La Fontaine	1854–1943	Belgium
1917	International Committee of the Red Cross	1863–	Switzerland
1919	Woodrow Wilson	1856–1924	United States
1920	Léon Bourgeois	1851–1925	France
1921	Karl Branting	1860–1925	Sweden
	Christian Lange	1869–1938	Norway
1922	Fridtjof Nansen	1861–1930	Norway
1925	J. Austen Chamberlain	1863–1937	Great Britain
	Charles G. Dawes	1865–1951	United States
1926	Aristide Briand	1862–1932	France
	Gustav Stresemann	1878–1929	Germany
1927	Ferdinand Buisson	1841–1932	France
	Ludwig Quidde	1858–1941	Germany

YEAR	WINNERS	BIRTH/DEATH	COUNTRY
1929	Frank B. Kellogg	1856–1937	United States
1930	Nathan Söderblom	1866–1931	Sweden
1931	Jane Addams	1860–1935	United States
	Nicholas Murray Butler	1862–1947	United States
1933	Norman Angell	1873–1967	Great Britain
1934	Arthur Henderson	1863–1935	Great Britain
1935	Carl von Ossietzky	1889–1938	Germany
1936	Carlos Saavedra Lamas	1878–1959	Argentina
1937	Robert Cecil	1864–1958	Great Britain
1938	Nansen International Office for Refugees	1931–1939	Switzerland
1944	International Committee of the Red Cross	1863–	Switzerland
1945	Cordell Hull	1871–1955	United States
1946	Emily Greene Balch	1867–1961	United States
	John R. Mott	1865–1955	United States
1947	American Friends Service Committee	1917–	United States
	Friends Service Council	1927–	Great Britain
1949	John Boyd Orr	1880–1971	Great Britain
1950	Ralph J. Bunche	1904–1971	United States
1951	Léon Jouhaux	1879–1954	France
1952	Albert Schweitzer	1875–1965	France
1953	George C. Marshall	1880–1959	United States
1954	Office of the UN High Commissioner for Refugees	1951–	Switzerland
1957	Lester Pearson	1897–1972	Canada
1958	Dominique-Georges Pire	1910–1969	Belgium
1959	Philip Noel–Baker	1889–1982	Great Britain
1960	Albert Luthuli	1898(?)–1967	South Africa
1961	Dag Hammarskjöld	1905–1961	Sweden
1962	Linus Pauling	1901–1994	United States
1963	International Committee of the Red Cross	1863–	Switzerland
	League of Red Cross Societies	1919–	Switzerland
1964	Martin Luther King, Jr.	1929–1968	United States
1965	United Nations Children's Fund (UNICEF)	1946–	United States
1968	René Cassin	1887–1976	France
1969	International Labor Organization	1919–	Switzerland

YEAR	WINNERS	BIRTH/DEATH	COUNTRY
1970	Norman E. Borlaug	1914–	United States
1971	Willy Brandt	1913–1992	West Germany
1973	Henry Kissinger	1923–	United States
	Le Duc Tho	1911–1990	North Vietnam
1974	Seán MacBride	1904–1988	Republic of Ireland
	Eisaku Sato	1901–1975	Japan
1975	Andrei Sakharov	1921–1989	Soviet Union
1976	Mairead Corrigan	1944–	N. Ireland
	Betty Williams	1943–	N. Ireland
1977	Amnesty International	1961–	Great Britain
1978	Menachem Begin	1913–1992	Israel
	Anwar Sadat	1918–1981	Egypt
1979	Mother Teresa of Calcutta	1910–1997	India
1980	Adolfo Pérez Esquivel	1931–	Argentina
1981	Office of the UN High Commissioner for Refugees	1951–	Switzerland
1982	Alfonso García Robles	1911–	Mexico
	Alva Myrdal	1902–1986	Sweden
1983	Lech Walesa	1943–	Poland
1984	Desmond Tutu	1931–	South Africa
1985	International Physicians for the Prevention of Nuclear War	1980–	United States
1986	Elie Wiesel	1928–	United States
1987	Oscar Arias Sánchez	1940–	Costa Rica
1988	United Nations Peacekeeping Forces	1948–	United States
1989	The Dalai Lama	1935–	Tibet
1990	Mikhail Gorbachev	1931–	Soviet Union
1991	Aung San Suu Kyi	1945–	Myanmar
1992	Rigoberta Menchú	1959–	Guatemala
1993	F. W. de Klerk	1936–	South Africa
	Nelson Mandela	1918–	South Africa
1994	Yasir Arafat	1929–	Palestine
	Shimon Peres	1923–	Israel
	Yitzhak Rabin	1922–1995	Israel
1995	Joseph Rotblat	1908–	Great Britain
1996	Carlos Felipe Ximenes Belo	1948–	East Timor
	José Ramos-Horta	1946–	East Timor
1997	Jody Williams	1950–	United States
	International Campaign to Ban Landmines	1991–	United States

Appendix 2
A Short Peace Glossary

arbitration—the settlement of disputes by a neutral outsider, called an *arbiter*, or judge.

arms control—limiting, regulating, reducing, or eliminating a nation's armed forces and weapons.

conscientious objector—a person who refuses to participate in warfare for moral or religious reasons.

disarmament—giving up or reducing armed forces and weapons; supporters of *nuclear disarmament* want to ban all nuclear (atomic) weapons.

Geneva Conventions—a series of international agreements (the first was signed in 1864 in Geneva, Switzerland) providing for the humane treatment of prisoners of war.

internationalism—a policy of cooperation among nations; supporters of world government are called *internationalists*.

international law—a body of rules that regulate the rights of nations in their relations with one another.

pacifism—opposition to war or violence as a means of settling disputes; a *pacifist* is a person who supports pacifism.

Appendix 3
A Peace Timeline: Milestones on the Road to Peace

1625

Dutch jurist Hugo Grotius introduces the idea of international law in his book *The Law of War and Peace*

1668

Society of Friends (Quakers), first religious denomination created to work for peace, established in England by George Fox

1815

New York Peace Society founded; first nonreligious organization in the world dedicated to preserving peace; forerunner of the American Peace Society, established in 1828

1863

Red Cross Society founded in Geneva, Switzerland

1864

First Geneva Convention, guaranteeing humane treatment of prisoners of war, signed by 12 nations

1867

International League of Peace and Freedom founded in Paris

1873

Institute of International Law founded in Ghent, Belgium

1889

Interparliamentary Union founded in Paris

1891

International Peace Bureau founded in Rome

1899

First Hague Conference, international peace conference attended by representatives of 26 nations

1899

Permanent Court of Arbitration (the Hague Tribunal)—the first international arbitration court in the world—founded at The Hague, the Netherlands

1901

First Nobel Peace Prizes awarded

1907

Second Hague Conference, international peace conference attended by representatives of 44 nations

1915

Women's International League of Peace and Freedom (WILPF) founded at The Hague, the Netherlands

1919

League of Nations founded in Paris by the Versailles Peace Treaty, which ended World War I; although the League became inactive in 1938, it did not formally end until 1946

1921

Permanent Court of International Justice (World Court) founded in Geneva, Switzerland

1922

Washington Conference: U.S., Great Britain, France, Italy, and Japan sign a series of international arms-control agreements—the first in the world—in Washington, D.C.

1928

Kellogg-Briand Pact, also known as the Pact of Paris, signed by 15 nations, including the U.S.; the treaty renounced warfare as a means of resolving difficulties— the first such international agreement in the world

1945

United Nations founded in San Francisco

International Court of Justice, principal judicial arm of the UN, founded as successor to Permanent Court of International Justice

1946

U.S. presents Baruch Plan, the first proposal to control nuclear weapons, to UN General Assembly

1948

United Nations Peacekeeping Forces, world's first international "peace army," established by UN Security Council in New York City

1952

UN General Assembly establishes the UN Disarmament Commission to work for arms control among UN-member nations

1953

U.S. proposes Atoms for Peace, leading to the creation of the International Atomic Energy Agency, a UN-sponsored organization, in 1957

1961

UN-sponsored treaty establishes Antarctica as nuclear-free

1963

Limited Test Ban Treaty, prohibiting the testing of nuclear weapons in the atmosphere, in outer space, or underwater, signed by the U.S., the U.S.S.R., and Great Britain

1967

Treaty of Tlatelolco, signed by 21 Latin American nations in Mexico City, bans nuclear weapons in Central and South America

1968

United Nations approves Treaty on the Non-Proliferation of Nuclear Weapons, which prohibits nations from giving nuclear weapons to other nations; ratified by more than 120 nations, the treaty went into effect in 1970

1969

U.S. and U.S.S.R. begin SALT—Strategic Arms Limitation Talks

1972

First SALT Treaty (SALT I) signed by U.S. and U.S.S.R., limiting numbers of certain types of weapons that each nation can maintain

1975

Helsinki Accords—series of agreements supporting international cooperation and human rights—signed by 36 nations, including U.S. and U.S.S.R.

1979

Second Salt Treaty (SALT II) signed by U.S. and U.S.S.R., imposing further limitations on numbers of weapons held by each nation

1987

U.S. and U.S.S.R. sign the INF Treaty, which bans intermediate-range nuclear forces; to ensure compliance, the treaty allows representatives from each nation to inspect the other's weapons supplies

1990

Treaty on Conventional Armed Forces in Europe, providing for the destruction of numerous nonnuclear weapons in Europe, signed by U.S., U.S.S.R., and 20 other nations; treaty went into effect in 1992

1991

First Strategic Arms Reduction Treaty—START I—signed by U.S. and U.S.S.R., reducing number of long-range nuclear missiles held by each nation

Collapse of U.S.S.R. ends 45-year-long Cold War with U.S. and other Western nations

1993

Second Strategic Arms Reduction Treaty—START II—signed by U.S. and Russia, further reducing nuclear-missile holdings

1996

Comprehensive Test Ban Treaty (CTBT), signed by U.S. and Russia, bans all nuclear weapons tests and other nuclear explosions; to date, 146 nations have signed the treaty

Appendix 4

Major International Organizations Working for Peace

Albert Einstein Peace Prize Foundation
60 Revere Drive, Suite 250
Northbrook, IL 60062
Founded: 1979
International activities include funding the annual
International Pugwash Conferences on Science
and World Affairs.

Bertrand Russell Peace Foundation
Bertrand Russell House, Gamble Street
Nottingham NG7 4ET, England
Founded: 1963

Fellowship of Reconciliation (FOR)
Kuhlenstrasse 5A-7
25436 Uetersen, Germany
Founded: 1914
U.S. chapter: Fellowship of Reconciliation
P.O. Box 271
Nyack, NY 10960

Friends World Committee for Consultation
1506 Race Street
Philadelphia, PA 19102
Founded: 1937

International Peace Bureau
41, rue de Zurich
CH-1201 Geneva, Switzerland
Founded: 1891

International Peace Research Association
c/o Paul Smoker, General Secretary
Antioch College
Yellow Springs, OH 45387
Founded: 1965

International Physicians for the Prevention of Nuclear War
126 Rogers Street
Cambridge, MA 02142
Founded: 1980

Jane Addams Peace Association
777 United Nations Plaza
New York, NY 10017
Founded: 1948

Martin Luther King, Jr. Center for Nonviolent Social Change
449 Auburn Avenue N.E.
Atlanta, GA 30312
Founded: 1980

Pax Christi International
U.S. division: Pax Christi U.S.A.
348 East 10th Street
Erie, PA 16503
Founded: 1972

United Nations*
United Nations Plaza
New York, NY 10017
Founded: 1945

War Resisters League
339 Lafayette Street
New York, NY 10012
Founded: 1923

War Resisters International
Caledonian Road
London N1 9DX, England
Founded: 1921

Women's International League for Peace and Freedom (WILPF)
Case Postale 28
CH-1211 Geneva 20, Switzerland
Founded: 1915
U.S. division: WILPF
1213 Race Street
Philadelphia, PA 19107

For a complete listing of peace organizations, see *Encyclopedia of Associations*, 33th edition (1998).

*For names and addresses of individual UN agencies, see the *Yearbook of the United Nations*, published annually by the Department of Public Information, United Nations, UN Plaza, New York, NY 10017. To request a list of all UN publications, phone 800-253-9646 or 212-963-8302.

Further Reading

In addition to the books listed below, see book and article listings that follow each entry in text. Titles preceded by an asterisk (*) are especially appropriate for younger readers.

General

*Abrams, Irwin. *The Nobel Peace Prize and the Laureates*. Boston: G. K. Hall, 1988. (Brief profiles of Nobel Peace Prize winners, 1901–1987.)

Burns, Richard Dean, ed. *Encyclopedia of Arms Control and Disarmament*. 3 vols. New York: Scribners, 1993.

Gray, Tony. *Champions of Peace: The Story of Alfred Nobel, the Peace Prize, and the Laureates*. New York: Two Continents, 1976.

Josephson, Harold, ed. *Biographical Dictionary of Modern Peace Leaders*. Westport, Conn.: Greenwood Press, 1985.

Laszlo, Ervin, and Jong Youl Yoo, eds. *World Encyclopedia of Peace*. 4 vols. New York: Pergamon, 1986.

Nobel Prize Winners. New York: H. W. Wilson, 1987. (Profiles of Nobel Prize winners in all fields, 1901–1986.)

*Pauli, Hertha E. *Toward Peace: The Nobel Prizes and Man's Struggle for Peace*. New York: Ives Washburn, 1969.

Roberts, Nancy L. *American Peace Writers, Editors, and Periodicals: A Dictionary*. Westport, Conn.: Greenwood Press, 1991.

*Schraff, Anne. *Women of Peace: Nobel Peace Prize Winners*. Springfield, N.J.: Enslow, 1994.

*Wintterle, John, and Richard S. Cramer. *Portraits of Nobel Laureates in Peace*. New York: Abelard-Schuman, 1971.

Alfred Nobel and the Nobel Peace Prize

Bergengren, Erik. *Alfred Nobel: The Man and His Work*. New York: Nelson, 1962.

Fant, Kenne. *Alfred Nobel: A Biography*. Translated from the Swedish by Marianne Ruuth. New York: Arcade, 1993.

History of the Peace Movement

Allen, Devere, ed. *Pacifism in the Modern World*. 1929. Reprint. New York: Garland, 1971.

Andrew Carnegie's Peace Endowment. 2 vols. New York: Carnegie Endowment for International Peace, 1985.

Brock, Peter. *Freedom from War: Nonsectarian Pacifism, 1814–1914*. Toronto: University of Toronto Press, 1991.

———. *Pacifism in Europe to 1914*. Princeton, N.J.: Princeton University Press, 1972.

———. *Pacifism in the United States: From the Colonial Era to the First World War*. Princeton, N.J.: Princeton University Press, 1968.

———. *Studies in Peace History*. Syracuse, N.Y.: Syracuse University Press, 1991.

Ceadel, M. *Pacifism in Britain, 1914–1945*. Oxford: Clarendon Press, 1980.

Chamberlain, Austen. *Down the Years*. London: Cassell, 1935.

Chatfield, Charles. *For Peace and Justice: Pacifism in America, 1914–1941*. Knoxville: University of Tennessee Press, 1971.

Chatfield, Charles, ed. *Peace Movements in America*. New York: Schocken, 1973.

Chatfield, Charles, and Peter van den Dungen, eds. *Peace Movements and Political Cultures*. Knoxville: University of Tennessee Press, 1988.

Chickering, Roger. *Imperial Germany and a World Without War: The Peace Movement and German Society 1892–1914*. Princeton, N.J.: Princeton University Press, 1975.

Choate, Joseph H. *The Two Hague Conferences*. Princeton, N.J.: Princeton University Press, 1913.

Cooper, S. E., ed. *Internationalism in Nineteenth-Century Europe*. New York: Garland, 1976.

Davis, Calvin D. *The United States and the Second Hague Peace Conference*. Durham, N.C.: Duke University Press, 1975.

Davis, Hayne. *Among the World's Peacemakers*. 1907. Reprint. New York: Garland, 1972.

De Benedetti, Charles. *Origins of the Modern American Peace Movement*. Millwood, N.Y.: KTO Press, 1978.

De Benedetti, Charles, ed. *Peace Heroes in Twentieth-Century America*. Bloomington: Indiana University Press, 1986.

Falnes, O. J. *Norway and the Nobel Peace Prize*. 1938. Reprint. New York: AMS Press, 1967.

Hull, W. I. *The Two Hague Conferences and Their Contributions to International Law*. 1908. Reprint, New York: Garland, 1972.

Kelen, Emery. *Peace in Their Time: Men Who Led Us In and Out of War*. New York: Knopf, 1963.

Knock, Thomas. *To End All Wars: Woodrow Wilson and the Quest for a New World Order*. New York: Oxford University Press, 1992.

Martin, David A. *Pacifism: An Historical and Sociological Study*. New York: Schocken, 1966.

*Meltzer, Milton. *Ain't Gonna Study War No More: The Story of America's Peace Seekers*. New York: Harper & Row, 1985.

Moritzen, Julius. *The Peace Movement of America*. 1912. Reprint, New York: Garland, 1971.

Rappard, William E. *The Quest for Peace Since the World War*. Cambridge: Harvard University Press, 1940.

Stienstra, Deborah. *Women's Movements and International Organizations*. New York: St. Martin's, 1994.

Trueblood, Elton. *The People Called Quakers*. New York: Harper & Row, 1966.

Yarrow, C. H. Mike. *Quaker Experiences in International Conciliation*. New Haven: Yale University Press, 1978.

The League of Nations

Bonsal, Stephen. *Unfinished Business*. New York: Doubleday, Doran, 1944.

Jones, S. S. *The Scandinavian States and the League of Nations*. 1939. Reprint. Westport, Conn.: Greenwood Press, 1969.

Knudson, John I. *A History of the League of Nations*. New York: T. E. Smith, 1938.

Northedge, F. S. *The League of Nations: Its Life and Times, 1920–1946*. London: Holmes & Meier, 1986.

Walters, F. P. A. *A History of the League of Nations*.1952. Reprint, Westport, Conn.: Greenwood Press, 1986.

The United Nations

Osmanczyk, Edmund Jan. *The Encyclopedia of the United Nations and International Relations*. New York: Taylor & Francis, 1990.

*Patterson, Charles. *The Oxford 50th Anniversary Book of the United Nations*. New York: Oxford University Press, 1995.

Bibliographies and Peace Research Guides

Carroll, Berenice A. *Peace and War: A Guide to Bibliographies*. Santa Barbara, Calif.: ABC-Clio, 1983.

Cook, Blanche Wiesen, ed. *Bibliography on Peace Research in History*. Santa Barbara, Calif.: ABC-Clio, 1969.

Publications of the Carnegie Endowment for International Peace, 1910–1967. New York: Carnegie Endowment for International Peace, 1971.

van den Dungen, Peter, ed. *From Erasmus to Tolstoy: The Peace Literature of Four Centuries*. Westport, Conn.: Greenwood Press, 1990.

*Walter, Virginia. *War and Peace Literature for Children and Young Adults: A Resource Guide to Significant Issues*. Phoenix, Ariz.: Oryx Press, 1993.

The WISH List: A Bibliography of Books for Peace. Hammond, Ind.: Hammond Public Library/Women's Action for Nuclear Disarmament, 1987.

Index

References to main biographical entries are indicated by **bold** page numbers; references to illustrations are indicated by *italics*.

Ann T. Keene was born in Chicago and educated at Swarthmore College and Indiana University. She writes and edits nonfiction for both children and adults, specializing in biography, and has taught writing and literature at Indiana University and George Mason University. Keene is the author of five previous books for young adults, including *Earthkeepers: Observers and Protectors of Nature*, also in the Oxford Profiles series. She is the editor of the *Oxford American Children's Encyclopedia* (1998) and is a contributor to Oxford's forthcoming *American National Biography*.

Acknowledgments

The author wishes to thank Wendy Chmielewski, curator of the Swarthmore College Peace Collection, and Mary Ellen Chijioke, curator of the Friends Historical Library of Swarthmore College, for their invaluable assistance.

Picture Credits

Agence France Presse/Corbis-Bettmann: 290; American Friends Service Committee: 131, 132, 133; Amnesty International USA: 215; Archive Photos: 286; R. Steven Burns: 244; courtesy of the Jimmy Carter Library: 221; Corbis-Bettmann: 196; The Hague/Peace Palace Library: 36, 42, 44, 49, 50; © 1998 C. Herscovici, Brussels/Artists Rights Society (ARS), New York/Art Resource, NY: cover (background); Theodore Roosevelt Collection, Harvard College Library: 32; International Labour Office: 143, 144, 189, 190; International Physicians for the Prevention of Nuclear War: 247 (copyright Willem Diepraam), 248 (Yoshito Matsushige); courtesy Linda Pauling Kamb: 172; © Photo: Knudsen/Nobel Institute/Intra Media, Oslo: 2, 19, 20, 22, 27, 34, 40, 72, 88, 94, 107, 120, 127, 210, 218, 222, 236, 253; courtesy of the Leo Baeck Institute: 117; Library of Congress: cover (bottom left inset), 12, 16, 26, 30, 38, 52, 53, 54, 55, 56, 63, 67, 76, 78, 80, 82, 84, 86, 90, 92, 100, 101, 104, 106, 111, 135, 150, 156, 258, 260; Martin Luther King Jr. Library, Washington, D.C.: cover (top right inset), 225, 243; National Archives: 152 (306-NT-901-72), 200, 250 (courtesy of United States Holocaust Memorial Museum Photo Archives, Desig. # 12.325 W/S # 747870); courtesy of the National Portrait Gallery, London: 58; National Swedish Art Museums, Swedish Portrait Archives: 70 (photo by Richard Bergh), 93 (photo by Svante Nilsson); Peace People Headquarters, Belfast: 212; Photo Bibliothèque Nationale, Vienna, courtesy of the Comité International de la Croix-Rouge: 60 (HIST 1682/27); Photothèque Comité International de la Croix-Rouge: 14 (HIST 97, artist Horage Vernet), 59 (HIST 1446/10A, photo from Croix-Rouge britannique—Imperial War Museum, London), 75 (HIST 1061/27), 118 (HIST 1180), 119 (Photo Alb. GRIVEL), 177 (HIST 296); Project SAVE Armenian Archives, Watertown, Mass., courtesy of Margaret Kedonian Melickian: 116; Pugwash Conference on Science & World Affairs: 283, 284; Ronald Reagan Library: 262; reproduced with permission of the Library Committee of the Religious Society of Friends in Britain: 134; Reuters/Corbis-Bettmann: 207, 254, 265, 266, 271, 274, 276, 278, 280; Franklin D. Roosevelt Library: 188; Southern Evening Echo, Southampton: 216; Swarthmore College Peace Collection: cover (bottom right inset), 96, 98, 124 (Papers of Emily Greene Balch), 126 (Records of the Women's International League for Peace and Freedom, U.S. Section); UNICEF: 183 (#1680/Anders Engman), 184 (#ICEF-2371), 232 (#116,233/Balcomb/Mullick/Nelson-jr); UN Photo Library: 68 (#189150, Geneva), 121 (# 024477), 122 (R/ARA), 139 (#31216), 140 (#16037), 154 (#34991), 169 (#59778), 231 (#52532/SC/jt), 256 (#174113/J. Isaac), 257 (#188854/ A. Burridge), 261 (#172543/Y. Nagata), 269 (#182000/M. Grant); photo courtesy of United States Holocaust Memorial Museum: 249; UPI/Corbis-Bettmann: cover (top left inset), 113, 146, 148, 159, 163, 165, 166, 176, 178, 180, 182, 186, 193, 194, 198, 203, 206, 226, 228, 235, 239, 240; Photograph courtesy of Manis Collection, University of Nevada, Las Vegas Library: 174; Woodrow Wilson House, National Trust, Washington, D.C.: 64; YMCA of the USA Archives, University of Minnesota Libraries: 128.

BOSTON PUBLIC LIBRARY

3 9999 03555 553 9

WITHDRAWN
No longer the property of the
Boston Public Library.
Sale of this material benefited the Library.

Brighton Branch Library
40 Academy Hill Road
Brighton. MA 02135-3316